Resolving Disputes Between Nations

Resolving Disputes Between Nations

Coercion or Conciliation?

Martin Patchen

Duke Press Policy Studies
Duke University Press
Durham and London
1988

© Duke University Press 1988
All rights reserved.
Printed in the United States of America
on acid-free paper ∞
Library of Congress
Cataloging-in-Publication Data
Patchen, Martin.
Resolving disputes between nations: coercion and concession /
Martin Patchen.
p. cm.—(Duke Press policy studies)
Bibliography: p:
Includes index.
ISBN 0-8223-0764-2. ISBN 0-8223-0819-3 (pbk.)
1. International relations—Research. 2. Pacific settlement of
international disputes—Research. I. Title. II. Series.
JX1291.P375 1988
327.1′1′072—dc19 87-26845

To Jenny and Liza
May they and their children
live in peace

Contents

Tables and Figures

Figures

Preface

My work on this book grew out of a concern that all of us share: how can we avoid war? Since most people also want to defend what they consider to be their own country's vital interests and way of life, the more realistic question becomes: how can we avoid war while at the same time maintaining those things we hold dear? In the terms of a popular slogan, how can we manage to be neither Red nor dead?

For many years I have been interested in the accumulating body of theory and research on conflict and conflict resolution as general social processes. My own training and primary expertise is as a social psychologist. Much of the work on conflict resolution has focused on subjects of concern to social psychologists—for example, perceptions, decisionmaking, methods of influence, patterns of interaction, and bargaining.

Ideas and research findings concerning these topics have been applied to international relations by scholars in a number of fields. However, this has been done mainly with respect to specific single topics. For example, scholars interested in the credibility of deterrent threats by national leaders often draw on the general literature on perceptions, and those concerned with national decisionmaking sometimes draw on the general literature concerning group decisionmaking. But disputes between nations have not been analyzed in a broad and systematic way from the perspective of general conflict processes. In this book I present such an analysis. I consider a variety of specific topics—perceptions, decisionmaking, use of threat, use of force, etc.—within an overall theoretical framework that relates concepts and findings in one specific subject to those in other subjects. Thus, the intended contribution of this book is to provide an integrated summary of work on many topics that will contribute to an understanding of the interaction between disputing nations.

For each specific topic area, I attempt to summarize what we know about this topic that may be relevant to inter-nation disputes. I include ideas and findings both from the general literature on conflict, including many experimental studies, and evidence directly from studies of relations between nations. On some specific topics—e.g., the effectiveness of certain types of strategies used to influence an adversary—parallel data from experimental studies of conflict and studies of inter-nation conflict are available. Where both types of evidence are available, they generally show an encouraging consistency. Where results are available only from experimental studies (or those concerning units other than nations), it is clear that they cannot be applied uncritically to relations between nations. But such results, in the context of concepts about general conflict processes, are useful in formulating propositions that may help us to understand disputes between nations as well as conflict in other areas. The propositions stated within this book should be viewed both as summaries of available evidence and as hypotheses for future research.

In addition to whatever contributions this book can make to understanding the resolution of disputes between nations, it is my hope that it can provide some guidance for policy. The emphasis in much of the book is on seeing which types of actions and strategies work and which do not, and on the conditions under which a given strategy is most likely to be effective. The conclusions are necessarily general and do not provide a prescription for what national leaders should do in each specific dispute. But they do provide perspectives and guidelines for policy that go beyond the often-simplistic formulas that guide the thinking of large segments of the public and of some officials as well.

Clearly this book does not give complete and entirely proven answers to the questions of peace and war that are addressed. It does not provide a formal theory of conflict resolution between nations. The propositions it advances are subject to elaboration, revision, and, in some cases, to being discarded as more work on this subject is done.

Despite these limitations, it is my hope that this book's systematic summary of work relevant to inter-nation disputes, within a broad conflict perspective, will prove useful. It is my hope, too, that the book will stimulate discussion and further research on at least some of the specific propositions advanced. If this happens, then it will have achieved its main purposes.

Finally, I want to acknowledge the help I have received in working on this book. A fellowship from the Center for Humanistic Studies at Purdue enabled me to begin work on this project. A number of people read and made helpful comments on drafts of portions of the manuscript. These include Louis Kriesberg, Robin Williams, Louis Beres, Don Borden, Steve Caldwell, Harvey Marshall, Erich Weede, Sally Tanford, David Brownfield, Jenny Patchen, Susan Patchen, and Jorge Drevitz. Robert Jervis was the primary reviewer of the manuscript for Duke University Press and made constructive suggestions for improving the final product. Successive versions of various chapters were typed by the able clerical staff of the Department of Sociology and Anthropology, including Evelyn Douthit, Candy Lawson, Mary Perigo, Bonnie Wilkerson, and Kay Solomon. Gaye Matthews was helpful in coordinating the typing. I thank all of those mentioned, and anyone I have inadvertently neglected to mention, who contributed their time, effort, and suggestions.

Martin Patchen
West Lafayette, Indiana

1 Disputes Between Nations:
An Analytic Framework

How can disputes between nations be resolved peacefully, without the use of force? Obviously this question is of crucial importance to us all. To help answer it, it is important to understand why national leaders act as they do in the course of a dispute. How does each side perceive the situation and its adversary? How does each choose among alternative actions? How do the actions of one nation affect those of its adversary? For example, when does a threat lead to compliance and when does it lead instead to counter-threat?

To answer these and related questions, it is very helpful to have a general theoretical framework for analyzing the interaction between leaders of nations. Such a framework can direct our attention to the important variables and processes at work. It can help us to describe the processes of interaction between nations in a systematic way. And it can help us to pose specific questions and hypotheses about the conditions related to peaceful or violent resolution of disputes.

In this chapter I will present such a theoretical framework.[1] This framework is based on the view of conflict and cooperation as a process of strategic interaction between two parties who are interdependent. This viewpoint has been developed by game theorists and by some social psychologists, most notably by Harold Kelley and John Thibaut (1978). This same general perspective has been brought to bear on international relations by some political scientists. Glenn Snyder and Paul Diesing have made an especially important contribution in applying the approach to international crises in their book *Conflict Among Nations* (1977). The theoretical framework to be presented here is influenced heavily by these lines of work. At the same time, it is distinctive in some ways, as will become apparent.

In presenting this theoretical framework, I will illustrate the ideas by using the case of the Cuban missile crisis between the United States and the Soviet Union in 1962 (Abel, 1966; Kennedy, 1969; Allison, 1971; Detzer, 1979). This case is not necessarily typical of international conflicts or crises, but it should serve to make the general points more concrete.

Actions and Statements of Intent

The actions of each party to a dispute may be categorized in terms of whether (or the extent to which) they provide rewards or penalties to the adversary. Rewarding behavior may involve concessions on the disputed issue (e.g., removing one's troops from a disputed area) or it may not be related directly to the dispute (e.g., granting the other nation a loan). Likewise, behavior that penalizes the other may be directly relevant to the dispute (e.g., blocking supplies to the other in a disputed territory) or not directly relevant (e.g., blocking an international loan to the other). Penalizing actions may or may not involve the use of violence against the other. (However, we will want to give special attention to violent actions.)

As the term is used here, actions may include statements. As with physical actions, statements may be rewarding or punishing. For example, statements by American leaders that acknowledge that the Soviet Union is a superpower on a par with the United States satisfy the long-felt need of Soviet leaders for recognition of their nation (and themselves as leaders) as equal to the United States. Conversely, statements that question the legitimacy of their regime or of their control over Eastern European countries are damaging to Soviet leaders not only symbolically but because they could potentially stimulate unrest. Of course, statements rarely are equal in reward or punishment value to physical actions—e.g., opening up markets for trade or dropping bombs.

Threats and promises are not viewed here primarily as actions. While they may have some direct reward or punishment value (e.g., threats may be seen as insulting), their main importance is as expressed intentions to take actions in the future, usually under certain conditions. Likewise, offers by one side concerning terms on which they are willing to settle the dispute are treated here as promises to take certain rewarding actions (reflecting concessions) if the other side will agree to the terms.

To illustrate, when the United States discovered the construction of Soviet missile bases in Cuba, it considered several types of options at various times. One was to take (or promise to take) actions that represented concessions (or rewards) to the Soviets—specifically to remove our own missiles from Turkey and to refrain indefinitely from invading Cuba. A second option was to do nothing new—i.e., ignore the Soviet base on the grounds that it represented no significant change in the military balance. A third basic option was to impose some penalty on the Soviets or to threaten to do so. Those penalties considered by the president and his advisers included a blockade of Cuba and direct military action (bombing and/or invasion).

For the Soviets, too, the basic options can be viewed as ones that were either rewarding or penalizing to the other side. A basic option (once they were challenged) was to remove the missiles as the United States demanded, an important concession that would have been rewarding to the United States. A second basic option was to take some action that was further penalizing to the United States. The possibilities included completing and expanding new bases in Cuba, taking military action in the Caribbean (e.g., sinking a blockading U.S. ship) or taking counter-military action elsewhere in the world (e.g., cutting off Western access to Berlin). A third option was to do nothing after being challenged but rather to stall and hope that the United States would only bluster and would take no effective action to force removal of the missiles.

The Set of Outcomes

At any time during the course of the interaction, the outcome for each side depends on the joint actions of the two sides at that time. The set of outcomes, and the preferences of each side among outcomes in the set, may be represented in the form of a payoff matrix, as shown in table 1.1.

The basic types of possible actions for nation B are listed down the left column of table 1.1 while the parallel actions of nation A are indicated across the top. The entry in each cell of the matrix indicates the outcome that results from a particular combination of actions. For example, if both sides take actions rewarding to the other (make concessions), the outcome will be a compromise, as indicated in the upper left cell.[2]

The rank order preference of each side for each outcome also is indicated in each cell. (B's preference is shown at the bottom left while A's preference is shown at the top right of each cell.) The preferences of each side among the various outcomes will depend on its particular values—e.g., how vital to its welfare each believes winning its demands to be, how much each cares about the possible costs of a stalemate or a fight, how much each cares about the welfare of the other side. In the particular illustration shown in table 1.1, each side's first preference is exploitation of the other (the outcomes in cells C and G), compromise (cell A) is the fifth preference of each, a fight is just lower in preference (sixth) for both, and so on.

Table 1.1 The Basic Options and Possible Outcomes in a Dispute (with Possible Preferences by Each Side Among Outcomes)*

Options of nation B	Options of nation A		
	Action rewarding to B	No action	Action penalizing to B
Action rewarding to A	5 Compromise 5 A	2 Unilateral advantage to A 8 B	1 Exploitation of B by A 9 C
No action	7 Unilateral advantage to B 3 D	4 No change in situation (stalemate) 4 E	3 B hurt but does not retaliate 7 F
Action penalizing to A	9 Exploitation of A by B 1 G	8 A hurt but does not retaliate 2 H	6 Fight 6 I

*The number in the lower left-hand corner of each cell represents the rank order preference of nation B for this outcome. The number in the upper-right corner of each cell represents the rank order preference of nation A. The number 1 is the highest preference.

Table 1.1 represents the simplified essentials of the options available and the possible outcomes for the two sides in the dispute. But it may be expanded to indicate various types or degrees of rewarding or penalizing actions by each. For example, actions imposing physical damage on the other side may be distinguished in terms of the magnitude and extensiveness of the damage. If a larger number of possible actions by each side are considered, then the number of possible outcomes that may result from the combined actions of the two sides also will increase. For example, the use of token military force by each side may result in small skirmishes while a full-scale attack by one or both would result in a major war.

An outcome shown in a cell of the matrix may be a temporary one, reflecting the current status of a struggle between the two sides. For example, the outcome in cell I—a fight—is likely to be temporary, pending settlement of the dispute. Other outcomes, such as possible settlements of the dispute by negotiation or by the tacit acceptance of each side, may be more permanent.

The terms of each possible settlement will reflect certain rewarding (or penalizing) actions that side A takes toward side B and that B takes toward A. For example, in cell A of table 1.1, a compromise agreement would entail the two sides trading certain rewards (presumably at some cost to each side). While only one compromise outcome (cell A) is shown in table 1.1, there are in fact a variety of possible compromise agreements in cell A, some of which would be more advantageous to side A (B rewards A more than vice versa) and some of which would be more advantageous to side B (A rewards B more than vice versa). Possible settlements of the dispute may be found as well in other cells of the matrix. Thus, for example, side A may be able to force side B to accept an agreement that falls in cell C. Such an agreement would entail rewards to A but penalties to B and could be said to reflect A's exploitation of B.

The nature of the strategic situation—in terms of the options available to each side, the outcomes of possible joint actions, and each side's preferences among possible outcomes—often will not be clear to the parties, especially at the start of the dispute. As the interaction between the sides progresses, new options may be considered and old ones discarded as impractical. The possibility may arise that the other side may take actions not previously considered. Conceptions of particular outcomes—e.g., how much cost a stalemate will entail—may be uncertain and may change. Most important, each side—especially at the outset—may be uncertain about the preferences of its adversary or even of its own preferences. For example, does the other side prefer war to giving in? Or will it, in a crunch, choose surrender to war? And how about one's own side? Is it better to give in if necessary than go to war?

In addition to possible uncertainty by each side about the basic situation, there also may be differences in the two sides' perceptions of the options available to each side, of the nature of outcomes (e.g., how extensive and lengthy a fight would be), and especially of the preferences of each side. Thus, each side may believe that the other would prefer to give in on the issues in dispute rather than to fight. So long as both sides hold such

Table 1.2   Main Options, Possible Outcomes, and Preferences Among Outcomes for the United States and the Soviet Union During the Cuban Missile Crisis*

United States	Withdraw missiles	Continue present actions only (build missile bases)	Soviet Union Use limited force In Caribbean	Elsewhere	Fight general war
Give concessions (missiles out of Turkey; refrain from invasion; withdraw own Cuban base)	2 Compromise 2 A	1 Soviet victory 6 B	1 Soviet victory; U.S. humiliated 6 C	1 Soviet victory; U.S. humiliated 6 D	1 — E
Do nothing new	4 U.S. victory 1 F	1 Soviet victory 6 G	1 Soviet victory 6 H	1 Soviet victory 6 I	1 — J
Blockade	4 U.S. victory 1 K	3 Imminent completion of bases; danger of fight 3 L	5 Small-scale fighting; danger of wider fight 4 M	5 Small-scale fighting; danger of wider fight 5 N	7 Big war starts 7 O
Bomb-invade	6 U.S. victory; Soviets humiliated 1 P	6 U.S. victory; bases destroyed 1 Q	5 Small-scale fighting; bases destroyed; danger of wider fight 4 R	5 Small-scale fighting; bases destroyed; danger of wider fight 4 S	7 Big war starts 7 T
Fight general war	 — U	 — V	7 Big war starts 7 W	7 Big war starts 7 X	7 Big war 7 Y

Table 1.2   (continued)

*The number in lower-left corner of each cell represents the rank order preference of American leaders for this outcome; number in upper-right corner of each cell represents the rank order preference of Soviet leaders. The number 1 is the highest preference. Blank in cell indicates that the combination of actions by two sides is very improbable.

different perceptions, no settlement of the dispute is likely.

As interaction between the parties continues, each side gains information that may clarify or change its view of the situation. Moreover, each side attempts to influence the preferences of the other side among possible outcomes and the expectations of the other side concerning its own actions. For example, side A may attempt to convince B that it will never make concessions and will fight if necessary to get its way. Thus, much of the series of events in a dispute can be understood as a process by which each side's perceptions of the basic interdependence situation are clarified and their perceptions may eventually converge.

In the case of the Cuban missile crisis, the set of possible outcomes at the time U.S. officials were deciding on a course of action is shown in table 1.2. In each cell of the matrix, my own estimates of the rank order preference of each side for this outcome are given. The estimates of the preferences of central U.S. officials (ultimately, the president) are based on the accounts of their deliberations during the course of the crisis. The estimates of the preferences of central Soviet leaders (particularly Premier Khrushchev) are more speculative but are based on general information about their objectives at that time.[3] My aim is not to provide a completely accurate and detailed picture of the preferences of the two sides but, rather, to illustrate how the general approach may be applied to this type of situation.[4]

As table 1.2 indicates, American officials preferred to accept the prospect of a local armed conflict with the Soviet Union (i.e., to be in cells M, N, R, or S) rather than to give in to the Soviets on this issue (i.e., to be in cells B, C, D, G, H, or I). This was because of the great political cost they believed the United States and their administration would suffer if the United States did not react forcefully to what they saw as a brazen Soviet challenge to long-standing American predominance in its own "backyard." President Kennedy was quoted as saying he believed he would be impeached by the Congress if he did not act forcefully in this situation (Allison, 1971:195).

The preference order shown for the Soviet leaders, on the other hand, reflects the estimates of most observers that they preferred to give up their prospective Cuban missile bases rather than accept a dangerous armed confrontation with the United States if such a withdrawal was not carried out under humiliating circumstances (i.e., the Soviets preferred the outcomes in cells F and K to those in cells M, N, R, and S). While the missile bases would have improved the strategic and political position of the Soviets, they had no long-standing stake in such bases and had not even admitted to building them. In other words, they would be giving up something that they had not had anyway. In addition, the Soviets knew that they would lose an armed confrontation in the Caribbean (though not necessarily elsewhere).

This difference in the preference order of the two sides gave the United States an advantage in the bargaining that followed. It meant that the United States was able to credibly threaten actions that would provoke an armed confrontation while the Soviets were less willing to do so. It should be noted also that each side—if it could not have its own way in the dispute—preferred a compromise (cell A) to an armed fight. Though this did not guarantee a peaceful settlement (there was always the possibility of miscalculation about the chances of the other backing down completely), it provided the opportunity for an eventual peaceful settlement.

Table 1.2 shows the situation—i.e., the options and outcomes seen by each side and the approximate preferences of each—after several days of confrontation between the United States and the Soviet Union. But both sides' views of the situation they faced were not completely formed at the start of the crisis. American leaders at first did not consider the option of a blockade, the action they eventually chose. The desirability of various outcomes were debated; for example, Secretary of Defense McNamara argued early in the U.S. discussions that Soviet missiles in Cuba would have little effect on the overall military balance while other American officials maintained that the Soviet bases would have great military and political significance. American leaders were uncertain about general Soviet intentions and about how they would react to a firm stand by the United States. On the Soviet side, Khrushchev and his colleagues were unsure about whether the ultimatum of the United States that the missiles had to be removed really reflected an American preference for war rather than concession on this issue or whether it was merely a bluff.

Initially, there were differences in the perceptions of leaders on the two sides about their mutual preferences among outcomes. In particular, there was a key difference in perceptions about American preferences. Khrushchev's decision to put missiles into Cuba reflected his judgment that, while

Kennedy would be upset about such a development, he would prefer to accept it as a fait accompli rather than to provoke an armed fight with the Soviet Union. The actual preferences of Kennedy and his key advisers were different: they preferred to risk war with the Soviets rather than accept the sudden fact of Soviet missiles ninety miles off American shores.

During the crisis, each side took actions and made statements that were intended to influence the preferences and expectations of the other. For example, Kennedy's tough address to the American people, the blockade of Cuba, the mobilization of American troops and planes in the southeastern United States, and Robert Kennedy's warning to the Soviet ambassador all were intended to convince Khrushchev that the United States was going to invade Cuba if he did not agree quickly to remove the missiles.

Additional possible outcomes—not initially among the outcomes considered—also were suggested by each side. The Soviets suggested a possible settlement in which they would remove the missiles while the United States would pledge not to invade Cuba and (in a later proposal) also remove U.S. missiles from Turkey. The United States proposed the deal of "missiles out for a pledge of no United States invasion" supplemented by a tacit pledge to remove the U.S. missiles from Turkey soon. As the perceptions of the two sides about the actual situation became more similar, and as new outcomes emerged as possible solutions, chances for resolution of the dispute increased.

Bargaining

The processes of influence and bargaining may be viewed in the context of the type of payoff matrix confronting the two sides. Influence moves may be of two types—overt action or statements about future overt actions. First, each side may be able to induce the other to change its behavior (in a more rewarding direction) by taking some overt action itself. Thus, for example, by instituting a blockade (moving the situation from cell G to cell L in table 1.2), American officials hoped to make the present situation less desirable for the Soviets and thus induce them to withdraw their missiles. However, for the Soviets, withdrawal without getting anything in return (cell K) was no better, and maybe worse, than a continuation of the crisis (cell L). The Soviets might have chosen to counter the blockade of Cuba with a blockade of Berlin (moving the situation from cell L to cell N), thus making the U.S. outcome poorer and providing a possible incentive for the United States to drop its resistance to the missile bases in Cuba. However, such a surrender by the United States in the face of Soviet military pressure (cell I or cell D) would have been extremely repugnant to American leaders, and the Soviets undoubtedly realized this.

Each side also may threaten to take actions that penalize the other if the other does not take more rewarding actions (make concessions) on the issue in dispute. Thus, the United States threatened to bomb or invade Cuba, or both, if the Soviets did not withdraw their missiles (which would have moved the situation from cell L to cell Q). If this had occurred, the outcomes for the Soviets would have been worse than they were in cell L, and the Soviets would have had no options at that point that could have improved their outcomes substantially. Thus, it was in the Soviets' interest to withdraw the missiles rather than to suffer the consequences of the United States' carrying out its threat.

Promises are an alternative verbal means for influencing behavior. In the latter stages of the Cuban crisis, the United States promised to take actions desired by the Soviets—i.e., to remove its own missiles from Turkey and not to invade Cuba—if the Soviets withdrew their missiles. These promises were intended, of course, to make the outcome of such withdrawal more attractive to the Soviets (compared to other alternatives).

In addition to threats and promises, persuasion may involve A pointing out to B the possible advantages to B of taking actions desired by A and the possible disadvantages of not doing so (i.e., advantages and disadvantages not due directly to A's future actions). In the Cuban missile crisis this type of persuasion was not prominent but probably was used by Kennedy to some extent when, in urging Khrushchev to accept an agreement, he pointed out some possibilities of mutually beneficial cooperation between the two nations that might follow a resolution of the crisis.

The process of bargaining in its narrower sense—i.e., the exchange of offers and demands—may be viewed within this same framework. Offers are promises to take future rewarding actions, usually on condition that the other side take actions rewarding to oneself (or stop actions punishing to oneself). Thus, Khrushchev's initial offer to settle the crisis was a promise to remove Soviet missiles from Cuba if the United States would promise not to invade (and, of course, remove its blockade). A demand made of the other side usually is linked to a threat. It asks the other side to take a given action or face unpleasant consequences. Thus, the U.S. demand that the Soviets remove their missiles from Cuba was explicitly linked to a threat to take action that would penalize the Soviets (e.g., invasion) if they did not comply.

Note that this conceptual framework makes a clear separation between overt actions that have an impact on the other side and verbal statements (threats, promises, offers, etc.) about possible actions. This approach differs from that of many writers who group together positive or conciliatory actions and statements and combine negative or belligerent actions and statements. The reason for the separation here of overt action and statement is that the basic structure of the situation (i.e., the set of possible outcomes) depends on various combinations of overt actions only. Verbal statements such as threats or promises are means of getting the other side to change its overt actions and thus to change the outcome. One of our concerns will be with differences in situations (i.e., patterns of preferences among actions) that lead to the use of overt action as a means to influence the other side versus those situations that lead to the use of threats or promises of overt action. Thus, it is important to keep overt action and verbal statement separate.

The approach presented above also permits us to study within a single conceptual framework several basic processes that often have been studied separately. Since verbal statements of threat and promise refer to the overt actions that each side may take and to the outcomes of those actions, the processes of influence and of interaction are intimately related in this perspective. Moreover, since offers are seen as specific promises to take overt action, and demands are viewed as requests for overt actions by the other (accompanied by threats of one's own actions), bargaining or negotiation in its narrow sense fits within the same framework as the processes of influence and interaction.

Choosing an Action

At any given time during the course of a dispute, the two sides are at a given cell in the outcome matrix—i.e., they are each taking certain actions that result in a certain outcome. The next action a given side will take (or whether it takes any action at all) will depend on (1) its own perception of the present outcome and its preference for that outcome compared to other possible outcomes; (2) its perception of the alternative actions open to it; (3) its expectation about the actions the other side is likely to take—perhaps in response to its own actions; and, (4) its perception of the possible outcomes that would follow from various combinations of further actions (or inactions) by the two sides. Given these perceptions, expectations, and preferences, each side's leaders have to use some decision rule or criterion to make their choice. The exact nature of the decision rule used by a particular leader at a particular time is an important topic for investigation and one that I will discuss in detail later (see chapter 4). For the present, we may note only that national leaders will choose an action that they believe is likely to meet their most important objectives.

In the Cuban missile crisis the problem facing U.S. officials was what action stood the best chance of meeting their objectives of getting rid of the missiles and demonstrating American resolve while at the same time avoiding war with the Soviet Union. The difficulty was that they could see no course of action that would assuredly do both. Almost all of the Americans quickly agreed that diplomatic pressure alone was not likely to be successful in getting the missiles removed. An offer of mutual concessions was seen as not meeting the objective of demonstrating American resolve. Bombing of the bases or invasion of Cuba (or both) was the course of action preferred initially by some of the officials. The combination of bombing and invasion in particular was seen as sure to lead to destruction of all the Soviet missile sites. However, this course of action, which probably would lead to killing some Soviet personnel, was seen by some of the policy group as having a substantial chance of provoking a violent Soviet response and even the possibility of a Soviet nuclear attack on the United States.

After long days of discussion a majority of the executive committee came to favor initiating a blockade, at least as a first step. American officials perceived that a good chance existed that the blockade would be successful in forcing removal of the missiles (though this outcome was far less certain than for bombing). They also perceived some chance (between one in three and even, President Kennedy said at one point) that it would lead to a violent confrontation with the Soviets. But this possibility was seen as less likely in the case of a blockade than in the case of bombing or invasion. However, if the blockade did not succeed in achieving removal of the missiles, then the Executive Committee was prepared to move to the stronger option of bombing and invasion.

The American leaders in this crisis, like other national leaders in other crises, chose an action they thought had a good chance of meeting all their major objectives. Since no action was certain both to lead to removal of the missiles and to avoid war, and since the focus of their attention was on getting rid of the missiles, they relaxed the constraint of avoiding war by requiring only that an action have a good (perhaps better than even) chance of avoiding war. In doing so, they were taking an enormous gamble with the lives of their countrymen in order to achieve their primary objective. (Some of the reasons why they were willing to take such a gamble are discussed in chapter 4.)

The question may be raised as to whether the theoretical framework being used here assumes too much rationality by national decisionmakers. What about decisions made in anger, or in fear, or by national leaders —like Adolf Hitler—who may be somewhat unbalanced mentally? I make no assumption that the decisionmakers' objectives and their preferences among outcomes (e.g., compromise, victory, stalemate, fight) are based only, or even primarily, on pragmatic considerations of national well-being and security. While such pragmatic considerations are common, the objectives and preferences of national leaders may be affected also by emotions of anger, hate, and fear, by a desire for personal prestige or success, and by wishes to enhance their self-images (e.g., to see themselves as courageous and bold). Leaders may not even be fully aware of the impact of such personal emotions and motives on their goals.

What is being assumed here is that—however rational the underlying reasons—national leaders, like other people, have some ideas of their preferences among outcomes (e.g., whether they would rather have a compromise agreement or a stalemate that might lead to war). No great rationality is assumed regarding the accuracy of national leaders' perceptions of the possible options each side possesses, of the nature of possible outcomes, or of the likely actions an adversary may take. Under stress and time pressures, decisionmakers may ignore effective options possibly open to them. Because of faulty information or distortions of available information, they may misperceive the nature of possible outcomes (e.g., see a fight as leading to their own victory when a more objective analysis would suggest a probable loss). And, because of hope, fear, hatred, preconceptions, or even paranoia, their expectations about the future actions of an adversary may be quite unrealistic. The only minimal assumptions being made here are that decisionmakers make some choice among options (including that of doing nothing) and that they choose the option they expect will yield the results they most prefer.

In making a choice among possible options, national leaders sometimes make a careful analysis of the likely consequences of each action, weighing the likelihood that the adversary will react in alternative ways, considering the consequences of various combinations of actions by the two sides, and even constructing possible scenarios to see where a series of actions by the two sides may lead. During the Cuban missile crisis American decisionmakers went through this kind of careful deliberative process before choosing what they believed to be the best course of action. However, not all decisions may be made in this deliberate way. A national leader may act impulsively, as the German kaiser did in 1914 when giving a "blank check" of German support to Austrian punishment of Serbia. Or he may act by following a standard rule, as President Truman essentially did when he ordered American troops into Korea in 1950 in accord with the rule that aggression in one place must always be resisted so that it is not repeated.

The present framework does not assume that decisionmakers always (or even usually) make a search of all available options and analyze the advantages and disadvantages of each. Nor does it assume careful deliberation by decisionmakers in which they carefully weigh the value of possible outcomes by the likelihood of their occurrence in an attempt to "maximize expected utility."[5] What is assumed here is simply that a decisionmaker tries, either by careful analysis or by intuition, to find an option that he believes—given his preferences and his expectancies—will meet his basic objectives.

Patterns of Outcomes

The choice that is seen as most desirable by each side's leaders will be affected strongly by the pattern of their own preferences among possible outcomes together with their perceptions of the preferences of the other side. Some preference patterns will provide incentives for the use of reward, some for coercion, some for threat, and some for promises or offers of concessions.

In the Cuban missile crisis American decisionmakers chose first to use coercion and threat in part because they believed that the Soviet leaders would prefer the outcome of losing their bases to the outcome of a serious military confrontation with the United States. But American leaders were not certain that the Soviets would make this choice. The Americans were willing to take this gamble in part because they themselves preferred the possibility of limited armed conflict to the prospect of allowing the Soviet missile bases in Cuba to remain. Given a different rank order of their own preferences, or a different rank order of perceived Soviet preferences, the American leaders might have chosen concessions, or promises of concessions, in return for reciprocal concessions as their first move. As the crisis progressed and the American leaders saw that the Soviets might prefer armed conflict to a humiliating total surrender, American leaders modified their strategy to include offers of concessions if the Soviets would make the major concession of removing the missiles.

These remarks are intended only to introduce the subject of how the pattern of preferences among outcomes may affect the actions of each side and interactions between them. This subject, along with other aspects of the situation faced by the two sides, will be discussed at much greater length in chapter 2.

Interaction Over Time

So far we have considered the factors that affect the overt actions and statements of the sides at a given time in a dispute. But we also need to take into account the process of interaction over time. How does the action (or statements) of side A at time 1 affect the action of side B at time 2, and how does this, in turn affect the action of side A at time 3, etc.? Figure 1.1 presents a simple model of this process of interaction.

To illustrate how this general model may be applied (with nation A being the United States and nation B the Soviet Union), let us begin at the time that President Kennedy announced the U.S. blockade of Cuba and demanded that the Soviets remove their missiles (box G-1 at top left of figure 1.1). These actions changed first the Soviets' perceptions of possible outcomes in the present situation (box E-2). In particular, it was now clear to Khrushchev that an armed clash with the United States was possible if the Soviets attempted to move more military supplies to Cuba. In addition, the American statements and actions shook the Soviets' previous expectations that the United States would not take any direct military action against their bases (box D-2). But the Soviets at this point were not sure that the Americans would take any action beyond a blockade. They hoped that the Americans were bluffing or that they could be dissuaded from further military action by Soviet threats. The Soviets decided to stall for time (box G-2). They turned around some of their ships that were heading for Cuba so as not to force a showdown with the U.S. Navy. They made threatening statements about the dire consequences that would ensue if the United States took military action. At the same time they continued work on the missile bases.

The United States interpreted the Soviet actions to mean that the Soviets did not want to provoke an immediate confrontation but that they also were not prepared to surrender the missile bases (box H-2). Thus, the Soviets' initial responses to the blockade reduced American expectations that the blockade would in itself force a Soviet withdrawal (box D-1). Given the absence of a Soviet withdrawal, the Americans now saw direct military action as the only way to accomplish their goal of removing the missile bases. They were prepared to accept the risk that the Soviets would react with counter-violence to such U.S. actions; but they also believed that a stronger threat of direct military action might persuade the Soviets to give in. By verbal communication (especially by Robert Kennedy to the Soviet ambassador in Washington) and by military preparations (massing troops and planes in the southeastern United States), they threatened an immediate bombing of the bases and invasion of Cuba if the Soviets did not remove the missiles (box G-1).

These American actions next had to be interpreted by the Soviets (box H-1). The combination of the previous blockade action, the public position of Kennedy, the U.S. preparations for attack, and the new U.S. warn-

Figure 1.1   A Framework for Analyzing the Interaction Between Two Nations

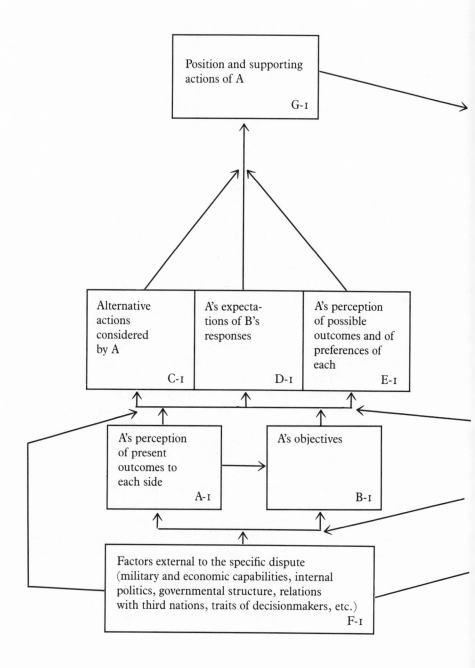

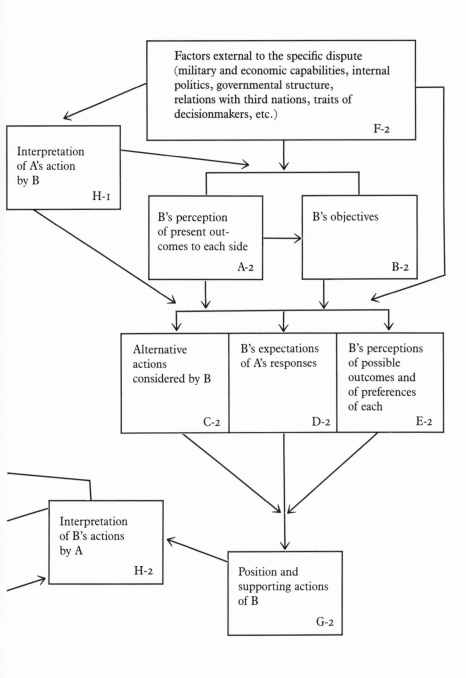

ings of imminent attack combined to convince Khrushchev that the threats of bombing and invasion were no bluff. Thus the Soviet expectations of U.S. actions, in the absence of a Soviet withdrawal of the missiles, changed (box D-2). Their perception of the possible outcome of an armed confrontation may also have become more grave in light of such developments as the United States putting its strategic nuclear forces on alert (box E-2). Given this newly perceived probability of imminent U.S. attack and possible disaster, the Soviets shifted their objectives (box B-2). They now sought not a political-military coup but, rather, a chance of retreat without humiliation. Khrushchev's next action was to offer a deal whereby the Soviets would remove their missiles in exchange for a noninvasion pledge by the United States (box G-2). (In a second letter, he asked also for removal of U.S. missiles from Turkey.) Such an outcome of the dispute was preferred by U.S. officials to the armed confrontation that would have resulted from an invasion of Cuba. Moreover, the Soviet messages did not lead U.S. officials to expect that the Soviets would withdraw peacefully if the United States refused its offer. Thus, the United States accepted and the crisis was over.

The specific case we have been looking at illustrates the dynamics of the general model presented in figure 1.1. As interaction in a conflict proceeds, the actions of each side affect the other side's perceptions of the situation and its objectives. Most importantly, each side's expectations of how far the other side is willing to concede (or how far the other can be pushed) may be modified. Such changes in perception will produce a changed expectation about what it is realistically possible to attain in the situation without excessive losses or risks. As a result, the terms that each party is willing to accept will be modified. Eventually, this process will cause the positions of the two sides to converge sufficiently for the conflict to be settled. (The convergence in positions may represent a compromise or a capitulation by one side.) What varies is how long the process takes and whether the convergence occurs without the use of force by either or both sides.

The terms of the eventual settlement are likely to reflect the relative power positions of the two sides as they appear to the participants following their interactions. The terms of the missile crisis settlement were generally acknowledged to favor the United States. The United States was able convincingly to threaten military actions that, if countered by the Soviets, would result in a situation undesirable for both sides but worse for the Soviets. This was mainly because the United States enjoyed unchallenged military superiority in the area of the conflict (the Caribbean) and was also superior in strategic (long-range nuclear) weapons at that time.

Moreover, as U.S. words and actions slowly made clear, it preferred a military confrontation to acceptance of Soviet bases in Cuba. For the Soviets, however, a military confrontation with the United States was not necessarily preferable to a pullback. Given this imbalance in capability and in preferences, the United States was more effectively able to threaten military moves, and the Soviet Union was willing to give up more to avoid a military showdown (Trachtenberg, 1985).

The Assumption of a Unitary Decisionmaker

In discussing the way in which the U.S. and Soviet governments arrived at their crucial decisions, I have treated each government as essentially a single actor—having objectives, considering alternatives, anticipating responses of the other, etc. Yet it also has been mentioned that there was a group of men on the American side who discussed what actions the United States should take. And while very little is known about the internal deliberations on the Soviet side, it seems probable that Khrushchev did not deliberate alone throughout this grave crisis. (For example, American analysts believed that while Khrushchev's first letter to Kennedy was his own composition, his second letter bore the marks of the Soviet bureaucracy.)

In view of the involvement of many persons on both sides, in this case and in others, how realistic is a model (such as that in figure 1.1) that assumes a choice of action based on the extent to which the perceived outcomes of various actions meet the decisionmaker's basic objectives? Some have argued that often this is not the way in which decisions are made by governments. Rather, decisions may be made by a process of bargaining and compromise among persons and factions with different preferences. Thus, the strategy finally chosen may not be a coherent action chosen rationally to meet objectives but may rather be an amalgam and compromise among action elements preferred by various participants (Allison, 1971).

In the case of the Cuban missile crisis there were at least three alternative courses of action advocated during the last stages of the American decisionmaking. One was the strategy of conciliation and compromise advocated solely by UN ambassador Stevenson. More importantly, there was a group of officials who supported the blockade option while another group continued to advocate a bombing strike. But in his discussion of the application of the "governmental politics" model to the Cuban crisis, Allison's account makes it clear that, after the case for each option was made by its adherents, the final choice was made by a single decisionmaker,

President John Kennedy. As Robert Kennedy recalled later: "It was up to one single man. No committee was going to make this decision" (Kennedy, 1969:47). Moreover, President Kennedy's decision was not some amalgam of or compromise between the major options of blockade and bombing but a clear choice—at least as a first step.

In analyzing decisions for war, Bruce Bueno de Mesquita argues that the assumption of a single central decisionmaker for such major decisions is a reasonable one. "Of course, no leader can afford to ignore completely the desires and interests of those who follow him. Without some support, even the most coercive dictator cannot hope to muster sufficient resources to wage a successful war. Still, it is ultimately the responsibility of a single leader to decide what to do and how to do it" (Bueno de Mesquita, 1981a:28). However, even when he has the authority to make final decisions, the central decisionmaker (president, king, prime minister, etc.) may modify his decision in order to win broader support within his government.

Whether it is realistic to assume that a single decisionmaker exists may depend on a number of circumstances. Snyder and Diesing (1977) suggest that the applicability of problem-solving theories versus bureaucratic politics theory depends on the type of decisionmaking structure involved. They propose that problem-solving approaches apply best when one or two persons make decisions and that a bureaucratic politics perspective may be more useful when decisions are made by a committee or a divided government. They suggest that either approach, or a combined approach, would fit situations in which there is a central decisionmaker with advisors or where one person makes decisions within "collegial limits" (Snyder and Diesing, 1977:357).

Whether decisions are made by a single individual may depend also on the importance of those decisions. Hoagland and Walker (1979:130) state that evidence indicates that "a government's decisionmaking process in a crisis situation is likely to become centralized under the control of its principal leader." Bueno de Mesquita comments that while major choices for war or for peace are made by a central decisionmaker, less critical decisions, such as the best way to conduct a war, may be made by a more bureaucratic process (Bueno de Mesquita, 1981a:16).

In some cases where final decisions are a collective responsibility—e.g., are made by a majority vote of a cabinet—it may still be realistic to use a model that assumes a single decisionmaker. This would be the case where there is a cohesive majority faction, the members of which have basically similar perceptions and preferences.[6] It would be the case also where responsibility for foreign policy decisions has been largely delegated to one person, whose decisions are subject only to approval by the group.

The framework I have presented for analyzing conflict interaction assumes an essentially single actor (a central decisionmaker, a cohesive dominant faction, or an individual—such as a foreign minister—acting with delegated authority). The effects of the political and bureaucratic environment are reflected in this framework in two ways. First, political-bureaucratic pressures affect the objectives of the decisionmaker. In particular, the objectives of his policy probably include satisfying important political factions within his nation and also satisfying elements within the government (e.g., the military). Second, the decisionmaker's selection of a policy or action may be determined not only by his perception of how well it will meet his objectives (including internal political ones) but also by whether or not he can gain enough support within the government to carry out this policy successfully. As many observers have pointed out, even presidents and dictators—whatever their formal powers—need the cooperation of their bureaucracies in order for their policies to be executed successfully.

To say that major policy decisions usually are made by a central decisionmaker does not necessarily mean that such decisions will be carried out effectively by their subordinates. Thies (1980:chapter 8) has described the way in which orders by American presidents have been distorted in their execution by military bureaucracies. For example, while President Kennedy sought to avoid the use of force during the Cuban missile crisis, Navy ships forced several Soviet submarines to surface. And President Johnson's orders concerning which North Vietnamese targets were to be bombed were often undermined by the operating procedures of Air Force units. Thus, while basic outlines of a leader's decisions—e.g., put a blockade in place around Cuba, bomb North Vietnamese cities—are followed, they often are not executed in the way intended.

Even with these attempts to include bureaucratic realities, the present framework probably would not be appropriate in some situations. Where there is *not* a single dominant decisionmaker and where decisions are made by a process of bargaining, the resulting decision may be some amalgam or compromise that bears little relation to the original preference of any single individual. In such a case, the approach proposed here would be useful only in understanding the action preferences of each individual involved in the final bargaining about the decision. The internal bargaining process would have to be analyzed separately. However, for reasons already suggested, it seems likely that a central decisionmaker usually will make major foreign policy decisions. Moreover, the assumption of a single decisionmaker has proved useful in research on decisions for war (e.g., Huth and Russett, 1984; Bueno de Mesquita, 1981a). Thus, an approach based on this assumption seems appropriate in most cases of serious international disputes.

Other Variables

The discussion so far has focused on the way the world looks to individuals (especially national leaders)—for example, the options they see, their expectations of the actions of others, and their perceptions of present and future outcomes. As figure 1.1 indicates, the perceptions of each side in a dispute at any given time are affected by the actions of the other side. In addition, as figure 1.1 also shows (boxes F-1 and F-2), each side's perceptions, expectations, and objectives are affected by other factors that are outside the pattern of the present interaction between the parties. These factors include past experiences, the internal political situation, governmental structure, relations with third parties, and the economic and military capabilities of each side, as well as cultural, ideological, and individual psychological factors. These factors (and others) have their effects on national actions by influencing the key cognitive variables on which the previous discussion has focused.

In the Cuban missile crisis, for example, the Soviet objective of establishing missile bases in Cuba was shaped by its inferiority in strategic nuclear capability at that time and by its internal economic and political situation. Khrushchev wished to satisfy the military factions that wanted to establish strategic equality with the United States. But economic constraints made him reluctant to spend the money and time necessary to do this by a large-scale buildup of Soviet capability on its own soil.

The Kennedy administration's objective of getting rid of the Soviet missile sites was based not only on the possible impact of these bases on the military balance between the two countries but also on the presence of powerful political pressures from conservative factions in the United States. In addition, beliefs rooted at least partly in ideology, such as the long-held dictum that foreign powers should be kept out of the Western Hemisphere and that the spread of communism had to be resisted, helped to strengthen Kennedy's determination to eliminate the Soviet bases.

The expectations each side held of the other also derived from factors outside the current interaction between them. Khrushchev's initial expectations that Kennedy would take no effective action to remove the Soviet bases apparently were influenced in part by his prior meeting with Kennedy in Vienna and by Kennedy's "weak" actions in two previous crises

—his refusal to give air support to Cuban exiles in the Bay of Pigs invasion and his acquiescence in the building of the Berlin Wall. Khrushchev's expectations may have been influenced also by information and analyses presented by the Soviet foreign policy and intelligence agencies concerning U.S. priorities and intentions.

As the crisis progressed, the expectations of each side concerning whether the other would use military force were influenced by both the local and strategic ratio of forces. The fact that the United States had much greater air and naval power around Cuba and also had a much stronger strategic nuclear force made the Soviets give greater credibility to Kennedy's statements that he would not permit the bases to remain. This fact also made Kennedy believe that the Soviets were not likely to challenge the U.S. blockade of Cuba.

Similarly, the preferences of each side's leaders among various possible outcomes of the dispute were influenced by factors external to the dispute. The fact that both Khrushchev and Kennedy felt vulnerable to attack by opposition within their own nations made each more reluctant to suffer a defeat on this issue than he would have been had he considered solely the political-military consequences of the outcome. While both Khrushchev and Kennedy recoiled from the prospect of a general war, a limited fight in the Caribbean was less unattractive to Kennedy because he knew the United States had the capability to prevail in such a fight. In addition, the psychological traits of each leader may have affected the strength of their preferences among the possible outcomes. For example, Kennedy's family background, which stressed successful competition in everything from touch football to politics, may have added to the unattractiveness of accepting defeat on this issue.

In later chapters I will discuss the role of various personal, ideological, organizational, political, and international system factors that may affect an individual leader's actions. But I will continue to focus attention on a limited number of key variables at the cognitive level. This strategy is intended to make the analysis manageable and to keep it within a single theoretical framework. Other factors are seen as having their effects on national actions by influencing the key cognitive variables on which I have focused.

Other types of analysis, at other levels, are possible. In particular, it is possible to study variations in the structure of the international system (alliances, power distributions, trade relations, etc.) as these relate to outcomes like war (see, for example, Russett and Starr, 1981, chapters 4 and 5).[7] While there are points of contact between the two types of analysis (e.g., system variables may affect the bargaining position and thus the decisions of individuals), they represent analyses at different levels. My concern here is with action and interaction between national leaders and not with the operation of international systems as systems.

The Number of Nations Interacting

The reader may have noticed that the discussion has been limited to the interaction between the leaders of two nations. Since there are a great many nations, and disputes sometimes involve more than two of them, how can we handle this fact? In principle, the theoretical framework outlined above can be applied to interactions among three or more parties (see, for example, Thibaut and Kelley, 1959; Kelley and Thibaut, 1978). However, such an expansion of the analysis becomes complex and somewhat unwieldy. Since my main interest in this book is in the type of interaction that occurs between two nations—such as the United States and the Soviet Union—I will usually use a framework that focuses on the interaction between two parties.

The role of other nations can be represented in this analysis in several ways. First, they can be seen at times as basically members of a fairly unified alliance. In this case, the analysis can focus on interaction between two alliances, or, more commonly, between the two nations that lead and represent each alliance. To illustrate, in some arms negotiations, the United States represents the North Atlantic alliance while the Soviet Union represents the Warsaw Pact countries.

In some instances third nations can be seen as an important part of the environment in which the decisions of two interacting nations are made. The leaders of each side may be influenced by the anticipated reaction of other nations to its actions. In negotiating a peace treaty with Israel, for instance, Egypt had to take into account the reactions of its Arab neighbors. Where the possibility of an armed fight with an adversary is present, the leaders of each side may need to assess the likelihood that one or more third parties will give political or military assistance to either side. In addition, third parties may affect the interaction between two nations by acting as mediators or by facilitating communication between the two. In a few cases this strategy of handling the role of third nations within a two-nation framework may not be tenable. For example, if the United States, the Soviet Union, and China were competing for dominance in an African country, it would probably be necessary to extend the framework to include the possible actions of all three, the set of outcomes that might occur as a result of various combinations of action by the three, etc. However, my main focus will be on the interaction between a pair of adversary nations.

The Task of This Book

I have presented above a framework for analyzing (a) the overt and verbal actions of each nation at a given point in time and (b) the interactions between the nations over time. This framework identifies in a broad and general way the types of variables and the relationships between these variables that may be crucial in understanding the interaction between the parties in a dispute.

The framework leads us to raise questions about the exact nature of the relationships between more specific variables that may be encompassed within the general scheme. These questions center on the following topics:

(1) *Variations in the Situation*. Different patterns of preferences among outcomes by the parties result in variations in the extent of conflict of interest and in the relative power of the two sides. How are these and other variations in the situation related to the use of different types of actions—e.g., threat, force, or concessions—by each side? Are there ways of modifying conflict situations that will promote the nonviolent resolution of disputes?

(2) *Perceptions of the Situation*. How do the leaders of each nation define the situation they face? For example, how do they come to perceive their own options, the preferences and the likely actions of the other side, and the possible outcomes? Are there ways to improve the accuracy of leaders' perceptions so that dangerous miscalculations can be avoided?

(3) *The Choice Among Options*. Faced with a particular situation (i.e., a set of possible outcomes that may occur with different probabilities) how do national leaders choose among actions (e.g., to use force or to make concessions)? Under what circumstances do they take risky actions that may lead to war and when do they make less risky choices? What can be done to encourage decisionmakers to make choices that do not risk war?

(4) *The Effectiveness of Alternative Strategies*. When are particular types of actions—e.g., threat, coercion, concession—effective in securing cooperation from the other side and when does each lead instead to coercion (or the threat of it) by the other? Under what conditions will attempted deterrence of attack from an adversary be successful? What types of general strategies—e.g., consistent firmness, consistent cooperation, reciprocity (tit for tat), combining firmness and conciliation—are most apt to elicit concessions from the other side?

(5) *Escalation and De-escalation*. What is the process by which threats, arms buildups, or use of force may escalate to dangerous levels? Under what conditions does the reverse process of de-escalation occur? What are the implications for national policies such as arms acquisition, deterrence, and use of coercion?

(6) *Settling Disputes*. When is agreement reached and when is it not reached? What determines the terms of an agreement—who gets what? What are the advantages and disadvantages of alternative bargaining strategies? What can be done to increase the chances that a dispute will be settled successfully without the use of force?

In the chapters to follow I will consider each of these sets of questions and for each will attempt to summarize in an integrated way what we know about the issues in question. In doing so, I will draw on relevant theory and research—especially from international relations and from social psychology—without attempting to provide an exhaustive review of all relevant work. Building on previous work, I will present a set of conclusions concerning the conditions under which inter-nation disputes are more or less likely to result in violence. These propositions—sometimes made with some confidence and sometimes rather tentatively—are intended both as a convenient way of summarizing what we know and for guiding further inquiry.

On the basis of the conclusions reached concerning each set of issues examined, I also will discuss the implications for national policy. The knowledge we have is clearly not sufficient to enable one to make policy suggestions with assurance that they will always be useful in particular situations. But what we know is relevant for policy and these implications need to be spelled out.

Summary

This chapter presents a theoretical framework for studying the interaction between two nations engaged in a dispute. The outcomes for each side in a dispute depend on the joint actions of both sides. The action chosen by each side at any time depends on the values it places on different outcomes and on its expectations about the actions of the other side. As interaction between the parties continues, each side attempts to influence the current outcomes for the other side, the preferences of the other for possible outcomes, and the expectations of the other side concerning its own actions. Such changes in perceptions lead one or both sides to change its expectations about what it is possible to attain in the situation without excessive costs or risks. Eventually, this process causes the positions of the two sides to converge sufficiently for the conflict to be settled.

Characteristics of the nations involved in a dispute (such as their military capabilities and their politics), personal traits of leaders, and features of the broader environment (e.g., relations with third nations) affect the actions of the disputants by affecting their perceptions of possible outcomes, their preferences among outcomes, and their expectancies concerning what actions will lead to what outcomes.

Within the broad theoretical framework presented in this chapter, succeeding chapters will explore what determines the actions of national leaders in disputes and what kinds of actions are most effective in avoiding war while also defending the interests of one's nation. These chapters will focus on the following topics: the conflict situation, perceptions of the situation, choosing among options, the effectiveness of alternative strategies, and the settlement of disputes.

2 The Situation

When nations are involved in a dispute, how are their actions affected by the nature of the situation they face? In this chapter I consider this question in the context of the more general issue of how variations in conflict situations affect the ways in which the conflicts are resolved. This more general perspective will be applied to the subject of inter-nation conflicts in particular.

The situation facing each party in a dispute may be defined by (a) their basic alternatives of concession and firmness;[1] (b) the possible outcomes (a win for side A, a win for side B, compromise, and continuing struggle) that may result from possible combinations of actions by the two sides; and, (c) the pattern of preferences of the two sides among these outcomes. These elements form the type of outcome matrix discussed in chapter 1. The conditions under which interaction between the parties occurs—e.g., whether each side can reverse its actions and the amount of communication between the two sides—also are part of the basic situation. Other circumstances—e.g., the economic and military capability of each side, the support of third parties for each side, domestic political pressures —are important primarily insofar as they affect the significance of various outcomes (e.g., how humiliating a defeat would be or what the results of a fight are likely to be) and therefore affect the strength of the parties' preferences among outcomes.

The nature of the situation the parties face will not necessarily determine their actions completely. Much depends on the perceptions the participants have of the situation. Also, the actions of each side in a given type of situation are likely to be influenced by the behavior of the other side. But the situation provides a set of constraints on the actions of each side. It poses a set of problems and challenges for each side individually and for the disputants as a pair. In particular, the situation will shape: (a) incentives to take conciliatory or competitive actions; (b) incentives to act first or to wait for the other to act; (c) expectations about the likely behavior of the other side; (d) the power of each side to influence the actions of the other; (e) the ease of reaching and keeping agreements; and, (f) the balance of individual versus mutual interests. Let us consider each of these topics in turn as well as the related topic of communication between the parties.

Incentives for Cooperation and Competition

When two parties have a dispute, there usually are a variety of specific actions each may take toward the other. However, it often is useful to group the specific actions into two general types: those that involve making concessions and that represent firmness or toughness (Snyder and Diesing, 1977). The firmness strategy is likely to be accompanied by vigorous attempts to influence the other to accept one's position (by persuasion, threat, etc.), although such influence attempts also may accompany concessions. The possible combinations of these two strategies by the two sides and the resulting outcomes are shown in table 2.1. If both sides make concessions, the likely outcome is a compromise (cell A). If both stand firm, the outcome is a deadlock, with the possibility of a fight resulting (cell D). If side 1 makes concessions while side 2 stands firm, the end result (assuming the concessions are large or sustained enough) is that 1 will get its way (cell C). If 1 concedes while 2 stands firm, the outcome is that 2 gets its way (cell B). The value, or payoff, of each outcome to each side is indicated in each cell. For example, the value of a compromise to side 1 is indicated by the notation R_1.

Whether a given side will concede or stand firm will depend in part on the relative size of the payoffs associated with each of the four possible outcomes (R, S, T, and P). The incentive for side 1 to make concessions becomes greater as: (a) the value of a compromise solution (R_1) increases; (b) the value of letting side 2 get its way (S_1) increases (or becomes less negative); (c) the value of 1 getting its own way (T_1) decreases; and, (d) the value of no agreement (P_1) decreases. The incentives for side 2 are similar.

The relative size of the various payoffs is also important. Social psychologists who have studied cooperation and conflict in laboratory situations have tried to provide an overall characterization of the extent to which the possible outcomes (payoffs) in a situation favor either cooperation or conflict. For example, Boyle and Bonacich (1970) have characterized the situation in terms of three aspects. The first is the gain from cooperation, g, which is equal to R-P. The second is the risk in cooperation, r, which is equal to P-S.

The third is the "temptation" (the possible advantage of winning), t, which is equal to T-R. Boyle and Bonacich found that the likelihood of making a noncooperative choice in the initial plays of different laboratory games was predicted very well by the following formula: the risk from cooperation multiplied by the temptation to try to win, divided by the possible gain from cooperation (with the square root of this term then taken).

Other investigators have used other formulas that combine the four possible payoffs to predict cooperative or noncooperative behavior (e.g., Steele and Tedeschi, 1967; Rapoport, 1967; Wyer, 1971). Several writers have gone beyond characterizing the incentives for each single player to cooperate and have proposed ways to describe the overall correspondence of outcomes between the two sides (Axelrod, 1967; Kelley and Thibaut, 1978). Such measures have been shown to be related to the proportion of cooperative choices in different experimental situations (Axelrod, 1967). Without attempting to assess the relative validity of various specific formulas, it seems reasonable to conclude that the incentives for one party in a dispute to make concessions becomes greater as the values of a compromise agreement and of a loss increase relative to the values of a win and of a deadlock (with its present, or potential, struggle).

In international relations there is little systematic evidence concerning the ways in which behavior is affected by the pattern of outcomes in the situation and the relative values each side assigns to these outcomes. Also, it is obviously a simplification—sometimes an oversimplification—to describe the actions of each side in terms of two basic categories —conciliatory versus standing firm—and the resulting possible outcomes for each in terms of four basic categories (win, lose, compromise, stalemate). Yet, investigators using historical evidence from many international disputes have found that this simplified approach is useful for understanding the basic dynamics of most inter-nation disputes (Snyder and Diesing, 1977; Gamson and Modigliani, 1971; VanEvera, 1985). By indicating the relative magnitude of the incentives each nation has for either concession or firmness, the basic framework helps to account for actions taken in international crises.

We may illustrate the way in which the relative attractiveness of various outcomes may affect the behavior of nations involved in disputes by considering the situation faced by Israel and the Palestine Liberation Organization (PLO).[2] Table 2.2 shows the possible outcomes of conciliatory and firm action by the two sides with respect to their dispute about control of the land west of the Jordan River. The table also shows what are hypothesized to be the preferences for the two sides among the possible outcomes.

Table 2.1   Set of Possible Outcomes Resulting from Concession or Firmness by
Each Side in a Conflict Situation*

	Side 2	
	Make concessions	Stand firm
Make concessions	Compromise R_1, R_2 A	2 gets its way S_1, T_2 B
Stand firm	1 gets its way T_1, S_2 C	Deadlock, no agreement (possible war) P_1, P_2 D

Side 1 (labels on the left: "Make concessions" / "Side 1" / "Stand firm")

*The entries in the center of each cell indicate the value to each
side of that outcome.

Both Israel and the PLO, it is assumed for the sake of this illustration, have
the following rank order of preference:

win > stalemate (continuing struggle) > compromise > lose

In other words, we are assuming that for either side to compromise—for
ideological, religious, political, security or other reasons—would be so
painful that a continuing struggle is deemed preferable. Given such a
pattern of preferences, it would clearly be in the best interest of each side
to continue to stand firm in its position. Making concessions can lead at
best to compromise, which is seen as worse than the present deadlock. At
worst, making concessions could result ultimately in complete victory for
the other side. On the other hand, standing firm may result in the best
possible outcome (victory) and, at worst, in continuing stalemate, which is
still better than either compromise or defeat. Given such a pattern of
preferences among possible outcomes by both sides, deadlock would be
the result.

   The strength of the incentives for each side to make concessions or to
stand firm depends not only on the rank order of their preferences but on
the *strength* of preference for each outcome. For example, if Israel or the
PLO saw some type of compromise as almost as desirable as the present
deadlock, its incentive for making concessions would be stronger than if a
compromise was seen as far worse than deadlock.[3]

   If we want nations to choose conciliatory rather than intransigent courses
of action, it is important to try to manipulate the relevant incentives or

Table 2.2　The Israeli-Palestinian Dispute: A Situation in Which Incentives Favor Standing Firm*

| | Israel | |
	Make concessions	Stand firm
Make concessions (Palestinians, e.g., PLO)	*Compromise* Division of land between Jews and Arabs 3, 3	*Victory for Israel* Arabs give up claim to (almost all) of land 4, 1
Stand firm	*Victory for Arabs* Major portion of land transferred to control of Palestinians 1, 4	*Stalemate* No agreement; military and political struggle continues 2, 2

*Number 1 is preferred most, and number 4 is preferred least.

their perceptions of these incentives. First, it may be possible to increase the (perceived) value of a compromise solution. Sometimes this may be made possible by either side (or third parties) providing additional information about the advantages of further cooperation to which today's agreement may lead. Second, it is sometimes possible to create new compromise solutions that offer advantages to both sides. For example, a disagreement between Israel and Egypt in 1982 on the Sinai border was resolved by placing a multinational force in control of the disputed area until the matter could be arbitrated.

Third, the disadvantages of a deadlock may be emphasized. One or both of the parties may not have fully considered the economic, political, and possibly physical losses that could result from deadlock and a possible armed conflict. European leaders in 1914, for example, all thought of a possible war as an event that, though perhaps regrettable, would be quickly decided. If they had been better informed about the new military realities that would lead to an agonizing mutual slaughter for four long years, their readiness to stand firm rather than to compromise in 1914 might well have been lessened.

Steps might also be taken to reduce the possible penalties of making

Table 2.3   A Situation Favoring Preemptive Attack*

	Nation A	
	No military action	Takes military action
Nation B — Takes military action	1, 3	4, 4
Nation B — No military action	2, 2	3, 1

*Number 1 is preferred most, and number 4 is preferred least.

one-sided concessions. For example, when the principal cost of backing down is the loss of prestige or face, it may be possible to make the concession appear to be a magnanimous acceptance of the wishes of some legitimate international body (e.g., the United Nations) rather than bowing to the coercion of the other side in the dispute.

Finally, it may be possible to reduce the value of winning for each side. For instance, the disadvantages of completely humiliating and frustrating the opponent in terms of future relations between the two sides can be emphasized. In addition, it sometimes is possible for third parties to arrange for the gains of victory to be reduced. For example, when Israel tried to win a complete victory over the Egyptians in 1973, rather than making concessions for cease-fire arrangements, the American secretary of state told the Israelis that the United States would not allow Israel to destroy the surrounded Egyptian Third Army (Kissinger, 1982).

Incentives for Acting First

If one side in a dispute is able to act first—as is usually the case—some situations provide an incentive for first, or preemptive action (Rapoport and Guyer, 1966; Kelley and Thibaut, 1978:151–155). Consider, for example, the situation shown in table 2.3. Let us suppose that A and B are two antagonistic nations disputing some piece of territory (say, Britain and Argentina quarreling over control of the Falkland/Malvinas Islands). If nation A takes military action first (perhaps by occupying the territory), it forces nation B to choose between not retaliating (which will give B a poor

Table 2.4 A Situation Where First Attack Improves Each Nation's Outcomes in the Event of a War*

		Nation A	
		Fight only when attacked	Attack first
Fight only when attacked			
Nation B		2, 2	3, 1
Attack first		1, 3	4, 4

*Number 1 is preferred most, and number 4 is preferred least.

outcome) or of taking military action, which will give B an even worse outcome (although also reducing A's outcome). If nation B takes military action first, it forces the same unpleasant choice on nation A. Each side thus has a double incentive to attack preemptively—first to attempt to get the other to allow it to win unopposed and, second, to prevent the other from putting it in the same undesirable position.

A preemptive action also may be taken in order to improve one's own outcomes in the event a fight does occur. Table 2.4 shows two antagonistic nations that may either attack first or fight only when attacked. (Israel and Egypt in 1967 might fit this situation.) The nation that attacks first may thereby enjoy a decisive advantage and get a better outcome even though the other side fights when attacked. Thus, each side has a strong incentive to strike first. Such a situation is especially likely to occur when the technology and terrain of war give a marked advantage to the offense (Snyder, 1985; Quester, 1986: chapter 13).

However, in some situations it is (or is perceived to be) in one or both side's interest to wait for the other to act first. Consider the situation in October 1973 just prior to the Egyptian attack on Israel. For the Egyptians, a surprise attack was seen as essential for any degree of success in another war with Israel. But the Israelis, when they learned that an Egyptian attack was imminent, decided that the final outcome would be better for them if they fought only when attacked rather than striking preemptively as they had in 1967. This is because they now had more defensible borders than they earlier had and because they were anxious to retain the support of other nations, especially the United States, by showing that they were the victims of attack (Kissinger, 1982). In summary, the more that the pattern of outcomes is such that the side that moves first may permanently improve its outcomes at the expense of the other, the more likely each side is to make a coercive move.

Today, the all-important deterrence of nuclear attack by each super-power on the other depends in part on the absence of an incentive by either to strike preemptively. A number of writers (e.g., Schelling and Halperin, 1969; Harkabi, 1966; Quester, 1986) have discussed the danger of a nuclear war being launched preemptively by a nation that fears attack and believes that it must strike first. These writers have suggested various measures that may be taken to reduce the incentive for preemptive attack. These include improving each side's information about the other's prepara-tory actions, avoiding actions that appear as preparations for attack, reduc-ing the vulnerability of each side's retaliatory forces to attack, and other collaborative measures to reduce the advantage to an aggressor of surprise attack. Such measures, if successful, would permit each side to continue with a peaceful course of action in the knowledge that its policy could be changed if necessary without unacceptable penalty for delay.

Expectations of the Other's Responses

The discussion so far has focused on the value of possible outcomes to one side with little attention to the expected actions of the other side. But a particular outcome—e.g., a compromise agreement—obviously depends on the joint actions of both sides. In some cases an actor may disregard the actions of the other side when making his own action choices. He may believe that he cannot predict the action of the other side or that a particu-lar action of his own is best regardless of what the other does. However, in many other cases the choice of each side will be influenced by the antici-pated action of the other. And one of the major determinants of the other's expected action is the pattern of incentives faced by the other side. Results from several experimental studies provide relevant evidence. Wyer (1971) found that if the incentives for B to make a cooperative choice are high, A is likely also to make a cooperative choice—apparently because of his expectation that B will be motivated to do so. Mogy and Pruitt (1974) found that compliance to a threat was less likely if the costs of enforcement of the threat were high. Those threatened often did not believe that it was in the threatener's interest to carry out his threat, and so their own actions were based on this assumption.

In the international arena as well the actions of one nation often may be influenced greatly by its perceptions of the incentives that are present for and thus likely to affect the actions of another. For example, in 1973 Israeli leaders disregarded the mobilization of Egyptian and Syrian troops along Israel's borders and the statements by Egypt's President Sadat that he intended to go to war. Their basic reasoning was that it was not in Egypt's (or Syria's) interest to go to war since they would only suffer another crushing defeat. Therefore, the Israelis did not take the threat seriously and did not mobilize their own forces. In this case of course they were mistaken, not realizing that Sadat was playing for political stakes rather than for military victory over Israel (Maoz, 1982:206–208).

Power

The outcome matrix in any relationship determines the power that each side possesses to affect the outcomes of the other. Two basic types of vulnerability are possible: threat vulnerability and force vulnerability.[4]

Threat vulnerability. Suppose that side A, by threatening to change his own behavior, can make it in B's interest to change first rather than to suffer the consequences of A's shift. Suppose also that if A carries out his threat he will lose less than B (relative to their present outcomes), thereby making his threat credible. In such a situation, B is "threat-vulnerable."

To illustrate a threat-vulnerable situation, table 2.5 shows a situation that might exist in the relations between the United States and China as they concern the U.S. link to Taiwan. Let us suppose (as was the historical case) that China has been conciliatory about establishing and maintaining diplomatic and other relations with the United States, despite the fact that the United States remained firm in its policy of supplying arms to Taiwan (which China, of course, claims as part of its own territory). Thus, the two nations are in cell A and neither can improve its payoff by a unilateral action. However, China may be dissatisfied with the present outcome in cell A because that outcome ranks low in its preference order, while it is the number one preference of the United States. But China is in a position to threaten the United States with a move—increasing firmness about breaking off ties with the United States if the latter continues supplying arms to Taiwan—that will result in a decrease in payoff for the United States (in cell C) that is greater than the decrease for China. To avoid this result, the United States might be induced to make concessions—such as reducing arms supplies to Taiwan in return for continuing relations with China (cell B). Although this outcome is not as desirable for the United States as the outcome in cell A, it is preferable to that which would have occurred in cell C if China had carried out its threat. If side B in a dispute is vulnerable to

Table 2.5   A Threat-Vulnerable Situation: Actions by the United States and
Mainland China on the Issue of Taiwan*

United States

		Firm	Concede
China	Concede	U.S. supplies arms to Taiwan; China maintains ties to U.S. 3, 1 A	U.S. stops arms to Taiwan; China maintains ties to U.S. 1, 2 B
	Firm	U.S. maintains ties to Taiwan; China breaks ties to U.S. 4, 3 C	U.S. stops arms to Taiwan; China breaks ties to U.S. 2, 4 D

*Number 1 is preferred most, and number 4 is preferred least.

threat from side A, then A is more likely to use threat and, if it does so, B is more likely to submit to A's demands than if B were not threat-vulnerable.

Force vulnerability. Suppose that by actually changing its behavior (not merely threatening a change), A can change B's outcomes in such a way that it then becomes in B's interest to change its own behavior. Suppose also that A can do this while suffering little, if any, loss (thus making this a realistic option for A). In such a situation, B is force-vulnerable—i.e., vulnerable to a penalizing action by A.

To illustrate a situation in which one side is vulnerable to the use of force by the other, consider table 2.6. This table shows a hypothetical situation involving spending by the United States and its NATO allies on the defense of Europe. Let us suppose that the action starts in cell A—i.e., that the United States is spending much on defense but that the West European countries are spending relatively little. The result (cell A) is a good outcome (first preference) for the Europeans but a relatively poor outcome (next-to-lowest preference) for the United States.

If the United States would lower its spending to match the low spending by the Europeans, the outcome would be even worse for the United States, presumably because of the high value it puts on maintaining a credible

Table 2.6   A Force-Vulnerable Situation: Spending by the United States and Its NATO Allies on Defense*

| | | NATO allies | |
		Low spending	High spending
United States	High spending	3, 1 A	1, 3 B
	Low spending	4, 4 C	2, 2 D

*Number 1 is preferred most, and number 4 is preferred least.

deterrent to the use of Soviet power. However, by actually changing its action to one of low spending (thus moving the action to cell C), the United States can lower the payoff for the Europeans greatly (they might feel vulnerable to Soviet attack) and thus make it in their interest to increase their own spending. If they did so, this would move the situation to cell D, where the outcomes to both are relatively good. (Once in cell D, the United States can improve its payoff by switching its behavior again, but it is unlikely to do so since it will recognize that the Europeans would in turn be motivated to change again, thus bringing the action full circle to cell A.) If side B in a dispute is vulnerable to force used by side A, then A is more likely to use force and, if it does so, B is more likely to submit to A's demands than if B were not force-vulnerable.

Force vulnerability and escalation. When each side in a dispute is vulnerable to the use of force by the other, a pattern of mutual escalation of the use of force may result. Side A may take an action that penalizes B in the hope that B will then see that changing some "undesirable" behavior is in its self-interest. But A may also be vulnerable to the use of force. Rather than concede to A, B may counter with a move that penalizes A and makes it (B believes) in A's interest to concede. If at this point A believes that B is vulnerable to still another (perhaps stronger) forceful move, it may act to penalize B again, at which point B may move again, and so on. (See chapter 8 for a fuller discussion of the escalation of force.)

Relative power. The actual use of threat or force in securing compliance will be affected greatly by the relative power of the two sides (i.e., the

ability of each to affect the outcomes of the other). The question of how
the relative power of nations affects their behavior in resolving disputes has
been much discussed. Some have argued that the use of coercion to settle
disputes is most likely when the parties are about equal in power (e.g.,
Organski, 1958; Blainey, 1973; Rummel, 1979). For example, Rummel
advances the proposition that power parity makes escalation to war more
likely. He states: "If one side is clearly superior in will and existing military capability and potential, then the other side is likely to avoid escalation, if necessary by negotiating a resolution to the conflict. . . . . Power
parity is an ambiguous situation of coercive power in which both sides
simultaneously can believe that war will be victorious. War clears up this
ambiguity" (Rummel, 1979:386).

However, other writers have argued the reverse—that war between two
nations is most likely when one is much more powerful than the other
(e.g., Claude, 1962; Morgenthau, 1963; Ferris, 1973). For example,
Ferris hypothesizes that "Given an interstate conflict, the greater the disparity in the power capabilities relationship between the two sides to the
conflict prior to the occurrence of the conflict, the greater the probability
the conflict will escalate to the level of military hostilities" (Ferris, 1973:22).
He reasons that "A state confronted with equal power capabilities is less
likely to initiate war than if it is confronted with weak power capabilities"
(Ferris, 1973:24). As for the weaker state, Ferris argues that it "may still
find it rational to wage war if it attaches great importance to the interest in
conflict" (Ferris, 1973:24). More importantly, he says, the leaders of the
weaker state may have other reasons not to appease the stronger nation,
including not whetting its appetite for further advantage and maintaining
their own positions of authority.[5]

Evidence concerning the way in which relative power affects the likelihood of overt conflict is available both from experimental laboratory studies and from studies of international relations. Experimental studies generally have found equal power to be associated with cooperation rather than
with conflict between the parties (Rubin and Brown 1975:214–221).
However, a number of studies have found that when both parties have a
high and equal capacity to injure the other, an overt conflict occurred more
often than when only one party (or neither) had such a capability (e.g.,
Deutsch and Krauss, 1960; Tedeschi, Schlenker, and Lindskold, 1972).

Evidence based on historical records from several centuries of international relations indicates that the relative power of two states in conflict is
not a good predictor of whether or not war will occur. Rummel reviewed
evidence from thirty-seven relevant studies and found that 65 percent of
the evidence supported the proposition that power parity makes escalation

to war more likely (Rummel 1979:287). However, some studies (e.g., Ferris, 1973; Singer and Small, 1979) have found an opposite relationship and some have found that power parity was associated with war during one time period but that power imbalance was associated with war during another time period (Singer, Bremer, and Stuckey, 1979).

Additional studies indicate that nations that are stronger than their neighbors do not thereby avoid war (Naroll, 1969; Weede, 1970; Raser and Crowe, 1968). It is undoubtedly true that, other things being equal, a strong nation is less likely to be attacked than is a weak nation. But it also appears to be true that strong nations act assertively and their resulting disputes with other nations often result in war.[6]

Overall, it seems clear that relative power in itself is not associated reliably with the occurrence of overt conflict. However, there are certain consistencies that do seem to occur. When one side is more powerful than the other, it usually is willing to use threat and coercion to settle a dispute (Tedeschi, Schlenker, and Lindskold, 1972). But when two parties are equal in power, each is more cautious about initiating an overt conflict with the other. In several experimental studies, Thibaut and his associates have shown that two parties are more likely to devise norms of behavior to regulate their behavior and avoid conflict when both have the power and willingness to affect the welfare of the other (e.g. Thibaut and Faucheux, 1965; Thibaut, 1968; Thibaut and Gruder, 1969).

Similar findings come from the real world of international relations. Wright (1965) found that where power between adversary nations is equal and the capacity for damage is great, war is unlikely. Jensen (1965) has shown that progress in reaching agreement in arms control negotiations has been greater when the parties are about equal in strength. Raymond and Kegley (1985) found that norms supportive of mediation between nations are stronger when relative parity in power exists among the major powers. It appears, then, that a high and equal capacity by each side to damage the welfare of the other is likely (other things being equal) to lead the parties to be cautious about initiating conflict and to try to build safeguards against such an event.[7]

On the other hand, there is evidence suggesting that if one party uses coercion against a second then the second is more likely to reciprocate when there is power equality between the two than when the initiator is more powerful. Experimental studies have found that higher-power persons tend to use coercion while lower-power persons tend to submit when a more powerful adversary uses coercion against them. When the parties are more equal in power, coercion is more likely to be resisted, and an increasing spiral of conflict often ensues (Rubin and Brown, 1975:214–221;

Tedeschi, Schlenker, and Lindskold, 1972). In international relations Leng (1980) found that when one nation threatens another, the nation threatened is more likely to respond defiantly when the adversaries are equal in power than when the threatener is stronger. Moreover, Leng found that defiance of threats was associated with the occurrence of war.

Thus, equality of power appears to have two separate effects that may work in opposite directions. On the one hand, when nations have equal power (especially when this power is high and each perceives the other as willing to use its power), both sides will tend to avoid the use of mutually damaging coercion. On the other hand, if one side uses coercion or the threat of coercion, the other side—being equal in power—is likely to retaliate in kind, and an overt conflict that often escalates to high levels of coercion tends to ensue. The evidence suggests, therefore, that equal-power relationships offer both special opportunities and dangers for the nations involved. The opportunity arises from the reluctance to use coercion and the tendency to accept noncoercive ways to settle disputes in equal-power situations. National leaders in such situations may be able to exploit these natural tendencies to develop noncoercive mechanisms (mediation, arbitration, norms, agreements, etc.) to settle disputes. It also appears important for nations to be especially cautious in their use of coercion or even threat of coercion in their relations with equal-power adversaries. The use of such tactics in these relationships will often result in counter-threat and counter-coercion and may escalate to a high level of mutual destructiveness.

Change in relative power. The likelihood of overt conflict between two parties may be affected not only by their relative power at a given point in time but also by *changes* in their relative power over time. In the area of international relations, Rudolph Rummel has placed great emphasis on what he calls "changes in the balance of power." He writes: "For war to occur . . . there must be a significant change in the balance of powers supporting the status quo. Interests, capabilities, and will singly or in combination must have changed sufficiently that the *status quo* is now felt to be unjust, threatened, or ripe for readjustment. . . . This change has created a tension, a cold or hostile climate between the parties" (Rummel, 1979:252). Changes in the relative power of the parties means that one party now has greater control over the outcomes of the other party than was true previously. It now is in a better position to change the behavior of the other side (and thus the distribution of benefits) by using threat or actual coercion. However, the status quo party is likely to resent efforts by the "revisionist" party to force changes and may well resist.

Rummel reviews some evidence in support of the idea that change in relative power leads to greater tension and hostility as well as to more overt conflict between nations (Rummel, 1979:268–270). Organski and Kugler (1980) also studied the relation between relative power and war in the international system between 1860 and 1975. They found that war was more likely among the most powerful when one of the contenders was in the process of passing the other in power. However, they did not find a similar result among the less-powerful nations. Ferris (1973) also reports that a change in the relative power position of two nations in either direction was associated with intense conflict (though not necessarily war) between those nations. In addition, Ferris found that a widening of the power gap was especially likely to lead to international conflict. However, Wallace (1982) examined a set of ninety-nine serious disputes between great powers from 1816–1965 and did *not* find that the outcomes of a dispute (war or not) could be predicted from the relative rates of military growth in the five years prior to a dispute. Overall, this evidence supports the idea that changes in relative power are likely to lead to tension and strain between two nations. Whether this tension will result in overt conflict, such as war, is less predictable and will depend on a variety of other factors, such as the dissatisfaction of the parties with the status quo, their sociocultural similarity, and their decisionmaking structures (Rummel, 1979:251–255).

The evidence suggests that it is important for nations to be aware of the strains that changes in relative power can exert on their relationship. A nation growing in power may feel that it is not getting the share of benefits —economic advantages, political influence, etc.—that are commensurate with its new status. It may believe that it is in a position, by threat or coercion, to force other nations to concede greater advantages to it. A good example is Japan in the 1930s. The Japanese had grown in economic and military power relative to the Western powers and they felt that they were not being accorded international status or economic and political position commensurate with their strength. They attempted to force the Western nations to modify the status quo in the Pacific. The Western nations resisted, and the result was war.

When changes in relative power do occur, and the nation growing in power has grievances it wishes redressed, other nations would be well-advised to try to adjust their behavior and the distribution of benefits to reflect the new power situation. Otherwise, there will be a constant temptation for the nation growing in power to use that power to change the situation in a way that reflects these new realities.

Reaching and Keeping Agreements

The pattern of outcomes that are possible in any situation affects not only the incentives for cooperation and the power of each side but also whether they are able to reach and keep an agreement. First there is the question of whether there are any outcomes that both parties prefer to having no agreement at all. If there is only one such outcome, and both sides are aware of this fact, it may be easy for the parties to coordinate their actions to reach this outcome. However, there may be more than one outcome that both prefer to no agreement, and the two sides may differ widely in their preferences among these possible outcomes. Since it may be difficult for them to coordinate their behavior, they may end up with the outcome each least prefers (i.e., no agreement).

Prominent outcomes. The likelihood of two parties reaching agreement may be increased by the existence of one or more "prominent" or "focal" outcomes (Schelling, 1960). A prominent outcome is one that stands out perceptually and may seem to be a natural point of agreement. For example, in a territorial dispute, a river, a line of latitude, or a previous boundary might be a perceptually prominent point. Principles like an equal division, a return to the status quo at the start of the dispute, or adherence to a UN resolution also may be perceptually prominent points.

Such a point is one on which the expectations of both sides may converge. One or both sides may use such a prominent point as one beyond which it will not concede further. ("If we don't take a stand here, where will concessions stop?") The other side may not expect to get its partner to concede beyond this prominent point. If the expectations of both sides converge on some prominent or focal point, then it may become the outcome on which they agree. In particular, the existence of a prominent point may make it easier to find a compromise agreement that both sides will accept.

However, the existence of a prominent point will not guarantee reaching an agreement. A number of prominent points may be present, each of which differs in how much advantage it would give to one side or the other. If this is the case, it would be hard for the two sides to coordinate their expectations on one of these outcomes. In addition, it is important to realize that a prominent point of possible agreement is not necessarily an "equilibrium outcome" (Rapoport and Guyer, 1966); that is, one side may be able by unilateral action to improve its position relative to that prominent outcome. For example, while a river might be a prominent point of agreement in a boundary dispute, one side (or both) may believe that, by the use of threat or force, it can achieve an outcome more favorable to itself. To be an acceptable outcome for both sides, a prominent outcome must reflect—at least roughly—the power balance between the two sides.

Stable settlements. The matrix of possible outcomes in a dispute may affect not only the chances of reaching an agreement but also the likelihood of the agreement being stable. The concept of a stable settlement in international relations has been discussed by Snyder and Diesing. Using a concept equivalent to that of equilibrium outcome in game theory,[8] they state:

> A settlement is stable if it dominates all other options for bargainers, that is, if no side has any option available that would improve its own position. In practice, this means that a settlement is stable if each side has a sanction available that can punish any attempt by another bargainer to improve his position unilaterally. . . . Bargaining is not simply a matter of reaching agreement; it is a matter of finding an agreement that cannot be unilaterally broken, an agreement that each bargainer can defend. (Snyder and Diesing, 1977:162)

As an example of an unstable agreement, they cite the agreement reached between Chamberlain and Hitler on 20 September 1938 to settle their future differences by negotiation. Since the British could not bring sanctions to bear on Germany in the event that Hitler changed his mind, the agreement was unstable and Hitler soon ignored it.

Snyder and Diesing also argue that the stability of an agreement should not be judged solely in terms of whether either side can unilaterally improve its position at present. They point out that if a party is dissatisfied with an agreement, it will continue to search for new options by which to improve its position, even if it has to wait for a while to do so. They mention as examples the Versailles treaty of 1919, the Saar agreement of 1945, various agreements in Palestine, and the 1973 Vietnam agreement. In each case, one of the parties to the settlement remained aggrieved and, though it could take no immediate action to improve its position, it bided its time until an opportunity to do so arose. Thus, in the long run a stable settlement is one that meets the basic aspirations of both parties. However, it should be added that stability in the previous sense—of an agreement that neither side can unilaterally improve upon—will continue to be relevant even when the parties are satisfied with an agreement. If one side sees the possibility of unilaterally bettering its position, it may raise its level of aspiration and become dissatisfied with the present arrangement.

Can anything be done about the pattern of possible outcomes in order to promote agreement between two parties to a dispute? Our analysis suggests first, not surprisingly, that it may be important for the parties (or third parties) to locate possible outcomes that they both would prefer to no agreement. Also, if an outcome can be found that is uniquely prominent in the perceptions of both sides, their agreeing on this outcome may be greatly facilitated.

However, our discussion also suggests that it is not only necessary that agreement be reached but that arrangements be made to make the agreement stable; i.e., in the sense that neither side has incentives to try to improve its position by violating the agreement. This might be accomplished by the parties themselves or third parties removing possible rewards from violations or arranging sanctions for violations. For example, when the United States entered into a peace agreement with North Vietnam in 1973, the American government attempted to keep the agreement stable by arranging for sanctions (withdrawal of economic aid, military retaliation) if the North Vietnamese violated the agreement (Kissinger, 1982). As events turned out, the weakening of President Nixon's authority as a result of the Watergate scandal and the weariness of the American public with involvement in Indochina removed the presence of most of the intended sanctions. The result was that the North Vietnamese soon ignored the peace agreement and sent their army south.

We also have noted that the stability of an agreement in the long run depends also on both parties being reasonably satisfied with the agreement. Again, the case of the United States–North Vietnam peace treaty is a good illustration. While coercion (especially bombing) by the United States forced the North Vietnamese to accept a divided Vietnam, they were not satisfied with this outcome, feeling that it ran contrary to their history as a single nation as well as to their basic political aims. When the opportunity to overturn the agreement arose they seized it. Thus, it is important that an effort be made to find agreements that both sides can accept as at least minimally satisfactory and fair. Such outcomes, if they also are ones from which the parties have no strong incentive to deviate in order to better their position, are likely to be truly stable.

Self-Interest and Mutual Interest

In some situations the pattern of outcomes is such that each of the parties, in seeking to maximize its own competitive self-interest, ends up with poorer outcomes than it would have if both sides had cooperated. These situations pose a problem for each side and for the two sides as a pair. Two types of situations merit special attention, both because they are fairly common and because they clearly are relevant for many inter-nation disputes. One type of situation has been labeled "Prisoner's Dilemma," the other "Chicken."[9]

Prisoner's Dilemma. In a Prisoner's Dilemma situation, the order of preference among outcomes for both sides is as follows:

T (Own win)>R (Compromise)>P (Deadlock or Fight)>S (Other's win)

To illustrate, the situation shown in table 2.7 represents the dispute between the United States and the Soviet Union over Berlin in the years 1958–1962. In this situation the best move from each nation's individual standpoint was a competitive one, regardless of what the other side did. For the Soviet Union, if the United States made concessions, its better move would be to stand firm in order to obtain a win rather than a compromise. But if the United States stood firm, the Soviet Union would also do better to stand firm, thus achieving a deadlock rather than a defeat. The same is true for the United States; whatever the Soviet Union did, the United States would benefit by competitive firm actions. However, if both sides followed this logic of where their own unilateral interest lay, they would both take a firm competitive stand, resulting in a deadlock, which was a worse outcome for each than a compromise would have been. This is the dilemma inherent in a Prisoner's Dilemma situation: if both sides in such a situation follow their individual competitive self-interest, they each end up with a worse result than they would have obtained by mutual cooperation.

Such a dilemma also characterizes many other disputes between nations (Jervis, 1972; Snyder and Diesing, 1977; Brams, 1985).[10] A similar dilemma is present in many arms races (Brams, 1985). When two or more competing nations each builds arms to advance its self-interest, they may end up with poorer outcomes (high costs, high tension, neither superior) than if they had cooperated to limit arms (neither superior, low tensions, low costs). In order for two antagonists to get out of the Prisoner's Dilemma, they must be able to coordinate cooperative actions. This often requires that each side is confident that the other side will reciprocate cooperation. When each side expresses its own intention to cooperate and communicates its expectation that the other will cooperate, coordination is more likely to occur (Loomis, 1959). In the Berlin crisis both the Americans and the Soviets at various times communicated a desire to solve the crisis by compromise rather than by confrontation.

Coordination also is more likely when each side does not have to rely heavily on trust but can verify cooperation and can switch to competitive moves if the other cheats. An experimental study of cooperation and conflict has found that cooperation is more likely when each side has the capability of reversing its actions after learning of the other's actions (Deutsch,

Table 2.7   The Berlin Crisis of 1958–1962: A Prisoner's Dilemma Situation*

United States

	Make concessions	Stand firm
Make concessions	*Compromise* Western access to West Berlin retained; closing of East German border (Berlin Wall) 2, 2	*Western Win* East Germany continues to weaken; West Berlin remains independent 4, 1
Stand firm	*Soviet win* West forced out of Berlin; East Germany recognized as independent 1, 4	*Deadlock* East Germany continues to lose people; West's access to West Berlin remains insecure; danger of conflict. 3, 3

Soviet Union (labels **Make concessions** / **Stand firm** on the left of the rows)

*Number 1 is preferred most, and number 4 is preferred least.

1957:97–98). In such situations, neither side has to trust completely in the good faith of the other. Each can afford to make a cooperative move without too much risk of being exploited. And, neither can hope to gain an advantage by tricking the other into taking a unilateral and unreciprocated cooperative action.

In the Berlin crisis, such actions as the openness of access routes to the city and the building of a wall there did not require verification. Moreover, neither side had to take any action that was irreversible if the other ceased cooperating. In other cases, however—such as those concerning cooperation to limit arms—the ability to verify cooperation and to change course without great danger if the other stops cooperating may be crucial to the possibility of cooperation occurring.

Chicken. In a "Chicken" situation, the order of preference among outcomes for both sides is as follows:

T (Own Win)>R (Compromise)>S (Other's Win)>P (Deadlock or Fight)

Note that each of the parties in a Chicken situation would prefer to see the other win than to face a deadlock or fight. (This is the reverse of the

Table 2.8   The Munich Crisis of 1938: A Chicken Situation*

| | Britain-France | |
	Concede	Firm
Germany **Concede**	*Compromise* Peaceful German occupation of Sudetenland, but some violation of due process 2, 2	*Western "victory"* Peaceful occupation of Sudetenland, following diplomatic due process; German humiliation 3, 1
Firm	*German victory* Immediate occupation of Sudetenland as unilateral action of Germany 1, 3	*War* German invasion of Sudetenland brings Britain and France to defense of Czechs 4, 4

*Number 1 is preferred most, and number 4 is preferred least. This table is adapted from G. Snyder and P. Diesing, *Conflict Among Nations*, 1977:112.

preference order between these two outcomes in a Prisoner's Dilemma situation.)

An example of an inter-nation dispute that appears to represent a Chicken situation is the Munich crisis of 1938 between Germany on one side and a British-French alliance on the other side (Snyder and Diesing, 1977). This situation is represented in table 2.8. By the time of the Munich conference Britain and France had agreed to German demands for annexation of that part of Czechoslovakia (the Sudetenland) that had a mainly ethnic German population. The issue in dispute was whether this would be accomplished by diplomatic and legal means (thus salvaging Czech sovereignty and Western honor) or by the force of German arms (giving Germany enhanced power and humiliating the West).

In a Chicken situation each side has the incentive to be competitive and firm in order (a) to win a complete victory and (b) to prevent the other from winning a complete victory. But if both sides remain unyielding, they will have a "collision," which is the least desirable outcome for both. Thus, Britain, France, and Germany were most anxious to avoid war in 1938 (Germany primarily because she had not completed her rearmament program). A compromise based on mutual concession was preferable to war for both sides. However, since each side in a Chicken situation knows, or at least strongly suspects, that the other would rather give in than endure a fight, each is tempted to try to convince the other that he is inflexible and will make no concessions. He may try to maintain this firm posture until the last possible moment in hopes that the other side will "lose its nerve" and concede.

In the Munich crisis Hitler knew that the British and French were very anxious to avoid war and thought that they would, in the crunch, permit Germany to have its way rather than fight another war. Even though Hitler himself preferred to back down from his most extreme demands rather than to go to war at that time, he blustered and threatened to send his army into action in an effort to get the Western powers to capitulate, as they had in previous showdowns. Only when the British showed evidence of being serious in their commitment to a "legal" settlement of the Sudeten issue did Hitler agree on a last-minute compromise (one that still gave him the territory he desired).

Thus, while a Chicken situation makes compromise eventually possible, it provides incentives for each side to take competitive, possibly coercive actions in an effort to frighten the other side into submission. A Chicken situation also provides a double incentive for each side to take a competitive action *first*. By doing so, one side presents the other with a choice between submission, which it doesn't like, and initiating a fight, which it likes even less. By acting first, the initiator also prevents the other side from forcing it to make the same unpalatable choice. For example, by placing British troops on the Sudeten border, Britain would have made Hitler choose between accepting British terms or going to war. Similarly, in the Cuban missile crisis, there was advantage to either side in moving first. For the Soviets, a swift fait accompli establishing the missile bases would have forced the United States to choose between accepting a strategic defeat or attacking the bases. When the bases were discovered before completion, the blockade by the United States forced the Soviets to choose between accepting the blockade or provoking a war.

The danger in a Chicken situation is, of course, that competition and coercion may get out of control. Either or both sides may confidently continue to use threat or coercion in the expectation that the other side will "chicken out" and thereby a fight will be avoided. Like two drivers playing "Chicken," speeding toward each other on the road, each may wait too long for the other to swerve. Or, if one believes that the other is intent on a fight, he may conclude that he must hit first in order to gain some military advantage.

Many inter-nation disputes are essentially Chicken situations (Jervis, 1972; Snyder and Diesing, 1977; Brams, 1985; Sonnenfeldt, 1986). The United States and the Soviet Union have on a number of occasions confronted each other in disputes that appear to represent Chicken situations: these include the Berlin crisis of 1948, the Cuban missile crisis of 1962, and the nuclear alert crisis during the 1973 Yom Kippur War. In each of these situations each of the two superpowers threatened the other, directly or implicitly, with war to try to get its way, despite the fact that a major war was the worst outcome for both. In fact, the basic relationship between the United States and the Soviet Union is, in some important respects, one of Chicken. War between them would be the worst outcome for each side—in fact, a clearly catastrophic outcome. Yet each has an incentive to be tough and intransigent in political disputes—and sometimes acts in such ways—in order to frighten the other into concessions. The possibility of an unintended and possibly catastrophic clash occurring has been and continues to be present.

Discussing the common interest of the United States and the Soviet Union in avoiding war, Helmut Sonnenfeldt (1986:27) writes: "Sometimes this problem of responsibility for the peace of the world acquires the characteristic of a tough game of 'chicken.' Who can be pushed the furthest given the fear of cataclysmic war? Moreover, while fear of a nuclear war helps to sustain nuclear arms talks, it has not produced effective mechanisms to reduce the risk of war, as distinct from the efforts to defuse crises that have occurred in such situations as the 1962 Cuban missile crisis and the 1973 Yom Kippur War."

Coordination by two sides to avoid disaster in a Chicken situation is inherently very difficult. So long as each side believes that the other will submit in time to avoid disaster, it will be tempted to continue to apply pressure. The more information that can be made available to each side about the limits of the concessions the other side would actually be willing to make rather than go to war, the less likely each is to push the other beyond the point where a collision will occur. Also, it may be possible for the two sides to agree on limits to the use of force in their relationship. For example, to avoid the possibility that conflict between the United States and the Soviet Union could escalate into a nuclear war, both nations have made several agreements to minimize the use of force. In a 1972 agreement on Basic Principles of Relations between the two countries, the United States and the USSR promised to exercise "restraint in their mutual relations" in order to prevent dangerous situations from arising (Frei, 1982).

In both Prisoner's Dilemma and Chicken situations, as in situations with other patterns of outcomes, the situation does not in itself determine the actions of the parties. Each of these situations presents a problem that they can handle more or less effectively. To assure a good outcome for itself in such situations, some cooperation with the other side is necessary for each. Whether the two sides will be able to achieve such cooperation depends in part on how clearly and how accurately each perceives the true situation, especially with respect to the other's preferences (see chapter 3). Cooperation depends also on the features of the situation referred to previously in this section—the opportunity to communicate cooperative intent, the verifiability of actions, and the chance to reverse cooperative actions without great penalty if they are not reciprocated. In addition, success in achieving cooperation to promote joint interests depends on the types of actions and strategies pursued by the two sides—a topic to be explored at length in chapter 10.

Communication

We have noted that when it is mutually beneficial for two parties to coordinate their actions, effective channels of communication between them are often crucial. What types of communications are most useful and when are communicative channels used effectively? Rubin and Brown (1975:92) comment:

> the effectiveness of bargaining depends in large part upon the exchange of sufficient credible information between the parties. When the information exchanged appears to be insufficient or distorted, bargainers have no real basis on which to assume good or equitable intentions on the part of the other. Nor is there a sufficient basis for recognizing common interests . . . thus communication isolation, whether it results from physical or psychological conditions, imposes constraints on the development of cooperation and is likely to promote mistrust and suspicion.

Communication of several types of information seems especially important. Morton Deutsch and his colleagues have found that cooperation is facilitated if each of the parties communicates (a) his expectation that the other will cooperate; (b) his own intention to cooperate; (c) his intention to retaliate against noncooperation; and, (d) his absolution of the other party for any past noncooperative acts (Deutsch, 1973). Communication also may give each party a better understanding of the motivational structure (goals, values, constraints) of the other party. Such insight may help to better predict the future reactions of the other side. An understanding of the other side's thinking may also help each side devise possible solutions to their problems that will be acceptable to both. By providing these types of information, effective communication can greatly help the parties coordinate their actions in order to reach mutually agreeable outcomes.

Many experimental studies have found that cooperation is increased when people can communicate freely (e.g., Loomis, 1959; Swingle and Santi, 1972). Similarly, a computer simulation study by Sisson and Ackoff (1966) found that communication reduces the probability that conflict will escalate. Communication in which each side can hear the other speaking seems to be more effective than written communication. Arranging for the two sides to see each other face-to-face also tends to enhance effectiveness of communication, but visibility seems to be less important than voice contact (Rubin and Brown, 1975:96–99).

While communication usually is necessary to attain cooperation, the fact the communication occurs does not necessarily mean that it will be effective. Intentionally or unintentionally, the messages that are communicated may be ambiguous or misleading. They also may be provocative, containing statements that reflect hostility or goals opposed to those of the recipient. Communications with unclear or negative content are likely to be sent by persons who are competitively motivated or who are exploitive in their orientation toward the other (Rubin and Brown, 1975:102–104). Because of ambiguities in the messages, plus perhaps his own preconceptions about the situation, the recipient of the message may not understand it correctly. Even if he understands it, he may not believe it. This is particularly true when there is lack of trust between the parties. Moreover, if the content of the message is negative, it may reduce the recipient's motivation to be cooperative (Pruitt, 1981:172). Thus, the availability of communication channels does not guarantee that their use will enhance cooperation. In the field of international relations, there is only limited evidence about how the availability and use of communications channels affects the resolution of conflicts. But the evidence we do have suggests that the general advantages and limitations of communication that have just been discussed apply in international affairs.

Sometimes the introduction of communications channels aids inter-nation cooperation. One fairly obvious case in which this is true was the establishment in 1971 of diplomatic contacts between the United States and China. Talks between leaders of these countries resulted in agreement and coordination of action on a variety of issues, such as mutual resistance to Soviet expansion. Another case in which the introduction of better communication channels facilitated cooperation is that of recent relations between Egypt and Israel. Following almost thirty years of lack of direct communication between these two nations, a series of meetings took place from 1975 to 1978 that resulted in a peace treaty. At these meetings, each side gained a clearer understanding about the vital goals and constraints of the other as well as about the other's intentions. This information clarified for each side what concessions it could expect from the other and helped them to reach an agreement acceptable to both sides.

During the Cuban missile crisis the lack of direct communication channels between the United States and the Soviet Union was a potential impediment to a peaceful solution of the crisis. Holsti (1972:188) recounts:

> Some extraordinary means were devised in an effort to overcome this problem. Reference has already been made to an important message affirming American desires to slow down escalation of the crisis which was sent to patrolling ships in the clear rather than in code. . . . Later, Premier Khrushchev announced acceptance of President Kennedy's formula for settlement of the crisis by a public broadcast in order to shortcut the time required to encode, transmit, and decode messages through the normal diplomatic channels. Several private citizens were also used to transmit important messages during the missile crisis.

Holsti indicates that this use of improvised channels of communications helped each side to see conciliatory actions by the other side as genuine efforts to delay or reverse escalation. These events also led the United States and the Soviet Union to soon after establish a direct communications hot line between their respective capitals.

On the other hand, there is evidence that communication between nations does not always facilitate cooperation. Again, some historical cases illustrate this point. For example, the American president, Kennedy, and the Soviet leader, Khrushchev, met in Vienna in 1961 to discuss outstanding issues between their countries. However, both sides were dismayed by the other's statements of its goals and intentions. The meetings ended in an atmosphere of gloom and were followed soon by a crisis between the two countries over Berlin and an even more serious confrontation over Soviet missiles in Cuba.

In studying the communications between the great powers of Europe just prior to the outbreak of World War I, Zinnes and her associates (1972) found that the number and intensity of hostile messages increased in a crisis as compared to a noncrisis situation. Zinnes also found, both in the crisis of 1914 and in a simulation study, that national leaders were more likely to express hostility toward another nation when they perceived unfriendliness and threat from that nation (Zinnes, 1966). In another inter-nation simulation study, Brody (1963) also found that expressed hostility toward another nation was greater when leaders perceived threat from that nation. In 1914 the hostile content of messages between nations appeared to contribute to escalation of the crisis since each nation tended to reply to hostility with counter-hostility (Zinnes, Zinnes, and McClure, 1972). In such cases communication between nations leads each to perceive hostile intentions from the other, to which—in self-defense—it feels compelled to respond in kind.

The use of communication channels. For communication to occur there must of course be the necessary physical arrangements or facilities—e.g., a meeting place, a telephone linkage, etc. But the availability of communication channels does not necessarily mean that they will be used. Studies of interpersonal relations and bargaining indicate that where competitiveness, hostility, or lack of trust exists, communication is likely to be reduced (Rubin and Brown, 1975:93–95; Pruitt, 1981:180). Deutsch (1969:12) comments:

> Typically a competitive process tends to produce the following effects: Communication between the conflicting parties is unreliable and impoverished. The available communication channels and opportunities are not utilized or they are used in an attempt to mislead or intimidate the other. Little confidence is placed in information that is obtained directly from the other; espionage and other circuitous means of obtaining information are relied upon. The poor communication enhances the possibility of error and misinformation of the sort which is likely to reinforce the preexisting orientations and expectations toward the other.

Several simulation studies of international relations also have found some evidence that hostility may lead to reduced communication. In one such study Zinnes (1966) found that the interaction between national leaders decreased as hostility and perceptions of threat and unfriendliness rose. In another study of a simulated international situation Brody (1963) also found that interaction declined as perceptions of threat increased and that there was more interaction within than between blocs of nations for much of the time period studied. However, a study of the 1914 crisis by Holsti (1972) provides only slight support for the hypothesis that each nation will interact more with its own allies and less with members of the other alliance as a crisis progresses. Moreover, in another study of the 1914 crisis Zinnes (1966) found essentially no relationship between the amount of communication between each pair of nations and their mutual hostility or their perceptions of unfriendliness or of threat by the other nation.[11]

Data presented by Holsti (1972:104) concerning changes in communication between specific pairs of nations as the 1914 crisis progressed may provide some clues as to when interaction between potential antagonists does or does not decline. They show that Austria-Hungary and Russia, the two nations that played a central role early in the crisis, substantially and uniformly reduced their communications to members of the other alliance as the crisis progressed. Both Austria-Hungary and Russia were clear on their central purposes in the dispute over Serbia and were not to be swayed by the actions of other nations. The nations that had not been directly involved in the early stages of the 1914 crisis—Germany, France, and Great Britain—did *not* substantially decrease their communications across alliance lines. In fact, Germany and Great Britain increased their communications with each other from the early to late periods of the crisis. These nations were less committed to specific courses of action regarding the dispute and, prior to making further decisions, were trying to learn more about each other's intentions. For example, German leaders were anxious to learn if Great Britain would enter any larger conflict. Moreover, while there was some hostility between Britain and France, on the one hand, and Germany, on the other, there were also positive ties of culture, commerce, and even kinship (the king of England and the kaiser were relatives) between these countries.

These considerations suggest that potential antagonists may continue to communicate with each other so long as hostility is not at high levels, and especially if they feel the need for more information about each other's actions and intentions prior to making a final decision on action. The tendency to close off communication with antagonists may operate most clearly when leaders decide early (perhaps prematurely) on a course of action, probably believing that they know what the other side is likely to do or are so suspicious of the other that they will not believe what it says.

To sum up, our discussion of communication indicates that in order for two parties to cooperate effectively it is usually important for them to communicate freely with each other. It also seems clear that if they want to reach agreement they need to communicate clearly and accurately certain kinds of information, especially their goals, expectations, and intentions. However, there often are pressures on parties in conflict to communicate in ways that are ambiguous, misleading, or negative. While such communication tactics may sometimes be helpful in gaining some advantage, they may be counterproductive in the long run when both sides have a mutual interest in reaching an accommodation. If they have learned not to trust the other, or are too confused by previous communications to understand the other's real goals and expectations, it may be very difficult for them to coordinate their actions sufficiently to reach necessary agreement.

Our review of the evidence suggests also that there is a tendency for two conflicting sides to close off communication with each other when antagonism between them increases. While this tendency is understandable (it is unpleasant to talk with an adversary who has done things to anger oneself), communication may be most important when tensions and hostilities are high in order to avoid an outbreak of violent action. Nations, like other parties in conflict, should resist the tendency to break off diplomatic contacts or to stop communicating through usual channels when tensions increase. In fact, there may be good reasons for increasing the communication of mutually important information when tensions rise. One proposal in this direction is that the United States and the Soviet Union should establish a center at Geneva to exchange information about any movement of nuclear weapons, especially at times of crisis (Blechman, 1985). Such information exchange might allay false anxieties by either side about an impending first strike by the other side, which might otherwise lead one side to launch a preemptive attack on the other.

Summary

In this chapter we have considered the ways in which the behavior of two sides in a conflict—especially that of nations—is likely to be affected by the situation they confront. The most basic aspect of any situation is the set of outcomes that will occur as a result of the actions of the two sides and the relative attractiveness of these outcomes to each of the parties. Different types of situations—i.e., different patterns of outcomes—will provide incentives for different types of behavior by national leaders.

First, the situation will affect incentives for conciliatory or competitive behavior. The greater the potential gain from cooperation as compared to the gain from competition the more likely it is that a party to conflict will be conciliatory. The net potential gain from concessions will increase especially as the value of a compromise (and of a loss) increases relative to the value of a win and of a deadlock. To increase the likelihood that nations in a dispute will act in a conciliatory way, it may be possible to find more attractive compromise solutions, to increase or make more apparent the disadvantages of a deadlock or fight, and to reduce the value of complete victory.

The pattern of outcomes also determines whether it is in the interest of each party to move first or to wait for the other to move first. The more that the pattern of outcomes is such that the side moving first will permanently improve its outcomes (perhaps at the expense of the other side), the more likely each side is to make coercive moves. To reduce the incentives for a preemptive attack by one side on the other, the adversaries can take steps to reduce or eliminate the advantage that such an action would bring. In addition to the effect on its own behavior, the pattern of incentives for each side also is likely to affect its expectations of the other side. If one side sees that the other has strong incentives for cooperative behavior, then it is likely to expect such behavior and to adjust its own actions accordingly.

The pattern of possible outcomes also determines the power that each side can exert on the other. If side B is vulnerable to threat or the use of force by side A, then side A is more likely to use threat or force, and side B is more likely to submit to such influence than if B were not vulnerable. When both sides are vulnerable to the use of force, mutual escalation of force is more likely to take place than under other conditions. The actual use of threat or force by either side is affected greatly by their *relative* power. When there is a marked imbalance of power, the stronger will often use threat or force and the weaker will usually submit to the stronger's demands. However, superiority of strength does not necessarily lead to peace. Nations that are stronger than their neighbors do not thereby avoid war; rather, they tend to throw their weight around and often end up embroiled in wars.

When adversaries—including nations—are about equal in power, they tend to be cautious in using threat or force and often try to develop rules to limit such actions. Thus, the equal-power situation presents national leaders with an opportunity for developing rules to regulate the use of force. When one side does use threat or force against an equal-power adversary, the other tends to reciprocate. An escalating spiral of mutual aggression may then occur. National leaders should, therefore, be extremely cautious about threatening or using force against an adversary of equal power. Change in the relative power of two nations often leads to strain in their relationship. Such strain may lead to overt conflict if the distribution of benefits in the relationship is not changed to reflect the changed power situation.

The nature of the situation facing two disputants also affects the ease of reaching and keeping agreements. Where a unique outcome exists that both sides prefer to a deadlock, the chances for a settlement increase. Finding or devising a prominent outcome (e.g., a river boundary, an equal division of territory, terms of a UN resolution) on which the expectations of the two sides can converge may help agreement to be reached.

For agreements to be stable, neither side should be able to improve its outcomes by unilateral action. Thus, it is desirable for any agreement to be made in such a way that neither side will have incentives to violate it. The long-run stability of agreements between nations depends not only on their incentives to change their behavior but also on whether the outcomes meet their basic aspirations. To be enduring, any status quo must be seen by each side as fair and meeting its basic needs, as well as in its immediate self-interest. In many cases the pattern of outcomes in a situation is such that by trying to maximize their individual outcomes, both sides end up with outcomes lower than each would obtain if they cooperated. Two notable examples of such situations are Prisoner's Dilemma and Chicken.

In the Prisoner's Dilemma situation, by following their individual inter-ests the two sides end up in a deadlock (or fight) that, while preferred by each to a loss, is worse for each than mutual cooperation or compromise would be. Mutual arms buildups often are an example of this type of situation. In trying to maximize its own military advantages, two nations may end up in a worse position (high costs, danger for both, superiority for neither) than if they had agreed on mutual restraint in arms buildups. It often is difficult for two sides in a Prisoner's Dilemma to coordinate their actions for mutual cooperation. Their chances of success in achieving a solution to their mutual problem are increased by greater opportunity for communication, by the chance for each to verify the cooperation of the other, and by the possibility for each to switch from cooperation without great penalty if the other does not reciprocate cooperation.

A Chicken situation is one in which, while each side would like to win over the other, its worst outcome is a collision (deadlock or fight) rather than a loss. The relationship between the United States and the Soviet Union has the character of Chicken in many situations. Each side would like to win in particular disputes (Berlin, Cuba, the Middle East, etc.) but each knows that a major war would be a worse outcome than losing on the specific issue. In a Chicken situation each has an incentive to act initially as firmly and as toughly as possible in order to frighten the other into giving in and avoiding a fight. The danger is that both sides will commit them-selves strongly to belligerence, expecting the other to give way, and that it will then become too late to avoid a collision. To prevent such an unwanted catastrophe, national leaders must agree to limit their coercive behavior toward each other.

Communication between the two sides usually is important to facilitate coordination of their actions. However, there is a tendency for adversaries to reduce communication between themselves when tension and antago-nism rise. Moreover, communication, when it occurs, must have certain kinds of content in order to facilitate cooperation. Exchange of information about goals, expectations, and intentions seems to be especially helpful. Those who are competitively motivated tend to send communications with unclear or negative content. Such communication is likely to have negative effects on cooperation.

3 Perceptions

We have seen that the actions of national leaders during a conflict with another nation will be affected by their perceptions of several crucial matters: (a) the alternative actions available to them; (b) the other nation's probable response to each of their own possible actions; and, (c) the outcomes that will result from various combinations of actions and the other side's preferences among these outcomes. In this chapter, I examine some of the factors that may affect these crucial perceptions. I will consider also some of the circumstances that may lead to changed perceptions and some of the reasons why national decisionmakers may resist such changes. This discussion will point up ways in which leaders' perceptions may become distorted and therefore may lead them to take ineffective and possibly dangerous actions in disputes.[1]

Perceptions of Alternatives

The actions of a given party in a dispute may depend in part on what alternatives it sees as possible. Does it see any specific conciliatory proposals it can make? Any plausible threats it can make? Any actions it can take to try to win its way by force?

In disputes between nations it sometimes happens that important alternatives for one's own nation, or for one's adversary, are not immediately perceived or perhaps not perceived at all. When the Soviet Union closed access by the Western nations to Berlin in 1948, neither side perceived the possibility that the United States could supply West Berlin entirely by air. When the same nations disputed the status of Berlin again in 1961, neither side considered at first that the Soviets and their East German allies might construct a wall to separate East and West Berlin. When American officials considered how to react to the introduction of Soviet missiles into Cuba in 1962, they did not at first consider the possibility of a blockade. In all these cases, the option not considered at first was used eventually and was important to a peaceful resolution of the crisis. It seems likely that in some other international crises that developed into warfare, one or both nations may have failed to perceive options that could have led to a peaceful resolution of the crisis. For example, it is possible that Germany or Russia could have conceived proposals that would have satisfied both Austria and Serbia in the 1914 crisis that led to World War I.

Why should the leaders of nations fail to perceive some of the possible alternative actions open to them — or, if they are aware of such options, see them as not realistic or not appropriate? First, as Pruitt (1965:394) points out, national leaders develop conceptions of appropriate ways of dealing with another nation. For example, the Israelis have come to believe that the appropriate way of dealing with any armed provocation by an Arab nation is a swift retaliatory response. Thus they are not likely to consider alternative actions when such a situation arises.

Second, there is a strong tendency for individuals to see certain actions as being forced on them by the situation while their adversaries are more free to choose among a variety of actions (Jones and Nisbett, 1972). This same perspective appears to be found among national policymakers who tend to see the range of alternatives open to their adversaries as relatively large while their own are restricted by external constraints (Mitchell, 1981:116). One important example of this phenomenon is provided by Holsti's study of the perceptions of national leaders in the European crisis of 1914. Holsti (1972:151–152) writes:

> The 1914 documents are filled with such words as "must," "compelled," "obliged," "unable," "driven," "impossible," and "helpless," but these rarely occur except when the author is referring to the policies of his own nation. . . . Even a cursory survey of the diplomatic documents reveals that with the exception of Austria-Hungary, European leaders consistently perceived fewer options open to themselves than to their adversaries. In at least one respect even the data for Austria-Hungary are similar to those of the other nations. In an overwhelming majority of references to alternatives, the decision makers in Vienna perceived themselves to be acting out of necessity and facing closed options rather than open choice. There are, however, only two statements regarding the alternatives of enemies, and none are perceptions of choice.

Despite British urging, the German chancellor said, "We cannot mediate in the conflict between Austria and Serbia." Meanwhile, the Russian foreign minister Sazonov said, "We have assumed from the beginning a posture which we cannot change" (Holsti, 1972:153). With such an overall perspective that their choices are governed by necessity, national decisionmakers are not apt to seek or attend to new options or to perceive those brought to their attention as realistic. Holsti (1972) also found that national decisionmakers will see the range of alternatives open to them as even narrower as stress increases.

Several other factors that may limit the range of alternative actions perceived by national decisionmakers are suggested by de Rivera (1968: 74–77). One is the frequent assumption that there is a single correct choice. If one "knows" what the correct action is (e.g., always to retaliate immediately to a provocation), then there is no need to consider other options. The number of options considered may be limited also by the difficulties of gaining adoption of a policy. When one has to win the consensus of a group for any option, only one or a few options that can be "sold" to the group may be perceived as realistic possibilities. Related to the need to gain approval within the organization is the tendency pointed out by Verba (1961) for national decisionmakers to consider initially only policies that are similar to past policy. Such familiar options are likely to win the necessary group approval. Finally, when decisions have to be made quickly, the number of alternatives considered may be constricted. Snyder and Paige see the time factor as important in explaining the fact that American policymakers considered seriously only one option at the time of their decision to resist militarily North Korea's invasion of South Korea (Snyder and Paige, 1958).

In summary, decisionmakers' perceptions of the options open to them tend to be restricted by the common tendencies to consider only familiar options and to feel forced by the situation to take particular kinds of action. The tendency to limit the number of options considered will increase as: (a) time is more limited; (b) stress on the decisionmakers is greater; (c) norms concerning appropriate or correct actions are stronger; and, (d) following any new option will require forming a new and difficult-to-achieve consensus.

Expectations of Other Side's Actions

The actions of one side to a conflict usually will depend in part on its expectations about the responses of the other side to these actions. Social psychologists have found that the likelihood of each side making a cooperative move in a "mixed-motive" situation (one in which there are both shared and opposed interests) often is increased if it expects the other side to reciprocate this cooperation (Deutsch, 1973; Wyer, 1969). A noncooperative move becomes more likely as trust in the other side declines. In describing the behavior of the typical experimental subject, Deutsch states, "His behavior toward the other is congruent with what he expects from the other and what he expects from the other is congruent with his behavior toward the other" (Deutsch, 1973:206).

In international affairs, also, whether national leaders choose a firm or a conciliatory action usually is affected by their expectation about the responses of their adversary. One of the key differences between the hard-liner and the soft-liner is in such expectations (Snyder and Diesing, 1977:297–310). The hard-liner believes that the adversary will interpret conciliatory moves as weakness and will therefore maintain or toughen his demands. He sees a policy of firmness, and even sometimes of force, as convincing the adversary that he cannot win his demands, thereby leading the adversary to concede on issues in dispute. The soft-liner, on the other hand, tends to see the adversary as a basically reasonable party who is likely to reciprocate conciliatory actions but who may be alarmed by extreme firmness by one's own nation and react belligerently to such firmness in order to defend his own interests.[2]

Expectations about the reactions of the other side may be held in terms of probabilities. Wagner (1974) found that Israel's top decisionmakers were able (at least after the fact) to assign numerical probabilities to the likelihood that the Arab nations would react in each of a number of ways to possible Israeli actions in the crisis of 1967. For example, the Israeli leaders estimated the probabilities that, if they did nothing and the status quo continued, there would be an Arab invasion and that, if such an invasion occurred, it would result in a victory for Israel. However, some researchers have maintained that there is a tendency for policymakers to try to reduce their own uncertainty and stress when making difficult decisions by assuming certainty regarding the opponent's intentions. For example, Jack Snyder (1978) argues that during the Cuban missile crisis President Kennedy (and his advisers) tended to make unwarranted assumptions of certainty about Soviet intentions (e.g., to test American resolve) and other matters (e.g., impeachment of Kennedy if he didn't act). However, it may be noted that Kennedy remained uncertain about the Soviet response to the American blockade and made a probabilistic assessment of the chances of war resulting.

It is possible to view the course of interaction between two nations from the perspective of how their expectations change over time. At the beginning of a dispute each side is expecting, or at least hoping, to get its own way. As Snyder and Diesing (1977:290) comment: "at least some reduction of differences in expectations is probably necessary to a settlement." It is important, therefore, to understand the ways in which the expectations of each side to a dispute are formed and the ways in which they may change during the course of the dispute.

Expectations about the actions of another nation are based on two fundamental judgments about the other: its capability and its intent (Handel, 1977). Writing about one type of expectation—that of being attacked by another nation—Singer (1958) has proposed that the perception of threat is determined by the capability of the other *multiplied* by the intent of the other. Perceptions of capability and of intent often are not completely independent of each other (Handel, 1977). For example, if a competitor nation begins to increase its military capability, this is likely to be seen as evidence of probable intent to take aggressive action (Jervis, 1976; Cohen, 1979). Thus, Germany's program to build a fleet of battleships in the early years of the century was viewed by many influential British as evidence of Germany's aggressive intent.

Nevertheless, the factors that affect perceptions of capability and of intent are different and we may consider the determinants of each separately. I will begin by discussing briefly perceptions of capability and then move on to a more extensive discussion of perceptions of intent.

Perception of Capability

In some ways the capability or strength of a nation is obvious, something that can be measured and counted. For example, the number of naval vessels, planes, and men under arms usually are listed in publicly available records. Likewise, elements of economic strength and self-sufficiency—tons of steel and numbers of barrels of oil produced, electric power capacity, and so forth—are publicly stated. Judgments of the capabilities of an adversary will be based in part on such objective information. However, there are many elements of a nation's strength—military, economic, and political—that are much more difficult to assess. While the number of men at arms may be known, what is the quality of their training, their motivation, their leadership? How rapidly can a nation transform its economy to wartime production? How unified are its people behind its political leaders, and how stable would its regime be in times of national stress? Such questions require judgment and interpretation about many tangible and intangible factors affecting national capability. Reviewing evidence concerning estimates by national leaders about the military capabilities of their adversaries prior to the two world wars, May (1984) concludes that perceptions generally were inaccurate, especially in the earlier period.

As Handel (1977) points out, even apparently hard data on a nation's capability is subject to deceptive manipulation by that nation. For example, the German battleship *Bismarck*, launched in 1939, was listed as 35,000 tons to comply with the London Naval Treaty of 1922 but was in fact at least 42,000 tons (Kennedy, 1974). Today strategists in both the United States and the Soviet Union are concerned about the possibility that the other side may underestimate the number and size of missiles it possesses—especially in categories for which limitations have been agreed upon. Given that some ambiguity about the capability of nation A is inevitable, the perception of this capability by those in nation B will be affected by their own beliefs and concerns. Leaders and officials of nations have images of their adversaries—their courage, tenacity, technical ability, discipline, etc.—that are relevant to their judgments of the other side's capabilities. Writing of the estimates by pre-1914 intelligence bureaus of the military capabilities of their potential adversaries, May recounts: "A formal intelligence appreciation from the German General Staff questioned the tenacity of French infantrymen, observing, 'The Frenchman is nervous; his voice easily rises.' And General Sir Alfred Knox, Britain's expert on the Russian army, explained his doubts about the tsarist officer corps by writing: 'Unlike our officers, they had no taste for outdoor amusements . . .'" (May, 1984:504–505).

Where the leaders of another nation are seen as having hostile intent, the perception that this nation has or is developing the capability of carrying out this intent may be heightened. Freedman (1977) has described how those in the American government who most distrusted the intentions of the Soviet Union perceived the Soviets in the 1970s as developing a much greater first-strike offensive capability than did those who saw Soviet intent as less aggressive. Where a potential threat is seen to exist, vigilance for any signs of the threat being imminent may increase. Therefore, decisionmakers may pay very close attention to any sign of growing capability in a nation that they see as having hostile aims. For example, American policymakers during the 1950s and 1960s undoubtedly paid much closer attention to evidence that the Chinese might be developing a nuclear-strike capability than they did to similar developments in, say, India. Jervis (1976:chapter 10) has discussed this phenomenon of perceptual vigilance as it may apply to inter-nation perceptions, but he also suggests that it tends to occur only when the perceivers feel that they can do something about the threat. (Otherwise, the perceiver may react in an opposite fashion, tending to ignore signs of impending threat.)

Another factor that tends to heighten perceptions of the capability (as

well as hostile intent) of another nation is the fact that decisionmakers
—especially those responsible for defense—usually feel that it is prudent
to plan for the contingency of hostile action by certain other nations. Pruitt
comments: "To do his job, the contingency planner must pay a lot of
attention to evidence that his nation is threatened and little to evidence that
it is safe. From such one-sided perusal of the evidence, it is only a short
psychological step to the conclusion that one's nation is really in danger"
(1965:401).

In addition to psychological factors, there are institutional forces that
usually tend to produce perceptions of high capability by adversary nations.
Such institutions include the uniformed military services, the civilian military bureaucracy, networks of defense contractors, and even veterans' and
other patriotic organizations dedicated to strong national defense. Again
Pruitt's remarks are relevant: "Institutions provide many services to people
associated with them, including such things as financial support, education, status, and a sense of personal identity. As a result people come to
have a 'vested' interest in their continuation. People associated with an
institution that is designed to cope with a threat have a vested interest in
the continuation of the threat, which may result in a predisposition to
perceive threat" (1965:401). In the case of institutions dedicated to national
defense this would lead to dispositions to perceive certain other nations as
having both hostile intent and high capability.

An example of these institutional pressures may be seen in the often-
remarked pattern whereby each time Congress makes its military appropriations, U.S. defense officials point with alarm to the growth of Soviet
military power (Barnet, 1981). Their Soviet military counterparts undoubtedly point with similar alarm to U.S. military forces when arguing for their
appropriations. In each country it obviously is in the organizational self-
interest of the military to portray the other side as strong. Moreover,
because of their roles and responsibilities, and because of pressures for
cognitive consistency, these military men undoubtedly are genuinely concerned with signs of growing strength by an adversary.

In summary, in addition to the effect of objective evidence, those in one
nation will tend to see an adversary as having greater capability at a given
time: (a) the more they hold general images of the other as strong; (b) the
more they perceive hostile intent by the adversary; and, (c) the more they
are engaged in planning for the contingency of attack by the adversary or
are a part of an organization whose mission is to defend against attack.

Perception of Intent

The second basic determinant of expectations about the future behavior of another nation is perception of the intentions of its leaders. Such judgments of an adversary's intent are often mistaken. For example, May finds that leaders of the great powers of the two world wars often misjudged their adversaries' intentions. He comments that "the available evidence supports a conclusion that, as of the 1930s, no great power evidenced much understanding of the proclivities of potential enemies" (May, 1984:525). Even more than perceptions of capability, intent cannot be known conclusively from any objective evidence. It must be inferred from many beliefs, perceptions, and experiences that are thought to be directly or indirectly relevant. The bases on which the leaders of nation A infer the intent of the leaders of nation B may be grouped into the following categories: (a) the general beliefs and experiences of those in nation A; (b) the past and present behavior of nation B; (c) the perceived motivations of leaders of nation B; (d) the perceived willingness of the leaders of nation B to take risks; and, (e) the perceived unity of nation B.[3]

Beliefs and experiences of the perceivers. The leaders of one nation often have beliefs about particular other nations that lead them to perceive those nations as having either peaceful or aggressive intent. One example involves U.S. Secretary of State Cordell Hull, whose image of Japan from the late 1930s to 1941 is described by Ben-Zvi (1975) as follows: "Hull tended to view Japan as an inherently aggressive power . . . a power that under no circumstances was to be trusted." Thus, when Japanese leaders attempted to negotiate a compromise with the United States over disputed issues in the Pacific, Hull tended to dismiss every Japanese approach as insincere.

Beliefs about the leaders of another nation may be rooted in ideology and ideological conflicts. The U.S. secretary of state in the 1950s, John Foster Dulles, had a firm and persistent belief in the aggressive intentions of the leaders of Communist countries, like the Soviet Union, which he saw as locked in battle with the capitalist, Christian West (Holsti, 1967). On the Soviet side, perceptions of U.S. foreign policy are influenced by Marxist-Leninist ideology right up to the present time (Lenczowski, 1982). (A comparison of Soviet and American leaders' views of the other is presented by Frei, 1984.)

Perceptions of intent also may be based on previous experiences of the perceiver. These previous experiences may not necessarily be with the nation that is currently being judged. Robert Jervis has discussed at length the many instances in which national decisionmakers form judgments about a current situation or adversary by drawing analogies with their previous experiences. For example, those who experienced the evidence of Hitler's unlimited aggressive intent after the unsuccessful efforts to appease him at Munich in 1938 tended to see later adversaries (e.g., the Soviet Union at the time of the Korean invasion, Nasser at the time of his takeover of the Suez Canal, China at the time of the Vietnam war) as having unlimited aggressive aims similar to those of Hitler. Jervis comments: "People living in a period characterized by a particular kind of actor will tend to see a new and different one as though it fit the familiar pattern. This perceptual readiness helps the decision-maker to reach better decisions if the original conditions continue to be present, but makes it harder for him to recognize and cope with change" (1976:271).

In their study of perceptions by international decisionmakers in a wide range of crises, Snyder and Diesing report finding that in many cases analogies influenced perceptions, including perceptions of intent. They report that "no examples in our sample or elsewhere in the cases of historical analogies produced a correct interpretation of a message. Jervis's hypothesis that statesmen usually draw incorrect or overgeneralized inferences from historical analogies is strongly confirmed" (1977:321).

National leaders are likely to draw analogies especially from those persons and events that were firsthand and important experiences in their early years. However, the extent to which experience with a given person or event will shape later perceptions will depend on the presence of other and different experiences. As Jervis puts it, "those who are familiar with multiple possibilities will be less influenced by any single historical case" (1976:270).

Overt and verbal behavior. The intent of another nation often is inferred from its past and present behavior. For example, the Soviet Union's invasion of Afghanistan in 1979 led some American officials to speculate that the Soviets might intend to attack other nations, such as Iran and Pakistan, in the same region. The fact that Libya's leader, Colonel Qadaffi, sent troops into neighboring Chad in 1980 led many African leaders to believe that Libya might send troops into other neighboring countries. In addition to overt action, perceptions of intent may be influenced by verbal statements. The perception that British Prime Minister Chamberlain (and many others) had of Hitler's intentions in the 1930s was based in part on Hitler's frequent declarations that he wanted nothing more than territories inhabited by ethnic Germans. The effect of stated intentions on others' perceptions and actions has been confirmed in experimental studies of conflict and cooperation by Morton Deutsch, who found that expectations of cooperation from another person rose as individuals received communication from the other of his intent to cooperate (Deutsch, 1973:195–199).[4]

However, neither the overt behavior nor the verbal statements of another nation's leaders will always affect perceptions of intent. Where a firm image of the other nation's aims and intentions has become established, new information that does not fit these images may be resisted. As Jervis points out, "because deception is common, many of the other's behaviors which do not fit his image can be dismissed as attempts to mislead" (1976:315). For example, the announcement by Soviet leader Gorbachev in 1986 of a unilateral halt to nuclear testing was greeted with great skepticism by American officials concerning Soviet sincerity about stopping the arms race.

Some sets of beliefs about the intentions of the other nation's leaders are especially resistant to change on the basis of new actions or statements by those leaders. Most notable of these is the "inherent bad faith" image (Jervis, 1976:310–315). This is a set of perceptions concerning hostile aims of and deceitfulness by the other side that is so general and so rigid that it cannot be contradicted by any behavior or statements of the other. Holsti describes how U.S. Secretary of State Dulles had such a bad-faith image of the Soviet Union that was impervious to any change in Soviet actions. Hostile, aggressive, or deceitful actions by Soviet leaders were a clear confirmation for Dulles of the correctness of his image. But friendly, cooperative, or truthful behavior also fit Dulles' image, since he believed that the Soviets would, when expedient, seek to lull and deceive the West by such actions. Holsti comments: "To the extent that each side undeviatingly interprets new information, even conciliatory gestures, in a manner calculated to preserve the original image of the adversary, they are caught up in a closed system with little prospect of changing the relations between them" (Holsti, 1967).

The opposite phenomenon of an "inherent good faith" image also may occur. Jervis notes several historical cases in which some persons had a belief that the leader of another nation was friendly and trying to help them, a belief that proved resistant to contrary actions by the other nation's leader. One example is the image of a friendly Soviet Premier Stalin that was held by some Western observers in the 1940s and 1950s. This image persisted despite hostile acts by the government which Stalin headed. Such evidence was discounted as indicating the presence of militant hard-liners in the Soviet Union whom Stalin had to accommodate despite his own supposedly benign intentions.

Perceived capability. The capability of another nation to take some action often will be seen as evidence of intent to take such action. Most notably, those in one nation are likely to see a high (and especially an increased) military capability by another nation as evidence of aggressive intent (Handel, 1977; Jervis, 1976). For example, the buildup by the Soviet Union of its missile force in the 1970s was seen by many American officials as evidence of possible Soviet intent to launch a first strike against the United States (Freedman, 1977). On the other hand, where another nation lacks the capability to take some military action, it is likely to be seen also as lacking the intent. In a study of the views that Soviet leaders have of the United States, Hough (1980) describes their view of the United States as basically aggressive but as having a reduced aggressive intent in the 1970s because it had lost the military superiority necessary to launch a successful attack on the Soviet Union.

Motivation of the other nation's leaders. Regardless of another nation's capabilities or what its leaders say about their intentions, perceptions of their intent will be strongly influenced by perceptions of their motives. Such judgments of motives, in turn, will be affected by perceptions of (a) their morality; (b) their similarities to and attitudes toward one's own nation; and, (c) their incentives for peaceful or belligerent behavior.

(a) Morality. Those who are seen as evil are likely to be seen as having hostile motives. Ralph White (1968; 1984) has described the tendency of national leaders to see their adversaries in "diabolical" terms—i.e., as evil men making dangerous plans. Of course, there *are* real devils in the world —those who wish to ruin others. But White points out that images of the evil nature of adversaries are likely to be greatly exaggerated. Among the examples he cites of such exaggerated perceptions are the German kaiser's belief in 1914 that England wished to destroy Germany, Hitler's belief in a world conspiracy of the Jews, and the images that American and North Vietnamese leaders had of each other during the Vietnam war.

Another example of the way that perceptions of morality may influence judgments of motivation and intent is provided by U.S. Secretary of State Dulles. Dulles's beliefs about Soviet intentions (described previously) were based in substantial part on his view that Soviet leaders were basically immoral. Dulles felt that their materialism and atheism motivated them to act in immoral, brutal, and deceitful ways (Holsti, 1967).

(b) Attitudes. In discussing the conditions that promote trust, Deutsch hypothesizes that "an individual is more likely to perceive that another person has an altruistic intention to benefit him if he believes that the other person likes him than if he does not have this belief" (1973:158). Later he hypothesizes that a person will expect those who have similar characteristics or attitudes to his own to be more oriented to help him than are those with dissimilar attitudes (1973:159). This latter proposition is consistent with a large body of research that shows that interpersonal attraction and help for others generally increases with similar beliefs and characteristics

(Byrne, 1971; Middlebrook, 1980:chapter 9). Since people are apt to experience more helpful behavior from those who like them (usually those similar to themselves), they will come to expect such persons to be most motivated to help them.

I am not aware of systematic evidence on this matter in the realm of international affairs. But clearly there are many instances in which perceptions of the motivations of other national leaders have been influenced by perceptions of their attitudes toward one's own nation. For example, American leaders tend to assume that most leaders of Western European nations, who share basic cultural similarities and political beliefs with Americans, will be basically sympathetic to the United States and can therefore be counted on to cooperate with us in important matters. Even leaders of those foreign countries that are very different from our own are sometimes seen as having a positive personal relationship with American leaders and therefore somewhat more motivated to cooperate. For example, President Nixon stressed the importance of his cordial personal relationship with Soviet Premier Brezhnev and seemed to feel that this might influence Brezhnev toward greater cooperation (Kissinger, 1982). On the other hand, those foreign leaders—such as Qadaffi of Libya, or even de Gaulle of France—who have been seen as disliking the United States may be seen as motivated to act in ways that will harm our interests.

(c) *Incentives*. Whether individuals are seen as being motivated to act in a conciliatory or in an unyielding and belligerent way will depend also on the incentives they are perceived to have for alternative actions. In his experimental studies of cooperation and conflict, Deutsch (1973) found that individuals were more likely to expect their partners to take benevolent action when the partner had nothing to gain by an alternative choice. How much a party is seen as having to gain by any given action should depend on perceptions of that party's preferences for various outcomes and its expectations that particular actions will lead to its preferred outcomes. Judgments of the other party's expectations about the consequences of its actions should depend, in turn, on perceptions of one's own power over that party and on what actions the other party expects one's own side to take. Consistent with these speculations, Deutsch (1973:chapter 8) found that when a person has some power to influence the outcomes of his partner, he is more likely to expect trustworthy behavior (and to make a trusting choice himself).

These ideas and findings, based on experimental studies, seem to be applicable to relations between nations as well. For example, perceptions by American decisionmakers of the extent to which Isreal will be conciliatory or unyielding in a policy difference between our countries will depend in part on their perceptions of what the Israelis' incentives are. These perceptions would depend, in turn, on how strongly the Israelis are seen to prefer various outcomes in the situation (e.g., do they think their very survival depends on a given course of action), on what the Israelis expect the United States to do (e.g., do they think we would withhold arms or UN support if they refuse to give in to our requests), and on the extent of power that we have to affect their outcomes (usually great).

An additional factor that may affect perception of the other party's motivation is whether it has committed itself to a given course of action. Deutsch hypothesizes that "the stronger a person's commitment to his intention is perceived to be, the more reliable it is perceived to be" (1973:155). An individual is committed to an action to the extent that he will suffer negative consequences if he does not take the action. For example, if he has put down a deposit that will be forfeited if he does not act, or if he has made a public declaration of his intention, he will suffer negative consequences (loss of money, loss of face) if he does not follow through with the action. In the case of nations, too, commitments affect perceptions of intent and in fact are often made for that purpose. For example, the United States has committed itself to the defense of West Berlin by repeated presidential declarations and by placing troops in that city. If the United States were not to fulfill this stated intention, in the event of a Soviet attack on Berlin it would suffer both the loss of its credibility and the almost intolerable humiliation of abandoning its own soldiers. Thus, the United States has some clear motives to defend Berlin and these motivations are certainly perceived by the Soviets. The ways in which various commitment tactics can be used to affect perceptions of intent have been discussed at length by Thomas Schelling (1960).

Finally, perceptions of the other side's motivation may be affected by whether it is seen as following a well-planned strategy. Snyder and Diesing (1977:chapter 4) found that the hard-liners in each nation are more apt than the soft-liners to see the actions of an adversary nation as part of such a coherent long-term strategy. This strategy is often seen as aggressive or one calculated to advance the other's interests at the expense of those of one's own nation. The soft-liners, on the other hand, are more likely to see the other's specific behaviors as a series of isolated, perhaps improvised, actions—often in reaction to one's own nation's actions. They are thus more likely to see the other's actions as more limited, more varied, and more defensive in intent.

Risk-taking. In addition to perceptions of the capability of another nation and the motivation of its leaders, the perceived intentions of those leaders may be affected by perceptions of their readiness to take risks. Some statesmen, like President Sadat of Egypt, acquire a reputation as risk-takers. Others, like Jordan's King Hussein, are generally seen by others as cautious in their actions. The reaction of the U.S. Secretary of State Dean Acheson to the invasion of South Korea by North Korea (backed by the Soviet Union) in 1950 was influenced by his perception of the future aggressive intentions of the Soviet Union. This perception of aggressive intent, in turn, was affected by his assumption of a high readiness of Soviet leaders to accept serious risks. In testimony before a Senate committee, Acheson said: "The very fact of this aggression . . . constitute(s) undeniable proof that the forces of international communism possess not only the willingness, but also the intention, of attacking and invading any free nation within their reach at any time that they think they can get away with it. The real significance of the North Korean aggression lies in this evidence that, *even at the resultant risk of starting a third world war*, communism is willing to resort to armed aggression, whenever it believes it can win" (Acheson, 1951, emphasis added).

Unity of other nation. Finally, perceptions of another nation's intent may be influenced by the extent to which it is seen as a single, unified entity or as split into competing factions having differing aims. A good example is provided by Ben-Zvi in his description of the varied images of Japan held by different groups within the U.S. government prior to the outbreak of war in 1941. Several of these groups saw Japan as a single unified actor and even as part of a single unified Axis alliance (Germany, Italy, and Japan). Another group was much more sensitive to the difference in aims of various groups within Japan—the army, the navy, the foreign office, the industrialists, the emperor, etc.—and of differences within the Axis alliance. Ben-Zvi says of the first group: "these policy-makers maintained a static, rigid, and unchangeable image of the situation. Their perceptions enabled them to ignore the changes, fluctuations, and shifting dynamics which characterized the Japanese domestic scene . . . they remained totally unresponsive to the groups and factions in Japan which opposed war with the U.S. . . . these officials persisted in holding onto a vision of unity and harmony between the two aggressor powers cooperating in their united effort to conquer the world" (Ben-Zvi, 1975:244).

Whether a nation is perceived as unified or as divided into contending factions does not determine the type of intent (e.g., cooperative or aggressive) that is perceived. But as the example just discussed illustrates, it does affect the complexity and certainty of these perceptions. More importantly, it may affect the extent to which the perceivers consider possible actions of their own that may strengthen certain factions in, and thus influence the overall intent of, the other nation. For example, it is possible

Figure 3.1   Factors Affecting Expectations of Other Side's Actions

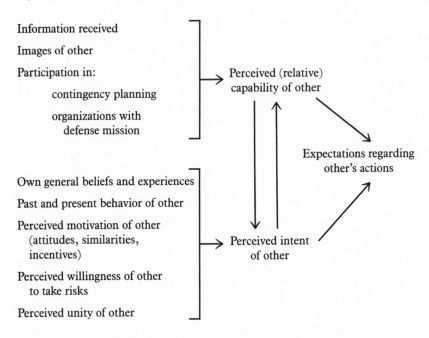

that if the United States had agreed to a Japanese proposal for a summit meeting between Japanese Premier Konoye and U.S. President Roosevelt and made modest concessions to Japan, the strength of those in Japan who favored moderate, nonbelligerent aims might have become predominant.

To summarize this section, the likelihood that national leaders will perceive the intent of an adversary at any given time as aggressive rather than benign may be expected to increase as:

(1) The adversary(ies) with whom they have had experience in the past have been aggressive.
(2) The (present) adversary has been aggressive in the past.
(3) The adversary has expressed aggressive intentions or, at a minimum, has not expressed cooperative intentions.
(4) The adversary has the capability to carry out aggression.
(5) The adversary is perceived as having the motivation to carry out aggressive acts. Such motivation is more likely to be perceived as the adversary is seen as:
   (a) immoral,

(b) dissimilar in attitudes and not liking oneself,

(c) being able to gain benefits (or avoid losses) by aggression,

(d) willing to take substantial risks.

A graphic summary of the factors that affect perceptions of capability and of intent, and thus affect expectations of the other side's actions, is shown in figure 3.1

Perceptions of Outcomes and Preferences

Outcomes

We have considered so far the perceptions that national leaders have of the options available to them and their expectations about the actions of other nations. Combinations of such actions by their own and another nation will of course lead to certain outcomes for each. National leaders will form conceptions of what these outcomes will be. For example, they may believe that intransigence on a given issue by both sides will lead to continuation of the status quo or that it will lead to war.

In some instances the immediate outcomes of particular combinations of actions may be obvious. For example, if nation A demands a piece of nation B's territory and nation B agrees, then the outcome obviously is a territorial loss for nation A and a corresponding gain for nation B. However, the outcomes of some combinations of actions are not necessarily so clear. For example, if nation A demands a piece of nation B's territory and nation B refuses, the outcome might be a protracted stalemate or an immediate war. Even when the immediate outcome seems clear, the longer-range outcome may be less clear. For example, if A takes over some of B's territory, will the population in that territory cooperate with nation B? Will nation A try to regain its territory when it is stronger? Will a third nation, C, become alarmed at nation A's expansion and try to restrict the growth of A's power?

Expectations of outcomes may be influenced by past experiences in situations that are perceived as analogous. For example, those who experienced the events of Munich and its aftermath in the late 1930s came to believe that when an aggressor nation makes demands and another nation acquiesces, the inevitable result is not peace but further demands and eventual war. Those who experienced the events of Vietnam in the late 1960s and early 1970s came to believe that an attempt by a major power to impose its will on a small nation, which is resisted by a significant segment of the small nation's people, will result in the defeat of the major power.

The "theories" that national decisionmakers hold about international affairs may shape their perception about specific persons and events (Jervis, 1976:chapter 4), including those that bear on probable outcomes in a given situation. Such theories may be part of a broader set of beliefs that such decisionmakers hold, which have been termed their operational codes (George, 1979).

Another way of understanding decisionmakers' perceptions of the outcomes that will follow from given actions is in terms of their "cognitive maps." Axelrod (1976) describes the concept of a cognitive map as being designed to capture the structure of the causal assertions of a person regarding a particular policy domain. For example, Axelrod describes the thinking of members of the British "Eastern Committee" that deliberated in 1918–1919 about possible British policy in Persia. He traces the causal chains perceived—e.g., that a policy of British withdrawal would reduce the amount of internal security in Persia, which would reduce the ability of the Persian government to maintain order and in turn would adversely affect British interests. Hart (1977) has elaborated further the concept of cognitive maps and applied these ideas to the perceptions of several Latin-American policymakers. While emphasis in this line of work has been on the chain of consequences generated by the actions of one nation, the approach seems applicable also to perceptions of the consequences of actions by two nations. In the simplest case, the action of nation A is seen as leading to action by nation B, which is seen to result in consequence 1, etc.

Preferences Among Outcomes

Perceptions of the outcomes that will follow from the actions of one's own and other nations are important primarily because the leaders of each nation prefer certain outcomes over others. The pattern of one's own side's preferences and the preferences of the other side define the basic aspects of the situation, including the degree of conflict of interest and the power of each side over the other (see chapter 2).

Though the leaders of each nation may need to decide on their own preferences, and may change these over time, generally their own preferences are known to them. Much more problematic are the preferences of the other side. The way in which nation B's preferences are perceived often is fundamental to nation A's actions. For example, if nation A thinks that nation B is bluffing in a crisis and if its bluff is called would prefer to accept humiliation and defeat rather than to enter a war, nation A is likely to stand firm in its own position. However, if it believes that nation B would prefer war to defeat and humiliation on the issue in question, then nation A might propose some compromise solution it believes nation B would prefer to war.

Writing about the perceptions and behavior of nations in crisis, Snyder and Diesing comment: "when a player misestimates another's payoff ordering, a common occurrence, he thinks that he is playing a different game than he actually is. As we shall see, a good part of crisis behavior can be explained in terms of the correction or non-correction of such estimates" (1977:85). Among the types of situations discussed by Snyder and Diesing are Prisoner's Dilemma (PD)—where each side prefers war to surrender —and Chicken—where each side prefers surrender to war.[5] They state: "It is important to note that a PD crisis is always characterized by an initial misperception, by the challenger at least, that the opponent is in Chicken, that he would rather accept one's demands than push the dispute to the point of war" (1977:95–96).

Snyder and Diesing give several examples of this type of misperception. In the Morocco crisis of 1911 both the French and the Germans initially thought that the other side was "playing Chicken" (bluffing) when, in fact, each saw the other's claims on Morocco as intolerable and was willing to go to war over the issue. In the Berlin crisis of 1958, Khrushchev mistakenly believed that the Western powers would not risk a war in order to defend West Berlin. Only gradually did he realize his error. In the crisis of 1914 the Central Powers (Germany and Austria) believed that the Russians were bluffing in threatening to go to war if necessary to support Serbia, while the Russians hoped that Austria would back down if confronted by a partial mobilization by Russia. In this case the misperceptions were not corrected quickly enough and events careened out of control, with World War I the result.

The more information decisionmakers possess about their adversaries concerning their personal values, the political pressures on them, their economic needs, etc., the more accurate one would expect their perceptions of the adversary's preferences to be. In general, greater communication with the adversary may be expected to increase the amount of information necessary for judging the other side's preferences.

The perceptions that national leaders have of an adversary's preferences also may be affected by general beliefs that adversaries prefer conceding to fighting or vice versa. Lockhart (1977) has discussed the tendency of some hard-line statesmen to see all conflicts as ones in which the opponent has a Chicken preference ordering—preferring to give in rather than to go to war over an issue in dispute. These hard-liners tend to see the opponent as bluffing and as one who can be faced down in a crisis. Dean Acheson, U.S.

secretary of state under President Truman and later adviser to President Kennedy, was one who tended to see things this way—as, for example, in the Cuban missile crisis. Other statesmen, usually soft-liners, are more likely to see an adversary nation as being in a Prisoner's Dilemma situation —especially as being reluctantly willing to go to war rather than suffer the loss of values important to them and the accompanying humiliation. British Prime Minister Chamberlain in his relations with Hitler is an example.

Lockhart points out that there may be unfortunate, perhaps disastrous results if a statesman persists in applying stereotyped views (specifically regarding the pattern of the opponent's preferences) to situations in which they do not fit. In such cases his misperception of the situation may lead him to use an inappropriate and ineffective strategy. Lockhart suggests, for example, that in the years before World War I, German foreign minister Kiderlen applied a coercive strategy indiscriminately, sometimes with unintended consequences. As an example on the other side, he suggests that Adlai Stevenson, U.S. presidential candidate and later UN ambassador, was "prejudiced" against the use of coercion, even in situations in which it might have been effective.

Stability and Change in Perceptions

So far in this chapter we have considered some of the factors that affect perceptions relevant to interaction in a conflict situation. Now we consider the question of stability and change in these perceptions.

Changes in perceptions are a crucial element in the process by which conflicts are resolved (or exacerbated). As participants in a conflict perceive the possibility of new alternative actions, as they change their expectations about the response the adversary may make to their actions, and as they change their view of the benefits and costs associated with different outcomes, the type of action they take may change.

Such a change in action may reflect a changed expectation about what it is realistically possible to attain in the given situation without suffering excessive losses or taking excessive risks. As the parties interact and their perceptions about the options, interests, capabilities and intentions of the other become clearer, their expectations about the likely outcome of the dispute (i.e., what each can realistically attain) tend to converge. When this occurs peaceful agreement should follow. When this convergence does not occur peaceful agreement is not apt to take place. (A fuller discussion of the process by which agreement is reached is presented in chapter 11.)

Are there forces that tend to keep perceptions unchanged, even when new and conflicting evidence is presented? Are there other forces that

Figure 3.2 Factors Affecting Stability and Change in Perceptions

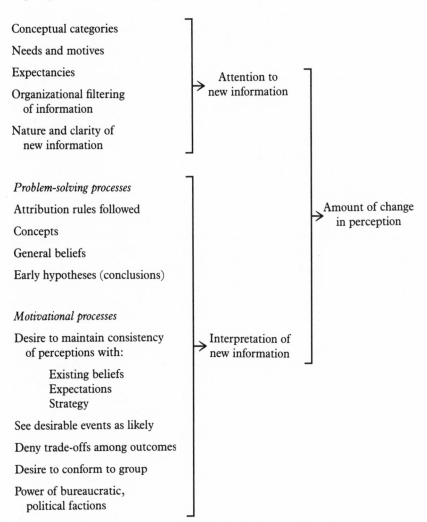

encourage change? In discussing these questions, I will examine two separate though related processes. The first is that of attention to new information; the second is that of interpreting this information. (A summary of factors affecting stability and change in perceptions is presented in figure 3.2.)

Attention

Whether an individual's perceptions are influenced by some piece of information depends in the first instance on whether or not he attends to—i.e., becomes consciously aware of—the information. Attention is influenced by the nature of the stimuli. For example, psychologists have found that large, bright, or moving objects, and also novel objects, are more likely than others to be noticed (Dember and Warm, 1979:chapter 5). In international affairs as well some types of stimuli—e.g., the flamboyant rhetoric of a dynamic leader, an unusual military maneuver —undoubtedly are more likely than others to be noticed.

However, as Dember and Warm point out, stimulation does not fall upon a passive receiver. The individual is prepared, implicitly or explicitly, for certain kinds of input. A simple illustration occurs when persons are shown a figure that can be seen either as a glass goblet or facing profiles. If the possibility of faces is mentioned, they will see the profiles; if the possibility of glasses is mentioned, they will see a goblet (Dember and Warm, 1979:340–341). The national leader who is concerned about an attack by another nation will be alert for any sign of military movement by the other side. A leader who is not so concerned is less likely to pay attention to such activities. The extent to which individuals attend to certain kinds of information may be affected by (a) their conceptual categories; (b) their needs and motives; or, (c) their expectancies.

Conceptual categories. Psychologists who study perception have pointed out that what we are set to notice in the environment depends in part on the concepts in our language. A classical example is the many categories that Eskimos have for snow, which helps to direct their attention to many characteristics of snow that most other people would not notice (Dember and Warm, 1979:354). In international affairs too conceptual categories may affect what individuals attend to and what they do not. For example, if contending factions in another country are labeled as Communist (therefore hostile) and anti-Communist (therefore friendly), important information about them that doesn't fit these categories—e.g., their desire to follow a policy independent of any bloc—may receive insufficient attention. This appears to have been true in the case of American policymakers' perceptions of North Vietnam in the 1960s. Because they were labeled as Communist, it was assumed that they would act in concert with other Communist countries. Evidence of their desire to remain independent of China (a desire that later led to war between those countries) was ignored.

Jervis (1976:162–163) has discussed the impact of categorization on perception in international affairs. He points out that the label put on an event or person influences the way in which it or he is perceived. He points out also that the availability of a piece of information depends on the category in which it has, literally or figuratively, been filed. He cites as an example a report the American ambassador to South Korea sent to Washington in the Spring of 1950 concerning the increased capability of the North Korean army. His superiors considered this report to be part of a wider campaign to increase military aid to South Korea and filed it with other such appeals. When, soon afterward, North Korea attacked South Korea and the U.S. government sought information about the North's military strength, the detailed information that the ambassador had provided was not found because it had been filed in a different category.

The concepts (categories) that individuals have for important features of their world are likely to remain fairly stable over time. New information is most likely to be noticed when it fits into these preexisting categories and is likely to be seen in terms of these categories. This is one of the factors that tends to promote stability and prevent radical change in perceptions.

Needs and motives. A second important influence on attention is peoples' needs. People pay attention most to what is most relevant to their needs and the satisfaction of those needs. For example, experiments have shown that people who have a high need for achievement are more likely than others to quickly identify achievement-related words (McClelland and Liberman, 1949). People who value one area of life (e.g., religion) are more likely to perceive words relevant to that area than to other life areas (Postman, Bruner, and McGinnies, 1948). National leaders who are especially concerned about economic development are most likely to notice actions, including internal actions, by other nations that may affect their own economies. Leaders who are most concerned with territorial expansion are more likely to notice those actions by other nations that bear on military capability and alliances.

In national governments the attention of particular officials also is directed by their particular position and responsibilities (Gibson, 1984). For instance, if a dispute arises between the United States and Western European countries over which country will provide planes for NATO forces, the U.S. defense secretary will probably attend most to military implications of the dispute, the secretary of state to its effects on the alliance, and the treasury secretary to the impact on the U.S. balance of payments.

By affecting what is attended to, needs do not necessarily make for stability (or for change) in perceptions. But in many cases needs do operate to direct attention in such a way as to preserve existing beliefs. Ralph White has described the process of "selective inattention" in international conflicts, which, he argues, helps those of each nation—including its leaders—to maintain nationalistic but satisfying images of their own side as moral and virile and of the other side as evil. He writes (1968:198):

> Call it resistance, repression, ignoring, forgetting, non-learning, inhibition of curiosity, evading, card-stacking, perceptual defense, blind spots, or plain not paying attention. By whatever name, it is omnipresent. . . . On each side of every acute conflict, the tendency appears; we have seen it in the minds of the Austrians in 1914, in Hitler's mind in 1939, in the minds of Communists today, in the minds of non-militants in the United States, and in this chapter and the last one we have seen it, in many forms, in the minds of militants.

White mentions a number of specific ways in which selective inattention manifests itself. These include not paying enough attention to the thoughts of others, ignoring third parties, denouncing those who raise unpleasant ideas as traitors, and ignoring potential dangers (such as nuclear war) to which one's own policy may lead.[6]

In addition to the need to maintain a favorable image of one's nation, attention to information also may be affected by a more general need that people have for their perceptions to be consistent with each other (Wicklund and Brehm, 1976). Sometimes consistency can be preserved by the kind of selective inattention just mentioned. But many times a person cannot help becoming aware of some information that is inconsistent with some belief he has or action he has taken. When this occurs, he will be uneasy, especially if the subject involved is important to him. Among the ways by which a person can reduce the inconsistency is by seeking additional information that will resolve the inconsistency and, usually, remove the challenge to his prior beliefs. One way to do this, which has been called bolstering (Jervis, 1976:294–295), involves seeking new information that supports existing beliefs. For example, during the Vietnam war, when American policymakers began receiving information that cast doubt on their belief that the war could be won, they eagerly sought additional information—on body counts, cutting off enemy supply routes, number of villages "pacified," etc.—that would confirm the viewpoint to which they had committed so much (Halberstam, 1972). Another way to reduce inconsistency is to seek additional information that will cast doubt on the information that created the inconsistency. Thus, disturbed by reports of failure of the pacification program, U.S. policymakers sent teams of fact finders sympathetic to the original policy to provide additional information that would disparage the disturbing reports. By directing attention to information consistent with existing perceptions, such techniques help to resist changes in them.

Expectancies. What a person notices in his environment is influenced also by his expectations.[7] Jervis (1976:359–372) discusses the ways in which the expectations of national statesmen have affected their perceptions. He cites as one example the perceptions of American officials during negotiations with the British aimed at ending the War of 1812. The British made a major concession, but the Americans, not expecting this, failed to perceive it correctly. If the Americans had been *expecting* a major British concession, they would certainly have been more apt to notice it when it came. Another example mentioned by Jervis is that in 1931 German officials ignored reports that the American president, Hoover, would propose a moratorium on the debt Germany owed to other nations. This information did not fit with the Germans' expectations about American policy.

Expectations are likely to reflect the effects of past experiences or of the individual's belief system; that is, they reflect existing perceptions. By influencing the kinds of new information the person attends to, expectations are another factor that tends to limit change in perceptions.

Organizational filtering of information. The processes that focus attention on some types of new information and direct attention from other information do not operate solely within individuals. Since organizations are information-processing mechanisms, they pass through some types of information while filtering out other types. Snyder and Diesing have studied the way in which messages between governments may be distorted in times of crisis. They found that "the chances of a message getting through untarnished to *someone* in the receiving government are about four in ten" (1977:316). In a number of cases they found that information that conflicted with existing expectations had been filtered out at lower government levels. The result is that higher officials may never get information that would lead them to change their present beliefs.

Advisers to President Johnson "protected" him from information that cast doubt on the wisdom and success of his Vietnam policy. Gibson (1984:223) comments: "President Johnson was not very receptive to views contrary to his own and his National Security Advisor, W. W. Rostow, usually was quite careful in screening information coming to the Oval Office that President Johnson might find incompatible with his thinking."

Interpretation of Information

Whether new information will produce change in perceptions depends not only on whether it is noticed but also on how it is interpreted. Interpretation is especially important when the information is ambiguous. For example, the mobilization of Egyptian forces along the Suez Canal in October 1973 was an ambiguous piece of information that was consistent with a past pattern of non-belligerent maneuvers but also with an imminent crossing of the Canal. (It was interpreted by the Israelis as maneuvers but turned out to be a prelude to invasion.) The way in which information —especially ambiguous information—is interpreted may be understood in terms of two general types of processes: problem-solving and the effects of motives.

Problem-solving. Like scientists, practical men may attempt to understand the meaning of events around them by applying their problem-solving skills (George, 1979; Jervis, 1976). For example, statesmen often are faced with the task of inferring the intent of those with whom they interact. As Jervis points out (1976:chapter 2), they are likely to make attributions about intent by using the same principles that others use. For example, people generally will not attribute a hostile intent to a harmful action by another if they perceive the other to have been forced to act in the way it did by forces beyond its control. Thus, a vote by Egypt for an anti-American resolution at a Pan-Arab conference might not be seen as evidence of hostile intent if Egypt was seen as being under great pressure to go along with its Arab brethren.

Interpretation of events and actions will be affected also by the concepts that people have and by the explicit or implicit theories they hold. In addition to drawing the person's attention to certain types of information, his concepts or categories help him interpret the information he receives. For example, if weapons are categorized as either defensive or offensive, then a particular weapons system that has some offensive potential may be seen as an offensive (perhaps a "first-strike") weapon even though it is suitable primarily for retaliation against attack.

The general beliefs about causation, or theories, that people hold will also affect their interpretation of information. For example, if an official of a capitalist nation believes that a Marxist regime will always try to establish totalitarian controls over its people, he is likely to view efforts by such a regime to extend roads and communication to outlying areas as part of an attempt to impose central control. He might interpret the same actions by a non-Marxist regime as part of an effort at modernization.

Since a person will tend to fit a new information into existing categories and interpret it according to his prior theories, the potential of new information to bring cognitive change may be minimized. Related to these processes is the phenomenon of "premature cognitive closure." An initial incorrect hypothesis has been found to delay accurate perception. To illustrate, subjects in one psychological experiment (Engel, 1961) viewed a fuzzy slide that was brought into clearer focus in stages. Some subjects watched from the start and were asked to guess what they were seeing even if they were unsure. These subjects maintained their interpretation of the images—usually incorrect—far past the time when others, who had not formed an early hypothesis, were able to identify the object correctly.

Jervis has discussed premature cognitive closure as it is found in international affairs (1976:195–197). He offers a number of interesting examples of cases in which this phenomenon appears to have been present. One concerns the Japanese ambassador who in the spring of 1941 formed the conclusion that President Roosevelt was willing to begin negotiations on Japanese terms. Despite the fact that he was told later by persons better informed than his original source that this was not the case, he continued to interpret later information in terms of his original belief. Writing of the way in which premature conclusions inhibit change in perceptions, Jervis says: "In policy-making, actors of course know that an incorrect image that leads to an incorrect policy is apt to have high costs, but they do not realize that an incorrect image will delay the development of accurate perceptions. Thus statesmen underestimate the cost of forming preliminary hypotheses and so form images more quickly than they would if they understood the process at work" (1976:195).

Motives. The interpretation of information is not a completely rational process of attempted problem-solving. It is influenced also by peoples' motives—what they want (or fear) to see. Two types of motivational influences on the interpretation of information seem especially important: the desire to maintain consistency in one's perceptions and the desire to conform to the perceptions of important others.

One kind of cognitive consistency that is important to people is that between new perceptions and existing beliefs. It is disquieting to have one's beliefs, especially those that are central, brought into question by conflicting information. There is, therefore, motivation to interpret new information in a way that fits with important beliefs. For example, if an American official believes that America represents the aspirations of all mankind for freedom, he may prefer to interpret evidence of hostility to the United States in El Salvador as limited to a small radical element of the population. Information that is inconsistent with prior expectations or existing strategies is also likely to be disturbing. Such information may call into question the rationale for one's present line of action, to which much effort and resources may have been devoted. For example, in South Vietnam in 1968 the Viet Cong launched a sudden large-scale offensive against South Vietnamese and American units. Their ability to do so was inconsistent with the expectations of American policymakers and with the American strategy of pacification. However, some of these officials preferred to interpret this event as a victory for the United States that showed the success of their current strategy (Milstein, 1974).

Discussing the impact of expectations and strategy on perceptions in international crises, Snyder and Diesing comment: "Since the bargainer desires the strategy to succeed, his desires and hopes make him reluctant to accept evidence that his expectations are mistaken. What seems to happen is that the bargainer tries to fit new information into his pattern of expectations with varying degrees of success" (1977:325).

Motivation to avoid inconsistency in perceptions also may affect perceptions of both the outcomes of a given policy and the probability of those outcomes occurring. When a person believes that the policy he favors contributes to an outcome that is important to him, he tends to see the same policy as contributing to other outcomes he values—despite the reality that trade-offs among values often are necessary (Jervis, 1976:128). For example, those who favor a continued buildup in American arms usually see such a policy as contributing not only to greater power relative to the Soviet Union but also to (eventual) disarmament and perhaps to other values such as economic well-being and a strong Atlantic alliance. A choice or trade-off among desired outcomes can thus be avoided.

Those who value an objective highly may also tend to see a high probability that it can be attained and estimate the costs of attaining the outcome as low (Jervis, 1976:130). Those who value an arms-limitation treaty between the United States and the Soviet Union, for instance, tend to see the chances of effective verification procedures as high. Those who, for other reasons, are not anxious to have an arms-control treaty are likely to see the chances of implementing effective verification procedures as low.

Individuals can use a variety of psychological mechanisms to interpret information so that it is not inconsistent with other perceptions they hold (Mitchell, 1981; Jervis, 1976; White, 1965). These mechanisms include rejecting the validity of discrepant information, dismissing the source as untrustworthy, changing the real meaning of the information, using euphemisms (such as liquidate for kill) to blur the meaning of the information, and differentiating objects into several parts (e.g., a government into several factions) so that perceptions about one part may change without perceptions of the other parts changing.

The tendency to assimilate new information to preexisting images appears to become stronger as the information is more ambiguous, as the actor becomes more confident of and more committed to his existing views, and as inconsistency becomes more painful—e.g., an action aimed at furthering one important value seems to threaten another important value (Jervis,

1976:chapters 4, 11). Also, those with certain personality traits—e.g., intolerance for ambiguity—appear more likely than others to try to reduce inconsistency in their perceptions (Rokeach, 1960). Individuals, including national decisionmakers, usually are not aware of the strong influence preexisting beliefs exert on their present perceptions. Jervis writes: "Because people do not understand the degree to which their inferences are derived from their expectations, they tend to see their interpretations of evidence as "compelling" rather than "plausible". . . . Most important for international politics are the cases in which a state takes as evidence of another's hostility actions that if it carried them out itself, it would have believed were consistent with its own peaceableness" (Jervis, 1976:182).

One example is found in the U.S. State Department view that resupplying North Vietnamese troops during a truce in February 1967 showed that North Vietnam was not interested in a cease-fire. But the United States also had resupplied its forces during this time and the North Vietnamese action could have been seen as defensive. Nevertheless, a State Department spokesman stated that North Vietnam's activity was "clear evidence of their intent to continue their aggressive action" (Jervis, 1976:186).

Efforts to reduce cognitive inconsistency may lead to unfortunate policy decisions. In an attempt to justify their previous policies, decisionmakers may distort their perceptions of what has been achieved and what the costs have been. This may lead them to take further actions along the same road (Jervis, 1976:406). Again the Vietnam war furnishes a good example. In an attempt to justify a policy to which they were heavily committed, American officials for a long time exaggerated the stakes involved, inflated their achievements, and minimized the costs. This facilitated a continuation of a probably unwise policy and later its extension into Cambodia.

Conformity pressures. The interpretation of information that individuals make is affected also by the views of others in their groups. Social norms develop about the correct interpretation of events. In part, group norms may exert a direct effect on what individuals believe they see. Experimental studies have shown for example that many persons' judgments about the length of lines or the movement of light sources are strongly affected by the near-unanimous judgments of their peers. As one would expect, this is especially true when the truth is somewhat ambiguous (Asch, 1951; Sherif, 1936).

Group norms may also exert their influence by affecting the readiness of people to voice their true opinions and interpretations of events. Irving Janis (1982) has investigated the ways in which such conformity processes have affected the actions of participants in important foreign policy decisions. For example, Janis describes the failure in 1961 of President Kennedy's advisers to recognize that the plan for the invasion of Cuba at the Bay of Pigs was diplomatically unwise and militarily doomed. Later accounts of the deliberations by the participants revealed that they shared an illusion of unanimity and that participants in crucial meetings suppressed their doubts. Freedman (1977:187) has described how the interpretations made by U.S. intelligence officers of Soviet capabilities and activities are influenced by the viewpoints dominant in their agencies. He writes:

> There are certainly plenty of examples of a neat fit between the inter-
> pretations of Soviet activity provided by the military intelligence agen-
> cies and the interpretations that their service chiefs desire to see. . . .
> A military intelligence officer is liable to wish to act as a "team player,"
> and to have internalised the adversary image peculiar to his service.
> He will not need to check with his superiors the position he ought to
> take in any particular intelligence debate. It will come quite naturally
> to him.

Another example of conformity pressures on perception and expression may be seen in the views that Israeli military intelligence and other parts of the Israeli government formed of Arab military intentions in October 1973 (Handel, 1977). There was a virtually unanimous, but mistaken, belief that the Arab nations were not planning an attack. While Handel mentions a variety of causes for these Israeli misperceptions, he cites group thinking and conformity as among the reasons. (The subject of decisionmaking in groups is discussed further in chapter 4.)

Bureaucratic and political power. The way in which information about another nation is interpreted by top government officials may depend also on bureaucratic and political struggles within a government. Freedman (1977) has studied the process by which official estimates of Soviet capa-bilities and intentions were formulated over several decades within the American government. He describes the way in which the views of particu-lar agencies— e.g., the Central Intelligence Agency, the separate military services, and the Defense Information Agency—come to be accepted by top officials at a given time, depending on changes in bureaucratic struc-ture and in the power of the political support for various agencies. More-over, political and bureaucratic pressures may cause a given agency to change its intelligence estimates. For example, in 1976 political pressures forced the CIA to accept the creation of an outside group (team B) to make an independent estimate of Soviet capabilities and intentions parallel to an estimate made by the CIA (team A). Team B, made up of known hard-liners, concluded that the Soviet Union was well on the way to developing a capacity to carry out a successful first strike on the United States. Team A (the CIA people) doubted that the Soviets could achieve either the quantity or quality of weapons necessary for them even to contemplate a first strike.

Nevertheless the existence of Team B, with the general support for its position from the Pentagon, set the terms of the debate for the CIA. In its estimates it moved some way towards the hard-line estimate, making the NIE (National Intelligence Estimate) much grimmer reading than it had been for many a year. This shift, it should be emphasised, was a consequence of the politics in the estimating process rather than any new information concerning Soviet forces, though the cumulative impact of the Soviet build-up of the past years was an important factor. (Freedman, 1977:197)

When Change in Perception Occurs

In much that has been written about perceptions (and in much of this section), emphasis has been placed on the forces that tend to keep perceptions stable and unchanging. But change does occur. For example, British leaders changed their image and expectations of Hitler after he occupied all of Czechoslovakia. American leaders changed their perceptions of the Soviet Union—its aims and expected behavior—in the years from about 1945 to 1947. Soviet Premier Khrushchev changed his image and expectations about U.S. President Kennedy during the few days of the Cuban missile crisis. Such changes have an important effect on the progress of conflicts, their development and their resolution.

How do these changes in perceptions come about, despite the tendencies for stability that have been discussed? In their study of international crises, Snyder and Diesing found that when confronted with new and discrepant information, national leaders usually initially resisted change in their expectations. But in some instances a continuing series of discrepant information gradually lowered the leaders' confidence in their expectations. In other cases some dramatic event occurred that, as Snyder and Diesing put it, was "too clear and urgent to be ignored or wished away" (1977:328). For example, in November 1956 an American ultimatum to British Prime Minister Eden that demanded British withdrawal from Suez after their invasion of that area made Eden realize that his expectation of tacit U.S. support (or at least neutrality) in this venture was mistaken. The dramatic visit by Egyptian President Sadat to Jerusalem in 1977 brought a swift change in the expectations of Israeli leaders and citizens concerning the Egyptian president's future actions.

Snyder and Diesing indicate that background images—e.g., general

images of an adversary—change more slowly than do immediate images—
e.g., what the adversary's intentions are in a specific instance. Background
images, they suggest, are affected by changes in the structure of international systems—for example, changes in alliances or defeat of a common
enemy.

Snyder and Diesing also discuss differences between "rational" and
"irrational" national decisionmakers with respect to their capacity to change
their perceptions. Rational decisionmakers are those whose judgments are
open to revision in the light of new information. Irrational decisionmakers'
perceptions, on the other hand, are tied firmly to their belief systems and are
relatively unshakable by new information. Snyder and Diesing write: "Our
rational bargainer is not one who 'knows' at the start of a crisis what the situation is, what the relative interests, power relations, and main alternatives
are, since there are few such people. He is rather one whose initial judgment
may be mistaken and who knows it, but who is able to correct initial mis-
judgments and perceive the outlines of the developing bargaining situation
in time to deal with it effectively" (1977:333). These same authors mention a number of national leaders who were either rational or irrational in the
sense described. An example of a more rational leader is U.S. President
Kennedy, who kept his expectations of Soviet action and other judgments
flexible during the Cuban missile crisis. British Prime Minister Chamberlain is an example of a more irrational leader, to the extent that his judgments about Hitler's basic peaceableness remained constant for a long time
in the face of a series of disconfirming events (Middlemas, 1972).

On the basis of this review of stability and change in perceptions, the
following propositions seem justified:

There are strong tendencies for national leaders to resist changes in their
perceptions of their adversary in a dispute and of other aspects of the
dispute (e.g., probable outcomes). These general tendencies to resist changes
in perception will be greater to the extent that:

(1) New information contrary to existing perceptions is ambiguous and
neither long-sustained nor dramatic.
(2) The leaders have concepts, beliefs, or theories that they hold with
great firmness.
(3) The leaders are highly committed to their present perceptions (i.e.,
they would suffer a high psychological and/or practical loss if those
perceptions are incorrect). Commitment to present perceptions is likely
to increase as:
(a) Greater resources have been devoted to current strategy, based on
present perceptions.

(b) Personal prestige or political standing are tied to the correctness of present perceptions (and strategy).

(c) Incorrectness of present perceptions would threaten beliefs and goals that are central to the leaders (e.g., the morality of their own nation, success by their nation in a conflict).

(4) Incorrectness of the present perceptions would force a (painful) choice between goals that are both (all) highly valued (e.g., between gaining one's objectives in a dispute and avoiding war).

(5) Significant others are unanimous in their expression of belief in the present perceptions.

(6) Government information-gathering agencies, in a conscious or unconscious attempt to support the official line, ignore or misinterpret contradictory information.

(7) Leaders are personally dogmatic, inflexible, and closed-minded.

Summary and Implications

Actions of nations in a dispute depend greatly on their perceptions of the conflict situation and of the likely actions of the other side. National leaders tend to perceive only familiar options and to feel forced by situational processes to restrict the actions they consider. The general tendency to limit the number of options considered increases as time is more limited, as stress on the decisionmaker(s) is greater, as norms concerning appropriate actions are stronger, and as choosing a new option will require forming a new difficult-to-achieve consensus.

Expectations about the actions of an adversary depend on perceptions of the adversary's capability and intent. National leaders will tend to see an adversary as having greater capability in specific ways the more they have a general image of the other side as strong, the more they see it as having hostile intent, and the more they are involved in (or members of) an organization devoted to defending against attack. They will tend to see an adversary as having more aggressive intentions the more that the adversary (or others) has been aggressive in the past, has not communicated cooperative intentions, has the capability to carry out aggression, and is seen as having the motivation to be aggressive. The adversary is more likely to be perceived as having aggressive motives the more it is seen as immoral, as dissimilar in attitudes and as not liking one's own side, as being able to benefit from (or avoid losses by) aggression, and as willing to run risks.

Leaders' expectations of the outcomes of joint actions by the two sides will be influenced by their previous experiences, their theories, and their cognitive maps of causal connections among actions and outcomes. Perceptions of an adversary's preferences (e.g., between conceding and fighting) are affected by a leader's general beliefs. But the more information decisionmakers have about their adversaries, the more accurate their perceptions of the adversary's preferences may be expected to be.

National leaders tend to resist changes in their perceptions of an adversary and of other aspects of a dispute. Resistance to change will increase as: new information is ambiguous, is not repeated often, and is undramatic; leaders hold their beliefs firmly or are personally dogmatic; leaders are committed to their perceptions because they have a large national and/or personal stake in the correctness of these perceptions and the strategy based on them; changed perceptions would force a painful choice between desirable goals; significant others unanimously support the present perception; and information-gathering agencies ignore or distort contradictory information, perhaps because changed perceptions would be an impediment to their agency's goals.

The matters discussed in this chapter are clearly relevant to the conduct of foreign policy. Let us consider some of their implications. First, it is important for officials, from a president on down, to be aware of the psychological and organizational forces that shape the perceptions of all persons, including themselves. For example, they need to be aware of the tendency to see one's own options as more limited than may be the case, of the tendency to hold sets of beliefs—e.g., the "bad faith image" of the opponent—that are impervious to new information, and of the fact that quick tentative conclusions about events are likely to distort the interpretation of later information. Such awareness among government personnel and others may be fostered by formal training programs and by in-service training programs.

But it is not enough for government officials to be aware of their personal and organizational fallibility. It is important to establish organizational mechanisms to try to improve the accuracy of the perceptions upon which important decisions may rest. First, it may be possible to increase the amount, quality, and range of information that is introduced into a foreign policy organization. The introduction of information is affected, first, by the ways in which personnel are selected. While it might seem a truism that foreign policy officials should know as much as possible about other nations and about foreign relations, high officials are sometimes chosen on the basis of other criteria—general administrative ability, political loyalty, etc. This occurred, for example, in the selection by President Reagan of William Clark, a longtime associate with no foreign policy or defense expertise, to be his first national security adviser. Compared to those who are more knowledgeable about foreign affairs, such persons are likely to form their judgments more on the basis of general beliefs and assumptions and less on the basis of wide information. It would seem desirable to choose high foreign policy officials who, whatever their other qualities, have extensive knowledge specifically in this area.

The diversity of personnel selected also can have an effect on the range of information and experiences available in a foreign policy organization. Since those who are familiar with a limited set of historical experiences will tend to interpret new events in terms of this limited experience, a foreign policy organization needs to contain information about a wide variety of events that can serve as a more adequate context for interpretation. This can be done partly by formal education but also by having personnel with a wide spread of ages, different educational backgrounds, and different experiences in various parts of the world. Increased direct contact with those in other nations, including adversary nations, also seems important in order to give the officials of one nation a better understanding of the thinking and perspectives—and thus ultimately the behavior—of their counterparts.

In addition to improved selection and training of personnel, as well as arranging for them to acquire the broadest possible range of information, a number of organizational innovations may improve the accuracy of perceptions. One possibility is to give certain persons or units responsibility for attention to matters that are often neglected. For example, the tendency to ignore some options could be countered by giving certain individuals responsibility for developing as many different and new alternatives as possible in important policy areas. The tendency for officials to notice only information compatible with their existing beliefs might be countered by giving certain persons the job of finding and disseminating a wider range of information, including that which is likely to be unpalatable. The tendency for officials to see events in ways that are consistent with existing beliefs and policies could be countered by establishing individuals or units in the role of devil's advocates to point out inconsistencies and mistakes in assumptions, beliefs, and actions. Such persons also should have access to a wide range of incoming information in order to counteract an organization's tendency to filter out information that doesn't fit its biases. Such devil's advocates are likely to be most successful if they are outsiders who are not committed to current policy and whose careers do not depend on conformity to established ways of thinking. President Johnson made use of such outsiders ("wise men") during the Vietnam war. The advantages of such a group can be institutionalized so that it can contribute fresh thinking more continuously.

In addition to trying to improve the accuracy of one's own perceptions, it often is important to improve those of the leaders of other nations. For example, leaders of one nation often assume that those in other nations recognize their intent, and it may sometimes be vital that this is so (e.g., that their intent is *not* to attack preemptively). However, their adversaries may put a very different interpretation on an action than the actors intended (Thies, 1980). The evidence reviewed here indicates that a helpful first step is simply to communicate one's own intentions very clearly. Since leaders of nation B will judge intent also on what they perceive A's incentives to be, the leaders of nation A might find it useful to provide more complete information about the advantages to them of the option they intend to follow.

Another matter that may be important for the other side to perceive correctly is one's own preferences. If, for example, nation A would rather fight than give up some territory or privilege, it is very important that it communicate its preferences clearly to its potential adversary. There are times of course when one nation wishes to mislead an adversary with respect to its preferences, capabilities, or intentions. Some of the ideas presented in this chapter concerning the determinants of perceptions can be used in this way also—to purposely make the opponent's perceptions inaccurate. This may sometimes be useful in winning an advantage but it is a dangerous game. In general, accurate perceptions on both sides appear to be necessary to resolve conflict.

4 Making Decisions

When one nation is engaged in a dispute with another, the basic choice its leaders have at any time is whether to take actions that are (a) beneficial to the other side, giving it more of what it wants, or, (b) harmful to the other side, punishing it or giving it less of what it wants. The first set of actions represents concessions (rewards) or promises of future concessions if the other side responds as desired. The second set of actions represents coercive actions, including military attack, or the threat of coercion if the other side does not respond as desired. A further possible choice is to stand pat for the present, making no further concessions but exerting no further coercion. (See chapter 1 for a discussion of the basic types of national behavior in disputes.)

When will the leaders of a nation choose to employ each of these means in pursuit of their objectives? Under what circumstances are they likely to use rewards, or promises of reward? When will they instead choose coercion or the threat of coercion? In trying to answer such questions, case studies of inter-nation disputes often are suggestive (e.g., Feis, 1950; Davison, 1958; Abel, 1966; Maghoori and Gorman, 1981). But such historical studies are too specific and diverse to permit useful generalizations unless they are placed in the framework of general theories of decisionmaking.

Psychologists and those in other social science disciplines (e.g., economics) have developed a body of theory and research on decisionmaking under risk that appears relevant to national decisions. Efforts to apply some of these ideas to national decisionmaking have been made (e.g., Snyder, 1960; Wagner, 1974; Horelick, Johnson, and Steinbruner, 1975; Bueno de Mesquita, 1981a). However, some important recent advances in the study of decisionmaking under risk have been applied little (if at all) to foreign policy decisions.

In this chapter I will outline some of the main research findings and theoretical conceptions that have been emerging in the study of decisionmaking. As the discussion proceeds, I will consider the ways in which these general ideas may be relevant to decisions in international conflict situations. In particular, I will try to see how these ideas may help us to understand choices to use or not use coercion.

The discussion in this chapter will center on the way in which choices are made at the actual moment of decision. Other aspects of the total decision process—including the way in which alternatives are identified, values are given to different outcomes, and expectancies about the actions of the adversary are formed—are discussed more fully in chapters 3 and 5. The main focus will be on the individual decisionmaker—e.g., a president or prime minister who bears the main responsibility for action in a serious international crisis. However, to understand the actions of any individual, it is necessary to consider the political and organizational context in which he is embedded. Therefore, the influence of such factors will be considered as they become relevant. The role of groups in making decisions also will be discussed briefly toward the end of the chapter.

Use of Standard Rules

Because the environment presents an unending series of occasions for choices, both individuals and organizations develop standard rules for dealing with recurring choice situations. For individuals, for example, the rule of thumb when presented with an aggressive act by another person may be turn the other cheek, or get away from the situation as soon as possible, or retaliate with interest. In foreign policy too individual leaders and governments may develop standard rules for dealing with conflict situations without a serious analysis in each particular case of the possible outcomes of alternative actions. For example, when presented with a demand by Hitler, British Prime Minister Chamberlain followed for a time the rule of "make concessions" on the assumption that such a policy would result in eventual German satisfaction and peace. A very different example is provided by the Israeli government, which for many years followed a standard policy of responding to every major terrorist raid against Israel with a military attack on Palestinian camps in Lebanon.

American military commanders have sometimes been given orders to respond with force if a certain event (e.g., an apparent threat of attack) occurs (Gibson, 1984). American aircraft apparently had such orders in

August 1981 when they shot down Libyan planes they believed posed a threat to U.S. forces in the area. Gibson (1984:242) says of that incident: "President Reagan was not informed of the American responsive action until well after it took place; therefore, one can infer that the contingency was preplanned, as was the almost automatic American response."

The U.S. government has plans for retaliation against Soviet targets (and the Soviet Union undoubtedly has similar plans) that would probably be activated almost automatically in the event of enemy attack, without analysis as to whether or not such action would best serve the national interest (e.g., hold down the number of deaths) at that time. Coercive action by any nation is more likely the more it has formulated, formally or informally, rules that call automatically for use of coercion in particular situations.

Beach and Mitchell (1978) have discussed the circumstances under which decisionmakers are likely to use nonanalytic strategies involving "fairly simple, preformulated rules," versus strategies based on analysis.[1] They indicate first that personal characteristics of decisionmakers may affect the type of strategy used. In particular, they suggest that "the more intelligent, cognitively complex and analytic the individual is, the easier it should be to use analytic rather than non-analytic strategies" (Beach and Mitchell, 1978:446). In addition, they suggest that a person who is impetuous or anxious to "get the matter settled" is more likely to choose on the basis of a simple rule rather than of careful analysis. Kaiser Wilhelm II of Germany was one such volatile person. After the Austrian crown prince had been assassinated in June 1914, the kaiser assured Austrian leaders that Germany would support them in punishing Serbia for this act, setting in motion a series of events that culminated in World War I. While the kaiser probably was influenced by certain policy aims of German officials, his action appears to have been affected also by his acceptance of the simple rule that assassins of royalty must be punished and by his "characteristic impetuosity" in acting without sufficient deliberation (Stoessinger, 1982:3–5).

Beach and Mitchell also argue that the use of an analytic versus a nonanalytic approach to choice will be affected strongly by the nature of the decision task. As this task becomes more difficult—i.e., the decision problem is unfamiliar, ambiguous, complex, and changing—analytic strategies are more likely to be used. For example, when North Korea invaded South Korea in June 1950 the problem seemed to President Truman a fairly simple one. A clear act of naked aggression, similar to ones the world had recently experienced in the 1930s, had occurred. Without extensive analysis of the consequences or of alternatives, Truman applied the rule that Americans had learned from the 1930s: resist, do not appease, aggressors

(Snyder and Paige, 1958). However, when faced later with a more unfamiliar and complex situation in Korea—i.e., the presence of a Chinese army aiding the North Koreans, the indirect participation of the Soviet Union, the involvement of the United Nations, and the possibility of atomic weapons being used—American actions became much more deliberate. Truman and his advisers weighed carefully the possible consequences of alternative actions (e.g., bombing Chinese bases in Manchuria).

While more difficult decision tasks are likely to result in the use of analytic decision strategies, this may not be true at the extreme of task difficulty. Beach and Mitchell suggest that if the task becomes extremely difficult the decisionmaker may despair of an analytic approach and revert to a simpler "standard rule" strategy. Perhaps this may occur in arms-control talks, where the complexity of many varying and changing weapons systems may lead the decisionmaker to fall back on simple rules like "cut all weapons by 20 percent."

In addition to characteristics of the person and of the task, Beach and Mitchell argue that the process of decisionmaking may be affected by features of the environment. They suggest that the more irreversible the decision, the greater its significance, and the more accountable the decisionmaker is for the results, the more the pressures to use an analytic strategy. On the other hand, time or money constraints may lead to the use of a simpler strategy of following standard rules or rules of thumb. The types of foreign policy decisions with which we are concerned are ones that are significant and for which the decisionmakers are accountable to their countrymen. These factors would favor an analytic approach to most important foreign policy decisions. On the other hand, where a decision has to be made quickly, standard rules for particular contingencies may be used. For example, when the Russians announced a partial mobilization in July 1914, German leaders felt pressured to act quickly themselves and fell back on the long-standing rule that if the Russians mobilized, the German army must mobilize too—without making a substantial analysis of the advantages of alternative actions (Stoessinger, 1982).

We would expect that the more that national decisionmakers have established rules that dictate the use of coercion under specified conditions, the more likely is coercion to be used by that nation in disputes. Having standard rules about when to use coercion permits quick action and avoids the necessity for a difficult process of decisionmaking. The problem with such general rules, however, is that they may not fit well a particular circumstance. Options not previously considered may be possible in the particular case. New negative consequences of the "programmed" action may now be foreseeable. In the light of new information, other negative consequences may be more likely than estimated when the rule was established. Thus it seems likely that careful assessments about the possible use of coercion on particular occasions will result in fewer actual decisions to do so than in cases for which there is a standard rule.[2]

It seems important for top officials to identify and review policies that have found their way into the civilian and military bureaucracies about the circumstances under which force will be used automatically. Such a review should include examination of the standard policies that are explicitly or implicitly followed by top leaders. Most important, national leaders should be very cautious about permitting subordinates to order the use of force without specific authorization from the top civilian officials. One vital example concerns rules for response in the event that signals of possible attack by another nation are received. In such an event it seems crucial that a decision about the nature of the response should be made by top officials on the basis of the specific facts of the situation rather than by having military commanders (or a computer) respond automatically. Otherwise, a nuclear holocaust could be triggered by following inappropriate rules or even by a computer malfunction.[3]

Choosing Among Options

In most serious disputes between nations, leaders will deliberate about which action, if any, to take at a given time. In doing so they will take into account the value that they place on various possible outcomes of the dispute (i.e., possible terms of settlement, continuing stalemate, and a (wider) fight between the two sides). They will consider also the likelihood that various possible actions they might take (issuing threats, using coercion, making concessions, etc.) will lead to given outcomes.

How do decisionmakers combine such information about the value of different outcomes and their expectancies that particular outcomes will follow particular actions in order to make a choice among actions? Often they proceed in phases or stages (Slovic, Fischoff, and Lichtenstein, 1977; Svenson, 1979; Abelson and Levi, 1985). In an initial screening phase, the individual rejects those options that do not appear to meet a minimum level on all, or the most important, of his criteria. Later he may use any of various decision rules—probably involving a comparison of the advantages and disadvantages of each option—on a reduced set of alternatives.

The Screening Phase

The minimum criteria an option must satisfy in order to survive the decisionmaker's initial screening will be determined by his initial level of expectation or aspiration. He may have as a target a minimum level of positive outcome. He also may have in mind a maximum loss that he is willing to accept as a possible result of any decision. Kahneman and Tversky (1979) have discussed how such levels of aspiration may have a marked effect on the value the decisionmaker places on specific outcomes. In their model of decisionmaking under risk, MacCrimmon, Stanbury and Wehrung (1980) suggest that there occurs a type of screening process in which sets of alternatives are first put in the following order of preference, according to whether they provide: (1) chances of desirable gains (above one's target) and of acceptable losses; (2) a chance of mediocre (below target) gains and a chance of acceptable losses; and, (3) the chance of unacceptable losses (regardless of possible gain).[4]

The process of screening possible options by testing them against minimum targets for gain and maximum acceptable losses appears to be very relevant to decisions in international conflicts. Snyder and Diesing (1977) found that the decisions of national leaders often were guided by their minimum or maximum goals and by their willingness to accept the possibility of the negative outcomes of war. For example, Stalin's provocative action of cutting surface traffic to West Berlin in 1948 was motivated by his hope of blocking Western plans for a unified West Germany and his aim of including West Berlin in the east zone. However, his unwillingness to run a serious risk of war with the Western nations led him not to challenge the airlift that kept West Berlin supplied (Davison, 1958).

Lebow's discussion of various international conflicts also points to the importance of whether decisionmakers are willing to accept the possibility of war (Lebow, 1981). He comments: "But when war loses its horrors, then fear of it no longer exercises a restraining influence on policy. Conversely, when war is defined as a calamity, politicians are likely to be more cautious in crisis situations regardless of their expectations of the outcome of a possible war. Positive attitudes toward war prevailed among the policy-making elites in initiators of three of our five brinkmanship crises that led to war" (Lebow, 1981:248).

A contrary perspective was held by Cyrus Vance, the U.S. secretary of state under President Carter. Zbigniew Brzezinski, who as national security adviser worked closely with Vance, states his agreement with a remark by the secretary of defense in the Carter administration that "Secretary

Vance was persuaded that anything that involved the risk of force was a mistake" (Brzezinski, 1983:44).

Snyder and Diesing (1977) see changes in levels of aspiration and constraints as crucial to the process of interaction and bargaining in a dispute. As a nation's leaders lower their aspirations for gain or become less willing to accept the possibility of war, they may moderate their demands and consider compromise solutions to the conflict that they would not consider before. On the other hand, if decisionmakers decide to accept a greater risk of war than they were willing to accept previously, they may consider (or reconsider) coercive actions and harsh demands they previously had ruled out.

Snyder and Diesing make a number of other interesting observations about the levels of aspiration and the perceived constraints found among foreign policy decisionmakers. One is that their levels of aspiration may be vague, especially at the beginning of a dispute. In other words, the decisionmaker may not be clear at a given time about just what outcome he would be willing to accept. Presumably the same thing would be true with respect to constraints. The decisionmaker may not be completely clear on whether he is prepared to accept the possibility of war until he is faced with taking some action that will run that risk.

A decisionmaker may find no option that appears to satisfy all of his major aspirations and constraints. For example, during the Cuban missile crisis, American decisionmakers perceived no action that would be sure to eliminate Soviet offensive missiles from Cuba and also would be sure to avoid war. Faced with such a situation, the decisionmaker must decide which of his positive goals and negative constraints have the highest priority. It is not usually necessary to completely eliminate an important aspiration or constraint. Rather, it may be possible to modify the extent to which, or the probability with which, a given outcome may be acceptable. For example, in the Cuban missile crisis the United States could have been satisfied with an air strike that eliminated most (but not all) of the Soviet missiles or that had a 90 percent chance of eliminating them. With respect to constraints the American decisionmakers could have been satisfied (as they were) with an action (the blockade) they saw as having only a moderately high probability of avoiding war.

Snyder and Diesing (1977:347) point out that since a crisis arises because a situation has become intolerable for at least one of the parties, the focus of the decisionmaker's attention tends to be on the objective of changing that situation (or blocking the other side from doing so). Therefore, other objectives and constraints, such as avoiding war, tend to be given secondary attention. In many cases such a focus of attention may be inappropriate in terms of national interest. For example, it can be argued that the objective of removing Soviet missiles from Cuba was much less vital to American interests than was avoiding war, despite the greater focus (and apparently higher priority) put on the former by American officials.

The nature of the objectives and constraints that decisionmakers accept, and the relative importance they assign to them, will be affected by a variety of personal, social, organizational, and political factors. Personal experiences and motives can make certain objectives especially important to particular individuals. For example, the early experiences of Prime Minister Menachem Begin of Israel, who saw his family and Jewish community in Poland destroyed by the Nazis, made the objective of protecting Jews in Israel from physical harm of very high salience to him.

The objectives of decisionmakers may be affected also by the beliefs and ideologies of social groups to which they belong. For example, Lebow (1981:chapter 7) describes a general belief among the aristocratic classes of Russia and Germany prior to World War I that war is a noble, purifying enterprise and would, moreover, rally their sometimes disunified nations. Such beliefs would of course tend to downgrade the importance of avoiding war when pursuing national objectives. Varying emphasis on particular objectives may also derive from the particular concerns and influence of various units within a government bureaucracy. For example, within the U.S. government, the State Department, the Defense Department, and the national security adviser had varying objectives for American policy when Iran under the Shah faced internal revolt (Brzezinski, 1983:chapter 10).

Finally, the goals of decisionmakers may be affected by political pressures within their nations. Lebow (1981:chapter 6) describes, for example, how the decision of President Truman to permit U.S. forces to advance beyond the 38th parallel in Korea (resulting in war with China) and the decision of Indian Prime Minister Nehru to send troops into a disputed border area with China were affected strongly by domestic political pressures on each to act firmly in the particular situation. Demonstrating firmness thus became an important objective for each of these national leaders. Neither, however, wanted or expected the war that resulted from their actions.

The preceding discussion suggests that the choice of coercive actions by national decisionmakers is more likely when: (1) they do not make the avoidance of war a constraint on policy; or (2) the constraint of avoiding war is not given a sufficiently high priority relative to other goals; or, (3) the constraint of avoiding war is relaxed to permit a low level of fighting or some substantial probability of war. When constraints of avoiding war are weak in such ways, potential actions that may lead to war will not be screened out as unacceptable options.

It is important for government leaders to try to build into their decision processes an early consideration of what priority they wish to give to avoiding war (relative to other goals) and how much risk of war they are prepared to take in order to win other objectives. Clarity about these vital questions would help to avoid the possibility that national leaders would, without clear reflection and intent, take excessive risks of war that are not justifiable even in terms of their own priorities.

Many thoughtful people today believe that a policy that carries even a small chance of leading to a nuclear war should be seen as unacceptable by national leaders (e.g., Fischer, 1984). This view is based on available information concerning the terrible devastation that such a war would bring and on the likelihood that any victor in such a war would reign only over radioactive rubble. If this case can be made persuasively both to the public and to government officials, then decisionmakers may come to judge any policy that increases the chance of nuclear war to be unacceptable.

Choice Among Final Options

The process of screening out unacceptable options by testing each option against aspirations and constraints may result in a single "passing" option. For example, a national leader engaged in a dispute with another nation may believe that an acceptable policy must (a) get some minimum of political support at home; (b) achieve some minimum level of advantage with respect to the issue in dispute; and, (c) avoid (with high probability) a war with the adversary. Each of these requirements may constitute a level of aspiration or—in the case of negative requirements such as avoiding war—a constraint to be met by any action. If he finds a possible action that appears to satisfy all three of his requirements, he may accept this option, usually without searching further for a possibly better option. Such a process of decisionmaking has been termed bounded rationality (March and Simon, 1958; Cyert and March, 1963). Snyder and Diesing (1977: chapter 5) have found that national decisionmakers often appear to act in this way during the course of an inter-nation dispute; i.e., search until they find an option that meets their major aspirations and constraints.

However, a decisionmaker may be able to find no option that meets all of his key criteria. Or he may find that there are *several* possible options that meet all of the criteria. In either case, he needs some way to choose among the several possibilities. He may attempt to resolve the problem by applying essentially the same screening method again with more (or fewer) criteria or with new minimum levels on the criteria. For example, he may decide that an acceptable policy must be politically popular and stand a good chance of gaining the prize in the dispute but that it no longer need avoid war. Or he may reduce (or raise) the minimum level of political support a policy must have (for a U.S. president, perhaps enough support to prevent impeachment). Or he may tolerate a larger (or smaller) risk of war than he was prepared to accept initially.

However, the decisionmaker often will see no clear reason to drop certain criteria from consideration or to change greatly his level of aspiration on particular criteria. When an important choice must still be made among several remaining options, he often will make a comparison of the overall attractiveness of each option in terms of its possible advantages and disadvantages and the likelihood of these outcomes occurring (Wright and Barbour, 1977; Payne, 1976). In such a comparison among options he will consider the extent to which the greater advantages of option A on criteria 1 and 2 (or the greater likelihood that those advantages will result from option A) compensate for the greater advantages of option B on criteria 3 and 4, or their greater likelihood of occurring following option B (Abelson and Levi, 1985).

One often-used theoretical model that deals with a decisionmaker's attempt to assess the overall attractiveness of each option postulates that the individual attempts to "maximize (subjective) expected utility" (Wright, 1984).[5] According to this theory the decisionmaker assesses the possible outcomes of an action and places a value or utility on each. The expected utility of action 1 is the sum of the utilities of all outcomes of that action, with the utility of each outcome being weighted by the decisionmaker's subjective probability that action 1 will lead to that particular outcome. The model predicts that the decisionmaker will choose whichever action has the highest expected utility.

The expected-utility approach has been used by researchers to try to understand a number of foreign policy decisions (Horelick, Johnson, and Steinbruner, 1975). For example Wagner (1974) used this approach to try to understand (retrospectively) the Israeli decision to launch a preemptive attack against Egypt in 1967. He asked members of the Israeli cabinet to judge the relative importance of six outcomes, such as ending the threat of invasion by Egypt, opening the blockaded straits of Tiran, and ending terrorist raids. On the basis of this information, he estimated the utility of each outcome to each decisionmaker. He also asked the Israelis to make numerical estimates of the probability (as they had seen it) that each possible Israeli option (diplomacy, all-out attack, etc.) would lead to each relevant outcome. Wagner aggregated the data for individuals to reflect the collective utilities and subjective probabilities of the Israeli cabinet as a whole. He then found that the alternative that actually had been chosen—a preemptive attack—had the highest expected value for the Israeli decisionmakers. (Wagner does note that other decision models also may be able to explain the Israeli decision.)

An ambitious effort to use expected-utility theory to predict decisions for war has been made by Bueno de Mesquita (1981a). Using data on several hundred inter-nation conflicts during the past two centuries, Bueno de Mesquita made estimates of the expected utility for war by each nation involved in a conflict. He finds support for the "proposition that positive expected utility is necessary—though not sufficient—for a leader to initiate a serious international dispute, including a war" (Bueno de Mesquita, 1981a:129).

The attack–no attack decision by national leaders also has been analyzed by Huth and Russett (1984) in terms of the expected utility of each option for the decisionmakers. Huth and Russett have focused on the effectiveness of deterrence attempts—i.e., on whether a potential attacker will carry out his attack on a small nation in the face of deterrent threats by a defender of that small nation.

The idea that a decisionmaker acts to maximize his expected utility has been questioned as a general model of decisionmaking. Critics have questioned such assumptions of the theory as the following: (1) that people really apply a common yardstick of utility when judging diverse outcomes, such as gaining territory, maintaining self-esteem, and improving one's political position; (2) that people will allow a high utility on one outcome to compensate for a low utility on another outcome—i.e., that utilities of various outcomes are interchangeable; and, (3) that people will perform the sometimes complex calculations required to assess the expected utilities of various options. Moreover, psychologists and others who have reviewed recent evidence on decisionmaking have concluded that the expected-utility approach is seriously deficient in explaining how people actually make decisions (Kahneman and Tversky, 1979; Fischhoff, Goitein, and Shapira, 1982; Simon, 1979).[6]

The applicability of the model to foreign policy decisions also has been controversial. For example, collaborators Glenn Snyder and Paul Diesing have disagreed on this issue. Diesing believes that in most of the foreign policy crises he and Snyder studied, national leaders did not act in accord with the utility-maximization model. In his view, they did not compare the advantages and disadvantages of each option in terms of some implicit common denominator of benefit. He believes that national decisionmakers behaved more in accord with the bounded-rationality model—assessing each option to see if it met each of their separate constraints—without trying to compare the relative value of each constraint against the others (Snyder and Diesing, 1977:405–406).

Snyder, on the other hand, finds the utility-maximization approach to be more relevant to understanding how national leaders make decisions in crises. He states:

> In the cases for which we have most data on internal decision making, we do find decision makers at certain points listing the pros and cons of all reasonable alternatives in fairly systematic fashion, then choosing the "best." This took place most clearly in the [cases of] United States, Cuba, 1962; also in United States, Berlin, 1948; United States, Berlin, 1961; and England, Munich, 1938. . . . In these instances it is very difficult if not impossible to judge whether the participants compared the alternatives to each other in terms of some implicit common denominator of costs and benefits or tested each one separately against constraints. . . . This is not so much because the data are ambiguous as because the intellectual procedures postulated by each theory are quite easily translatable into the other at difficult choice points (Snyder and Diesing, 1977:408, comment by Snyder).

Snyder suggests that in many cases a "complementary synthesis" of the "bounded rationality" and the "maximizing expected utility" theories would most accurately reflect the facts.

On the basis of evidence about decisionmaking in general and about foreign-policy decisionmaking in particular, it seems fair to conclude that decisionmakers often do not behave as utility-maximizers. They may make decisions by following standard rules or by habit. Even when deliberating on their choices, they often accept or reject options in terms of whether they meet each of several separate criteria, without trying to compare the overall value or utility of several options. However, the evidence also indicates that when decisionmakers have to make important decisions and when unacceptable options have been screened out, some comparison of the overall benefit of each remaining option is likely to occur. This is apt to involve some assessment of the relative value of the advantages and disadvantages each option may bring and of the likelihood that these results will occur.

One does not need to assume that the decisionmaker assigns some common abstract utility value to each positive and negative outcome. Rather, he may think in terms of trade-offs between different types of advantages and disadvantages. A national leader may consider, for instance, whether a gamble involving the moderate chance of eventually winning a territorial advantage along with a high probability of a continued stalemate of a dispute (the possible outcomes of an unyielding policy) is preferable to the certainty of a given compromise agreement of the dispute (the outcome of a conciliatory policy). More formally, the attraction for a decisionmaker of a particular acceptable action (one that meets minimal criteria) may be expected to be as follows:

(4-1)   Attraction
    of action 1 = (value of outcome A × weight associated with sub-
                                       jective probability of out-
                                       come A following action 1)

        + (value of outcome B × weight associated with sub-
                                       jective probability of out-
                                       come B following action 1)

    . . . + (value of outcome N × weight associated with sub-
                                       jective probability of out-
                                       come N following action 1)

The decisionmaker may be expected to choose the action that promises the highest overall value according to equation 4-1.

It should be noted that this description of decisionmaking is not identical to the formulation of those who have stated that people will select among options so as to maximize expected utility. The approach taken here recognizes that choices may be made by following rules and that possible options may be screened out at a preliminary stage (see previous discussion). In addition, in accord with recent work on decisionmaking (Wright, 1984), the equation presented above does not assume (as the expected-utility model does) that the weights decisionmakers attach to the value of different outcomes correspond to their subjective probabilities of these outcomes occurring or that these weights add up to one. It may be instead that certain subjective probabilities (e.g., those close to one or to zero) are given extra weights and that the sum of probabilities does not add up to one (Wright, 1984).

Equation 4-1 indicates that the likelihood that a national leader will use coercion in a dispute will depend on the values he gives to various outcomes of the dispute (winning, losing, compromise, stalemate, or fight) and his expectancies that coercion, as opposed to other means, will lead to the various outcomes. The likelihood that coercion will be used by a decisionmaker increases as (a) he places greater value on winning on the issue in dispute; and/or (b) the prospect of war seems less repugnant to

him; and/or (c) possible compromise agreements (or even giving in completely) seems more desirable. Alternatively (or in addition), a decisionmaker
will be more likely to choose a coercive option if his expectations of the
likely outcomes of such an action become more optimistic—e.g., if he sees
a greater chance that coercion will lead to winning on the issue in dispute
and a lesser chance of its leading to a fight.

The likelihood that coercion will be used will increase also as a
decisionmaker comes to expect that noncoercive options (e.g., making
concessions or promises) will not lead to desirable outcomes.

The factors that shape the values decisionmakers place on different
outcomes, and affect their expectancies about the effects of various actions,
will be discussed in chapter 5.

Making Risky Choices

Most important choices in foreign policy, as in other areas, involve risk.
The decisionmaker usually chooses among actions that may or may not
lead to particular outcomes—such as submission by the other side on the
issue in dispute or war. But some actions are more risky than others.
Because they are more likely to result in a (wider) fight, coercive actions
usually involve greater risk of large losses than more conciliatory actions,
such as making concessions. Especially in the present age of nuclear weapons, to run even a small risk of war is to run the risk of a very large loss
indeed. And yet sometimes national leaders still have been willing to run
large risks—as leaders of both the United States and the Soviet Union did
during the Berlin crises, the Cuban missile crisis, and the Arab-Israeli war
of 1973. At other times, national leaders have chosen more cautious
options—as when American leaders refrained from interfering in the Soviet
invasion of Hungary in 1956 or in their building of the Berlin wall in 1961.

Recent work on decisionmaking—most notably the work by Kahneman
and Tversky (1979, 1982, 1984) that they label "prospect theory"—has
advanced our understanding of decisionmaking under risk. Among the
topics discussed by Kahneman and Tversky that seem relevant to decisions
in inter-nation disputes are (a) the frame of reference of the decisionmaker
and (b) choices involving losses as compared to those involving gains.

The frame of reference. Kahneman and Tversky stress the importance of
the frame of reference against which people judge the possible outcomes of
each action they consider. Outcomes are usually judged, they state, in
terms of gains and losses from the status quo rather than in absolute terms.
For example, at the last horse race of the day, the typical bettor will judge
the outcomes of alternative bets not in terms of what he will have in his

pocket following the race but in terms of what he will have won or lost at the track for that day. (This perspective can account for the observed tendency for heavy betting on long shots in the last race, as many people try to recoup their losses and come out ahead for the day.) The importance of this phenomenon is that it may lead those who have lost something to date to make more risky choices at present. As Kahneman and Tversky put it, "This analysis suggests that a person who has not made peace with his losses is likely to accept gambles that would be unacceptable to him otherwise" (1979:287).

The possible relevance of this point to decisions in cases of international conflict seems apparent. Many national leaders have *not* made peace with their country's recent (or not-so-recent) losses. For example, Hitler in 1936 seethed with fury over the territory Germany had lost in 1919, and Syrian leaders in 1973 were unreconciled to the loss of the Golan Heights to Israel. It seems plausible that such leaders will be more likely to take risky actions—as Hitler did in reoccupying the Rhineland in 1936 and Syria did in attacking a strong Israel in 1973—than leaders whose nations had not suffered recent losses.

One way in which risk-taking can be minimized is for people to formulate the decision problem in terms of final assets rather than in terms of gains and losses. (This is true regardless of whether gains and losses are judged from the present or from some other time point.) Kahneman and Tversky (1979:287) comment, "The explicit formulation of decision problems in terms of final assets is perhaps the most effective procedure for eliminating risk-seeking in the domain of losses."

The case of the Cuban missile crisis is an interesting one to examine from this perspective. American decisionmakers looked at the possible outcomes of the crisis primarily in terms of possible losses or gains relative to the preceding status quo. What would the United States lose in prestige and political influence? What would the administration lose politically at home? From this perspective the substantial losses loomed large—large enough to justify in the decisionmakers' minds running the risk of nuclear war to get rid of the missiles and avoid these losses. But what if the outcome had been viewed primarily in terms of the final position of the United States? Even with Soviet missiles in Cuba, the United States would still have held a military advantage in the world (though a reduced one). The United States would still have had a large margin of economic superiority and many political advantages over the Soviets. From that perspective of final assets it might have seemed less justifiable to risk nuclear war in order to avoid having a Soviet base in Cuba.

Kahneman and Tversky point out that there are situations in which outcomes and losses are judged relative to an expectation or aspiration level rather than to the status quo at a given time. In this respect, their theoretical approach is consistent with bounded-rationality theory, which emphasizes that choices are made to try to meet aspiration levels. Kahneman and Tversky's basic point about risky choices to try to eliminate losses would still apply. When a decisionmaker sees his present position as lower than his level of aspiration, he may take considerable risks to try to reach the aspiration level. For example, German leaders in the first decade of this century aspired to a world position on a par with Great Britain and France —especially with respect to colonial possessions in Africa. However, they found themselves frozen out of this arena by the fact that their European rivals had acted earlier to establish spheres of influence in Africa. To try to fulfill their colonial aspirations, German leaders took a number of challenging actions that ran the risk of war with Britain and France (Gooch, 1938). The Soviet Union under Khrushchev furnishes another example. Khrushchev and his colleagues aspired to strategic equality with the United States but found themselves far short of this goal. To try to redress their undesirable position, the Soviet leaders took the risky action of moving missiles into Cuba.

Losses versus gains. One of the most interesting and important findings to come out of recent research on decisionmaking is that people generally choose very differently when they must decide between possible losses as compared to possible gains (Hogarth, 1980; Kahneman and Tversky, 1979). For example, consider a person who must choose between two options: (a) an 80 percent chance of winning $10 versus (b) a 20 percent chance of winning $40. Although the "expected values" of the two bets are equal, most people faced with this choice will pick the conservative option (a).[7]

However, when faced with a choice between (a), an 80 percent chance of losing $10, versus (b), a 20 percent chance of losing $40, most people will choose the riskier option (b). In other words, they are willing to take the chance of suffering a large loss in order to avoid any loss at all.[8] Kahneman and Tversky's work can account for this observed phenomenon in terms of two underlying processes. One is the certainty effect—the tendency of people to give more weight to outcomes that are certain (or almost certain) than to outcomes that are not very probable. (Such overweighting would go beyond the difference in objective probabilities.) This tendency would make a sure small gain more attractive (thus leading to a conservative choice among positive outcomes) but would also make a sure small loss less attractive (thus leading to a more risky choice among negative outcomes).[9]

A second principle that can help explain observed patterns of risky choices is the tendency of successive objective increases in either gains or losses to result in successively smaller increases in subjective value. Thus, an increase from $10 to $20 in winnings would be valued more than an increase from $110 to $120. Similarly, an increased loss from -$10 to -$20 would be valued more than the change from -$110 to -$120. The relatively small subjective value of a large gain would tend to make a risky choice for a large gain less attractive. On the other hand, the relatively small (negative) subjective value of a large loss would tend to make more attractive a choice risking that large loss.[10] It has been found also that the value function for losses is steeper than that for gains (Kahneman and Tversky, 1979). For example, the loss of $100 would be valued (negatively) by most people more than a gain of $100 would be valued positively.

Are these results from experimental studies relevant to the foreign policy decisions made by national leaders? In considering this question our interest is mainly in choices that involve the risk of serious negative outcomes, particularly war. While it is not possible to prove a general rule by citing specific cases (which may not necessarily be representative), it is not hard to find cases that reflect the tendencies found in experimental studies—i.e., for decisionmakers to take an action that risked large losses in order to avoid the certain (or almost certain) prospect of a smaller but very unpalatable loss. Japan in 1941 is a good case in point. Japanese leaders were faced with the basic options of (1) doing nothing in the face of U.S. embargoes on scrap iron and oil, which would have led surely to reduced Japanese economic and military strength, or (2) launching a program of military expansion in Southeast Asia, which offered the prospect of retaining (and strengthening) Japan's position but also ran the risk of a catastrophic defeat by the United States. The Japanese decided to take the risky course (Hosoya, 1974).

The factors that produced the German decisions that led to World War I are more complex and include some important misperceptions (including the belief that Britain would remain neutral in the event of war). However, German leaders' choices (as they saw them) also tended to be between accepting a certain loss (a weakened Austrian ally and a serious rift in their Austrian alliance) versus trying to avoid that loss (by backing Austrian "chastisement" of Serbia) and taking a risk of a larger loss (a wider European war that Germany might lose). As Lebow puts it, "German leaders faced a serious dilemma: they had to make a choice between a risky continental war and what promised to be an equally disastrous peace" (Lebow, 1981:134). Basically, the German leaders decided to stand firmly behind Austria (and risk war) until the last moment, when it was too late to reverse the momentum of events leading to war.

The possible losses that may be involved in foreign policy decisions are sometimes domestic political ones. Lebow describes in some detail two rather parallel situations in which a national decisionmaker had to choose between a policy involving political losses at home and a policy that stood a good chance of avoiding those losses but risked war. The first case concerns the decision made by U.S. President Truman to send American troops across the 38th parallel (the boundary between North and South Korea) in the fall of 1950. Truman had been under attack by some factions for his Asian policy, which critics said had recently lost China to the Communists. With American troops victorious in South Korea, Truman was warned by advisers that a failure to push further to "liberate" North Korea would be denounced by critics as further appeasement of communism. Although there were disturbing signs that China might enter the war if the United States pushed close to China's border (thus involving the United States in a war with the massive Chinese army), Truman took this risk and permitted the American commander in Korea to advance right up to the Chinese border. (The Chinese then crossed into Korea, inflicting a serious defeat on the exposed American forces and involving the United States in a long, costly—and, for Truman, politically disastrous—war.)

A few years later, in 1961, a similar scenario was enacted in India. Prime Minister Nehru was faced with a decision between compromising on India's border dispute with China or sending Indian troops into a disputed territory. Because of an inflamed public opinion in India on this issue (which Nehru himself had unwisely aroused), a "soft" policy toward China at this time would have meant that Nehru's political prestige would suffer damage. Such political loss could be avoided by firm military action, but such action entailed the risk of an unwanted and potentially very costly war with China. Faced with this choice, Nehru—like Truman—chose to try to avoid the sure (though modest) loss and gamble that a military action would not be resisted by the Chinese. Like Truman, Nehru also lost his gamble. The Chinese took military action to expel Indian troops and a costly though limited war ensued.

Another example of a nation's leaders trying to improve a negative situation by actions that risked an even more negative outcome is described by Shlaim and Tanter (1978). In 1969 Israel was locked in a low-level war of attrition with Egypt along the Suez Canal. While the current military situation posed no threat to Israel, it was causing casualties among her troops. A proposal was made by some military officials that Israel escalate the war by bombing military and industrial targets deep inside Egypt. If successful, this policy would force Nasser to call off the war of attrition (and perhaps even topple him from power). However, the "deep penetration bombing" policy ran some serious risks, chief of which was that the

Soviet Union would intervene in some way to help Egypt, its ally at that time. If this occurred, there could be serious political and even military setbacks for Israel. Despite the risks (which apparently were not explored in sufficient depth), Israel did gamble in hopes of eliminating a somewhat negative current situation. The result was Russian intervention that left Israel in a worse political and military position than she had been in when she initiated the deep-penetration bombing.

In their analysis of international crises, Snyder and Diesing make a relevant comment on risk-taking by national leaders: "When the objective is very highly valued, as in the Cuban (missile crisis) instance, decision makers will tend to act on the certainty of that valuation and gamble with the risks attached to negative constraints" (Snyder and Diesing, 1977:385). The evidence on decisionmaking suggests that such gambles, involving the possibility of large losses, are more likely to be made when the objective being sought is to avoid a sure (though smaller) loss rather than to make a gain.

Accepting losses. Decisionmakers will not always take the risk of a large loss in order to avoid the certainty of a smaller loss. Sometimes they will accept the small loss instead. Whether or not they are willing to do this will depend on the combination of (a) the value of the certain smaller loss, (b) the value of the possible larger loss, and, (c) the probability of the larger loss occurring. Kahneman and Tversky (1979:276) have proposed a precise formula that shows the attractiveness of an option or prospect as a function of these factors.[11]

In some cases there are points beyond which the negative value of losses takes a sharp jump (Kahneman and Tversky, 1979). For example, Israeli decisionmakers might feel able to live with a surrender of some of the West Bank territory but, if the territory to be surrendered included Jerusalem, this might make the prospect much more obnoxious and therefore unacceptable. To take another example, while the negative value attached to war would probably increase as its scope widened, the occurrence of nuclear war might bring a sharp rise in negative valuation and perhaps be seen as too great a catastrophe to risk.

Where there is a sure small loss, and a possible larger loss, the latter is more likely to be so great that it cannot be risked. However, the smaller loss also may be unacceptable and a national leader may make a risky choice in order to avoid it. This appears to have been the case in 1941 with the Japanese leaders who felt that giving up Japanese control over China and Indochina was unacceptable and risked a much greater catastrophe in order to avoid this loss.

The likelihood of a decisionmaker risking a large loss in order to avoid a smaller loss would, of course, diminish as the probability of incurring the larger loss increases. Thus, after discussing the frequent willingness of national decisionmakers to risk war in order to win some valued objective, Snyder and Diesing note: "However, in certain other cases (Russia, Bosnia [crisis] 1908; France, Fashoda [crisis] 1898) where war, and especially a losing war, was seen as a virtually certain consequence of firmness, this negative constraint triumphed over the positive goal at stake" (Snyder and Diesing, 1977:385).

To summarize, the discussion in this section on risk-taking suggests that:

(1) National leaders will tend to take an action that risks a large loss (such as might result from war) when they believe that other actions will result with near certainty in a smaller but painful loss (or, more generally, in an outcome below their minimum level of aspiration).

(1a) When a nation has recently suffered a loss, to which its top decisionmaker is not reconciled, he will be more likely to take a risky action (i.e., a coercive move that runs the risk of war) than if there has been no such loss.

(1b) When a national leader perceives his nation to currently occupy a position below his minimum level of acceptability, he will be more likely to take a risky (coercive) action than if he perceives his nation to be at or above a minimally acceptable level.

(2) The tendency to make a choice that risks a large loss in order to avoid a small loss decreases when the magnitude of the larger loss passes a threshold of unacceptability and/or the larger loss becomes very probable.

This discussion suggests that we should try to avoid situations in which national leaders define their choices in terms of either (a) accepting the inevitability of a loss (or negative outcome) or (b) taking a risk in order to avoid the loss. One step in this direction is to have outcomes presented to decisionmakers in terms of their absolute value as well as (or in addition to) the extent to which they represent gains and losses. For example, if U.S. decisionmakers were considering actions to head off the creation of a Marxist government in El Salvador, that possible outcome should be described in terms of its overall consequences for the United States rather than (or in addition to) the extent to which it would represent a political loss for the United States.

In addition, it may sometimes be apropriate to try to persuade decisionmakers to change their point of reference for gains and losses so that the status quo is no longer seen as unacceptable. For example, West German leaders may be coming gradually to see their nation as part of a Western European community and to judge political changes in relation to this present situation. From this perspective they might see the division of Germany into two separate states as something that, though not desirable, can be "lived with" indefinitely.

While it may sometimes be possible to modify decisionmakers' frames of reference against which outcomes are judged, this will not always be possible. Some perspectives are not very flexible, and some outcomes are realistically negative by almost any standards. Rather than attempt to change an adversary's perception of his outcomes, the leaders of a nation may instead attempt to make the present situation of the adversary less negative. For example, the United States might have been able to do more in 1941 to make Japan's situation less unendurable to her leaders—e.g., by easing the embargo on oil. Such actions to reduce or eliminate the sure loss facing an aggrieved nation will reduce the chance that this nation will use coercion in a risky gamble to change a situation it finds unbearable.

Personal, Organizational, and Political Influences

In discussing some basic principles that underlie decisionmaking under risk, I have stressed the importance of the decisionmaker's frame of reference for judging outcomes, the value he places on various outcomes (both positive and negative), and the various expectancies he has of these outcomes occurring. These key elements of decisionmaking will in turn be affected by the personal characteristics of the decisionmaker and by the organizational and political milieu in which he functions.

The background and world view of particular leaders may affect, first, their frame of reference for judging various outcomes. Mussolini, the Italian dictator of the 1930s, sometimes judged the outcomes of his foreign policy against the backdrop of the "glorious" Roman Empire of a millennium and a half earlier. After World War II, British leader Winston Churchill judged the declining state of the British Empire against the reference point of 1900, when he first knew and fought for it. Some of his less imperialist-minded contemporaries, such as Labour party leader Clement Attlee, were more likely to judge Britain's current state in more absolute terms or perhaps relative to the near-catastrophe from which it had just escaped. For Americans the outcomes of the Korean and Vietnam wars —both "draws" at the time peace negotiations were concluded—were viewed very differently by those whose level of acceptable outcomes for the United States in any war was to win ("The United States has never lost a war" was the boast) compared to those who saw withdrawal without real humiliation as an acceptable, even desirable, outcome.

Individuals, including leaders, also may differ in the values they attach to particular gains and losses or to gains and losses in general. For example, persons with a high need for achievement tend to focus on possible successes while those with a strong fear of failure are particularly concerned with avoiding failure (Atkinson, 1964). Given a situation in which one must choose between accepting a sure loss and taking a substantial risk in order to avoid failure, one might expect that the decisionmaker who is motivated strongly by fear of failure would be more likely than others to take the very risky course.

Finally, individual characteristics may affect the weight the decisionmaker gives to various probabilities of an outcome occurring. While there appears to be a general tendency to give greater weight to outcomes that are certain (or near-certain), persons who are uncomfortable with uncertainty or ambiguity may be particularly apt to do so. At the other end of the continuum, where probabilities are very tiny, there appear to be contrasting tendencies for persons either to round off a very small probability to zero or to give it greater weight than is merited objectively (Kahneman and Tversky, 1979). Which of these tendencies applies in a particular case may also depend on the individual's personality. For example, the self-confident optimist may tend to overweight the long shot.

Organizational processes and political pressures also may affect basic elements of the decisionmaker's thinking. Groups and organizations within the government help to define the frame of reference within which outcomes are judged. One way they do this is by setting policy goals. For example, at the start of the Carter administration in the United States, the national security adviser, Brzezinski, in consultation with other officials, developed a set of ten major foreign policy goals, such as "to push United States–Soviet strategic arms *limitation* talks into strategic arms *reduction* talks" and "to normalize United States–Chinese relations." Brzezinski comments that subsequent outcomes were judged, at least in part, with respect to how well they reflected achievement of these goals (Brzezinski, 1983:53–57).

Public opinion and political pressures in a nation may also help to establish the frame of reference against which decisionmakers judge outcomes. Public opinion in Germany would make it difficult for any German chancellor to accept a permanently divided Germany; the unified Germany of an earlier time is a continuing reference point in this matter. Similarly, public opinion in Syria would make it difficult for a leader in that country to accept the loss of the Golan Heights and to use any reference point for judging outcomes other than the time when Syria controlled that area. In the United States some political groups dedicated to strengthening America's military strength tend to use as a point of reference the period 1945 to

1970, when the United States enjoyed strategic military supriority in the world. They have attempted to pressure U.S. policymakers to pursue policies that would result in military outcomes favorable to the United States by that standard.

Organizational processes and political forces may also be important in establishing the values decisionmakers attach to various outcomes. For example, how serious a loss it would be if El Salvador fell under the control of a Communist government would be judged by a president partly on the basis of the information presented to him by the Central Intelligence Agency, the State Department, and the National Security Council concerning the impact of such an event on U.S. interests. The seriousness of such an event probably would be judged also by perceptions of how much public outcry and political damage would follow such an event.

In the next chapter I will discuss at much greater length the specific factors that influence decisionmakers to choose one type of action over another (e.g., coercion over concession) during the course of a dispute. In particular, I will consider the factors that affect the value decisionmakers place on various outcomes—such as settlement of the dispute and war —and their expectancies about what actions will result in what outcomes.

Decisionmaking in Groups

Throughout this chapter, I have focused on the way in which individuals make decisions. The rationale for such a focus (discussed in chapter 1) is that most important foreign policy decisions are made primarily by the chief executive of a nation—a president, a prime minister, the general secretary of the Communist party of the Soviet Union, etc. There is empirical support for such an assumption. In their analysis of decisionmaking in international crises, Snyder and Diesing (1977:chapter 4) found that most decisions were made by one (or at most two) people. In nine instances decisions were made by the head of government alone (e.g., Hitler in the 1938 Munich crisis) or by the head together with one other person, usually a foreign minister (e.g., U.S. President Eisenhower with Secretary of State Dulles in the 1958 Quemoy crisis). In eleven instances, decisions were made by one person "within collegial limits" (e.g., British Foreign Minister Grey in the 1911 Agadir crisis acting within broad guidelines set by the British cabinet). In four instances (mainly U.S. cases) decisions were made by a central decisionmaker with advisers (e.g., President Kennedy meeting with an ad hoc executive committee in the 1962 Cuban missile crisis).

However, in some of the international crises studied by Snyder and

Diesing, decisions were made by groups. In ten instances decisions were made by a "committee"; for example, during much of the dispute between the United States and Japan in 1940–41, U.S. policy was decided by a group that included the secretary of state, the undersecretary of state, the secretary of war, the secretary of the navy, and the senior adviser on Far Eastern Affairs. (Of course, President Roosevelt had the ultimate authority for each executive action.) In three other historical instances, decisions were made by a government that was composed of divided factions (e.g., Japan in 1940).

When decisions were made by committees (or by a central decisionmaker with advisers), more options usually were considered than when only one or two persons were deciding. However, when decisions were made by a group, the group often was seriously divided. Snyder and Diesing (1977:377–78) comment: "a committee that is initially divided on strategy usually reaches decisions either by vacillation, postponement, an ambiguous, meaningless compromise that evaporates in practice, or one faction outmaneuvers the other and pushes its view through without serious discussion of alternatives." Other studies of decisionmaking in government bureaucracies indicate that the process of reaching agreement within a group may involve negotiations that rest more on the prestige and power of individuals and subgroups than on the power of their arguments (Halperin, 1974). Moreover, the final decision may be a compromise no one sees as an adequate solution to the problem. When decisions are made by compromising or combining divergent viewpoints, the description of individual decisionmaking needs to be supplemented by a description of how individual preferences are combined (e.g., of the power of each person or faction within the group).

Though decisionmaking groups sometimes have difficulty in reaching consensus, an opposite phenomenon sometimes occurs. In highly cohesive groups, especially those with directive leaders, there often is a tendency for members to refrain from questioning what they perceive to be a group consensus. There is a shared illusion of unanimity and pressures on members not to dissent. Members, who feel a strong sense of loyalty to the group, tend to believe in the higher morality of their own group and have negative stereotypes of outgroups. In such an atmosphere of high morale, group members tend to see their group as invulnerable and believe that its chosen actions will be successful. Therefore they fail to search fully for information, fail to examine other alternatives, and fail to examine or greatly underestimate the risks of the option selected.

This lack of critical judgment may lead to the selection of risky actions that turn out to be disastrous. Janis (1982) has labeled this type of group-decision process as "groupthink." He has described how groupthink may have contributed to some risky and highly unsuccessful foreign policy decisions by American officials. These include the decision by the Kennedy administration in 1961 to sponsor an invasion of Cuba by Cuban exiles at the Bay of Pigs; the decision by the Truman administration in 1950 to send American forces into North Korea (thus provoking Chinese intervention and prolongation of the Korean war); the decisions by American naval commanders in 1941 that led to the destruction of the U.S. fleet at Pearl Harbor; and decisions of the Johnson administration in the years 1964–1967 to escalate the war in Vietnam.

The way in which groupthink may operate is illustrated by the Bay of Pigs decision in 1961. The inner Kennedy circle was a bright, energetic, cohesive group characterized by buoyant optimism. According to presidential assistant Arthur Schlesinger, Jr., "Euphoria reigned; we thought for a moment that the world was plastic and the future unlimited" (Janis, 1982:35). They tended to dismiss the "enemy"—in this case, Cuba's Castro—with stereotyped images of weakness and stupidity. And while some members of the group had private doubts about the invasion plan, none voiced dissent and all shared in an illusion of unanimity. Schlesinger later observed that "our meetings took place in a curious atmosphere of assumed consensus" (Janis, 1982:38). Participants in the meetings felt reluctant to question a plan they thought was accepted by the whole group for fear of disapproval from the others. Presidential assistant Theodore Sorensen concluded that among the State Department men and White House staff "doubts were entertained but never pressed, partly out of a fear of being labelled 'soft' or undaring in the eyes of their colleagues" (Janis, 1982:39). The thinking of the group was dominated by wishful thinking and a downplaying of the limitations and dangers of the invasion plan.

From one perspective, groupthink is not so much inadequate group decisionmaking as the *absence* of group decisionmaking. It is, as noted, most likely to occur when there is a directive leader, such as a president, whose preference his advisers already know or think they know. Group members may simply be going along with what they see to be the official position. Janis has recommended that to help counter groupthink a leader should avoid stating his personal preferences among the options—at least early in the discussion. Other procedures to encourage diversity of opinion suggested by Janis include breaking down the group into subgroups to work separately on the same problem and then to reconcile their differences; hearing the opinion of outsiders, including those who disagree with the group; and making a "second chance" reevaluation of the rejected alternatives once a consensus has begun to emerge. During the Cuban missile crisis, President Kennedy used some of these techniques to encourage full consideration of U.S. options by the executive committee (Janis, 1982).

The decisionmaking that takes place when a powerful leader, such as a U.S. president, meets with his advisers or subordinates does not lie outside of our focus on individual decision processes. While a group may reach a consensus about the relative advantages and disadvantages of various alternatives, its evaluations (including the fact of consensus) are recommendations to the top decisionmaker. If the decision is important, he will not simply rubber-stamp the decision but will consider for himself the alternatives, the possible outcomes, his evaluation of these outcomes, and the chances that particular actions will lead to particular outcomes. In doing so he will take into account and perhaps be heavily influenced by the reasoning and recommendation of the group, but the final decision process will be his own. For example, while President Kennedy was undoubtedly influenced by the recommendation of the executive committee that the United States blockade Cuba and, failing that, strike directly at Soviet bases, eyewitness accounts make clear that he wrestled personally with the problem throughout the crisis (Kennedy, 1969; Schlesinger, 1965).

Summary

This chapter has considered how decisionmakers make choices—e.g., between the use of coercion and the use of more conciliatory actions in disputes. Some decisions are made by following preestablished rules—e.g., that a coercive act by an adversary must always be answered immediately by greater coercion. The more that national leaders have established rules that dictate the use of coercion under specified conditions, the more likely is coercion to be used by that nation in disputes. Some rules for automatically using force—e.g., in the event of signals of possible attack by an adversary —may be inappropriate in some circumstances and dangerous. Therefore, national leaders should try to avoid adopting policies or procedures that lead themselves, military commanders, or even computers to order the use of force without careful top-level consideration of the specific facts of the situation.

Most important foreign policy decisions are made by a central decisionmaker who considers the advantages and disadvantages of one or more options (often with the advice and consultation of subordinates). A common first phase in choice is the screening of options to eliminate those not meeting one or more of the minimum goals or constraints of the decisionmaker. The use of coercive means is less likely when the decisionmaker has made the avoidance of war a clear and high-priority constraint. Where avoidance of war is not given as high priority as some other objectives—e.g., gaining control of some territory—then the decisionmaker may be prepared to use coercion despite the risk of it leading to war.

It sometimes happens that decisionmakers focus on the goal of winning with respect to the issue that led to a dispute and give only secondary attention to the constraint of avoiding war. They may not face clearly—at least until very late in a crisis—the question of the relative priority of winning on the issue in dispute versus avoiding war or the amount of risk of war that is justifiable in the circumstances. Given the catastrophic nature of war today, national leaders should give early and central attention to the question of whether a policy increases the risk of war and whether such a risk is acceptable.

After unacceptable options have been screened out by a decisionmaker, he generally will consider the overall attractiveness of each alternative in terms of the value and the likelihood of the outcomes that may follow from it. The decisionmaker may be expected to choose the action he believes offers the most attractive combination of possible outcomes and likelihood of achieving those outcomes (as specified in equation 4-1). To make the choice of coercive actions less likely, it is helpful to try to reduce the importance to a decisionmaker of winning on the issues in dispute and to make war more repugnant. In addition, convincing him that coercion is less likely to succeed (e.g., that the adversary is not likely to submit to coercion) and more likely to lead to a costly war would reduce the attractiveness of coercion as an option. Since the choice among actions depends on their *relative* attractiveness, the use of coercion may also be discouraged by making alternatives more attractive. This may be done by making the possible outcomes of other actions—e.g., a compromise settlement —appear more attractive or making desirable outcomes of such actions seem more likely.

The choice among possible actions by national leaders often involves risks. Whether decisionmakers are willing to take the risk of a large loss may be affected by their frames of reference for judging outcomes. Decisionmakers tend to judge their outcomes not in terms of absolute value but in terms of how present outcomes compare to a previous status quo position or their levels of aspiration. When a decisionmaker has experienced a loss relative to a previous status quo and is unreconciled to this loss, he will tend to take a substantial risk of even greater losses in the hope of eliminating or improving his poor position. More generally, when a decisionmaker's current position is below his minimum level of aspiration, he will tend to take large risks in order to change his negative situation. Decisionmakers are more likely to take risks in order to avoid or eliminate a loss or negative situation than they are in order to try to make gains.

These principles derived from general research on decisionmaking appear to operate in many inter-nation cases. It seems important to avoid situations in which a national leader defines his choice in terms of either accepting a loss (or unacceptable situation) or taking a risk in order to avoid the loss. Sometimes it may be possible to modify the decisionmaker's frame of reference so that he judges outcomes more in terms of their absolute value than in terms of gain and losses. But when a nation has suffered serious losses or is in a poor position relative to reasonable aspirations, other nations would do well to try to improve the position of that nation so that its leaders are not tempted to take dangerous risks.

While important foreign policy decisions usually are made finally by a chief executive, sometimes they are made, at least provisionally, by a group of officials. Groups usually consider more foreign policy options than do one or two decisionmakers. Since it may be impossible for members of a group to reach consensus on a single option, their decisions may represent compromises between the options preferred by different individuals. On the other hand, in strongly cohesive decisionmaking groups, especially those headed by a directive leader, members tend to refrain from questioning a decision that represents an apparent consensus. Such reluctance by group members to voice dissent, coupled with tendencies to exaggerate the potency of the in-group and the weakness of out-groups, may lead to adopting highly risky decisions without sufficient deliberation. This breakdown in critical thinking appears to have occurred in a number of groups responsible for American policy decisions and led to catastrophic results.

This chapter has been concerned with the general process of decisionmaking, focusing expecially on how the values and expectancies of decisionmakers affect their choices. In the next chapter I examine the specific values and specific expectancies that lead to the choice of coercive and noncoercive actions in disputes and discuss how these values and expectancies are determined.

5 When Are Coercive Versus Conciliatory Tactics Used?

In the last chapter we examined some of the general processes underlying the choice by decisionmakers among alternative actions in a dispute. In this chapter we consider in greater depth and specificity the circumstances that promote the use of one type of action rather than another—e.g., coercion rather than concession. The circumstances to be examined include aspects of the situation (e.g., relative power or support from third nations); the overall relationships between the disputing nations (e.g., ties of positive interdependence between them); domestic pressures (e.g., political support for belligerent actions); and the perceptions that decisionmakers have of their adversary's goals and likely responses to their own actions. The aim here is to see what conclusions we can draw about the conditions that tend to produce belligerent as opposed to more conciliatory actions by national leaders engaged in a dispute.

The Options

At any given time the leaders or representatives of one side who are engaged in a dispute have a choice among the following options:

(1) Accept the other side's last demand (offer);
(2) Hold firm to one's own position and either
    (a) wait for the other to concede, or
    (b) use (additional) influence tactics to get the other side to concede (i.e., verbal persuasion, threat, coercion, or promise of reward outside the issue in dispute);
(3) Make a counteroffer (which may be combined with the use of influence tactics to get the other to accept).

Leaders of each side also may take steps to strengthen themselves in the event the dispute ends in a (wider) fight.[1] These steps can include such actions as mobilizing military forces, building additional arms, stockpiling strategic materials, strengthening defenses, and making alliances with other nations. Such actions are designed to affect the outcomes of a possible fight as well as the adversary's perceptions of such outcomes. They may be intended to permit one's own side to threaten the other, to defend against possible attack by the other, or for use in launching an attack if the other does not concede. By making such preparations for a fight, national leaders hope to make their adversaries more reluctant to risk a fight and therefore more willing to make concessions in the issues in dispute. However, building one's own strength for a fight is not a direct part of the bargaining that takes place during a dispute. I will concentrate therefore on the actions listed above—i.e., those that reflect each side's willingness to make concessions and its attempts to influence the other to do so. (The subject of arms buildups and their effects on the outbreak of war is discussed in chapter 7.)

The discussion will focus on three processes discussed in chapter 4: the use of rules for choice, the screening of acceptable options, and the choice among final options. For each of these processes, I will consider the conditions that tend to lead to coercive versus conciliatory actions.

Following Rules

In discussing the way in which choices are made by national decision-makers (see chapter 4), it was pointed out that choices are sometimes made by following rules rather than by a process of analysis and problem-solving. Some of the conditions—such as a limited time to act—under which action is likely to follow preestablished rules also were discussed.

When national decisionmakers follow standard rules in deciding an action, when are such rules likely to dictate that they should stand firm in their demands or that they should make concessions? When are the rules likely to call for the use (or threat of) coercion and when for more positive methods of influence (e.g., persuasion or promises of reward)?

First, as March (1982) has pointed out, rules that are currently used by decisionmakers may be based on their previous experiences. For example, in the two decades after World War II, it was an almost automatic rule of American foreign policy that the use of force by a Communist nation outside of its own bloc should be met by United States or other Western force. This rule derived from the lesson American leaders had drawn from the failure of the democracies to block Hitler's early aggressive actions. For example, following the principle that it was vital to show adversaries that aggression could not succeed, American leaders decided without great deliberation to use force to counter the invasion of South Korea and to defend Taiwan (Paige, 1968).

In more recent years (since about 1970), it has been a fairly clear rule of American foreign policy that U.S. troops should not be committed in a civil war of any Third World nation. This widely accepted rule clearly derives from America's experience in the Vietnam war. (Sometimes, most notably with respect to Nicaragua, the simultaneous use of both rules results in a policy of using force by proxy—e.g., backing the "Contras" in Nicaragua.)

Thus, when decisionmakers have experienced a series of events (or a single traumatic event) that show that the use of coercion is effective in achieving national aims (or that use of conciliatory actions is not effective), then they are likely to adopt (usually informally) a rule of using coercive means in similar circumstances. Conversely, when salient recent past experiences seem to show that conciliatory actions are effective, or that coercive actions are not effective, then an informal rule that one should use conciliatory actions (e.g., try for compromise agreements) in similar circumstances is likely to be adopted.

Decision rules may be based also on the decisionmaker's moral principles, ideology, or self-image (March, 1982). Some national leaders believe that it is necessary, right, and perhaps even a moral or religious duty to use coercive methods in order to win against adversaries. For example, Ayatollah Khomeini of Iran and his fellow Islamic fundamentalist leaders glorify the use of holy war against their perceived enemies. A few national leaders— e.g., former U.S. Secretary of State Cyrus Vance—see the use of force as wrong, even when provoked by another nation (as the United States was by Iran's holding of American hostages).

The self-images of some national leaders are consistent with (and may even require) that force be used in some circumstances. For example, the Israelis have long had a standard policy rule of responding to terrorist attacks with counter-violence (Blechman, 1972). While this policy undoubtedly is based in part on pragmatic considerations (i.e., the hope that it will discourage terrorism), it also reflects a deeply felt need among Jews following the Holocaust that never again will they be passive victims of violence.

The shared moral principles, ideology, and self-images of the citizens of a nation may create public norms that call for the automatic use (or non-use) of force in given circumstances. Thus, after the Japanese attacked Pearl Harbor in 1941 and after Germany invaded Poland in 1939, the decisions for war were almost automatic (Feis, 1950; Middlemas, 1972).

The strong expectation of a vast majority of Americans was that the United States should fight if attacked (whatever the net benefits of conceding to Japan control of the Western Pacific), and the strong expectation of most Britons was that Great Britain should stand by its pledge to aid an ally under attack.

Finally, the rules that decisionmakers sometimes follow are affected by the types of incentives consistently present in the situation they face. For example, if faced with a firm demand by the Soviet Union, Polish leaders are likely to assume without serious deliberation that they must concede rather than resist. Because of the much greater power of the Soviet Union, the presence of its military forces on Polish soil, and the demonstrated willingness of the Soviets to use force against Eastern European regimes, Polish leaders see little incentive to resist a demand the Soviets deem important. Having once considered the relative advantages of resisting and conceding Soviet demands, they can concede in a fairly automatic way on most occasions. (Of course, changes in the situation—such as pressures from Western nations that might make the Soviets more reluctant to use force—may lead Polish leaders to reexamine their options.)

Sometimes the situation is such that the side that uses force first in a dispute enjoys an advantage. Such incentives, combined with a lack of time to make decisions, tend to lead to rules stipulating that force should be used under specified circumstances. In the days prior to World War I, for instance, the government of Germany followed the established rule that if Russia mobilized, Germany must mobilize too and carry out its war plan. To delay, German leaders believed, would risk a Russian attack and military disaster (Stoessinger, 1982).

With the missile technology of today, national leaders have an incentive to launch their missiles against an adversary if they think they are likely to be (or are being) attacked. Otherwise, their missiles may be destroyed before they can be used. Leaders of both the United States and the Soviet Union, as well as those of other countries, have detailed plans for automatic retaliation should they be attacked. More dangerously, with accurate missiles being deployed closer to the borders of each nation and the time to make retaliation decisions reduced to just a few minutes, each of the superpowers seems on the verge of adopting "launch on warning" rules (Steinbruner, 1984). Such rules would make the launching of nuclear missiles automatic (by military personnel or even by a computer) when warning of an enemy attack is received. Should the warning turn out to be an error, it might be too late to recall the missiles.

In summary, when decisionmakers follow formal or informal rules about appropriate actions in disputes, such rules are likely to favor coercive actions when most or all of the following conditions exist:

(1) Recent salient experiences have indicated that coercive actions are effective.
(2) Their moral principles, ideology, or self-images favor use of coercive methods.
(3) Norms of their society favor use of coercion.
(4) A stable situation provides incentives for use of coercion or for first use when a fight seems likely to occur.

Rules are likely to call, instead, for conciliatory actions when most of the relevant circumstances (past experiences, morality, social norms, and incentives) are supportive of conciliation.

Narrowing the Options

Most important decisions by each of the parties to a dispute are not made simply by following preestablished rules of behavior. Usually decisionmakers will make a choice among several options, considering positive and negative consequences of each possible action. However, research on decisionmaking indicates that before a decisionmaker deliberates seriously among options, he often narrows the range of alternatives. He does this by dropping as clearly unacceptable any options that do not meet his minimum goals (see chapter 4).

Sometimes the process of preliminary testing of options against minimum goals leads to a quick rejection of acts of force. This would be the case if decisionmakers judged it essential to avoid war with a certain rival nation and believed that use of force in a given situation had a chance of leading to war which was beyond the minimum chance they were willing to accept. For example, in the Berlin crisis of 1948 (Davison, 1958) the United States eliminated the option of trying to break through the land blockade because such an action was seen as having an unacceptably high risk of leading to war with the Soviet Union.

In addition to the goal or constraint of avoiding war, the option of using force may be screened out early in the decision process because it is seen as failing to meet other minimal goals. For example, when Iranians seized a group of Americans as hostages in 1978, U.S. leaders dropped the use of force against Iran from the options considered initially because such action was seen as incompatible with the important goal of preserving the hostages' lives (Brzezinski, 1983).

Sometimes screening out options that do not meet basic goals may lead to discarding not acts of force or other coercion but rather to discarding alternatives to coercion. This is sometimes the case when decisionmakers deem it of great importance that they win with respect to certain outcomes at issue in the dispute. In such cases any option that does not promise a high probability of gaining this objective is likely to be quickly dropped from consideration. In the Cuban missile crisis the alternative of trying to resolve the dispute by bringing it before the United Nations was quickly rejected on the ground that such action would stand little chance of getting the Soviets to withdraw their missiles from Cuba. Such a withdrawal was seen as essential by Kennedy and most of his advisers (Abel, 1966).

A similar example was the dismissal by Israel in 1967 of the option of relying on diplomatic efforts to reopen the Straits of Tiran and to restrain Egyptian President Nasser in his other belligerent actions against Israel. After giving this option a trial, the Israelis concluded that diplomacy offered little chance of achieving their essential goals of removing Egyptian threats to their security. Thus the diplomatic option was dropped from further serious consideration (Brecher, 1980).

Whether or not force is considered seriously as an option may depend on the priority that is given to the goal of avoiding war as compared to the priority put on the goal of winning some objectives at issue in the dispute. In the Cuban missile crisis priority was given to the goal of gaining removal of the Soviet missiles and so the constraint of avoiding war was relaxed and force was not ruled out as unacceptable. If the goal of avoiding war had been given highest priority, then only actions that were (almost) sure to avoid war would have been considered, even though such actions were not sure to result in removal of the missiles. In general, the choice of coercive actions by national decisionmakers is more likely when the constraint of avoiding a fight is given lesser priority than other goals.

We considered in chapter 4 some of the conditions that may affect the relative priority decisionmakers place on winning with respect to the issues in dispute versus avoiding war. The more the attention of the decisionmakers is focused on the disputed issues (rather than on avoiding war), the more the beliefs and ideology of the decisionmakers emphasize values (e.g., gaining political advantage, preserving a reputation for resolve) that may be at stake in the dispute rather than other values (e.g., increasing cooperation, preserving life), and the greater the political pressures to win the dispute, the more likely are national leaders to place greater priority on winning on the disputed issues than on avoiding a showdown that may lead to war.

Even when decisionmakers believe that avoiding war is more important than gaining a certain advantage in a dispute, they may nevertheless be willing to run the risk of war. As pointed out in chapter 4, this may occur especially when decisionmakers are faced with a sure loss (or continuation of a negative situation) if they do nothing. Historical evidence suggests that national leaders—even though recognizing the importance of avoiding war—may be willing to run a substantial risk of war (so long as that risk is judged as not too high) in order to avoid a threatened loss or to escape an undesirable situation. The actions of American presidents in ordering the blockade of Cuba in 1962 and an alert for the U.S. missile force in 1973 are examples.

Selecting Among Possible Options

After decisionmakers have screened out any options that do not meet their minimum objectives, usually more than one option will remain. These may include standing firm and waiting for the other side to concede, making concessions oneself, making threats, using coercion, making promises, attempting persuasion, or some combination of these actions. How is the choice among final alternatives made?

Research on decisionmaking indicates that at this point in the decision process individuals will assess the overall attraction of each option. This assessment involves some comparison of the relative advantages and disadvantages of each option and of the likelihood that such positive or negative outcomes will result from different actions (see chapter 4). To understand decisionmakers' choices among different ways of acting in a dispute, we need to know how much they value various outcomes of the dispute[2] and their expectations that particular actions will lead to particular outcomes. The possible outcomes most likely to be of concern to decisionmakers are: (1) reaching agreement and the particular kinds of agreement reached (e.g., one favorable to one's own side, one favorable to the adversary); (2) continuation of a stalemate in the dispute; and (3) a (wider) fight with the adversary. The attraction of a particular action for decisionmakers will depend on how positively or negatively they feel about each of these possible outcomes and on their expectancies that this action will lead to one or more of the outcomes. In addition, each type of action is likely to have some intrinsic advantages or disadvantages (e.g., how costly the action is) that affects its overall attraction.

More formally, we would expect that the overall attraction of a particular type of action would be determined as follows:

(5-1)   attraction of a = intrinsic value of that action
        given action   + (value of agreement   × expectancy that action
                          per se   will lead to agreement*)

                        + (value of specific terms × expectancy that action
                          of agreement (winning,   will lead to these
                          losing, compromise)   terms*)
                          discounted by time to
                          agreement †

                        + (value of status quo of × expected length of
                          nonagreement   time nonagreement
                                                     will continue following
                                                     this action*)

                        + (value of (wider) fight × expectancy that action
                          with the other   will lead to fight*)

To understand decisionmakers' choices among actions, we need to know what these values and expectancies are and how they are shaped. Let us consider each of the values and expectancies included in equation 5-1.

Intrinsic Value of Actions

The attraction of an action for a decisionmaker may be affected by its intrinsic costs and benefits. These are outcomes that are likely to occur regardless of how the action affects the behavior of the adversary or the outcome of the dispute. These intrinsic costs and benefits include: (a) tangible costs, such as the financial expense of the act; (b) the emotional satisfactions that decisionmakers get from taking particular actions; (c) the effect on their nation's (and their personal) prestige and reputation; and, (d) the support or opposition of domestic groups or other nations.

Tangible costs of action. Any action has some cost—in time, effort, money, or other resources. For example, the U.S. decision to place ground troops in South Vietnam and to conduct an air war against North Vietnam meant a large expenditure of money. Inevitably it meant also some American casualties. Coercive actions that do not involve the use of force usually also have costs. For example, the American decision to stop the export of grain

---

*Strictly speaking, it is not the expectancy per se but a weight based on this expectancy that enters into the equation (see Kahneman and Tversky, 1979).
†The value of an agreement may be lower (or higher) as it is more delayed.

to the Soviet Union in 1980 (following the Soviet attack on Afghanistan) meant a direct loss in profits to American farmers and traders.

Making concessions to the other side—or rewarding the other in some other way for a desirable action—also involves direct costs. For example, to help improve relations with China, the United States has given China certain trade advantages in textiles that may be harmful to U.S. domestic producers.

The cost of an action will depend on the magnitude of the resources that will have to be used and how much such resources are valued—based on the actor's needs and the scarcity of the resources. In the case of the U.S. decisions to use force against Grenada and Libya, the resources to be expended were relatively small and could be well afforded by the United States. A larger military action—say, an invasion of Nicaragua by American forces—would involve much greater resources of scarce men and materials.

Similarly, the cost of a reward given or promised to another nation will depend in part on the size of the rewards, e.g., the amount of a loan. The cost of the rewards given will also depend on the resources a nation possesses (Kriesberg, 1982). For example, the United States (especially before the time of large budget deficits) has had the financial resources to promise economic and military aid to countries like Egypt and the Philippines in exchange for political and military cooperation. Other nations—e.g., Great Britain and China—have fewer resources available for such purposes. Other things equal, the more intrinsic costs an action entails, the less likely it is to be used. One of the reasons why threats tend to be used more often than promises to influence an adversary is that threats, if successful, involve few costs while promises, if successful, are costly to fulfill (Baldwin, 1971a, 1971b).

Emotional satisfactions. When the decisionmaker considers his options, the prospect of taking certain actions may be emotionally appealing while other actions may be emotionally repugnant. Actions have moral significance for decisionmakers. They are seen as right or wrong, appropriate or inappropriate, courageous or cowardly. Such judgments stem from the norms that decisionmakers accept, from their ideologies, and from their self-images.

Taking action that harms an adversary may be viewed as a fair and appropriate retaliation against some action of the other. There is a widespread norm of reciprocity that requires we return "harm for harm" as well as "good for good" (Tedeschi and Bonoma, 1977) and people often feel satisfaction at having "evened the score." National leaders often justify acts of coercion as retaliation for the alleged acts of their adversary. Undoubtedly, such statements often are partly rationalization of actions taken for other reasons, but the sense of appropriate reciprocity often may play a genuine part in prompting the action.

In some cases, decisionmakers have accepted an ideology that excuses or even glorifies the use of force. The Nazis in Germany glorified "blood and iron," while some Moslem leaders from the time of the Prophet to Ayatollah Khomeini of Iran have extolled "holy wars." On the other hand, the ideology or self-images of other national leaders have been opposed to the use of coercion and especially of violence. Gandhi in India was opposed in principle to the use of violence. Other national leaders, such as Prime Minister Neville Chamberlain of Great Britain—while not as categorical as Gandhi in rejecting force—have thought of themselves as men of peace to whom the use of violence is abhorrent.

Using (or supporting the use of) coercion is sometimes valued as showing toughness or even masculinity. In the discussions among U.S. officials about the Bay of Pigs invasion of Cuba in 1961, participants apparently were anxious to appear sufficiently tough (Schlesinger, 1965). Using force or other coercive action also may help to support a leader's own self-image as tough and decisive. Richard Nixon's descriptions of his own foreign policy decisions (e.g., ordering the Cambodian invasion) and the Christmas bombing of North Vietnam (Nixon, 1978) suggests that forceful action was satisfying to Nixon's self-image.

Feelings of anger toward (or of liking for) the other party also will make certain actions seem more satisfying. If decisionmakers are angry at an adversary—because they believe they have been harmed, deceived, betrayed, insulted, or humiliated—they are likely to anticipate satisfaction at the prospect of inflicting injury (Tedeschi and Bonoma, 1977). Writing of the mood in Austria-Hungary, Germany, and Russia just prior to World War I, White (1984:200–201) writes: "There are many indicators that both the leaders and the general public were aroused and angry as well as fearful during the crisis of 1914 . . . both were carried along on a wave of anger . . . the Kaiser, whose rage at Edward VII is well known, was perhaps the angriest of the national leaders, to judge by his many exclamations ('Liars!' 'Slippery eels!') on the margins of telegrams, but most of the German public and nearly all the German press seemed to be with him in his desire to 'punish Serbia.'" If, on the other hand, a decisionmaker feels goodwill toward the other—e.g. because the other has been helpful in the past—then coercive actions in a present dispute are apt to have less emotional appeal and conciliatory actions to have more appeal.

The quality of feeling toward the other party is likely to reflect the past history of relations between the two sides and the extent to which the other side's recent actions are seen as provocative or in violation of norms of proper conduct. For example, the anger Kennedy and his advisers felt toward the Soviet Union at the time of the Cuban missile crisis was based in part on recent Soviet challenges to the United States (notably over Berlin) and especially on their perception that the Soviets had lied in denying the placement of offensive weapons in Cuba.

Feelings of hostility toward an adversary may be affected by the availability and use of communication channels between the parties (see chapter 2). As a dispute intensifies, adversaries often communicate less (or not at all) with each other directly. When communication is cut off, the opportunity to understand and perhaps even sympathize with an adversary's concerns are greatly reduced. The opponent may seem more and more evil and even inhuman. Therefore, inhibitions about injury to the adversary may decline and the value of punishing him for perceived transgressions may increase.

In summary, decisionmakers are likely to anticipate emotional satisfaction from using harsh, coercive methods when (a) their norms, ideology, and self-images support the use of such actions as appropriate in disputes; and, (b) poor overall relations and poor communications with the adversary, as well as actions by the adversary that violate the decisionmaker's norms, lead to feelings of anger. When these conditions are different, more conciliatory methods will seem more emotionally appealing.

Effects on others' attitudes. Taking particular actions often is seen by decisionmakers as likely to affect the way in which the leaders of other nations perceive them and the attitudes of such leaders toward them. In particular, they may believe that by such actions as refusing concessions, making concessions, making threats, making promises, or using coercion, they will affect their prestige, their reputation for resolve, the attitudes of other national leaders toward themselves, and even the unity of those in other nations.

Giving rewards or making concessions may be seen as likely to produce positive attitudes toward the giver—especially if the rewards are seen as freely given. American leaders considering giving economic assistance to a developing nation may believe (or at least hope) that such actions will make the people and leaders of that nation more friendly toward the United States. However, in many cases, leaders may be concerned that offering rewards or concessions will lead the other nation to see them as weak and lacking resolve. The more that the current dispute is viewed as a test of strength and resolve in a more general and ongoing competition, the more the decisionmakers will wish to project an image of firmness. In their study of the decisions of national leaders in many international crises, Snyder

and Diesing (1977) found such long-term considerations of national prestige and image for resolve often to be important. The National leaders sometimes will refrain from making a concession they might otherwise make in
a dispute for fear it would endanger too much their overall reputation for
firmness. This concern is likely to be especially great when they have
recently made some unreciprocated concessions. One reason that Russia
refused to make concessions in her dispute with Austria in 1914 was that,
having made important concessions in some other recent disputes, Russian
leaders were anxious to repair the damage to their image (Lebow, 1981).
American leaders (President Ford and Secretary of State Kissinger) welcomed the opportunity to use force to rescue an American ship seized off
Cambodia in 1975 in order to show that, even though the United States
had withdrawn from Vietnam, it was still prepared to use force to defend
its interests (*New York Times*, May 15, 1975).

Coercive acts also may serve to affect the expectations of others when
they are used as a symbolic affirmation of one's rights and policies. For
example, the imposition of an economic boycott against Cuba in 1960
appears to have been motivated in part by a desire of American policymakers to affirm their policy in this hemisphere. Discussing the reasons behind
this action, Ann Schreiber (1973:405) says:

> The policy was a punitive reprisal against actions interpreted as being
> contrary to U.S. interests. In addition, economic coercion was applied
> and maintained as a symbolic affirmation of the U.S. belief in its right
> to maintain a pre-eminent influence in Latin America. It was a decla-
> ration of U.S. opposition to the spread of revolution and communist
> influence in an area deemed to be within its "sphere of influence." For
> more than a decade, successive U.S. administrations have felt that
> such a symbolic statement needed to be made in a forceful, concrete
> fashion.

Such symbolic acts were intended to influence the expectations not only of
Cuban leaders but also those in other Latin American nations.

While decisionmakers usually will perceive that their use of coercion
will have desirable effects on the expectations of others, there are times
when such effects may be seen as undesirable. Policymakers may not wish
to make the leaders of an adversary so fearful of one's own side as "trigger-
happy" that the adversary will strike first. Also, national leaders may not
wish to raise the expectations of allies that one is apt to use coercion too
quickly in a dispute. Allies may not wish to become embroiled in a fight
and may, therefore, try to weaken the ties of alliance. For example, the use
of force by the United States in Grenada and Nicaragua in 1983–84 raised

fears within some European allies that the United States might be too ready to use military force.

A nation making concessions usually will try to avoid having these seen as signs of lack of resolve. For this reason it often will combine concessions with threats of coercive action if cooperation is not forthcoming (Snyder and Diesing, 1977). Also, the specific concessions may be designed to create a perception of firmness in one's new position. For example, a concession by one side in an arms negotiation that calls for equality in weapons to the two sides might be intended to indicate new firmness because this position reflects a prominent and widely accepted principle (i.e., equality).

In addition to the effects that rewards may have on the attitudes and perceptions of an adversary, they may also have effects on its unity. The leaders of one side in a dispute may believe that by offering concessions they can divide the other side. For example, Kriesberg (1981) suggests that in negotiating about an Austrian peace treaty, Soviet leaders regarded their adversary as a coalition and believed that by offering rewards they could divide these nations. Such a hope will be more likely of course when there is evidence of the existence of factions within the other side, one or more of which favors accommodation.

Political costs and benefits. Any decision to take action in a dispute is likely to be made with some anticipation of the political costs or benefits it will bring. One very important political consequence is that of increased support or opposition at home. In many cases the national mood is such that leaders can anticipate that use of coercion against an adversary will be applauded. It may even be demanded by important segments of the population. In the Cuban missile crisis, U.S. President Kennedy perceived that he would face a complete collapse of support in Congress and of the public if he did not act forcefully to get the Soviet missiles in Cuba withdrawn; he even predicted his own impeachment in the circumstance (Abel, 1966). During the Iranian hostage crisis, President Carter perceived that using force in some way against Iran would raise his sagging popularity with the American public (Brzezinski, 1983).

National leaders may hesitate to make too many (or any) concessions for fear that they will be labeled soft or appeasers. For example, several French governments in the 1950s were reluctant to make extensive concessions to the Algerian independence movement for fear of political attack from French conservatives and even from the French army (Pickles, 1963).

As a conflict between two sides intensifies, specialists in coercion—e.g., military men—may come to the forefront and assert more influence. Moreover, competition between leaders may arise to show who is the toughest and most militant in his actions toward the adversary (Kriesberg, 1982). Advocacy of more and bigger coercion may then be valued by leaders in part as a way of maintaining or strengthening their political position. If a leader is not seen as militant enough to carry on an intensifying struggle, he may be replaced by someone more militant. Thus, soon after Britain was at war with Germany in 1939, the mild Chamberlain was replaced by the pugnacious Churchill.

While militancy against an adversary often brings political advantage, sometimes national decisionmakers can reasonably anticipate a negative public reaction against the use of coercive actions. President Nixon, believing that the American people were in a mood for conciliation in 1970, rejected recommendations for confrontational moves in the Middle East and instead made conciliatory overtures to the Soviet Union (Hersh, 1983). The public mood in the United States during the 1970s against the use of military force in Third World countries created important costs that later presidents (Ford and Carter) had to face when considering the use of force. These political costs probably help to account for the very mild American reactions to the assertive Soviet-Cuban moves into Angola, Ethiopia, and Somalia in the post-Vietnam years.

Political costs or advantages stemming from the use of coercion may also derive from the action of other nations. If other countries strongly oppose the use of coercion, then national leaders considering the use of coercion can anticipate being labeled as aggressors. Such anticipations raise the costs of using coercion and tend to discourage its use (Tedeschi and Bonoma, 1977). Quincey Wright (1965) has asserted that strong world opinion against use of military force is one of the factors that prevents inter-nation disputes from escalating to wars. On the other hand, support by other nations for initiating or continuing use of coercion raises the value of being engaged in a fight. For example, widespread early support for American armed intervention in Korea by members of the United Nations raised the prestige of the United States and gave confirmation to American leaders' self-images as defenders against aggression. The sending of Cuban troops to Angola was dictated in large part by the Cubans' desire to retain the support (especially financial) of the Soviet Union.

National leaders also may offer concessions or make promises to an adversary in order to appear reasonable in the eyes of the leaders of other governments. Kriesberg (1981) has described the role of third parties in directly or indirectly encouraging concession in disputes. Apparently one of the motives of the Soviet Union in agreeing to withdraw its troops from Austria was to convince other small, pro-Western nations that it was possible for them to be neutral. A central role was played by a third party (the

United States) in encouraging concessions by both Israel and Egypt in their peace negotiations of 1978 (Kriesberg, 1981). In their study of positive versus negative inducements in inter-nation disputes, Leng and Wheeler (1979) also found that in a number of cases third parties played a major role in encouraging the use of positive inducements that led to de-escalation of a dispute.

The importance of the actions of allies is illustrated by several historical cases of war escalation described by Smoke (1977). During the Spanish Civil War of the late 1930s the French government was sympathetic to the democratic forces (the Loyalists) in Spain and was tempted to intervene on their side. However, the British pressured France to hold back.

> The French role in Spain would almost certainly have been significantly greater than in fact it was, had it not been for Great Britain. The military alliance with Britain was the bedrock of security-conscious France's foreign policy in this period, and when on August 8th (1938) Sir George Clark, the English ambassador in Paris, informed the French cabinet that if French involvement in Spain led her into a general war, Britain would abrogate the alliance, French policy at once became extremely cautious. (Smoke, 1977:67)

A contrary example, in which allies pressured each other to launch a war, is that of the Crimean War (1854–1856). In their dispute with Russia, the leaders of Britain and France encouraged each other to join in an attack on Russia. "In part, the English decision was aimed at demonstrating to the French that Great Britain could be a strong and reliable ally—ironically, since Napoleon III for once was not advocating more forceful action. . . . A few months later, it would be Napoleon who would threaten to break up the alliance unless London went along with his insistence that their joint fleet sail into the Black Sea" (Smoke, 1977:177).

The overall political costs and benefits of using coercive methods may be expected to depend on: (a) how widespread support for or opposition to the use of coercive methods is; (b) the intensity of support or opposition; and, (c) the political importance to decisionmakers of those who support and of those who oppose.

Value of Agreement Per Se

The more decisionmakers value an agreement to settle a dispute and the more they wish to avoid lack of a settlement, the more likely they are to use conciliatory methods. On the basis of their analysis of eighteen inter-nation crises, Snyder and Diesing (1977) assert that accommodative tactics are likely to be used in a crisis situation when the decisionmakers' main goal is to settle the dispute peacefully rather than to win with respect to the issues in dispute. In their study of relations between the United States and the Soviet Union from 1946 to 1963, Gamson and Modigliani (1971) found that whether the actions of each side were conciliatory or refractory (i.e., belligerent) depended in part on that side's goals—e.g., whether it wanted to exploit or to have better relations with the other side. In particular, Gamson and Modigliani found that each nation's own goals were critical to how it responded to accommodative behavior by the other.

There are of course a variety of reasons why a nation may give great importance to reaching agreement with an adversary. It may recognize common interests with the other that, in Kreisberg's (1981) words, "justify a step away from coercion." For example, in the 1970s both Chinese and American leaders saw a common interest in combating Soviet influence in the Far East. Both were anxious to settle (or at least to defuse) their dispute over the status of Taiwan in order to improve the general relations between their two countries. Similarly, both Japan and the United States are anxious to settle trade disputes because they recognize their strong common interests in a continuing high level of trade between them. On the other hand, the fundamentalist religious leaders of postrevolutionary Iran did not want quick agreement with the United States concerning the release of American hostages. They saw continuation of the dispute as a tool to aid them in consolidating power (Ramazani, 1982).

National leaders also may see settlement of a conflict as necessary in order to pursue more effectively another conflict which has assumed higher priority (Kriesberg, 1981). For example, Arab nations such as Jordan and Syria have sometimes attempted to settle disputes among themselves in order to pursue their conflict with Israel more effectively. In addition, national leaders may wish to settle a dispute in order to use their resources to tackle domestic problems. For instance, an important reason for Egyptian President Sadat's effort to make peace with Israel was his desire to use Egypt's resources to try to raise the low living standards of its people.

Settlement of a dispute also will be seen by national leaders as more desirable when they believe that the chances for a desirable settlement (or of any settlement) will decrease over time. For example, Jordan's King Hussein said in 1985 that the last chance for a peaceful resolution of the Arab dispute with Israel over the status of the West Bank was at hand. As time goes by and Israeli settlement of the area increases, the possibility of any negotiated agreement on the subject may disappear.

A similar sense of a limited opportunity for settlement made American leaders in 1970 anxious to settle the dispute with Panama over control of the Panama Canal. They believed that anti-American feeling among Panamanians over the issue would increase and that chances for a peaceful agreement might decline. Where decisionmakers believe that reaching an agreement quickly is important they are likely to make concessions (as the United States did in surrendering sovereignty over the canal) in order to achieve this result.

In some cases, however, lack of an agreement will not be too disturbing to national leaders. For example, Syrian leaders in 1986 did not seem concerned about settling their long dispute with Israel, believing perhaps that "time is on our side" and that their chances of winning will be better at a later date.

In sum, agreement is most likely to be valued when decisionmakers: see important common interests with the adversary and wish to improve their general relations; wish to free their resources devoted to this conflict for other purposes, such as pursuing another conflict or achieving domestic goals; and believe chances for a desirable settlement will decrease over time.

Value of Winning, Losing, and Compromise

Whether a decisionmaker chooses to stand firm in his demands, to take actions that risk war in order to win his demands, or to make concessions to the other's position depends also on the value he places on getting his own way in the dispute. The value of a particular outcome of the dispute is affected by: the decisionmaker's frame of reference for judging outcomes; relevant norms; the decisionmaker's commitments or motivation regarding the issues at stake; and other benefits (costs) of a given outcome.

Frame of reference. The outcomes specified by a particular offer usually are not judged primarily in terms of their absolute advantages and disadvantages. Rather, they are likely to be judged in terms of the decisionmaker's particular frame of reference (see chapter 4). Often outcomes are judged in terms of gains or losses from the status quo as of a given time. Thus, the nations of the world judged the outcomes of the Versailles conference following World War I in terms of losses or gains relative to their prewar positions. An outcome that is seen as a loss relative to some relevant starting point is likely to have a very negative value regardless of the actual benefits or costs inherent in that outcome (Kahneman and Tversky, 1979).

Outcomes involved in any agreement may also be judged in terms of whether (and how much) they reach, fall short of, or exceed the decisionmaker's level of expectation or aspiration. This level may be thought of as a goal, thought to be attainable, against which outcomes are measured. For example, Japanese leaders in 1940–1941 judged any potential agreements with the United States at least partly against their goal of Japanese domination over Southeast Asia (Feis, 1950). At the start of a dispute a decisionmaker may or may not have in mind a firm goal he wants to achieve. If not, he may develop such a goal as the bargaining progresses.

In addition to a goal, a decisionmaker may have a lower limit of what he is willing to accept. This is the minimum below which he would prefer no agreement at all. For example, the British have said that they will accept no agreement with Argentina concerning the Falkland (Malvinas) Islands that does not give them sovereignty over this territory. (Such a public statement may or may not express a true limit.) As in the case of a goal, the decisionmaker may or may not have a firm limit in mind as he begins bargaining in a dispute. If he does have a limit but does not obtain his objectives soon, he may lower his limit as time goes on.

There is evidence from experimental studies that negotiators who have higher levels of aspirations will make higher demands and smaller concessions. The same is true for limits. The higher the bargainer's (lower) limit, the higher his demands and the smaller his concessions (Pruitt, 1981: 25–28).

A bargainer's level of aspiration is a function of what seems attainable in the situation. The greater he sees his own power to be relative to his opponent and the better the outcomes he has experienced in the past, the higher his present goals are likely to be (Pruitt, 1981:chapter 1).

A bargainer's lower limit is a function of the outcomes available to him if an agreement is not reached. The better the alternatives open to him (e.g., agreements with other parties), the higher his lower limit is likely to be. Similarly, the less the anticipated costs if negotiations break down (such as punishment from the other or deterioration of the relationship) the higher his limit is likely to be (Pruitt, 1981:chapter 1).

Norms. The possible outcomes of a dispute are likely to be judged also in terms of what is seen as fair and legitimate. As Gulliver (1979) has pointed out, the usual framework of a dispute is normative. At least one party, and possibly both, claim that its rights have been denied. Bartos (1978) maintains that each of the parties to a negotiation has two motives: to maximize its own utility and to reach a fair solution.

What is fair is defined to a considerable extent by norms—rules of behavior that are widely accepted. In relations between nations these norms may be stated in formal documents, such as those regulating each nation's control of the waters off its coasts. Norms may also be informal, arising from custom and precedent. Thus, for example, norms regarding legitimate spheres of interest exercised by great powers—such as that of the

Soviet Union in Eastern Europe and the United States in the Western Hemisphere—have been widely accepted by national leaders and publics.

Norms affect the value put on particular outcomes of a dispute for several reasons. First, by affecting decisionmakers' perceptions of what is legitimate, they affect the desirability to them of particular outcomes. Secondly, norms affect the extent to which making or accepting particular demands will win approval or disapproval by others, both at home and in other nations.

Existing norms, and the perceptions by the parties of legitimacy, are likely to affect their bargaining behaviors. Gulliver (1979:chapter 1) states that an appeal to norms by one or both sides is one of the causes of a convergence of bargainers' positions. In their study of crises between nations, Snyder and Diesing found that "perceptions of legitimacy are potent in determining bargaining power and outcomes. That is, the party that believes it is in the right and communicates this belief to an opponent who has some doubts about the legitimacy of his own position, nearly always wins . . . of course, the parties often differ about the justice of change or different kinds of change; what matters is the intensity of the beliefs" (Snyder and Diesing, 1977:498–499). Snyder and Diesing note, for example, that the outcome of the first Morocco crisis of 1905–1906 favored France over Germany despite the superior military strength of Germany ". . . because the legitimacy factor favored the French on the substantive issues" (Snyder and Diesing, 1977:499). The side that feels more intensely that its claims are legitimate values more highly the outcomes it seeks and is therefore less likely to accept the other side's demands and less likely to make substantial concessions. Moreover, the other side, sensing the determination of its "virtuous" opponent, will expect few concessions and thus is more likely to concede itself.

Importance of issues. The value to decisionmakers of particular outcomes of a dispute depends also on the importance they put on the issues in contention. For example, during the Cuban missile crisis American decisionmakers believed that it was of very great importance—for America's military-political position in the world and for the administration's own political position at home—that the Soviet missiles be removed from Cuba. In the dispute between Portugal and India over Goa (a Portugese colony on the Indian subcontinent), possession of Goa was not seen by Portugese leaders to be of vital importance.

Snyder and Diesing (1977:183–184) have divided the interests that nations have in a dispute into three categories: (1) strategic interests, derived from the material power content of the object in dispute; (2) reputational interests that concern the effects of the outcomes on others' images of one's resolve, trustworthiness, etc.; and, (3) intrinsic interests that are outcomes for their own sake, such as self-respect, prestige, or economic values. Bacharach and Lawler (1981:chapter 7) found in experimental studies that the greater the commitment of bargainers with respect to the issues at stake the smaller the concessions they made. Similarly, Druckman (1978) found that concessions depend in part on the importance of the topics under negotiation.

Coercion is most likely to be used in a dispute when both sides place great value on winning (or not losing) and when neither sees a compromise as very attractive. Under such circumstances, a stalemate or a fight may seem relatively attractive to one or both sides. Reviewing relevant social-psychological research, Tedeschi and Bonoma (1977:215) comment that "coercion is usually not a preferred mode of influence because of the obvious dangers of escalation. It is introduced only when it appears that something of great value will be lost by failure to gain agreement." Analysts of international relations have made a similar point, stating that when national leaders have strong motivation to get their way in a dispute they are more likely to use force (George, Hall, and Simons, 1971; Kaplan, 1981). The American readiness to use force in Cuba, even at the risk of a nuclear war, is a vivid example. Another example is the readiness of the Soviet Union to use force against rebellious East European satellites. Soviet leaders have seen the maintenance of their dominance over the Socialist bloc in Europe as a vital interest.

A refusal by both sides to a dispute to give in or even to compromise very much is most likely to occur when the goals of the two sides are incompatible, interdependent, and vital to each side (Tedeschi and Bonoma, 1977:229). In other words, each side has important goals, the fulfillment of which depends on the actions of the other as well as of itself, but both cannot reach their goals at the same time. Some inter-nation situations fit the pattern in which the goals of adversaries are vital, interdependent, and incompatible. For example, for both Israel and the PLO legitimate control over the same land is a vital goal, but the fulfillment of that goal for each side depends (at least in part) on the actions of both sides, and fulfillment of the goal by one side is incompatible with fulfillment by the other. Given this situation, both parties have preferred prolonged and violent struggle to losing or even to compromise.

Other motives for winning. Achieving one's goals in a dispute may be valued also for reasons other than the intrinsic importance of the issues. Winning may bring political benefits, raising the prestige of the nation and its leaders, while losing may lower their prestige. Winning may bring feelings of personal success for leaders while losing may cause them to feel personal failure. And winning may be seen as creating a precedent for future victories while losing may be seen as setting a pattern for further defeats.

The positive value that American leaders placed on winning in the confrontation with the Soviet Union over missiles in Cuba and the high negative value they placed on losing illustrate several of these points. President Kennedy and his advisers believed that vital military and political interests of the United States were at stake. But they were concerned also that losing (i.e., not being successful in stopping creation of a Soviet missile base in Cuba) would damage seriously the prestige of their administration, would constitute a personal failure for them as leaders, and would probably encourage the Soviets to pressure the United States further at other points around the globe. Winning in this dispute would, they believed, have the opposite consequences (Allison, 1971).

At the beginning of a dispute winning is usually defined primarily in terms of the issues involved. Each party wants to improve his own welfare and wants to avoid having his welfare damaged. However, as a dispute continues and intensifies, one or both parties may become more concerned with his outcomes *relative to the adversary* rather than his own absolute welfare (Deutsch, 1973). In other words, he becomes more concerned with winning in the sense of doing better than the other than in the sense of improving his own position. The German kaiser seemed to have this orientation in 1914 when he was preparing to enter a general European war. He wrote that, "If we are to be bled to death, England shall at least lose India" (Stoessinger, 1982:14).

Other evidence indicates also that the values decisionmakers assign to possible outcomes will differ with their attitudes toward their opponent. Bargainers who have positive feelings toward each other make greater concessions than others (Pruitt, 1981:39–40).

Those opponents in a particular dispute whose general relationship is friendly may prefer an outcome that is at least minimally beneficial to their partners. This preference may stem in part from an altruistic desire to see the other fare well and in part from the realization that one's own long-range self-interest lies in keeping the other fairly satisfied. In a dispute over trade barriers between the United States and Japan, for instance, each side may prefer an agreement that has at least minimal benefits for the other. At the other extreme, where a relationship of rancor and even hatred (e.g., Iraq and Iran, Syria and Israel, India and Pakistan), one or both sides may prefer an outcome harmful to the other side, even if this does not bring pragmatic benefit to itself. Alternatively, one party may not wish particularly to see the other suffer but may value instead an outcome in which it comes out *ahead* of the other. For example, some U.S. military strategists seem to be relatively ready to tolerate the destructive outcomes of a nuclear war so long as the United States emerges in some sense "ahead of" the Soviet Union.[3]

To summarize, the value of winning in a particular dispute will be higher and the value of compromise agreements (or losing) will be lower for decisionmakers as:

(1) Their levels of aspiration are high (and compromise outcomes are defined as losses).
(2) Their norms give little legitimacy to the position of the other side.
(3) The issue(s) at stake is of great intrinsic importance to them.
(4) Winning on the issues in dispute is seen as bringing other benefits because:
  (a) There is pressure from constituents to settle for nothing less than victory.
  (b) There is a continuing series of disputes between the parties that makes any agreement a precedent.
  (c) Decisionmakers' personal prestige has become involved in the outcome.
  (d) A rancorous relationship with the other side makes "beating" the other seem important.

Value of No Agreement (Status Quo)

One of the major factors affecting the behavior of participants in an ongoing dispute is the value they place on the present situation of no agreement. The value of nonagreement will depend on several major types of costs (and possibly some benefits) that accompany such lack of agreement: the costs of the disruption of the relationship; the costs of the resources committed to the dispute; the penalties imposed by the other side; and other costs (benefits) resulting from the ongoing dispute.

Given a lack of agreement, normal relationships between the parties may be disrupted; e.g., the dispute between Britain and Argentina over the Falkland Islands led to a disruption of trade and financial relations between those countries. The significance of such cost for each side is determined by its dependence on the other (see Bacharach and Lawler, 1981). Such dependence derives from the extent to which one side needs resources provided by the other and the alternative sources it has to fill its needs. Bacharach and Lawler (1981:chapter 7) found that negotiators who had more alternatives made fewer concessions.

Secondly, a lack of agreement often results in each party having to commit costly resources to conducting the dispute. In disputes between nations sometimes these resources are simply the time and energies of its leaders. In more serious disputes, the resources may be military equipment that is produced and perhaps destroyed and the manpower called up for military duty and perhaps killed and wounded. The costs of conducting a dispute should be seen not only in terms of resources being expended but also in terms of other uses for the resources being foregone (so-called opportunity costs). For nations, other uses for resources include building the domestic economy and prosecuting other disputes more effectively.

Lack of agreement frequently also brings direct penalties imposed by the other. In international disputes these may include condemnation by political bodies (e.g., the Arab-sponsored condemnations of Israeli actions in the United Nations), boycotts directed against the other's trade and economy (the American attempt to disrupt the Cuban economy), and military action to destroy facilities or population (the Iraqi bombing of Iran's oil terminal). It is evident that the costs imposed by the other side are likely to rise as the other's relative power increases.

Other consequences of a situation of no agreement include political ones. These may be negative; for example, the lack of a settlement in the Iran-Iraq dispute may have undermined the popularity of the Iranian regime (*New York Times*, 17 December 1983). However, a continuation of the dispute (at least temporarily) may sometimes be beneficial politically, as when the popularity of British Prime Minister Thatcher rose during the Falkland Islands dispute with Argentina.

The greater the net costs of nonagreement become, the more anxious the negotiator will be to bring the dispute to an end. He will be less likely to simply wait for the other to concede. In an effort to reach agreement, he may either accept the other's current offer or make a more attractive offer himself. On the other hand, he may try to end the dispute quickly by taking some action (e.g., stronger coercion) intended to force the other to concede. Which choice he makes will depend on the other factors in equation 5-1.

Value of a Fight

The flexibility or firmness of leaders during a dispute is affected also by the value they put on a fight (or an expanded fight).[4] Lebow (1981) has described the positive attitudes toward war that have been held by some national leaders. For example, he asserts (1981:249) that at the time of the European crisis that led to World War I:

Russian leaders during the fateful month of July 1914 . . . knew that their acquiescence in Serbia's destruction would have been a far greater humiliation than their inability in 1909 to prevent Austria's annexation of Bosnia-Herzogovina. Such a political setback was certain to have had profound domestic repercussions; in the opinion of most contemporary observers it would have alienated conservatives from the government and have given considerable encouragement to revolutionary elements. There was also something of a consensus that war on the other hand was bound to arouse patriotic sentiments and rally support behind the government as indeed it did, at least initially.

On the other hand, horror of war has led some national leaders to make generous concessions in an effort to resolve a dangerous dispute. For example, the almost total capitulation of the British government led by Neville Chamberlain to the demands of Hitler for the Sudetenland in 1938 was strongly influenced by British revulsion at the thought of fighting another war with Germany only twenty years after a whole generation of British youth had been decimated in World War I.

The overall value to leaders of a fight depends on (a) its direct value (i.e., its intrinsic costs and benefits); (b) the values to them of winning and of losing; and, (c) their expectancies about which side will win. We may state the following equation:

(5-2)   value of a fight = intrinsic value of fight
$$+ \text{(value of winning fight} \times \text{expectancy of winning fight*)}$$
$$+ \text{(value of losing fight} \times \text{expectancy of losing fight*)}$$

Next we will consider the factors that affect each of the terms in this equation.

Intrinsic value of a fight. In considering the possible use of coercion against another nation, national leaders will anticipate the direct costs (and possible benefits) that would result if their actions lead to a fight with the adversary. The anticipated costs of a fight will depend, first, on how much resources (in money, material, and men) would be required to carry on the fight and how scarce such resources are. A nation that is close to bankruptcy may hesitate to embark on an expensive war. Similarly, the leaders of a nation short of arms or of armed personnel may be reluctant to commit their limited forces to a fight unless absolutely necessary. On the other hand, leaders of a nation with budget surplus, a large standing army, and a

---

*More technically, this is the weight attached to the expectancy.

large stockpile of arms might be less concerned about the immediate costs of an armed conflict.

The more the capability of the adversary to impose penalties and the greater one's own vulnerability, the more costly a fight is likely to appear. For example, if American policymakers thought about the use of military force against OPEC oil producers when OPEC drastically raised prices and reduced oil supplies in 1973, they would have considered the ability of these producers to cut off oil supplies completely and the need of the United States and its allies for such imports.

When two sides are roughly equal in power, and especially when they also have great capacity to harm each other, they are likely to be cautious about using threat and coercion. Under such conditions each will expect the costs of a fight to be high and neither can be confident of winning. Often two parties in this circumstance will develop norms for resolving disputes without the use of coercion (Tedeschi and Bonoma, 1977; Kelley and Thibaut, 1978). Wright (1965) found that disputes between nations were less likely to escalate to war when both parties had a strong capability to inflict harm on the other. (However, if two adversaries are about equal in strength and one side does use coercion against the other, then the other is very likely to retaliate in kind.)

The overall material costs of a fight will depend on how long the fight continues. The more that decisionmakers believe that their own power is greater than that of their adversary (i.e., their ability to inflict harm is greater and their vulnerability to harm is less) the more they are apt to expect the fight to be over quickly. The potential user of coercion also will be more likely to expect a fight to be short and thus less costly if he has evidence (e.g., in media, in statements of opposition leaders) that indicates a lesser resolve within the adversary nation than within his own. Indications of support by third nations for one's own side also may contribute to expectations of a short, low-cost fight.

In addition to its financial, material, and human costs, a fight may bring other costs (and possibly benefits). The interruption of positive ties (in trade, tourism, scientific exchange, etc.) may entail costs for both adversaries. For example, the war between Argentina and Britain cost each side not only the direct expenses of the fight but also the benefits of trade with the other nation. Kriesberg (1982a) notes that force is more likely to be used in disputes when there are few positive ties between the parties (and thus little cost involved in disrupting the normal relationship).

Frequently a very important direct result of a fight between nations is its political consequences for leaders of both sides. Decisionmakers may anticipate criticism for getting the country into war, especially if the war is not won quickly. Alternatively, a war may be seen as a way to unify a divided nation and divert attention from unsolved domestic problems. For instance Argentina's leaders in 1982 saw seizure of the Falkland (Malvinas) Islands from Great Britain as a way to rally a discontented people. Whether an external fight will be seen as being politically costly or politically beneficial at home is likely to depend on the extent of political division and the extent to which it is thought that domestic opinion can be easily turned against an outside enemy.

In summary, we would expect that the direct value of a fight to a nation's leaders will increase as:

(1) The resources that would be used in a fight are more plentiful and their depletion would be less costly.
(2) Vulnerability to damage by the adversary is less.
(3) Power relative to the adversary (and/or evidence about the adversary's will to persist) is such as to lead to expectations that a fight would be short.
(4) The value of positive ties to the adversary (e.g., of trade) that would be disrupted by a fight is small.
(5) Political support for a potential fight appears to be high.

Values of winning and losing. The values of winning or losing a fight to a decisionmaker will depend mainly on the value to him of getting his way in the dispute that led to the fight. The value of the various outcomes of a dispute have been discussed earlier in this chapter.

In addition, the value of winning a fight may be enhanced by a rise in the reputation of one's nation (military or otherwise) and by political benefits to those who have led a winning battle. For example, Egypt's partial successes in the 1973 war with Israel not only succeeded in recovering some territory but also raised Egypt's military reputation and brought President Sadat (who pictured the outcome to his people as a great victory) a considerable boost in popular esteem. Conversely, losing a fight results not only in losses in the issues at stake but also in military reputation and in popularity for the defeated leaders.

Expectancies about outcomes of a fight. If a leader believes that his use of coercion may lead to a fight with the adversary, then his decision to go ahead anyway will depend in part on his expectancy about who will win such a fight. Will his own side finally gain its objective in the dispute or will it be forced eventually to concede all or part of that for which it initiated the fight?

As with perceptions of outcomes in general (see chapter 3), expectations about the outcome of a fight will be influenced by past experiences. For example, the expectancies of both Israeli and Syrian leaders about which side would win another war between their countries would undoubtedly be influenced by the fact that Israel has won four contests since 1948.

Probably the major determinant of expectations about who would win a fight is the expectation of the relative power of each side—i.e., how leaders see their own ability to damage the other side (physically, economically, etc.) and how vulnerable they see themselves to being damaged in turn. For example, American decisionmakers expected to win their fight with North Vietnam because of the great capacity of the United States to inflict material and economic damage on that country while the Vietnamese could do no direct damage to the United States.

The capability of each side to damage the other may depend in part on which side strikes the first blow. This would be especially true when the character and number of weapons and their deployment on each side enable the side that strikes first to cripple the retaliatory capability of the adversary. Where such a first-strike capability is possessed by one or both sides, it may believe that the probability of winning is quite high if it does in fact strike first.

Expectations of victory depend not only on perceptions of the relative ability of each side to impose damage on the other but also on perceptions of each side's willingness and ability to endure the hardship imposed on it by the other. American leaders thought that because of the great damage that North Vietnam would suffer in a fight with the United States it would soon give up the struggle to win South Vietnam (Milstein, 1974). However, the North Vietnamese, while they recognized that their own losses would be greater than those of the United States, expected to win eventually because they believed they would be willing to persist in the struggle longer than would the United States. Events proved the Vietnamese correct.

In addition to perceptions of the relative power of the adversary and of its likely persistence, expectations about the outcome of a struggle may be affected by expectations about the actions of third parties. For example, expectations of Israeli and of Syrian leaders about the probable outcome of another war would be influenced by their expectations about actions by the United States and by the Soviet Union in such an event. How actively would the Soviet Union intervene in Syria's behalf? If the Soviets showed signs of moving their troops into the region, would the United States take action to stop this move, as it did when the Soviets threatened to send troops into Egypt in 1973?

Finally, expectations about the outcomes of one's actions may be influenced by sets of beliefs about reality. In the case of the outcomes of war, military and civilian leaders develop sets of beliefs (military doctrines) about the nature and probable course of a war. French leaders in the 1930s envisioned that another war would follow a pattern of static defensive operations similar to that of World War I, probably producing no quick winner. On the other hand, German military leaders had developed a doctrine of mobile tank warfare that led them to expect a high probability of swift victory. Many Americans and many Russians believe that nuclear war between the superpowers would be so devastating to both sides that there would be no winner. But military strategists on both sides still consider scenarios under which they would be able to win a limited nuclear war. Some national leaders may even anticipate the outcome of a war on the basis of religious or other nonpractical beliefs. For example, Ayatollah Khomeini of Iran apparently expected victory in his war with Iraq because he saw it to be a holy war in which God was on the Iranians' side.

Expectations about the chances of winning a fight, as compared to the chances of success through other methods, will vary with different leaders. The importance of the expectations of a particular leadership is illustrated by the case of Japan in 1940–1941. For a time the top Japanese leadership—e.g., Prince Konoye—abhorred the prospect of a war with the United States, believing that it might be catastrophic for Japan. However, General Tojo, who took over as prime minister in 1941, represented a nationalist military clique that glorified war and saw it as the only means to reach Japan's imperial goals. Soon after Tojo's accession to power, the Japanese attacked Pearl Harbor (Feis, 1950).

To summarize, the leaders of a nation will see their own side as more likely to win a fight, and therefore more likely to initiate one, as:

(1) Their power relative to their adversary, the advantage of a first strike, and their beliefs about war lead them to expect greater damage to be caused to the adversary.
(2) The stakes, the ideology, the political situation, and the past behavior of each side lead them to believe that the resolve of their own side is greater.
(3) The actions and statements of third parties lead them to expect military and/or political support from other nations in a fight.

Expectancies About the Outcomes of Actions

The choice of a particular action depends not only on the value the decisionmaker places on various outcomes but also on his expectancies about the outcomes of alternative actions. For example, a leader is more likely to use coercion if he expects such action to result in the other side giving in rather than retaliating. Concessions are more likely to be made if they are expected to lead to an acceptable agreement rather than to an attempt by the other side to force still further one-sided concessions. Standing pat on one's position and just waiting is more likely if the decisionmaker believes that the other side cannot endure the status quo of nonagreement much longer rather than being able to hold out indefinitely.

What do such expectancies about the outcomes of alternative actions depend on? We have already discussed (in chapter 3) the general topic of expectancies about an adversary's behavior. Now we may consider more specifically the question of how decisionmakers will expect the adversary to react to their own actions. Such expectancies may be related to (a) the decisionmaker's general beliefs; (b) the statements and past behavior of the adversary; (c) the (perceived) current motives and incentives of the adversary; (d) the intensity of the conflict; and, (e) the safeguards against exploitation.

General beliefs. The general beliefs of leaders may influence their perceptions of the adversary's intent and their expectations about his actions. Snyder and Diesing (1977) have asserted that a major difference between hard-liners and soft-liners in foreign policy lies in differences in general expectations about the responses of any adversary to various actions of their own side. The hard-liner expects an adversary to respond to concessions with new demands while the soft-liner expects some reciprocation of concessions from the adversary. The hard-liner believes that taking a firm stand and demonstrating one's willingness to use coercion will cause an adversary to back down; the soft-liner expects that coercion will "get the opponent's back up," make him less willing to concede, and perhaps provoke him to counter-coercion.

The general beliefs that national leaders hold about the likely reactions of an opponent to their own behavior may stem from their personalities and personal backgrounds (e.g., lawyers versus military leaders), from their worldviews or ideologies (e.g., Marxist-Leninist views about the behavior of capitalist states or conservative views about the nature of communism), and from their past experiences. The effects of past experiences on expectations is illustrated by the generation that witnessed British and French attempts to appease Hitler with concessions in the 1930s. This experience led most of that generation to conclude that a policy of trying to satisfy an adversary with concessions would lead only to further demands and aggression. This was a very different kind of lesson than was learned by the generation whose central experience was that firmness, threat, and coercion had led to World War I.

Past statements and behavior of the other. Expectations about the likely behavior of an adversary will be affected by his past statements and especially by his past behavior. The expectations of Hitler and his lieutenants about the reaction of Britain and France in the event Germany attacked Poland in 1939 were affected by the statements of British and French leaders (Alexandroff and Rosecrance, 1977). The British cabinet had stated its intent to stand by Poland if she were attacked. But the past behavior of the adversary also had an impact. When confronted with firm German determination to occupy the Rhineland, Austria, and Czechoslovakia, Britain and France had backed away from a showdown. "I have seen them at Munich. They are worms," Hitler said (Wilmot, 1952:21). This past behavior made Hitler doubt for some time, despite the statements of Western leaders, that they actually would go to war in support of Poland.

Studies of bargaining indicate that expectations about whether and how soon the other side will accept a given offer will be affected by the other side's current demand (Pruitt, 1981). The higher the other's current demand and the greater the gap between that demand and one's own offer, the lower the negotiator's expectation that the other will accept that offer quickly, if at all.

A bargainer's expectations will be affected also by the other's previous concessions in this and other disputes. Larger previous concessions by the other side may lead a negotiator to expect that the other will continue to concede if he himself remains firm in his position. On the other hand, if the other side concedes a little, the negotiator may not expect much further concession and therefore may make greater concessions himself in order to reach agreement. Some experimental studies have found such a pattern of behavior; i.e., that larger concessions by one side were met with lack of reciprocity by the other (Bartos, 1974; Druckman, 1983; Pruitt, 1981). There is some evidence suggesting that such a pattern has sometimes occurred also in U.S.-Soviet arms negotiations. Jensen (1984) found that in several arms-control negotiations, the Soviets tended to increase their rate of concession in response to a hard-line U.S. position on the previous round of talks.

The effect of concessions by one side on the expectations of the other depends on the relative strength of the two sides. If a conceder is seen as acting out of weakness, then the adversary will expect further concessions and may wait for them. If, on the other hand, the conceder is seen as strong, further unilateral concessions are not likely to be expected. (See chapter 9 for a discussion of the effectiveness of conciliatory initiatives.)

Motives of the other. Expectations about the likely response of another nation will depend to a considerable extent on perceptions of the intentions of that nation's leaders. Writing of the choice by national leaders between coercion and accommodation, Snyder and Diesing say, "A rational resolution of this dilemma depends most of all on an accurate assessment of the long run interests and intentions of the opponent. If his aims are limited, conciliation of his specific grievances may be cheaper than engaging in a power struggle with him. If they are possibly unlimited, the rational choice is to deter him with countervailing power and a resolve to use it" (Snyder and Diesing, 1977:154).

In their study of Soviet-American interaction from 1946 to 1963, Gamson and Modigliani (1971) also stress the importance of leaders' perceptions of the goals of the adversary. They found that such perceptions are especially important for predicting how both Soviet and American leaders responded to belligerent behavior by the other nation. When the leaders of one side believed that the other was acting out of insecurity and defensive intent, they tended to respond to belligerence with conciliatory actions, apparently expecting that such behavior would reassure the other side and promote reciprocal cooperation. However, when one side saw the other as having aggressive, expansionist intent, it reacted to belligerence with counter-belligerence, apparently believing that conciliation would be exploited by the expansionist opponent.

George and his colleagues (1971) have found that coercive diplomacy is most likely to be used when the adversary's motivation to use force is seen as less strong than one's own side's motivation. They also state that national leaders are more likely to use coercion when they believe that the adversary fears escalation of the conflict and thus will refrain from responding to coercion in kind.

The adversary's motivation to use force will be seen as stronger as its possible benefits from such action increase and its possible costs decrease. Coercion will be seen as more in the adversary's interest as the stakes involved become more important to him, as his commitments to a firm stand increase, as political support (at home and abroad) for use of coercion increases, as its vulnerability to damage by the other decreases, and as its own capability to inflict damage on the other increases. Increased capability to damage the other and lesser vulnerability itself to damage will not only reduce its costs of fighting but also enable it to win the struggle. (See chapter 2 for a discussion of vulnerability to threat, vulnerability to force, and the tactics used by an adversary.)

To illustrate, when judging British motivation to fight in response to a German invasion of Poland, Hitler took into account the fact that Britain's economic and military stake in Polish independence was relatively small. Britain's concern with its vulnerability to German air attack, its general reluctance to bear again the terrible costs of war, and the uncertainty of the outcomes of war, also contributed to Hitler's initial doubt about the British will to fight. However, when Britain solemnly committed itself to fight if Poland was attacked, it raised greatly the costs to itself of standing aside. To renege on that commitment would have meant not only a loss of personal and national honor but also would have badly damaged Britain's standing as a great power. Furthermore, by that time in Anglo-German relations the British public was ready to support military action to stop Hitler. These factors finally convinced Hitler that Britain had the motivation to fight, though he went ahead with his planned invasion of Poland anyway (Alexandroff and Rosecrance, 1977).

Under certain conditions, national decisionmakers' expectancies that an adversary will attack first will be fairly high because they recognize that there is an advantage to that side in striking first (see chapter 2). For example, if the Soviet Union and the United States each were capable of destroying almost all of the nuclear weapons of the other side in a surprise attack, then in a crisis situation each side's leaders might be suspicious that the other side was about to attack. Each side's leaders then might be reluctant to wait before attacking. How much of an advantage the initiator of a war will have (and thus how high expectations about the likelihood of a surprise attack will be) depends on the types of weapons each side has, and the vulnerability of each, as well as on other factors (see chapter 7).

Intensity of conflict. Expectations may also be influenced by the seriousness of the conflict. Tedeschi and his colleagues (1972) assert that persuasion and promises of reward are most likely at low levels of conflict. One reason this may be true is that each side may expect a more positive response to promises of reward when the intensity of conflict is low than when intensity is high. Related to this point, Kriesberg (1982) has suggested that rewards and promises are unlikely to be used when there is great incompatibility between the goals of the two adversaries. In such a case, Kriesberg suggests, rewards and promises are not likely to seem adequate for getting the other side to cooperate.

Expectations about the effectiveness of conciliatory actions may be influenced not only by the seriousness of an immediate dispute but also by the general quality of relations between the two sides. A relationship that is generally cooperative leads to some degree of trust and understanding that, in turn, makes each side believe that conciliatory methods are likely to be successful in resolving a dispute (Kriesberg, 1982).

Safeguards against exploitation. Decisionmakers can have greater confidence that their own concessions or cooperative actions will *not* be exploited by an adversary the more that: (a) it is possible for them to verify that any agreement reached, or apparent mutual cooperation, is in fact being followed by the adversary; and, (b) it is possible for them to switch to more competitive tactics without suffering great loss if the adversary tries to exploit their cooperation. For example, when considering whether to make concessions in reducing armaments, national decisionmakers will have less expectation of being exploited if they can verify an adversary's reciprocation or, if reciprocation does not occur, build up their own arms without being at a dangerous disadvantage. (See chapter 2 for a discussion of these conditions for cooperation.)

In summary, national leaders are more likely to expect that firm (perhaps coercive) rather than conciliatory tactics against an adversary will have good outcomes the more that:

(1) They hold general beliefs in the efficiency of tough tactics and/or in the ineffectiveness of conciliatory tactics.
(2) The adversary in the past has backed down in the face of tough tactics.
(3) The adversary is vulnerable to coercion and/or is believed to fear a fight.
(4) The adversary has made unilateral concessions in the present dispute in a context (e.g., low power) that suggests his weakness and lack of resolve.
(5) The adversary has not reciprocated concessions in the past and has not promised to do so at present.
(6) The adversary is believed to have aggressive intentions.
(7) A highly rancorous relationship with the adversary exists.
(8) It is difficult to verify reciprocation of cooperation by the adversary and/or conciliatory actions that are not reciprocated will put one's own side at a disadvantage that is not easily reversible.

Conditions 2, 3, and 4 raise the decisionmaker's expectations that tough tactics will be effective in getting the adversary to give in. Conditions 5, 6, 7, and 8 lower his expectations that conciliatory tactics will be effective in eliciting a cooperative response and will be safe.

The Attraction of Specific Options

The attraction to the decisionmaker of taking each type of action depends on a combination of the factors specified in equation 5-1 and discussed above. We may consider next the circumstances under which the following options are more or less attractive: making concessions, doing nothing and waiting for the other to concede, using threat and/or coercion, and using promises and rewards. (Tables 5.1 through 5.4 summarize this, as well as the prior, discussion.)

Making Concessions

In making concessions to the other side (perhaps even accepting the other's last offer or demand), a decisionmaker suffers the loss inherent in reducing his own demands. On the other hand, he gains the possible benefits of obtaining an agreement, ending the costs of nonagreement, and avoiding a fight.

Making concessions will become a more attractive option as the value of what is conceded becomes less. The loss involved in reducing previous demands is likely to be more tolerable when the interests involved in the dispute are not vital, when one's aspirations are low, when accepted norms are consistent with concessions, and when other important interests (e.g., domestic political support) are not threatened by the concessions.

Making concessions also becomes more attractive as the value of having an agreement increases (e.g., because of the benefits of using one's resources for other goals), as the value of the present status quo of nonagreement decreases (i.e., as the continuing disagreement is more costly), and as the value of a fight decreases (i.e., as a fight becomes more costly or less likely to be won). This is true however only to the extent that the decisionmaker expects that concessions of the sort he is making will lead to agreement and avoid a fight. He is likely to expect concessions to lead to such a positive outcome if the adversary (or others) has in the past responded to concessions with cooperation and if he believes that the adversary now aims for cooperation and not domination.

Finally, the attraction of making concessions increases as this option is seen as having intrinsic advantages—e.g., that it is the morally correct or the politically popular thing to do. Conversely, making concessions will seem less attractive if they are seen as humiliating, damaging to one's reputation for resolve, or politically unpopular.

Table 5.1 Conditions Favoring the Making of Concessions (Seeking Compromise)*

Circumstances	Elements of decision
Strong common interests with adversary Resources, attention needed for other goals (other dispute, domestic aims) Chances for agreement seen as lower later	A. Agreement per se is highly valued
Stakes in dispute are not vital Level of aspiration is low Concessions required are not large Norms favor compromise Political support for concessions exists Dispute is not highly rancorous	B. Value of terms of possible compromise agreement is acceptably high
Normal relationship with adversary disrupted High level of resources being spent conducting dispute High level of penalties being imposed by adversary	C. Present state of nonagreement has very negative value (is costly)
General soft-line beliefs See goals of adversary as nonexploitive Adversary has reciprocated cooperation in past Adversary has communicated cooperative intent See adversary as having incentives to cooperate (political pressures, scarce resources, pragmatic advantages, nonsuperior power, etc.) Dispute is low-intensity Verification of cooperation is possible Change to firmness is possible without great disadvantage if necessary	D. Expect that own concessions (cooperation) will lead to acceptable agreement (mutual cooperation) rather than (attempt at) exploitation by other

Table 5.1   (continued)

Circumstances	Elements of decision
Ideology, self-images, norms favor concessions Interdependence with adversary makes positive attitudes by it toward own side desirable Dispute is nonrecurring; therefore not seen as creating precedent for concessions Political support for concessions from own public, third nations exists	E. Intrinsic value of making concessions (cooperating) is high

*Concessions become more likely as conditions A, B, C, and E are more present *and* as condition D also is present.

Table 5.2   Conditions Favoring Standing Firm and Waiting*

Circumstances	Elements of decision
Normal relationship with adversary not (completely) disrupted or not important initially Few resources being expended on conducting dispute Penalties being imposed by adversary are not great Dispute is politically advantageous for leaders	A.1. Value of present situation of nonagreement is *not* very negative (is not very costly)
General hard-line beliefs Adversary has conceded quickly in past disputes Incentives for adversary to concede quickly are great (high costs of dispute, political pressures, other uses for resources, etc.)	and/or A.2. Expect that adversary will concede very soon if one waits
(See table 5.3 for circumstances making winning highly valued)	B. Winning the terms one is demanding is valued at least moderately highly

Table 5.2   (continued)

Circumstances	Elements of decision
General hard-line beliefs Adversary has conceded eventually in past disputes Incentives for adversary to concede will be great eventually	C. Expect that adversary will concede eventually if one waits
Vulnerability to attack by other is low Power relative to adversary would remain high after attack by other Resolve of own side (based on stakes, unity, etc.) is higher than that of adversary Third parties would support own side if attacked by other	D.1 Value of a fight initiated by adversary is not very negative (i.e., cost would not be very high to one's own side or expect own side to win)
No substantial military advantage for first-strike is present Adversary has not attacked in similar circumstances in past Perceive that adversary does *not* seek domination Other incentives for adversary to attack are seen as low (possible tangible gains low, costs high, political support low, etc.)	and/or D.2 Expect that adversary will *not* attack if one stands firm and waits for other to concede
Self-image, ideology (e.g., of patience, steadfastness) supports waiting Lack of political pressure from domestic public, allies, for immediate action	E. Intrinsic value of standing firm and waiting is acceptably high

*Standing firm becomes more likely the more that conditions A.1 and/or A.2, B, and E are present, and C as well as D.1 and/or D.2 are present.

Standing Firm and Waiting

Standing firm and waiting for the other side to concede offers the decisionmaker the prospect that the dispute will be settled eventually on the terms he is seeking. The more he values the outcomes he has been seeking, the greater this advantage will appear. However, waiting for the other side to concede not only foregoes temporarily the benefits of an agreement but also means that the decisionmaker will suffer the costs of carrying on the dispute for as long as the adversary holds out. The smaller the costs of the status quo (nonagreement), the less urgency the decisionmaker will feel for the dispute to end. When no important relationship with the adversary (e.g., of trade) has been disrupted or an alternative partner has been found, when the resources being expended to pursue the dispute are few or affordable, when the penalties imposed by the adversary are small or easily bearable, and when other outcomes (e.g., political effects of the dispute) are not very costly (or even positive), then the decisionmaker will likely feel no great pressure to act to settle the dispute.

Standing firm also runs the risk that a fight (or a wider fight) may occur before the other side decides to give in. The less abhorrent a decisionmaker finds the prospect of a (wider) fight to be and/or the smaller his expectancy that a continuation of the status quo will lead to a (wider) fight, the more content he will be to wait. His expectations that the adversary will react to a continued stalemate by initiating (or escalating) a fight will depend especially on the adversary's past behavior and on his perceptions of the adversary's motives and incentives (e.g., whether the relative power of the two sides and political pressures create incentives for the adversary to attack).

The overall attraction of standing firm and waiting will be affected also by the intrinsic significance the decisionmaker gives to this option. If he views it as showing steadfastness rather than stubbornness and believes that his constituents and allies will support such a course, its overall appeal will be increased.

Using or Threatening Coercion

The leaders of one side in a dispute may value highly the prospect of achieving their basic demands. Therefore they may be very reluctant to make any substantial concessions in order to obtain an agreement. However, the costs of the ongoing dispute may be high for them—in terms of a drain on their resources, penalties imposed on them by the adversary, or other opportunities foregone. In such circumstances decisionmakers tend to find attractive the option of threatening or actually using coercion. Such actions are intended to make the lack of agreement more costly for the

Table 5.3   Conditions Favoring the Use (or Threat) of Coercion*

Circumstances	Elements of decision
Stakes are seen as vital Norms support legitimacy of position Levels of aspiration high (e.g., frame of reference makes non-win a loss) Political pressures for winning on issue Series of similar disputes makes outcome a precedent Decisionmakers' personal prestige involved Rancorous relationships makes beating other important	A. Winning on issues of dispute is highly valued
Normal relationships with adversary disrupted High level of resources being spent conducting the dispute High level of penalties being imposed by adversary	B. Present state of nonagreement has very negative value (is costly)
Sufficient expendable resources for fight are available Vulnerability to damage is low Remaining ties to adversary that would be disrupted by fight are small Political support for fight is high	C. Value of (wider) fight is relatively high 1. Intrinsic value (especially costs) of fight seen as acceptable
Power relative to adversary (i.e., relative capacity to impose damage) is high Relative resolve of own side (based on stakes, ideology, unity, past behavior, etc.) is high Third parties have indicated support	C. 2. Expect to win a fight
General hard-line beliefs Adversary has backed down in past because of apparent weakness Adversary is vulnerable to force and/or threat Perceive that adversary has little incentive to use coercion (stakes are low, commitments are weak, relative power is low, political opposition to use of coercion, etc.)	D. Expect that use (or threat) of coercion will lead adversary to back down

Table 5.3   (continued)

Circumstances	Elements of decision
Costs of coercion are low Beliefs favor use of coercion Adversary's actions violate norms Political support for use of coercion	E. Intrinsic value of using coercion is high

*Use of coercive methods becomes more likely as conditions A, B, and E are more present and as conditions C and/or D also are present. Threat is more likely to be used when the adversary is vulnerable to threat and actual coercion when the adversary is vulnerable to force (see chapter 2). When the adversary is vulnerable to both threat and force, then threat is likely to be used first, followed by actual coercion if the threat does not succeed.

opponent and thus force him to concede more quickly. If successful, the use of threat and/or coercion will permit the user to attain the outcomes he desires while shortening the time he suffers the costs of nonagreement.

Threat, being less costly and less provocative than actual coercion, is likely to be used first, especially when the opponent is "threat-vulnerable"—i.e., it would be in his interest to change his behavior rather than to suffer the consequences of the action threatened (see chapter 2). Coercion is likely to be used if the opponent does not concede in the face of threat and if he is "force-vulnerable"—i.e., by using coercion the user makes it in the interest of the opponent to change his behavior (see chapter 2).

Of course, using "tough" tactics (threatening or using coercion) entails the risk that a (wider) fight will result. The lower the decisionmaker believes the costs of a fight will be for his side, and the more he expects that his side would win a fight, the more willing he will be to take this risk. His perceptions of the costs of a fight and the likely winner will be determined by the relative power of the two sides, their relative resolve, support from third parties, and other factors discussed earlier.

Even if the value of a fight is low for a decisionmaker, he may still use threat and coercion if he believes that such tactics will elicit compliance rather than belligerence from the adversary. Such expectations of a compliant response to his own side's coercive action may derive from his general beliefs, from the past behavior of the adversary, or from his perception of the motives and incentives of the adversary.

There is evidence from both experimental studies and studies of international relations that threat and coercion are more likely to be used when one side is clearly stronger than the other than when the two sides are roughly equal in power (see chapter 2). Antagonists are especially likely to be cautious in using or threatening coercion when they are equal in power and have a high capacity to injure each other (Hornstein, 1965). Under these circumstances the risk of a fight would appear very negative to both sides: costs would be high and victory uncertain for each. However, equality of power is no guarantee that threat or coercion will not be used. While both sides may wish to avoid a fight, each may try to push the other as far as it can and may even try to take advantage of the other's reluctance to fight.

Finally, as with other options, the overall attraction of a coercive policy is affected also by the intrinsic value of the action. The more that

Table 5.4 Conditions Favoring Offering (or Promising) Extrinsic Rewards to Get Adversary to Make Concessions*

Circumstances	Elements of decision
(see table 5.3 for circumstances making winning highly valued) →	A. Winning on issues of dispute is valued highly
(see table 5.3 for circumstances giving present state of nonagreement a very negative value) →	B. Present state of nonagreement has very negative value (is costly)
Own resources are high Alternative demands for own resources are not high →	C. Value to own side of extrinsic rewards given (or promised) is fairly low
General beliefs about efficiency of positive incentives Adversary has conceded when offered extrinsic rewards in past Adversary has high need for rewards offered General relations with adversary are not very rancorous →	D. Expectancy that giving (promising) extrinsic rewards will lead other to concede on issues in dispute is high
Ideology, norms do not oppose giving rewards to adversaries Adversary's actions have not violated norms (provoked anger) →	E. Intrinsic value of giving (promising) extrinsic rewards is positive (or not negative)

*Giving (promising) extrinsic rewards becomes more likely the more that conditions A, B, C, and E are present and condition D also is present.

"toughness" is seen as morally correct and justified in the circumstances, and the more that it is seen as likely to win support from constituents and allies, the greater the overall appeal of this option will be.

Use of Positive Incentives

Sometimes the leader of one side may highly value getting his way in a dispute and find the continuing disagreement very costly but be reluctant to use coercive tactics to try to force his adversary to concede. This reluctance may stem from a desire to preserve good long-term relations with the other, from a perception that the other is not very vulnerable to his threats or coercion, or from a belief that a fight would be very undesirable—because it would be very costly or because one's own side might not win. In such circumstances a decisionmaker may find especially attractive the option of using positive influence techniques: persuasion, promises, rewards. He may try to convince the other side that the terms he is proposing have advantages that they have not recognized. He may promise them rewards if they make concessions. He may reward cooperative actions or concessions in hopes of eliciting further concessions.

When are positive incentives most likely to be an attractive option for influencing the other side? First, promises and rewards become more attractive as their costs become less. The greater the resources—money, markets, raw materials, military hardware, etc.—that are available and can be given up without great sacrifice, the more attractive it becomes to promise or give some of those resources in order to influence an opponent.

However, decisionmakers may consider not only immediate but long-term costs. They may be concerned that even though the adversary is influenced by their positive incentives he will demand similar payoffs for cooperation in the future. As Knorr (1975) has pointed out, national leaders also may be concerned that by using rewards to influence another nation they may be encouraging other national leaders to insist on similar rewards. When such concerns are strong, they may make the use of positive incentives seem too costly for the long run. This is especially likely to occur when disputes of the present sort are likely to recur often.

The attraction of promises and rewards also becomes higher as they are expected to be more effective in gaining compliance. The better the overall quality of the relations between the two sides, the less the incompatibility of their goals, and the less the intensity of the dispute, the more likely are positive influence methods to be used (Tedeschi, Schlenker, and Lindskold, 1972; Kriesberg, 1982). While there may be a number of reasons for these associations, it seems clear that in such circumstances the decisionmaker is more likely than otherwise to expect a positive response to his positive incentives. Such expectations that using positive incentives will be effective also will be greater when the adversary has responded positively to such actions in the past, is dependent on one's own resources, and is seen as having other incentives (e.g., political pressures) for cooperation.

Use of Several Types of Actions

While the preceding discussion has focused on the use of one specific class of actions in a dispute, leaders may use a mixture of different types of actions. One frequent combination in trying to influence the other side to make concessions is that of mixing threats or coercion with promises or rewards—the "carrot and the stick." For example, President Johnson tried to do this in Vietnam by combining bombing of North Vietnam with promises to give that country economic aid if it settled the dispute on American terms.

Disputants also may combine making concessions with the use of threat and coercion. In their study of inter-nation crises, Snyder and Diesing (1977:255) found that "although a coercive or an accommodative strategy is usually dominant for each party, it is often combined with elements of the opposite strategy." Coercive actions may serve to influence the other side to make concessions and thus enable the user to win more of his demands. Decisionmakers may, however, fear that coercive actions will provoke or anger the other side and lead to confrontation or even a fight, thus delaying settlement and perhaps incurring the large costs of a fight. Thus threat and coercion may be leavened with some accommodation (concessions) in order to promote the chances for settlement and to minimize the risk of war. But too exclusive an emphasis upon accommodation may also be seen as unattractive. Such an approach may lead the other side to doubt one's resolve and believe that one will surrender entirely. Decisionmakers may fear that an accommodative action will actually reduce the chances for acceptable agreement and even risk eventual war. To avoid this possibility, they may accompany any concessions with threats and possibly even actual coercion to show their resolve not to be exploited.

In chapter 10 I will discuss the effectiveness of various strategies that mix cooperation and coercion, reward and punishment.

Summary

This chapter has considered the conditions that affect the choice of actions by national leaders engaged in a dispute: whether to make concessions, do nothing and wait for the other side to concede, or try to pressure the other side (especially by coercive tactics) to give in. The choice among possible actions sometimes is made in accordance with explicit or tacit rules. Rules dictating the use of coercion are most likely to arise when salient experiences of decisionmakers have indicated that coercive actions are effective, the ideology and self-images of decisionmakers or the norms of their groups favor its use in disputes, and a stable situation provides recurring incentives for use of coercion or for first use when a fight seems likely to occur.

In most cases national leaders decide on their actions not by following rules but by evaluating the merits of alternative actions. The first step in this process is to screen out those options that would not achieve their minimum aspirations or constraints. Often decisionmakers search for an option that will permit them to win the dispute while avoiding a war. But they may need to give one of these objectives greater priority than the other. When the issues of the dispute have the greatest salience (as commonly happens), when ideology stresses the primacy of national principles or goals, (e.g, freedom, sovereignty, territorial integrity), and when political pressures to win are strong, then winning acceptable terms is likely to be given greater priority than avoiding war. In such circumstances coercion tends to be used in order to prevail on the issues. Even when avoiding war is given highest priority, national leaders may be willing to use coercive tactics if they believe that the risks of war are low and that coercion has a good chance of achieving what they believe to be an acceptable settlement of the dispute.

When several alternative actions (including doing nothing) are considered as viable options, decisionmakers may be expected to choose on the basis of how much they value different possible outcomes of the dispute and their expectancies about which actions will result in which outcomes. The action chosen may be expected to be the one with the greatest overall attraction, as specified in equation 5.1.

The specific values and expectancies that lead national leaders to choose particular kinds of actions (using coercion, making concessions, standing firm and waiting, etc.) are summarized in tables 5.1 to 5.4. These tables also summarize the circumstances affecting the values that decisionmakers place on various outcomes (winning, getting agreement, a fight, etc.) and their expectancies about what the outcomes of alternative actions will be.

This analysis of the choice among options suggests ways in which an adversary (or the leaders of one's own side) may be encouraged to take particular kinds of actions or discouraged from taking others. To discourage the leaders of a nation from using coercion in a dispute, one approach is to try to make winning on the issues of the dispute seem less vital. This may be done, for example, by reducing political pressures to win and by disengaging the leader's personal prestige from the outcome. Another way to reduce the attraction of using coercion is to make the value of a fight appear more negative. This may be done by making the costs of a fight appear very high or reducing the decisionmaker's expectancies that his own side will win the fight. Providing evidence of his own side's vulnerabilty, of the strong relative power of the adversary, of the high resolve of the adversary, and of support for the adversary by third parties are among the ways in which the prospect of a fight can be made to appear more negative.

Coercion will also tend to be a less attractive option the more a decisionmaker expects that coercive action (or the threat of it) will *not* cause his adversary to back down without a fight. An adversary can lead opposing decisionmakers to expect resistance to coercion by building a record of such resistance and by creating (and communicating) incentives to resist coercion (e.g., by making credible commitments). Finally, the use of coercion can be discouraged by making its use intrinsically less valuable and more costly. Among the ways in which this might be done is reducing anger-arousing provocations by an adversary and by building public opposition to the first use of coercive actions.

To increase the likelihood that national leaders will make concessions in a dispute, it is helpful first to make agreement per se more valuable to them. Proposing plans to pursue common interests (e.g., trade) and creating demands for resources to be used for goals other than the dispute (e.g., for domestic needs) are among the ways in which agreement per se can be made more attractive. Concessions can also be encouraged by actions that make the terms of possible compromise agreements appear acceptable. For example, trying to lower the decisionmaker's level of aspiration (e.g., by clarifying his lower-than-realized power position) and mobilizing political support for compromise may help to make concessions more attractive.

Another way of encouraging concessions is to try to raise the decisionmaker's expectancy that such actions will lead to acceptable agreements and mutual cooperation rather than to exploitation. For example, by establishing a record of reciprocating cooperation, and by communicating their present incentives and intent to cooperate, leaders of an adversary nation can raise their counterpart's expectancy that concessions will be reciprocated.

Finally, the overall attraction of making concessions can be increased by raising the intrinsic value of such actions. Placing emphasis on ideology and norms that support concessions (religious values, norms of equality and fairness, etc.) and separating the outcome of the present dispute from later disputes (thus reducing harm to the decisionmaker's reputation for resolve) are among the ways in which the intrinsic value of concessions may be raised.

While national leaders generally give one type of tactic (e.g., coercion or making concessions) greater emphasis in a dispute, they often use some mixture of tactics. Primarily coercive tactics may be leavened with some concessions in order to promote the chances for settlement and reduce the risks of war. When concessions are emphasized, they may be accompanied by threats and even by some coercion in order to demonstrate a resolve not to be exploited.

In the next section of the book, we will consider the effectiveness of various types of tactics in defending one's own interests while promoting cooperation and avoiding war.

6 Threat and Deterrence

I t is common for one nation to threaten harm to another nation in order to get the latter to do (or refrain from doing) something. Sometimes threat works as the threatener intends. For example, American threats to remove Soviet missiles from Cuba by force led the Soviets to dismantle their missile bases as the United States demanded (Abel, 1966). In other instances a threat does not influence the target's behavior as intended; it may even lead the target to respond with threats (or actual coercion) of its own. For example, Great Britain's threat to go to war did not deter Hitler from attacking Poland in 1939 (Alexandroff and Rosecrance, 1977).

When are threats effective and when are they ineffective? When do they lead instead to a spiral of threat and counter-threat, perhaps culminating in war? Jervis (1979:302–303) has commented about the lack of knowledge on this subject as it applies to international relations: "Two central questions are still without answers. First, under what conditions do threats and the use of force lead the other side to retreat and when do they lead it to reply with threats and force of their own? Second, when does a retreat or concession lead others to expect, and the state to make, other retreats?"

While our knowledge about the effects of threat is limited, there has been a considerable amount of work done on this subject. Social psychologists have investigated threat as a means of influence and the role that threat may play in conflict situations (Milburn and Watman, 1981). In the field of international relations there has been both theoretical analysis and some empirical study of the use of threat—especially in the context of deterrence (e.g., Snow, 1979; Weede, 1983; Huth and Russett, 1984; Quester, 1986; Jervis, Lebow, and Stein, 1985).

In this chapter, I will attempt to summarize and integrate what we know about the effects of threat as this information may be relevant to disputes between nations. My aim will be to draw some tentative conclusions about when threats against another nation are likely to work and when they are likely to be ineffective or even counterproductive. The conclusions will have particular relevance to the important subject of deterrence but will have other applications as well. (The subject of arms buildups, which is closely related to threat, is discussed in chapter 7).

Choices of the Target of Threat

The recipient of a threat has two basic choices: he can comply with the demands of the threatener or defy the threatener.[1] If he is defiant, he may try to avoid the penalty threatened by defending himself, issuing counter-threats, or attacking or trying to disarm the threatener.

Which of these options (or combination of options) is chosen in response to a threat from an adversary may depend on personal or organizational habits or rules. Some individuals have learned—as a result of personal experience or culture—that it is prudent to "back off" in the face of threats. Other individuals have learned that to back down signifies a weakness that one's adversary will exploit further. Some governments have developed more or less explicit rules that dictate acceding to certain external threats. For example, the governments of Poland and other East European countries now take it as axiomatic that a demand accompanied by a serious threat from the Soviet Union cannot be defied. On the other hand, it would be equally axiomatic for any Israeli government that a demand accompanied by a threat from an Arab country could not be acceded to, since to do so would be seen as showing weakness that would quickly be exploited.

While the response to threat may be almost automatic in some cases because of habits or rules, individuals and governments usually are not completely uniform in their responses to threats. In one situation they may accede to a threat; in another, they may defy the threat. (Moreover, habits and rules may differ for varying circumstances.)

The response that is made to a threat in particular circumstances will depend on the value the target of the threat places on possible outcomes of his actions and on his expectancies that each alternative action will result in particular outcomes. (See chapter 5 for a general discussion of the choice among different actions.) To understand the response to threat we need to know what benefits and costs the actor sees as likely to follow each of his major alternatives, which are either compliance or defiance. We need to know also how such perceptions of benefits, costs, and probabilities are likely to change as the situation varies and as the target's perceptions of the situation vary.

Benefits of Compliance

The major benefit of compliance under threat is avoiding the penalty or harm that is threatened. The motivation to avoid such penalty will depend on (a) how negatively the target values the penalty[2]; and (b) the target's perception of the likelihood that the adversary would carry out the threat in the event of the target's noncompliance.

Value of Penalty

How negatively a possible penalty is valued depends on its magnitude and on the target's abhorrence of the type of penalty threatened. It seems reasonable that the larger the magnitude of the penalty threatened for noncompliance the more likely is compliance to occur. Horai and Tedeschi (1969) have found this to be true in their experimental studies of threat. In international affairs as well, Leng (1980) found that as the magnitude of the threats made by one nation to an adversary increased, compliance with the threatener's demands also increased. However, Harkabi (1966) has noted that in some instances the magnitude of the penalty threatened may be too large for effective deterrence. If the threat is greatly disproportionate to the importance of the action to be deterred (e.g., if the United States threatened all-out nuclear attack if the Soviets made any interruption in truck traffic to West Berlin), the target of the threat may tend to doubt the threatener's seriousness.

The value of a penalty threatened will depend not only on its magnitude but also on the extent to which the type of penalty threatened is abhorrent to the target. For example, the possibility of an attack that would kill large numbers of people would have a much more negative value to Israel, which has a small population and a dedication to protecting its people, than to Iran with its much larger population and widespread acceptance of martyrdom in war.

Credibility of the Threat

It seems reasonable also that the more likely it is that the threat will be carried out, especially as perceived by the target of the threat, the more effective it will tend to be. This common-sense supposition has been confirmed in experimental situations (Horai and Tedeschi, 1969), and also in studies of threats between nations (Leng, 1980; Lebow, 1985a). It is important, therefore, to know what affects the target's perception that the threatener would carry out his threat if the target does not comply with his demands.

I have discussed (chapter 3) the general subject of how national leaders form expectations about the behavior of an adversary. Two major types of perceptions that affect expectations were considered: those of the other's capability and those of the other's intent. Now we may consider these types of perceptions in the specific context of the credibility of an adversary's threat.

Capability. It is clear that a threat can be credible only if the threatener has the capability of carrying it out and if this is perceived by the other. In order to deter attack by another nation, the threatening nation must have not only sufficient capability to do unacceptable damage to the potential attacker but to do this damage *after* suffering an attack. Thus, effective deterrence requires a sufficient second-strike or retaliatory capability that can survive a first strike by the potential attacker. Moreover, effective deterrence requires not only that the deterring nation have a survivable second-strike capability but also that the target of the deterrent threat knows this to be true (Quester, 1986:chapter 4).

While a nation's overall military capability, and especially its retaliatory capability, often is important for deterring attacks upon itself, such general strength may be less useful for deterring attack on a distant ally. Effective deterrence of attack by another nation against an ally is aided by having greater military strength in the locality of the potential conflict but not necessarily by the overall military balance or the possession of nuclear weapons by the defender (Huth and Russett, 1984).

Intent. What affects the target's perception that the threatener intends to carry out his threat if the target does not comply with his demand? First, a number of characteristics of the threatener, his situation, and his actions are relevant. These include (a) hostility to the target, (b) costs of carrying out the threat, (c) costs of *not* carrying out the threat, (d) past behavior, and (e) current preparations. In addition, (f) the target's beliefs about the threatener and (g) the specific form and source of the threat may be relevant.

(a) Hostility. In some experimental studies, threats have been found to be more effective when the threatener is seen by the target as hostile and exploitive and is not liked by the target (Rubin and Brown, 1975). Apparently, threateners who are seen in such a negative light are viewed as quite apt to follow through on their threats, while threats from persons who are seen as more benign and are better liked are believed less and may therefore

be less effective. It is easy to imagine a similar effect in international affairs. For example, Canadian leaders would probably view a threat from the Soviet Union with more alarm than a similar threat from the United States.

(b) *Costs to the threatener.* Compliance to threat has been found to decrease as the costs of enforcement to the threatener increase (Mogy and Pruitt, 1974). While the threatener still has the power to impose costs on the target, he is less likely to use his power, and the potential target is less likely to expect him to do so, as the costs of exerting power increase.

The costs to the threatener of carrying out a threat clearly are relevant to the credibility of threats between nations. The credibility of an American threat to cut off wheat supplies to the Soviet Union if the Soviets invaded Poland would be reduced by the fact (well known to the Soviets) that such a move would be costly to the United States as well—e.g., by depriving our farmers of a valued market for their crops. A Mexican threat to cut off oil supplies to the United States would have little credibility because the Mexicans so desperately need the revenues they would thereby lose. A Saudi threat to cut off oil supplies would have somewhat greater credibility because the costs of doing so would be less to the Saudis.

Costs of carrying out a threat may be political as well as economic. If important segments of the public do not support carrying out a threat, the political costs of doing so may be high. For example, in 1983 the West German government was faced with intense opposition from a large portion of the citizenry to carrying out their threat to permit the United States to deploy new intermediate-range missiles if the Soviet Union persisted in a similar buildup in Eastern Europe. Knowing of this political cost to the West German government of carrying out their threat, the Soviets were not convinced that the West Germans would actually do so (*Newsweek*, 24 October 1983).

Regardless of the actual costs to a threatener of carrying out his threat, the threat becomes more credible if the threatener seems to believe that these costs will be low. As Harkabi (1966) has pointed out, the threatener can reinforce his threats by proclaiming his ability to reduce (retaliatory) injury to himself and his conviction that he would emerge victorious in a showdown.

The costs of carrying out a threat may be increased if the threatener is vulnerable to counteraction by the target (Pruitt, 1981:78). This fact has been of concern to those concerned with the effectiveness of the American nuclear deterrent. Some strategic thinkers have been concerned for example that the Soviet Union no longer believes American threats to respond with nuclear weapons to a Soviet attack on Western Europe since the costs of such an action to the United States (in the form of Soviet retaliation) would be so enormous (Snow, 1979). Deterrence theorists have pointed out, moreover, that even the threat to respond massively to a Soviet nuclear attack on our missile bases in the United States may not be completely believable since it would be less costly to accept the blow than to retaliate against Soviet cities and thus trigger further Soviet attacks on our cities. Since the leaders of each side cannot be sure that the other side will react in such a restrained rational way if attacked first, they are not likely to take this chance. But it is sobering, nevertheless, that the doctrine of deterrence —supposedly relying on rationality—may ultimately be effective only if each side remains unsure of the ultimate rationality of the other side under extreme provocation.

To try to make a nuclear response in the event of attack more rational —and thus more believable—American defense officials have tried to develop the capability for fighting a limited nuclear war. Under such a strategy, nuclear attacks might be limited in the number of weapons fired and in the types of targets hit (e.g., military bases). Since the intent would be to deliver a serious blow to the enemy without leading to the annihilation of both sides' populations, a threat of a limited nuclear strike might be seen by an adversary as more credible than the threat of an all-out nuclear attack. However, as critics of the limited war concept have noted (e.g., Beres, 1980) such a policy involves two very serious problems: first, by making nuclear war more thinkable and acceptable, it may make it more likely. Second, a limited nuclear war could easily escalate into a full nuclear exchange and thus result in the final holocaust.

(c) Costs of not carrying out the threat. Just as the credibility of a threat is decreased when the costs of carrying it out are high, credibility is increased when the costs of not carrying it out are high. Possible costs include tangible ones, such as territory and economic advantages, and less tangible but important ones such as prestige and the reputation for resolve.

One of the major ways in which national leaders try to increase the credibility of their threats is to take public actions that increase the costs to them of not fulfilling their threats—e.g., by making public commitments. A number of writers have paid considerable attention to commitment as a factor affecting the credibility and success of threats in international affairs. Thomas Schelling has described a variety of ways in which people, including national leaders, can establish commitments (Schelling, 1960, 1966). And a number of writers have discussed commitment as a factor contributing to effective deterrence of attacks by other nations.

Commitments need not necessarily be explicit in order to be effective. Russett (1963) and Huth and Russett (1984) found that the success of larger nations in deterring attacks on smaller friends ("pawns") did not depend so much on formal commitments to defend the pawns as on the strength of economic and other ties with the pawn that established de facto commitments.

(d) *Past actions of the threatener.* Perceptions of the intent of national leaders to carry out a threat may be influenced also by their past actions. For example, in 1971 President Sadat of Egypt "promised" an attack on Israel during that year in order to recover the Egyptian territories then occupied by Israel. When Sadat failed to carry out this threat, the Israelis took much less seriously his stated intention to attack Israeli forces in 1973 (and were caught by surprise when Sadat did in fact launch an attack). When Soviet negotiators at the intermediate-range missile talks in Geneva threatened in 1983 to counter new American missiles with a further missile buildup of their own, Western observers expected them to do so because the Soviets had always carried out such threats in the past.

A study of the effectiveness of "gunboat diplomacy," including the threat of using naval force in order to gain political objectives, has been made by Mandel (1986). He found that such a display of force is most likely to deter unwanted actions by a target nation when it is employed by a nation that previously has engaged in war in the target's region and is also militarily prepared and politically stable compared to the target.

However, a record of following through on threats does not necessarily make such threats effective. In their study of effective deterrence, Huth and Russett (1984) found that whether or not a defender nation had fought in the past when a protégé was attacked did not affect the success of a current deterrence attempt. They suggest that success in deterrence does not "follow merely from establishing a record of 'standing firm' in the past" (Huth and Russett, 1984:524). Other factors, such as current incentives for carrying out the threat, may be more important. In addition, a potential attacker sometimes may believe that a defender who has backed down earlier will be less likely to do so again. The potential attacker is especially likely to hold such beliefs when a previous retreat by the defender led to negative results (e.g., domestic criticism) for the defender nation's leaders. Similarly, a nation that carried out a threat to defend a protégé at an earlier time might not be expected to repeat such an action if the previous defense led to very negative consequences for its leaders. For example, the actions of the United States in defending South Vietnam probably did not add to the credibility of American promises to defend other small nations (and may actually have reduced this credibility) because later potential attackers were aware of the enormous social and political costs the Vietnam war brought for American leaders. Thus, we may expect that the credibility of threats will be affected by the past actions of the threatener in combination with the success or lack of success of such actions.

(e) Preparations. Preparations by the threatener to carry out the threat also may have an important effect on the expectations of the target. In addition to enhancing the threatener's capability to carry out his threat, it may signal an intent to do so. For example, during the Cuban missile crisis, the United States engaged in a rapid buildup of its land, naval, and air forces in the southeastern United States close to Cuba. These obvious preparations to bomb or invade Cuba were undoubtedly helpful in persuading the Soviets that the United States intended to carry out its threat to remove the Soviet missiles from Cuba by force if the Soviets themselves did not remove them (Abel, 1966).

(f) Beliefs of the target's leaders. The perceptions of leaders of a nation that has been threatened about the intent of the threatener may be influenced also by these leaders' own beliefs about their adversaries. Snyder and Diesing (1977) have contrasted the beliefs of those national leaders who tend to be hard-liners with those who tend to be soft-liners. One of the differences is that the hard-liners tend to see the adversary as a bluffer who will back down if one's own side acts firmly enough. The soft-liners tend to be more sensitive to the adversary's interests, including his concern for his reputation for resolve, which might lead him to respond to firmness with firmness. Such different perspectives would, among other things, lead hard-liners more than soft-liners to believe that the adversary does not intend to follow through on its threats. An example of how such general beliefs may influence perceptions of threat is the case of U.S. General Douglas MacArthur (Higgins, 1960). After pushing North Korean troops back across the line from which they had invaded South Korea, MacArthur ordered his troops to go all the way to the Chinese border. China had threatened directly to intervene in the war if the United States went that far. However, MacArthur, who prided himself on knowing "the oriental mind," believed that the Chinese would inevitably be cowed by the firm use of force. MacArthur's beliefs were wrong and resulted in a military disaster for his overextended forces and in four long years of further war on the Korean peninsula.

(g) Nature and source of threat. Finally, it should be noted that the target of a threat may form his perceptions of a threatener's intent from the nature and source of the threat (Harkabi, 1966). First, the intent of the threatener is more likely to be seen as firm (and the demands on the target clear) when the threatener states a clear policy about the conditions under which a threat will be carried out. For example, a threat by the Soviet

Union to break off arms talks if the United States tests any weapons in space would be taken more seriously than a threat to end talks under the much vaguer condition of the United States "not negotiating seriously." Second, a threat that is explicit and unequivocal—e.g., "If the United States deploys an antisatellite weapon in space, we will certainly put up space mines to counter them—will signal more serious intent than one that is implicit or equivocal—e.g., "If the United States deploys antisatellite weapons, we will have to consider additional steps for our own defense." However, it should be noted that while an explicit threat is likely to increase credibility, it may be provocative, especially when made to a status equal. Snyder and Diesing (1977:218) state: "The threatener appears more resolved but this gain is offset by the 'stiffening' effect on the adversary —his prestige and resolve image are engaged as well as the threatener's. . . ."

The credibility of a threat may be affected also by its source. The more authoritative the source of the threat, the more it will signal serious intent. For example, a threat issued directly by the president of the United States will carry much more weight than the same statement by, say, an undersecretary of defense. A statement from the latter can be disavowed later as not reflecting official policy, if necessary; there is no such "out" if the president speaks.

While high-level statements of explicit, unequivocal threats and of the conditions under which they will be carried out are more likely to be taken seriously, they also carry the greatest risks. If the threat is not effective in securing compliance, it will either have to be carried out—perhaps resulting in an unwanted fight—or the threatener will have to suffer humiliation and a blow to his future credibility by backing down. Snyder and Diesing found that, in crisis situations, national leaders generally avoided committing themselves too definitely to carrying out explicit threats in order to preserve their freedom of maneuver (Snyder and Diesing, 1977: chapter 3).

Uncertainty by the Target

In their discussion of deterrence in American foreign policy, George and Smoke (1974) have stressed the importance of the view of the initiator (of a challenge to the status quo) of the exact nature of the defender's commitment—by which they mean the firmness of the defender's intentions to carry out his deterrent threats. George and Smoke point out that the initiator may believe that the defender's commitment is ambiguous or that it may weaken under pressure. They discuss several tactics the initiator may use to clarify or to change the defender's intentions. One is the limited probe, which involves a use of "limited force that will require [the] defender to clarify the ambiguity of his commitment." Another is controlled pressure, which attempts to "convince [the] defender that he will have great difficulty and incur unacceptable risks if he attempts to honor his commitments" (George and Smoke 1974:541).

While the target of a threat may try to reduce its uncertainty about the threatener's intentions, the very fact of such uncertainty may enhance the effectiveness of a deterrent threat. This is likely to be true especially when the magnitude of threatened loss is great, as it is with the possibility of nuclear war. Harkabi (1966) suggests that the greater the threatened loss, the less the inclination to gamble. Uncertainty, he asserts, is an integral part of the nuclear situation and increases the strength of deterrence above and beyond what calculations of gain and loss would seem to indicate. Harkabi's view seems consistent with a major point about deterrence made by George and Smoke. They propose that deterrence is more likely to fail when the target of the deterrent threat believes that the risks of his action triggering fulfillment of the threat can be calculated or controlled to make that action an acceptable risk. When there is some uncertainty about the exact nature of the threat and of the conditions under which it will be carried out, such calculation and control of risks is less possible.

Other Benefits of Compliance

In addition to the major benefit of avoiding a threatened penalty, compliance in the face of threat may have some other advantages. In particular, compliance may end a costly situation of nonagreement and restore good relations with the threatener. The more costly is the status quo of nonagreement and the more that compliance is expected to result in an end to such costs, the more attractive compliance will be. Similarly, the more that the target values reaching an agreement (i.e., restoring good relations with the threatener), and the more the target expects that its compliance will lead to restoring such good relations, the more attractive compliance will be. For example, for a South African government compliance, under threat of new economic sanctions, to the demands of Western nations for an end to apartheid would bring not only the benefit of avoiding the particular sanctions but also might reduce other economic and political costs resulting from this dispute and improve overall relations with Western nations.

Costs of Compliance

Compliance with a demand under threat also has costs. These include (a) what is given up by complying and accepting the terms the threatener is demanding and (b) the intrinsic costs of compliance in terms of its effect on one's self-image, prestige, and reputation.

The Terms Accepted by Complying

Compliance with a demand under threat may involve giving up something tangible one already has, such as money or territory. For example, President Sadat of Egypt threatened Israel with renewed war if it did not give up its control over the Sinai area. In other cases, what is lost is not what is already possessed but the opportunity to gain something desirable. Thus, for example, a threat by the United States to retaliate if the Soviet Union should invade Iran requires the Soviets to give up the possibility of gaining control over Iranian oil and other assets.

One would expect that, other things equal, the likelihood of compliance with demands under threat will *decrease* as the subjective importance or value of the tangible costs of compliance *increases*. One reason Israel was willing to comply with Egyptian demands for return of the Sinai is that the Israelis did not see that area as being vital to their national life or self-defense (as many Israelis view the West Bank and Golan Heights to be). An important reason why the Japanese did not comply with American demands (and accompanying threats) that they give up their colonial gains in China and Indochina in the late 1930s and early 1940s is that important segments of Japan's elite believed that control of Southeast Asia was vital to Japan's strength and prosperity (Feis, 1950).

The tangible costs of compliance to threat will depend mainly on the motivations and objectives of the target. In the case of pre-World War II Japan it is clear that the objective of building a Japanese empire to rival those of the European powers was an important one for top officers of the army and the navy as well as for other important leaders of the time. These objectives made the costs of withdrawing in the face of U.S. threats and coercion seem prohibitive. In discussing the requirements of effective deterrence, George and Smoke (1974:532) point out that one factor affecting the outcome is the strength of the target's motivation to change the status quo.

After reviewing a variety of inter-nation disputes, Lebow (1985b) also emphasizes the limitations of deterrent threats in affecting the actions of national leaders who are pursuing goals they feel are vital. He writes:

"These empirical findings raise serious questions about the utility of deterrence. . . . Even the most elaborate efforts to demonstrate prowess and resolve may prove insufficient to discourage a challenge when policy makers are attracted to a policy of brinkmanship as a necessary means of preserving vital strategic and domestic political interests. The Fashoda, July 1914, Korean (1950), Sino-Indian, and Cuban crises all attest to the seriousness of this problem" (Lebow, 1985b:183).

The costs of compliance to a target of threat may be affected also by whether the target sees any alternative ways of reaching his important goals. Reviewing the evidence of his own and colleagues' studies, Lebow (1985c) points out that attempts by one nation to deter military attack by another often fail because the target of deterrent threats sees no diplomatic alternatives to attack. He writes:

> According to Stein, two other considerations were crucial catalysts for the Egyptian decision to challenge Israel in 1974. These were the twin assumptions made by Sadat and his advisors that there was no chance of regaining the Sinai by diplomacy and that, the longer they postponed war, the more the military balance would favor Israel. . . . Japan's leaders opted for war only after it became clear that they could not attain their objectives by diplomacy. They were also convinced that the military balance between themselves and their adversaries would never again be so favorable as it was in 1941. . . . If there is any single example that drives home the point that challenges may be unrelated to the military balance, it is the recent war in the Falkland Islands. . . . Like the Japanese and the Egyptians, the Argentines had also lost all faith in the prospect of achieving their goal, sovereignty, over the islands, by diplomacy. (Lebow, 1985c:215–216)

To maximize the chance of deterrence being effective, the side to be deterred should be left an honorable alternative for reaching at least some of its goals. Otherwise, as Harkabi (1966) puts it, they may react like "cornered beasts."

Nontangible Costs

In addition to the tangible costs that may result from accepting the terms of the threatener, there may be intrinsic costs that are less tangible. These include loss of self-esteem, loss of status, loss of reputation for firmness, and the possible encouragement of new demands and new threats from one's adversary. Thus, the target of a threat may defy the threatener not because the immediate tangible costs of compliance are too high but, rather, because he views compliance as humiliating or as damaging to his long-term relationships with adversaries by creating an impression of weakness under pressure (Milburn and Watman, 1981:chapter 8; Snyder and Diesing, 1977:chapter 3).

In their study of sixteen international crises, Snyder and Diesing found that national leaders often were concerned with the effects of making concessions on their reputation for resolve. They write:

> in almost all of our crises, some participant warns that giving in or making a concession will be taken as evidence of general weakness and will encourage further challenges. . . . The concern is always voiced by "hard-liners." The hard-liner tends to focus on the power consequences of the outcome of the current dispute; the opponent's expectations about one's future firmness is an element of power. Furthermore, his image of the opponent is that he is a relatively permanent and aggressive opponent who is constantly probing for indications of weakness, and with whom one is engaged in a long-term power struggle that dwarfs in importance the "merits" of the immediate issue. (Snyder and Diesing, 1977:188)

Snyder and Diesing also found in their data what they term the "never again phenomenon." "A state that has backed down on several occasions finally comes to think that, if it yields once more, its future threats of firmness toward an opponent or pledge to allies will be worth nothing; therefore it *must* stand firm now, whatever the risk, to avoid political disaster" (Snyder and Diesing, 1977:189). As one example, they describe the unwillingness of Russian leaders to back down under German threats in 1914 as due in part to the fact that Russian leaders had backed down in several other recent confrontations with Germany and Austria and so believed that this time they had to stand firm. Similarly, the resolve of President Kennedy and his advisers to stand firm in the face of Soviet threats during the Cuban missile crisis was influenced by their perception that the United States had recently been weak in cold war confrontations (the fiasco at the Bay of Pigs and passivity concerning the creation of the Berlin Wall) and that it therefore was imperative to be firm this time.

The extent to which compliance under threat will be seen by the target as leading to the loss of intangible but valued assets such as status and reputation for resolve will depend on the nature of the action demanded to reduce the threat, the characteristics of the threatener, and the situational context in which the threat is issued.

Nature of the demand. A threat accompanying demands that the target *not* take a certain type of action—a deterrent threat—generally is more effective than a threat to take a punitive action unless the target *does* take a particular action—a compellent threat (Rubin and Lewicki, 1973). To comply with a deterrent threat usually involves little or no loss of status or reputation for resolve. Unless the target of the threat has publicly committed itself to take the "prohibited" action, it can claim that it never had any intention of doing what the threatener demanded it not to do. Thus, the failure of the Soviet Union to invade Poland in 1980 following warnings of retaliation from the United States was not seriously damaging to the prestige of the Soviet Union or its reputation for resolve. Nor was it likely to be so perceived by Soviet leaders. They had, after all, never said they intended to invade Poland.

On the other hand, compliance with a compellent threat, requiring that one take some particular action, is likely to be seen as humiliating and to reduce one's prestige. For example, compliance by the United States to a demand by Iran that the United States issue an apology or try the deposed shah (under threat to American hostages) would have been deeply humiliating and greatly damaging to U.S. prestige. Of course, while compliance to compellent threats brings such important intangible costs, this does not mean that the target of the threat will not comply if the possible costs of noncompliance are large enough. Thus, the Soviet Union complied under public threat with American demands that it withdraw its missiles from Cuba. But the costs to the Soviets in prestige and resolve reputation were high, as U.S. President Kennedy recognized. Kennedy tried to reduce these costs of compliance by avoiding incidents that would humiliate the Soviets (such as searching of Soviet flag ships) during the crisis and also by avoiding any "crowing" about the U.S. "victory" afterward.

Legitimacy. Threat is more likely to be effective if the target of the threat sees its use and the demands accompanying it to be legitimate—i.e., to conform to shared norms of proper conduct (Milburn and Watman, 1981; French, Morrison and Levinger, 1960; Cohen, 1979). Threats from an authority figure or even from a superior may be viewed as more legitimate than threats from an equal (Milburn and Watman, 1981:chapter 3). A threat may also be seen as relatively legitimate if it reflects some vital need of the threatener rather than just a capricious wish to influence one's will (Kelley, 1965).

When a threat is seen as not legitimate, the intangible costs of compliance increase. First, to comply with an illegitimate threat may lower one's status and self-esteem. Secondly, because illegitimate threats arouse feelings of anger (French, Morrison, and Levinger, 1960), they raise the psychological costs of giving in (as well as increasing the motive to hurt the threatener). Threats (as well as other actions) which are seen as illegitimate may also lead the target to become alarmed about the general intentions of the threatener. In his discussion of perceptions of threat in international crises, Raymond Cohen (1979:165) comments:

> The crucial inference, central to the appraisal of threat, is found in the recurrent argument that the opponent had in some way betrayed a trust or undertaken an illegitimate and unpermissible action—that he had somehow infringed a norm of behavior and that, as a *consequence* of this, he had ceased to be bound by existing restraints and was to be considered as bent on a policy of aggressive domination. . . . The observer was forced to conclude that the opponent was no longer playing the "game" according to the "rules" and had rejected those conventional and limited objectives of the diplomatic "game" for something far more sinister and unpredictable.

When a nation making a demand is perceived as bent on aggressive domination, it may appear that compliance will lead only to more demands and further threats.

The importance of perceptions of legitimacy in affecting the readiness of national leaders to make concessions in disputes also has been emphasized by Snyder and Diesing (1977:498–499), who state:

> Perceptions of "legitimacy" are potent in determining bargaining power and outcomes. That is, the party that believes it is in the right and communicates this belief to an opponent who has some doubts about the legitimacy of his own position, nearly always wins. Legitimacy often derives from defense of a long-term status quo against the attempt to change it by threat of force. In our cases, the defender always wins except when both sides share the belief that some change in the status quo is more legitimate than its perpetuation.

Snyder and Diesing (1977:499) also state that perceptions of legitimacy —being in the right—is "probably the most potent element in the 'balance of interest' component of the bargaining power equation." Such perceptions of legitimacy will affect the stakes that the target of a threat has in resisting and the costs of compliance.

The reaction of British leaders to the threats and demands of Adolf Hitler during the 1930s illustrates the importance of the perceived legitimacy of threats. Hitler's demands for control over ethnic German populations in the Rhineland, Austria, and the Sudetenland were seen by the British leaders as legitimate in terms of prevailing norms of national unity and self-determination. Concessions could be made to German demands, even under threat, without loss of British honor or at the cost (it was thought) of encouraging continuing demands. But when Hitler began to make demands and threaten actions the British considered illegitimate— e.g., his demands on Poland—they began to see Hitler's aims quite differently and the perceived costs of continued compliance to his threats rose precipitously (Middlemas, 1972).

Public nature of threat. The intangible, or symbolic, cost of complying to a threat should be greater when compliance is public than when it is private. In research using a bargaining game Brown (1968) found that the importance of maintaining face is greater when there is an audience of significant others. He also found that when audience reaction indicates that a person has lost face the person will take action against the party that made him lose face, even at the cost of greater damage.

In international affairs it seems clear that it will be less costly in terms of face for a national leader to comply under threat with a demand made privately rather than publicly. For example, when Syria moved troops into Jordan in 1970, Israel sent word to Syria that she would take counter military action unless the Syrians withdrew their troops (Kissinger, 1979). Syria did remove her forces from Jordan, but this compliance did not mean a loss of face for Syria as it would have had the Israeli threat been made publicly. As a counterexample, compliance by the Soviet Union to American demands during the Cuban missile crisis was more costly because the American demands and threats had been made publicly. Thus, compliance meant not only a pragmatic loss but also a serious loss of prestige for the Soviets. American policymakers were aware of this problem and tried to minimize the humiliation to the Soviets (Abel, 1966).

In their study of sixteen international crises, Snyder and Diesing found that national leaders most often made specific threats through private diplomatic channels. "The main reason is that the threatener wants to avoid the provocative effect of a public threat. Because it breaks a tacit rule of normal diplomatic intercourse, a public threat arouses anger and engages status values of the recipient so that he probably becomes more resolved to stand firm than before" (Snyder and Diesing, 1977:252).

Repetition of the situation. As Milburn and Watman (1981:110) point out, "One is more likely to submit to a threat if the situation is perceived to be a once-only affair rather than a habit." Where the situation is not likely to recur, compliance with a demand under threat does not carry the cost of encouraging similar demands at a later time.

When the United States threatened Great Britain with withdrawal of support during the British-French invasion of Suez, British leaders probably did not concern themselves with whether compliance with American demands for withdrawal would encourage future demands of the same kind. In general, the United States and Great Britain were close allies with common aims in international affairs; the Suez affair was a rare and rather unique moment of serious disagreement that was unlikely to occur again. At the other extreme, when Libya's President Qadaffi threatens to attack U.S. ships and planes in what the United States considers international waters, compliance by the United States at any one time might encourage threats by Libya and by other nations in similar situations in the future.[3]

A threatener may be able to reduce the potential future costs of compliance by assuring the target that "this is my last demand." Hitler used this ploy effectively in the Czech crisis of 1938 in order to help secure British and French compliance with his demand for German occupation of the Sudetenland.

Reducing the Intangible Costs of Compliance

The discussion so far has suggested some ways in which a threatener may be able to reduce the blows to the prestige and reputation of the target that compliance would bring. Specifically, I have noted that threats that are made privately, are clothed in the language of mutually shared values, and are presented as a "one-time only" event can be compiled with with relatively little loss of status and reputation.

In addition, there are other techniques for reducing the provocativeness of threats and making compliance easier. One technique is to frame the threat in the form of a warning. Snyder and Diesing describe the use of warnings in diplomacy between nations when the communicator attempts to portray his intent as providing information about what he will "have" to do in some contingency rather than as bringing coercive pressure. They comment that "the warning generates less hostility than a threat because the warner appears to be explaining, in a 'friendly spirit,' what he would have to do to make sure the recipient, out of ignorance, does not precipitate consequences harmful to both sides" (Snyder and Diesing, 1977:219).

Another technique for trying to reduce the status costs of compliance is to provide the target of threat with loopholes through which it can gracefully comply without seeming to bow to coercion. One example is the American statement in 1946 that it believed Soviet troops in Northern Iran were operating without official authorization. Such a pretense made it easier for the Soviets to comply with U.S. threats of coercive action if they did not withdraw their troops (Snyder and Diesing, 1977:221–222).

Finally, the threatener can couple his threat with a face-saving concession to the other side. Such a device makes it possible for the side that basically capitulates under threat to make it appear that it has only agreed to a compromise. In their studies of international crises, Snyder and Diesing found such a device to be used frequently and to be important in helping the weaker side to make the concessions necessary for the dispute to be settled. One good example is the Cuban missile crisis. Faced with a U.S. threat to bomb their missile bases in Cuba or invade the island, the Soviets were ready to comply with America's basic demands. But the Soviets' prestige had become engaged in a major way and it would have been extremely humiliating for them to simply announce their surrender under threat. That the United States was willing to make some counter-concessions—especially a pledge not to invade Cuba—enabled the Soviets to submit without excessive loss to their prestige and reputation for resolve.

To summarize the discussion in this section, the attraction of compliance with the demands of the threatener increases:

(a) the more negatively the threatened penalty is seen by the target and/or the more credible he believes the threat to be;

(b) the more the target values ending the dispute, avoiding a (wider) fight, and resuming good relations with the threatener;

(c) the less onerous to the target are the terms he accepts by compliance; and,

(d) the less the intrinsic costs of compliance to the target in terms of loss of self-image, prestige, and especially of reputation for resolve.

Alternatives to Compliance

The target of a threat may find compliance to the threat unattractive because of the tangible costs of accepting the threatener's terms and/or because of the costs in prestige and reputation intrinsic to compliance. Rather than comply, the target of threat may do one or more of the following: (1) defy the threat and accept the possible penalty; (2) try to defend against the threatened penalty; (3) issue a counter-threat, perhaps to try to discourage the adversary from carrying out its original threat; and, (4) take some coercive action against the threatener, perhaps in an attempt to neutralize the threatener's ability to carry out his threat.[4]

Accepting the Possible Penalty.

The leaders of a nation may decide that it is better to accept the possibility of a threatened penalty than to comply with a demand. For example, the white leaders of the South African government have stated that they would prefer to accept the possibility of economic sanctions from other nations than accept demands that they grant equality to blacks, a policy they view as suicide. Similarly, American threats to stop supplying India with nuclear fuel if the Indians did not accept international inspection were not successful in getting India to comply. The Indian leaders apparently preferred to accept the possible cutoff of nuclear fuel from the United States rather than suffer the practical costs of changing their nuclear program and the symbolic costs of giving in to what they saw as outside pressures and interference.

It seems probable that a nation will be most likely to defy a threat and accept a possible penalty under the following conditions: (a) the target's motivation to take action other than that demanded by the threatener is high; (b) the target can do little to defend itself against the threatened penalty; but, (c) the magnitude of the penalty threatened is not too high and/or the probability that the threat will be carried out is perceived to be low. Under such conditions, the expected costs of defiance would be less than the certain costs of compliance.

Defending Against a Threat

Rather than comply with a demand when compliance would be costly, national leaders may choose to try to defend their nation against a threatened penalty. In this way they may hope to reduce the probability that the threatener would carry out his threat or, if he did, to reduce the negative impact of the action. For example, when faced with implicit threats of invasion from the United States and its surrogates, the response of Nicaraguan leaders has been to defy U.S. demands for changes in the Nicaraguan government and its policies and to prepare to defend against attack. Such preparations, the Nicaraguans hope, may discourage the United States and its allies from attacking and, in the event of attack, prevent a quick or complete U.S. domination.

Defense against threatened penalties is more feasible in some situations than in others. While Nicaragua can realistically defend against a conventional attack by Honduras or even by the United States, it could not defend against a nuclear attack. NATO nations can defend against an attack by the Soviet Union, but it would be less feasible for Poland (which already has Soviet divisions on its soil) to do so effectively. The ability of a nation to mount an effective defense against a threat depends on its resources, its ability to mobilize such resources quickly, and the capability of the threatener to impose the penalties it threatens.

While defense against a threatened penalty may reduce the costs of defiance (by reducing the effectiveness and/or likelihood of penalties being imposed), defense itself is costly, requiring resources, manpower, etc. Thus, the attraction of a policy of defiance-plus-defense will be affected by the costliness of the defenses needed.

In general, we may expect that a nation's leaders would attempt to defend against a threat rather than comply with it under the following conditions: (a) the costs of compliance (tangible and nontangible) are seen as high; (b) the target has the capability to mount a defense that is at least partially effective; and, (c) the cost of mounting the defense is less than the expected costs of compliance.

Counter-Threat

Confronted with a threat but unwilling to comply with the accompanying demands, the target may respond also with counter-threat. In experimental studies, the use of threat has been found to lead often to the use of counter-threats (Hornstein, 1965; Tedeschi and Bonoma, 1977). Counter-threat is also frequent in the interactions among national leaders. Russell Leng (1980) studied influence attempts in fourteen disputes between nations. He found that actions taken to increase the magnitude and credibility of threats tend to be associated with extreme responses by the target — either outright compliance or defiance in the form of counter-threats and punishments. The sequence of threat and counter-threat may develop into what has been called a conflict spiral (Jervis, 1976; Bacharach and Lawler, 1981:chapter 4) or threat spiral (Milburn and Watman, 1981). In such a spiral, threats (and possible coercion) by each side continue to elicit similar responses from the other side, with the severity and explicitness of the threats increasing over time, perhaps culminating in a major fight.

When is counter-threat likely to be used? First, the target may find compliance with the demands of the threatener unacceptable because of its tangible and symbolic costs. In addition, the target may interpret the threat as a sign that the threatener has aggressive intentions and will continue to make further demands and threats if the present threat is successful (Jervis, 1976; Nardin, referred to in Bacharach and Lawler, 1981:125). Concern about the competitive or aggressive intentions of the threatener may lead the target to try to show that it cannot be "pushed around." Under these circumstances, a counter-threat will often be seen as the most appropriate way in which to show such firmness and discourage the original threatener either from carrying out its threat or from making additional ones. Counter-threat also is more likely when the target of the threat is resentful of being threatened himself (Milburn and Watman, 1981: chapter 8). Such resentment may arise from the feeling that the threat is illegitimate or that it is a challenge to the target's status (Snyder and Diesing, 1977:chapter 3). By responding in kind with a counter-threat the target is able to express anger and assert his equal status.

In order to make credible counter-threats, the target must of course have sufficient power. Bacharach and Lawler (1981:129) assert that punitive threats are least likely to be effective when power is equal. Milburn and Watman (1981) suggest that a slight inequality of power may be associated with conflict spirals. Leng (1980) found that defiant responses by national leaders to threats by other nations occurred most often when the adversaries were equal in power.

However, when the power of two sides to injure each other is high, the target of a threat may be cautious in issuing counter-threats. Hornstein (1965) found that, for bargainers having equal power, counter-threat was least likely to be used when the bargainers had great ability to harm each other. Wright (1965) has found that both equality of power and high destructive power of nations tend to inhibit disputes from escalating to war. Apparently recognition of mutual capacity for harm may lead to some restraint.

While counter-threat may discourage the other side from imposing penalties and discourage it from pressing present and future demands, the use of this tactic has some possible disadvantages as well. The primary disadvantage is that one's counter-threat may lead to a further escalation of threats and coercion by one or both sides. Thus, use of counter-threat is more likely when decisionmakers believe that it will not escalate the dispute to a higher level of coercion or they have little concern about this outcome occurring (e.g., because they believe that the costs of a fight will be low or because they expect to win a fight).

In summary, we may expect that national leaders will be most likely to respond to threats with counter-threats when the following set of conditions is present: (a) they judge that the costs of present compliance are high and anticipate that compliance will lead to future demands; (b) they see the threat against them as illegitimate or a challenge to their status; (c) their power relative to the threatener is at least equal but the destructive power of the two sides is not high; and, (d) they see counter-threat as a way of asserting their equal status and discouraging coercive action and demands by the other but do not see it as likely to result in a (wider) fight or do not give a very negative value to a fight.

Countering with Coercion

The circumstances that would lead the target of a threat to respond with coercion generally are similar to those that would lead it to respond with threat. (The response may of course be a combination of threat and coercion.) One key difference lies in the target's perception of the intent of the threatener. The target may perceive that the threatener has hostile intent and will (sooner or later) take some aggressive action regardless of whether the target complies with the present demands. Also, the target may have little confidence that defensive preparations or counter-threats will deter his adversary. Given such expectations, it may seem better to strike first at the threatener than to wait to be harmed. Such a preemptive action will seem particularly appealing if there is perceived to be an advantage for the side that uses coercion first. The events leading up to World War I provide a good illustration of this process. The major European powers engaged in a sequence of threats and counter-threats. As the crisis deepened, leaders of each nation perceived a high and increasing level of hostility by their opponents (North, Brody, and Holsti, 1964). Each became convinced of the hostile intentions of the other and eventually of the inevitability of war. Since there was a military advantage in quick military action, each responded to the threat of the other by hurrying to mobilize and to strike the first blow (Stoessinger, 1982).

Threat and Stress

In making a threat, the threatener often assumes (explicitly or implicitly) that the target will react rationally in terms of the benefits and costs of compliance versus defiance. However, when great punishment is threatened and especially if there is a need to make decisions quickly, the targets of threat may be under considerable stress. Much evidence has accumulated showing that a high level of stress typically interferes with efficient cognitive functioning (Janis and Mann, 1977).

Even under stress, the threatened decisionmaker will still be influenced by what he sees to be the likely outcomes of his actions and by how he feels about such outcomes (i.e., the analysis presented above should still be valid). However, his perceptions and evaluations may be distorted. Persons under high stress tend to see fewer options for action than actually exist. They tend to exaggerate their opponent's hostility. They may react fatalistically to their danger and are prone to anger and despair.

Such reactions under stress may mean that the target of threat may not react rationally. He may comply quickly out of panic or despair without considering fully alternatives of defense and counter-threat. On the other hand, he may refuse to comply because he fails to consider alternative means of reaching his goals while complying with the demand made, because of excessive anger at the threatener, or because of a defensive fatalism about the threat ("What will be will be"). Alternatively, because of his exaggerated perception of the threatener's hostility, the target may respond to threat with an attack on what he sees as a dangerous enemy. Even when stress is not high, misperceptions in conflict situations are likely to be common. But they are likely to be even greater when the decisionmaker is under great stress.

The main point here is that the target of threat may become unpredictable in his reaction to a threatener who assumes the target is making a cool, objective calculation of costs and benefits of all alternatives. This is one reason why threats are dangerous. If a threat is to be made, it will usually be wise to try to make it in such a way that it does not create great stress for the target. Steps to reduce stress might include giving the target ample time to respond, refraining from communicating hostility, and suggesting positive ways for the target to reach his goals without defying the demands. Making threats less stressful may reduce their frightening impact somewhat and also give the target time to prepare a strategy for countering the threat. But an effective threat is likely to remain effective, and reducing its stressful impact on the target may prevent his responding in an irrational and possibly disastrous way.

Positive Inducements

So far we have considered the effectiveness of threat in isolation. Discussions of important policies such as deterrence often focus exclusively on the effective use of threat, its magnitude, its credibility, etc. However, it is more realistic to view threat within a broader framework of influence (George and Smoke, 1974; Rosecrance, 1981; Baldwin, 1978). Viewed from this perspective, the answer to whether the leaders of another nation will comply with a demand (e.g., that they refrain from an attack on some small country) does not depend only on the magnitude and nature of the threats that can be made against them. It depends also on the positive incentives that can be created for compliance as well as on other possible sources of influence, such as the invocation of norms of legitimacy. The subject of influence through positive incentives will be pursued further in chapter 9. At this point it is sufficient to note that to make threats (including deterrent threats) most effective, it may be useful and at times crucial to combine them with other means of influence.

Summary and Policy Implications

Discussions of threat, and especially of deterrent threats, usually have focused on the magnitude and perceived certainty of the penalties threatened as keys to the effectiveness of threat. Our discussion also indicates that the perceived cost of defiance in terms of tangible penalties is important. However, we have seen that compliance with demands under threat depends also on a number of other important factors. These include the intangible costs of compliance (e.g., in prestige and reputation for resolve), opportunities to reach important goals by alternative means while complying, and the benefits and costs of alternatives to compliance (e.g., of defense, counter-threat and counter-coercion).

The tangible benefits for the target of complying with a demand under threat will increase as the magnitude of the possible penalty for defiance increases and as the credibility of the threat increases. A threat will be seen as more credible as: (a) the threatener becomes more capable of carrying it out; (b) the threatener states his intention explicitly and makes clear the conditions under which the threat would be carried out; (c) the threatener has carried out his threats and found the results rewarding in the past; (d) the motivation of the threatener is high in the issue at stake; (e) the costs to the threatener of carrying out the threat (e.g., from retaliation by the target) will be low; and, (f) the costs to the threatener of *not* carrying out his threat will be high (e.g., because of commitments previously made).

Compliance with demands under threat also has costs for the target of the threat. Part of such costs are tangible. By changing its (intended) behavior, the target must accept an outcome the threatener wants and forego moving toward the outcome it wants itself. The magnitude of this tangible cost of compliance increases as the importance of the goal sought increases and as alternative ways of reaching the goal are seen as lacking feasibility. Threats, including deterrent threats, tend to be less effective as compliance requires that the target give up what it sees as vital goals toward which there are no good alternative routes. A nation using threats (including deterrent threats) as a mode of influence would be well-advised not to back an adversary into a corner where it may take a risky gamble despite convincing threats. Rather, the threatener should try to leave open or even facilitate some means for the other nation to reach its important goals in permissible ways.

The costs of compliance to a threat also include nontangible costs often intrinsic to compliance, such as loss of prestige and loss of reputation for resolve. Such nontangible costs are likely to increase as threats (and accompanying demands) are seen by the target as less legitimate, as they involve demands for some action (compellent threats) rather than to refrain from some action (deterrent threats), as they are more public, and as they concern situations likely to be repetitive. Users of threat should try to reduce as far as possible for the target the costs in prestige and reputation that compliance will bring. Possible methods for doing this include emphasis on common norms relevant to one's demands, making threats privately rather than publicly, pointing to the uniqueness of the present situation (to make the other's resolve reputation less salient), and providing for face-saving formulas that will permit the other side to retreat gracefully rather than with humiliation.

Whether a nation's leaders comply with the demand of another under threat depends not only on the benefits and costs of compliance but also on the relative advantages of alternative actions. In cases where national leaders believe that the costs of compliance are very high but they cannot defend themselves against the threatened penalties for noncompliance, they may defy the threatener and simply accept the risks of punishment. Such a course becomes more likely as the magnitude of the penalty threatened becomes lower and/or their expectancy of it being imposed becomes lower.

In many cases, the target of threat, finding the costs of compliance to be too high but fearful of the penalties threatened, may try to defend against the penalties. An effective defense will reduce the potential costs of the penalties threatened and will raise the costs for the threatener to carry out his threat (possibly dissuading him from carrying out his threat). A target of threat is most apt to react with defiance and an attempt to defend itself when the costs of compliance are seen as high, the target is capable of mounting an effective defense, and the cost of defense is less than the expected cost of compliance. Clearly, threats—especially those that are very costly for the target to comply with—should not be made if their enforcement can be countered to any great extent by defensive measures that the target can take.

Frequently the target of threat responds with counter-threat or with coercion. Counter-threats are more likely when, in addition to the target seeing compliance as costly, he sees the threatener's actions as illegitimate and as a challenge to his own status. Counter-threats by the target serve to express his anger and to assert his equal status. The likelihood that the target of threat will react with counter-threat and/or counter-action is increased if the target interprets the threat as showing that the threatener is hostile or is embarked on a continuing policy of aggression. Given this interpretation of the threat, counter-threat or counter-coercion may be used not only to deter enforcement of the threat but also to show firmness—i.e., that one cannot be "pushed around." Counter-coercion, rather than just counter-threat, tends to be used when the target perceives not only hostile intent from the threatener (and thus an inevitable clash) but also an advantage to the side that attacks first.

Use of counter-threat or counter-coercion requires not only strong motivation for defiance but also the necessary power to threaten or use coercion effectively. Threat has been found to elicit counter-threat and counter-coercion most often when the two sides have about equal power. However, when the two sides have the capability of inflicting great damage on each other, they tend to be cautious in using threats or force.

Users of threat need to be alert to the possibility that, rather than securing compliance, they may provoke the other side to counter-threat and even to attack. This danger is especially great when dealing with an adversary of equal power and especially when, in the event of war, there is an advantage to the side that strikes first. To minimize such provocative effects, threats—if they are to be used at all—need to be made in a way that elicits minimum resentment from the target. Even more importantly, threats and accompanying demands need to be made in a way that signals clearly that they do not reflect hostile intent or unlimited demands. The threat (if it is necessary at all) should be put in a broader context of communications that recognizes the basic goals of the other side and shows willingness to be cooperative in reaching them, does not reflect lack of respect for the other side, and does not signal intention to harm the other or make more threats and demands. Although this context may be clear to the threatener, it may not be at all clear to the target. If the target believes otherwise, he may respond in a way that leads to an escalating spiral of threat and counter-threat and eventually to open conflict.

7 Arms Buildups: Deterrent
or Provocation?

When a nation is engaged in an ongoing dispute with another nation, it often builds up its arms. Such a buildup may be intended primarily to deter attack by its adversary. Stronger armaments may also be seen as useful for threatening other nations in order to win political or economic concessions. In addition, more arms may be seen as necessary for actually fighting a possible war—either one started by the adversary or by one's own nation. What effect is an arms buildup by one nation likely to have on an adversary?

One set of questions concerns the effect of an arms buildup by one nation on a possible arms buildup by its adversary (or adversaries). To what extent is the arms level of one nation a reaction to the arms level of an adversary? If an arms race between two (or more) nations begins, under what conditions does it level off or even de-escalate, and when does it continue to escalate, apparently unstable and perhaps out of control?

A second set of questions concerns the effects of arms buildups on the preservation of peace. Are arms buildups by a nation generally effective in deterring an adversary from attacking and therefore in preserving peace? Or do arms buildups generally have the opposite effect of leading to war? This chapter will consider these questions, with particular attention to the issue of whether and under what conditions arms buildups promote peace or war.

Effects of Arms Buildups on Arms of Adversary

When two (or more) nations are rivals for political or economic advantage, an arms buildup by one may be accompanied by a similar buildup by the other. Examples of adversaries who have engaged in apparent arms races since World War II are Greece and Turkey, Israel and several Arab states, India and Pakistan, Iran and Iraq, Argentina and Brazil, and the United States and the Soviet Union (Majeski and Jones, 1981; Smith, 1982).

What is the process that drives the buildup of arms by rival nations?[1] Some writers have described a process based on defensiveness and misperception on both sides (Jervis, 1976). A's defense preparations may be viewed with alarm by B's leaders, who may see them as showing a possible intent by A to attack B. Therefore B may increase its own military forces further (both as a cautionary measure and as a deterrent to A), which then leads A to further increase its forces, and so on.

Lord Grey, British foreign secretary before World War I, described the psychological dynamics behind this process in these words:

> The increase of armaments, that is intended in each nation to produce consciousness of strength, and a sense of security, does not produce these effects. On the contrary, it produces a consciousness of the strength of other nations and a sense of fear. Fear begets suspicion and distrust and evil imaginings of all sorts, till each Government feels it would be criminal and a betrayal of its own country not to take every precaution, while every Government regards every precaution of every other Government as evidence of hostile intent. (Grey, quoted by Jervis, 1976:65)

While an arms race may be the product of mutual fear, it may also begin with military preparations by one nation that reflect actual aggressive intent. For example, the arms race between Britain-France and Germany from 1936 to 1939 was begun by a German military buildup that reflected Hitler's plans for conquest.

While it seems clear that the arms buildup of a nation may be—at least in part—a reaction to the behavior of a rival, the nature of this process needs clarification. First, there is the question of what each nation is reacting to. Some arms-race models have posited that the level of one nation's arms is a function of the level of its rival's arms (Zinnes, 1976:chapter 14). Empirical studies of this phenomenon often have examined the way in which the military spending of one nation is related to that of a rival.

Ward (1984) found that the United States and the Soviet Union do tend to respond to one another in a race, but that this is not accomplished directly through military budget competition. Rather, they have reacted to the perceived difference between the level of weapons in their own stockpiles and those in the arsenal of their opponent. He asserts, "While there has been arms competition between the two major superpowers over the last thirty years, such competition is largely a consequence of hardware, not budget, comparisons" (Ward, 1984:6). There is evidence also that nations react more to *change* in their opponent's arms than to their absolute level (Hollist, 1977).

A nation may increase its arms in reaction to high tension between itself and a rival rather than to the rival's arms levels. Rattinger (1975) found military spending by the Warsaw Pact nations related to East-West tension (though this was not the case for NATO countries, which reacted more to their adversaries' arms spending). Cusack and Ward (1981) found that military spending by the United States and by the Soviet Union was related more to tension with the other than to changes in military spending by the other.[2] Zuk and Woodbury (1986) also found that arms spending by the United States was affected greatly by the state of American-Soviet relations.

Colin Gray (1976:chapter 4) has discussed several different patterns of possible interaction between nations with respect to their armaments. One is a "mechanistic" reaction pattern in which the actions of one nation trigger a specific reaction by the other to offset any advantage for the first (e.g., if nation A increases its bomber forces, nation B may quickly strengthen its air defense system). Another is a "macro-response" pattern that shows a series of "lagged, broadfronted, lurching responses" by each side as it perceives major shifts in the political intentions and capability of its adversary. The general U.S. arms buildup in the 1980s, which followed the major Soviet buildup in the 1970s and the expansion of Soviet troops beyond its borders in this period, is an example of this type of macro-response. Gray also notes a "differential response" pattern in which one side may be more reaction-prone than the other. Such a one-sided reaction pattern was found by Rattinger (1976) for some phases of the Israeli-Arab arms buildups and by Majeski and Jones (1981) for some of the arms "races" they studied.

As the discussion so far suggests, it has been assumed often that the military spending of one nation is primarily a reaction to a perceived threat (and in particular the arms buildup) of its rival(s). The term arms race itself suggests such a process. However, some studies have found internal factors *within* each nation generally to be more important than international competition in determining arms expenditures. Rattinger (1975) studied the defense spending of NATO and Warsaw Pact nations from 1951 to 1974. He found that, in general, bureaucratic momentum influenced defense spending more than did the spending of the other bloc or international tensions. Cusack and Ward (1981) found that changes in military spending by the United States and by the Soviet Union from 1949 to

1978 generally were explained better by internal forces (especially by war mobilization in the United States and by leadership changes in the Soviet Union) than by either changes in the defense expenditures of their rivals or by tensions with their rivals.[3] Allison and Morris (1976) have described the process by which the United States developed weapons systems such as Minuteman missiles and MIRV (multiple warheads on missiles). They conclude that weapons are developed and deployed as a result of a lengthy political-bureaucratic process in which the major units are the military services and their subunits. Allison and Morris also stress the pressures from Congress (especially from beneficiaries of arms projects) and from defense contractors as well as the limited power of any administration to change ongoing long-range weapons programs. They declare:

> While actions of foreign governments and uncertainty about the intentions of other countries are obviously important, the analysis above suggests that the weapons in American and Soviet force postures are *predominantly* the result of factors internal to each nation. Not only are organizational goals and procedures domestically determined, but the resulting satisfactions of political officials are to be found overwhelmingly at home. . . . Therefore, actions by the Soviet Union serve primarily as justification for American participants in the bureaucratic struggle to advance weapons that they favor for reasons only tangentially related to Soviet behavior. (Allison and Morris, 1976:126)

Gray (1976:chapter 2) has outlined a variety of the domestic forces that may drive arms spending. These include:

(1) *Interservice action-reaction processes.* Military services may compete for money, prestige, and expansion of their missions. For example, the U.S. Air Force and the U.S. Navy may each strive to be the leader in strategic nuclear weapons.

(2) *Electoral politics.* Arms spending decisions may be influenced by political processes. For example, there is evidence that President Johnson overruled his defense secretary and decided to proceed with an antiballistic missile (ABM) system at least partly to avoid attacks by Republicans on a "soft" defense policy (Halperin, 1972).

(3) *Organizational momentum.* Military organizations are engaged in activities that lead naturally to further arms spending. For example, the Special Projects Office of the Department of the Navy has the job of developing, procuring, and deploying ever more sophisticated missile-firing submarines.

(4) *"Follow-on imperatives."* Under this heading, Gray describes the

desire of the armed services to maintain steady work for important defense production lines.

(5) *Technological innovation.* Research scientists continually develop new ideas for weapons, which may then be produced in order to gain a lead over the other side or to counter the possibility of its developing this type of weapon. For example, the development of MIRV technology led to a large increase in the number of nuclear warheads deployed by the United States.

Whether and how much an arms buildup is affected by forces internal to each nation rather than by the actions of a rival nation may vary from case to case. Majeski and Jones (1981) studied arms expenditures of twelve pairs of nations involved in apparent arms races. They found arms expenditures to be independent in the case of seven of them (including the United States and the Soviet Union). But in five cases (e.g., Greece and Turkey, Iran and Iraq) the arms expenditure of at least one of the rivals was dependent on the arms expenditures of the other.

Hollist (1977) also found a competitive process underlying the arms procurement of some nations but not of others. Arms procurement by the United States responded to changes in arms by the Soviet Union, that of Israel to changes by Egypt, and that of Egypt to changes by Israel. However, Hollist found the importance of the "action-reaction" factor to be "less than clear" and internal factors more significant in the other cases he examined (Iran-Iraq,[4] India-Pakistan).

Whether an action-reaction process is found in a given case may depend on the measures of arms procurement that are used as well as on the period of time that is studied. In a study of arms races in the Middle East, Rattinger (1976) found no evidence of an overall action-reaction process in the arms buildup of Israel and its Arab adversaries from 1967 to 1973. However, he did find evidence of an Israeli-Syrian missile boat race during this period. Rattinger notes that, "By disaggregating overall military postures into individual services for which multiple indicators are available, it is possible for arms race research to identify reaction processes which not only would have gone unnoticed in aggregate data but also come closer to real world decision processes" (Rattinger, 1976:501). The sensitivity of results on the determinants of arms procurement to the specific data used is also indicated by the work of Cusack and Ward (1981). Using different estimates of total military spending by the United States, the Soviet Union, and China led to substantially different findings about the determinants of military spending.

It is possible of course that a nation's arms procurements may be determined by both the arms of its rivals and by internal forces within its own nation. After reviewing models of arms races, Moll and Luebbert (1980) conclude that both reaction to other nations' actions and internal bureaucratic factors need to be represented in such models. Hollist (1977) has used several "consolidated arms race models," which include both external determinants (such as arms buildups by the rival nation and grievances) and internal determinants (such as indicators of cost constraints and of technological capability). Ostrum (1978) has proposed another model that explains U.S. defense expenditures in terms of both external and internal forces. According to this model, initially the armed forces make a request that is based substantially on their anticipations of the future arms expenditures of the Soviet Union. This request then is subject to the pressures of bureaucratic and political processes as it is filtered through the executive branch and Congress. Both Hollist and Ostrum report some success in accounting for observed levels of arms expenditures.

On the basis of all the evidence, it seems reasonable to conclude that arms expenditures in any nation are likely to be determined by some combination of both external stimuli (arming by the other nation or tensions) and internal forces (political processes, bureaucratic momentum, etc.). The importance of external versus internal forces and of particular elements within each set of forces will vary among nations and different time periods. Further research is necessary to learn more about the conditions that tend to make particular determinants of arms expenditure more or less important in any given case and about the way the various determinants may combine in their efforts. What does seem clear is that—whatever the particular mix of forces—there are powerful processes that tend to drive arms expenditures of rival nations higher and higher.

Outcomes of Arms Races

What are the outcomes of an arms race? Do both sides eventually level off in their arms expenditures, and perhaps even eventually reduce their arsenals? Or do they arm at an ever-increasing rate, thus producing a "runaway" race? Most important, do arms races lead to war?

The Course of an Arms Race

An important characteristic of an arms race is whether it tends to be stable, in the sense of tending to reach equilibrium. An arms race tends toward equilibrium if the rate of change in the armaments of both countries tends toward zero. If, on the other hand, the arms race tends to move away from equilibrium (i.e., the two nations tend to continue increasing or decreasing arms) then the race is unstable (Zinnes, 1976).

Most discussions of the stability of arms races have been based on the work of Lewis Richardson (1960; see also Rapoport, 1957). Richardson's theory of arms races states that the change (increase or decrease) in the arms expenditures of nation X is described by the following equation:

$$\frac{dx}{dt} = ky - ax + g,$$

where $\frac{dx}{dt}$ is the change in X's arms over time,

x is the level of nation X's arms,

y is the level of nation Y's arms,

g is the level of grievance (or ambitions) that nation X has toward nation Y,

k represents the reactivity of nation X to the arms level of nation Y, and

a represents the strain (e.g., cost) imposed on X by its own armaments level.

The term ($+ky$) in this equation indicates that increases in the arms of nation X become greater as the arms level of its rival, nation Y, increases. (The effect of the arms level of nation Y is weighted by nation X's reactivity, or sensitivity, to the arms level of nation Y, indicated by the coefficient k.)

The term ($-ax$) in the equation shows that increases in X's arms level become smaller as its own arms level becomes greater. (The effect of its own arms level is weighted by the strain of its armaments, indicated by the coefficient a.) The term ($+g$) in the equation indicates that the total amount of X's arms spending increases as its grievances (or ambitions) vis-à-vis its rival increase. The grievance component of the equation affects the total amount of arms spending but not (as in the case of the other terms) the rate of change of spending.

The rate of change in the level of nation Y's arms over time is described by a similar equation:

$$\frac{dy}{dt} = lx - by + h,$$

where $\frac{dy}{dt}$ is the change in Y's arms over time,

l indicates the reactivity of nation Y to the arms level of nation X,

b indicates the strain on nation Y of its current level of arms, and

h represents the grievance (or ambitions) of nation Y toward nation X.

(As before, x and y represent the respective arms levels of the two countries.)

In the above equations k and l may be thought of as "stimulation" coefficients. They represent the extent to which each nation is stimulated to increase its arms spending by higher levels of armaments of its rival. On the other hand, a and b may be thought of as "restraint" coefficients: they represent the extent to which increases in each nation's arms spending is restrained by the strain (of cost, political turmoil, etc.) that its own arms level puts on it.

In order for an arms race to be stable (i.e., for the changes in the arms levels of both to tend toward zero) the following condition must be present: a b>k l. That is, the product of the restraint coefficients must be greater than the product of the mutual stimulation coefficients (Rapoport, 1957).

The length of time it takes for unstable arms races to "explode" (i.e., for the rate of increase to rise sharply) or for stable arms races to "damp down" (i.e., for the rate of increase to fall sharply) varies for different cases. Theresa Smith (1980) has estimated the "stability coefficients" for a sample of fourteen historical arms races. Some races are estimated to reach stability in a fairly short time. For example, the arms race between Norway and Sweden from 1895 to 1905 was estimated to reach approximate equilibrium (little increase by either side) in a little over four years. Some other races, though they are stable in the long run, would take decades to reach an equilibrium. For example, Smith estimates that the arms race between Israel and the Arabs from 1957 to 1966, though stable in the long run, would have taken over fifty-six years to damp down to near-zero increases by each side. (This race was, of course, interrupted by war.) Smith found that an arms race that does not damp down within the time span of the competition between the two parties, or that does not decline greatly in magnitude, tends to lead to war.

Arms Control

The Richardson-type model of arms races just described assumes that each nation acts independently of the other, leading in some cases to a result (e.g., a runaway arms race) that neither may want. However, nations may try to mutually limit or reduce their arms levels to their mutual benefit. In the twentieth century especially, as weapons have become more destructive, there have been many efforts to control or reduce armaments (Goldblat, 1983; Frei, 1982:chapter 8). There have been some limited successes— e.g., the Washington Naval Treaty of 1922, which limited the number and size of great power battleships for about a decade, and the U.S.–Soviet treaty of 1972 that limited sharply the number of antiballistic missiles each side could deploy. However, efforts at arms control and disarmament have been largely ineffective in stopping the overall long-term buildup of weapons (Taylor, 1982).

Part of the difficulty lies in the fact that arms competitions may reflect political competitions. Huntington (1958:80) states: "The most notable successes in arms limitation agreements have been combined, implicitly or explicitly, with a resolution of other controversies. . . . If both sides are to give up their conflicting ratio-goals and compromise the differences, this arrangement must coincide with a settlement of the other issues which stimulated them to develop the conflicting ratio-goals in the first place." Writing about the lack of progress in efforts to control the U.S.–Soviet Union arms competition, Trevor Taylor also emphasizes the importance of political considerations, asserting that "states will not agree to restrictions which are incompatible with their political goals, means, and conflicts" (Taylor, 1982:54).

Willingness by leaders of disputing nations to limit or reduce their arms will depend not only on the existence of disputes with rivals but also on whether they see military force as necessary or useful for reaching their policy goals in such disputes. The more that a stalemate in power with a rival exists and seems likely to continue into the future, and the more costly a possible test of military strength with a rival is perceived to be, the more attractive mutual arms control is likely to appear. Also, the more that nonmilitary means (e.g., negotiation) seem feasible for resolving existing disputes satisfactorily the more national leaders will be willing to forgo military methods and agree to arms-control measures.

The difficulties in controlling arms competitions, however, are not limited solely to the frequent desire of nations to acquire arms to pursue or defend their own national interests. Nations engaged in an arms competition (even one tied to political competition) may realize that it will be to their mutual benefit to control arms and yet be reluctant to agree to such a course. The key difficulty is that each nation may doubt the trustworthiness of the other, suspecting that the other would secretly violate the agreement and win a military advantage. As Brams and his co-workers (Brams, Davis, and Straffin, 1979) point out, an agreement can be reached only if it is verifiable. Thus, methods and procedures that aid in verification—e.g., photographic surveillance, on-site inspections, exchange of information—can be very valuable in facilitating arms-limitation agreements.

Schelling (1976) has pointed out also that the chance for arms-control agreements may be missed because either or both competing nations misperceive the preferences of the other. He discusses, for example, a situation in which both sides would like to acquire a certain weapon but would prefer that *neither* nation have it rather than *both* having it. However, each may believe that the other side prefers to have this weapon even if both sides acquire it. This misperception will lead both to believe that the inevitable outcome lies in both sides having the weapon. One side then acquires it, confirming the belief of the other. The result is one that neither side wishes. Schelling suggests that unilateral declarations by one side of its intentions—e.g., "We won't acquire weapon A if you don't acquire weapon A"—is likely to be the most effective way to promote arms limitation.

Overall, the chances for formal or tacit arms control between rival nations may be expected to increase as: (1) disputes between them decrease in importance or intensity; (2) equal power and high costs of a fight make military means appear more unattractive to both sides; (3) alternative means of resolving disputes appear more feasible; (4) each side indicates its intention to refrain from further buildups; and (5) effective methods for verifying arms levels are available.

Arms Buildups and War

Do arms buildups of rival nations lead to war? One view is that the spiraling of a mutual arms buildup brings with it a rapid increase in fear, suspicion, hostility, and tension, which sooner or later explodes into war. This position is explained by Paul Diehl as follows: "The arms competition and its accompanying hostility increase the probability that a dispute involving force will occur (Houweling and Siccama, 1981). The fear and suspicion of the spiral process erode the bases for a possible compromise in the conflict. War is an almost inevitable and rather ironical result of the misguided efforts of a set of nations seeking security" (Diehl, 1983a: 1-2).

But arms races are not always followed by war (Huntington, 1958; Lambelet, 1975) and some analysts have suggested that they may at times actually help prevent war. Huntington (1958) and Gray (1976) argue that arms races may become a substitute for war—e.g., that the United States and the Soviet Union may substitute competition in arms preparation for actual warfare. Gray also states that an arms race may provide time for conflict-resolution processes to work. To the extent that arms competition encourages hopes for victory tomorrow, he suggests, it reduces the incentive to fight today. Lambelet (1975) states that because an arms race may increase the stakes of war (i.e., the amount of death and destruction likely), the probability of rival nations actually going to war may be decreased.

The most influential argument that runs counter to the idea that arms races lead to war is that of deterrence. The argument is, of course, that by building up its arms, a nation can deter attack from an adversary. What is the evidence on the question of whether arms races lead to war? Michael Wallace (1979; 1982) investigated the question by studying ninety-nine serious disputes between great powers from 1816 to 1965. He found that when a dispute was preceded by an arms race, it was much more likely to result in war than when an arms race had not occurred.

However, Wallace's methodology has been criticized by several scholars (Weede, 1980; Altfeld, 1983, Diehl, 1983b), and Diehl has reanalyzed basically the same data used by Wallace but with the use of different methods. Diehl (1983b:8) concludes that "no meaningful covariation exists here between mutual military buildups and dispute escalation." Inspection of Diehl's tables indicates that there is a tendency for the presence of an arms race prior to a dispute to be associated with escalation to war, but this association is very much weaker than that found by Wallace.

Diehl (1983a) has also studied another set of data based on "enduring rivalries" between major powers in the period 1816 to 1980. An enduring rivalry was defined as one in which the two nations engaged in at least three serious disputes within a period of fifteen years. Diehl states that "There appears to be no significant association between the intensity or the duration of an arms race and the likelihood of dispute escalation [to war]" (Diehl, 1983a:7). However, Diehl's tables do show some tendency for arms races to be associated with war.

Another approach to investigation of the possible link between arms races and war has been made by Teresa Smith (1980), who has related the occurrence of war to the *stability or instability* of arms races. Smith identified cases in the late nineteenth and twentieth centuries in which bilateral arms races between rival nations had occurred for at least four years. She then computed coefficients indicating the stability of each arms race (i.e., whether arms expenditures were tending to decrease toward zero or to accelerate) and also noted whether or not each arms race was followed by war. Smith's data suggest that arms races that are unstable in the short run are more likely to end in war than are stable races. In another analysis of arms races Smith (1982) reports that a large upward surge in arms expenditures, especially by status quo nations, is typical of the final year before a war erupts. Smith also reports that of twenty-five terminated arms races, twenty-one (84 percent) ended in war. She comments that "Most but not all arms racing eventually ends in war."

Finally, Singer and his colleagues found that disputes between major powers were likely to escalate to war if two conditions were both present: a military buildup had preceded the dispute and the nations were about equal in military power. They found that "While only 13% of all major power militarized disputes since 1816 escalated to war, that figure rose to 20% when the parties were approximately equal in military terms, and to 75% if such parity was combined with a rapid military buildup during the three years prior to the dispute" (Singer, 1981:11).

The evidence reviewed above generally indicates some association between the occurrence of an arms race and the outbreak of war, especially when the race accelerates and when the adversaries are about equal in strength. However, there are some historical cases in which an arms race did not end in war and some in which the outbreak of a war was not preceded by an arms race. Moreover, there is other evidence that the mutual destructive power that results from the arms buildups of two rivals—such as that of the United States and the USSR from 1960 to 1982—may result in mutual deterrence of attack and thus in peace (Weede, 1982; 1983).

When, then does an arms buildup lead to war and when to peace through deterrence?

The Decision to Use Force

We may begin to explore this topic by asking the question: When will the leader(s) of one nation decide to attack another nation?[5] Our examination of how decisionmakers choose among options (chapters 4 and 5) indicated that usually their first step is to screen out actions that do not meet the objectives they feel are most vital. National leaders may rule out launching an attack if, for example, they believe that such action would result in a number of casualties that they view as unacceptable. Among actions not initially dropped as unacceptable, the attraction of each remaining option depends on the value given to possible outcomes, with each outcome value weighted on the basis of the decisionmaker's expectancy that this outcome will result from the action in question.

If A attacks B (or B's ally), certain outcomes may be expected to occur almost automatically, regardless of the reaction of the target of the attack. These intrinsic outcomes include the material costs of attack, political gains or losses, moral satisfaction or dissatisfaction from upholding or violating principles (e.g., acting courageously), and demonstrating one's own toughness. Other possible outcomes following an attack by nation A on nation B (or B's ally) depend on B's reaction. B may surrender without a fight, in which case A will win on the issues in dispute. Or B may resist and a fight (war) will ensue. In weighing the advantages and disadvantages of attacking B, A's leaders will be influenced by the value they place on each of these outcomes and by their perceptions about how likely each outcome is to occur. Thus:

(7-1) The attraction of attack = intrinsic value
on nation B (or B's ally) of attack
to leader(s) of nation A

+ (value of winning   perceived probabil-
on issues in   × ity that B will *not*
dispute without a   fight if attack
fight   occurs*)

+ (value of a fight × perceived probability that B will fight
if attack occurs*)

The value of a fight to national leaders will depend on several factors (see chapter 5). First, a leader will anticipate certain direct or intrinsic consequences from a fight. These may include some positive anticipated outcomes (e.g., solidarity in his own society), but the negative intrinsic outcomes—casualties, financial costs, material damage—are usually most salient. The overall value of a fight will depend also on the value to the leaders of winning that fight and on the value of losing it.[6] These values of winning and of losing the fight would each be weighted by leaders' expectancies of winning and of losing. Thus:

(7-2) Value to A's   intrinsic   (value of winning   perceived
leaders of a fight = value of + if it attacks   × probability
begun by A   fight   of winning
if it attacks*)

+ (value of losing   perceived
if it attacks   × probability
of losing
if it attacks*)

The attractiveness to nation A's leaders of the possible action of attacking nation B is meaningful only in comparison to the attractiveness of the alternative option, not attacking. (The alternative of not attacking actually

---

*Strictly speaking this term is a weight deriving from perceived probability but not necessarily equal to it (see chapter 4).

may include several suboptions, such as conceding all that nation B wishes, attempting to compromise differences with B, demonstrating one's military strength as a threat, and taking no new initiatives. For present purposes, however, we may treat the "no attack" option as a single alternative.)

The attraction to A's leaders of not attacking B will be affected first by its intrinsic value, which may reflect such benefits (costs) as political support for choosing a nonviolent policy. The attraction of not attacking B will be affected also by the value to A's leaders of the present peace. How advantageous (or disadvantageous) is the status quo and how much promise is there of things changing for the better (by evolution, compromise, etc.)? The value of the present peace will have to be weighted by a leader's expectancy that this peace will continue—i.e., that B will not attack and thus cause the present peace to disappear. The overall attraction of not attacking B will be affected also by the value of a fight if B attacks, weighted by the expectancy that B will attack. Thus:

(7-3) attraction to   = intrinsic   (value to A of   perceived
       A's leaders   value to   + present peace ×   probability
       of not   A of not   that B will *not*
       attacking B   attacking   attack*)

                                       + (value to A of a   perceived
                                          fight started ×   probability
                                          by B   that B will
                                                              attack*)

The value to A of a fight begun by adversary B will depend on the same types of factors that determine the value of a fight begun by A. Thus:

(7-4) value to A's   = intrinsic value (value to A of   A's perceived
       leaders of   to A of a   +   losing if B   ×   probability
       fight begun   fight begun   attacks   of losing if
       by B   by B   B attacks*)

                                          (value to A of   A's perceived
                                       + winning if B   ×   probability of
                                          attacks   winning if
                                                             B attacks*)

The magnitude of the relevant values and perceived probabilities for a fight begun by the adversary may differ from those begun by one's own side. Most notably, in some cases the probability of winning will be seen as less if one is the target of a first attack than if one initiates an attack at a time and under the circumstances of one's own choice.

If decisionmakers find the attraction of an attack greater than the attraction of not attacking, then we would expect them to launch an attack, otherwise not. This does not assume that decisionmakers necessarily make such momentous decisions as a result of cool, deliberate, rational calculations. As discussed in chapter 5, the values they attach to various outcomes (continuation of the status quo, war, winning over the other, etc.) may be influenced by strong emotions such as anger and fear, by ideology, and by personal needs. Their perceptions of the likely outcomes of their actions may be distorted by wishful thinking, by defensive avoidance of negative information, by bureaucratic filtering of information that doesn't fit official expectations, and so on.

Faced with awful choices, they may be under great physical and emotional stress. However, evidence on decisionmaking (see chapter 4) does indicate that decisionmakers—whatever the basis for their feelings and perceptions—will, either explicitly or at some intuitive level, take into account some possible outcomes of their actions, how they feel about (value) these outcomes, and what they expect the outcomes of their actions to be.

The Effect of Nuclear Weapons

What difference does the availability of nuclear weapons have on a decisionmaker's choice to attack another nation? If both sides have nuclear weapons—as the United States and the Soviet Union do today—does not the great destructive power of such weapons make initiation of war irrational for leaders of each side? Certainly the attraction to leaders of one nation of an attack on an adversary (equation 7.1) would usually be drastically lower if nuclear arms were involved. Their use by the adversary, as well as by one's own side, would make the intrinsic value of a fight appear extremely negative. Moreover, the anticipated death and destruction might be so extensive that the prospect of "winning" such a fight might appear meaningless; the victor would only preside over a vast graveyard. Yet, even when both sides have nuclear weapons, there are circumstances in which an attack on an adversary might appear attractive, or at least less unattractive than the alternative.

First, the leaders of a nation considering an attack may choose to use conventional weapons only in such an attack. For example, when American officials made plans to bomb Soviet missile bases in Cuba, only conventional bombs were considered. The intrinsic value of a prospective fight would then reflect (a) the value of a fight with conventional weapons, weighted by the expected probability that the fight would be conducted only with conventional weapons, plus (b) the value of a fight that involved nuclear weapons, weighted by the expected probability that the fight would escalate to nuclear weapons. If decisionmakers believed that a fight probably would remain at a nonnuclear level, they might judge the intrinsic value of a fight (i.e., its costs) to be acceptable. Presumably the Soviets would make such a calculation in deciding whether to attack Western Europe.

National leaders would be most likely to gamble on the probability that a fight they started would not escalate to a nuclear level if the status quo ("the value of the present peace" in equation 7.3) was seen as extremely undesirable and the value of winning as a result of their attack was high. As we saw in chapter 4, decisionmakers tend to run some risk of very large losses in order to avoid certain smaller losses or to escape very undesirable situations. This was true in the Cuban missile crisis, when American leaders were willing to run a substantial risk of a catastrophic nuclear war in order to be sure of avoiding a much smaller but painful political-military loss. Under certain circumstances, national leaders might find even an attack with nuclear weapons to be more attractive than the alternatives.

Another possibility is that the leaders of one side may believe that they can strike a swift crippling blow on the other side, leaving the other unable to retaliate effectively. The other side would then have to surrender without a fight or could only retaliate so feebly that the damage and casualties for one's own side would be acceptable. Both American and Soviet strategists have worried about the temptations of a successful first strike for the adversary if a "window of opportunity" for such action should be present. However, many analysts believe that a nuclear attack under such circumstances is very unlikely (e.g., Carnesdale et al., 1983:49–51; Allison, Carnesdale, and Nye, 1985:chapter 3).

A more dangerous set of circumstances that might lead national leaders to attack with nuclear weapons is one in which they fear being attacked themselves. Suppose that during the course of some crisis the leaders of the United States (or those of the Soviet Union) become convinced, or even highly suspicious, that the adversary was going to launch a nuclear attack on their country. Suppose also that if they were to absorb such a first strike they would suffer death and destruction that was far greater than the losses they would suffer from the smaller, more disorganized enemy forces remaining following a first strike of their own. In that case, even though the attack would not be an attractive option—i.e., the value of a fight begun by them would still be very negative—the attraction of doing nothing and probably being the target of attack would be even less. A president or premier might decide with some anguish that his responsibility to his own nation required that he order a nuclear first strike (see for example, Fischer, 1984:18–21).

Thus, while the presence of nuclear weapons creates the possibility that war may have an unprecedented negative value for national leaders, it does not rule out the possibility that the leaders of one nuclear-armed nation may find an attack on another nuclear-armed nation to be more attractive than other options.

When two nations are both armed with nuclear weapons, each is likely to find attack on the other to be an attractive option only under the special circumstances described above. What is more likely is that one nuclear-armed nation may be tempted to attack a small nation that is a client or ally of a nuclear-armed adversary. Thus, the United States bombed North Vietnam, a client of the Soviet Union, made plans to invade Cuba, a Soviet ally, at the time of the missile crisis, and might in the future find an invasion of Soviet-backed Nicaragua to be an attractive option. The Soviet Union to date has taken no direct military action[7] against American-backed regimes but might be tempted to do so in the future—e.g., against Pakistan if that nation's sheltering of Afghan rebel forces became intolerable for the Soviets. Either superpower may find a military action attractive if it believes it very unlikely that the other superpower would intervene directly. In that case, even if the attacked small nation resisted, the costs of a fight would be relatively low and—since the decisionmakers would expect to win—the overall value of a fight might be fairly high. However, such an action could be very dangerous. The other nuclear-armed nation, in an effort to support its ally, may get drawn into the fight, with possible horrendous consequences.

How Arms Buildups May Affect Decisions

An arms buildup by one or both sides may affect the attractiveness of the attack and of the no-attack option for each side (as shown in equations 7.1 and 7.3). They may do so by changing (1) each side's expectancies concerning the likely actions of the other and/or (2) its perception of the value of a fight initiated either by one's own side or by the adversary, based on perceptions of the costs of a fight and on expectations of which side would win. (Note, however, that some factors in the equations above—e.g., the value of the present peace and the value of winning over the other side —are likely to be determined primarily by factors other than arms buildups.)

Table 7.1   Conditions Under Which Arms Buildups Increase (Decrease) the
Likelihood of Attack and Defense

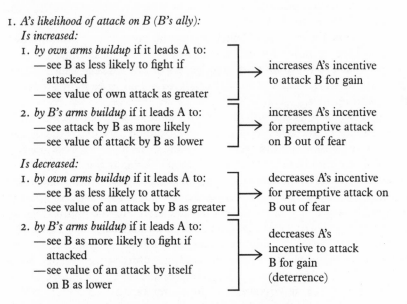

1. *A's likelihood of attack on B (B's ally):*
   Is increased:
      1. *by own arms buildup* if it leads A to:
         —see B as less likely to fight if   increases A's incentive
           attacked   to attack B for gain
         —see value of own attack as greater

      2. *by B's arms buildup* if it leads A to: increases A's incentive
         —see attack by B as more likely   for preemptive attack
         —see value of attack by B as lower   on B out of fear

   Is decreased:
      1. *by own arms buildup* if it leads A to: decreases A's incentive
         —see B as less likely to attack   for preemptive attack on
         —see value of an attack by B as greater   B out of fear

      2. *by B's arms buildup* if it leads A to:
         —see B as more likely to fight if   decreases A's
           attacked   incentive to attack
         —see value of an attack by itself   B for gain
           on B as lower   (deterrence)

2. *B's likelihood of defending itself (ally) against attack by A:*
   Is increased:
   —*by own arms buildup* if it leads B to see value of a fight
     when attacked by A as higher

   Is decreased:
   —*by A's arms buildup* if it leads B to see value of a fight
     when attacked by A as lower

Depending on the specific changes an arms buildup produces in the
perceptions of a nation's leaders, they may become either more or less
likely to attack the adversary. Table 7.1 summarizes the types of perceptual
effects an arms buildup may have and their effects on the likelihood of one
nation attacking another.

An arms buildup by an adversary (B) will *decrease* the likelihood that A
will attack B (or an ally of B) if B's buildup (1) leads A to see B as more
likely to fight if it (or an ally) is attacked and/or (2) if it leads A to see the
value of a resulting fight with B as lower (because B's arms buildup would
make a fight more costly to A or reduce A's chances of winning). These
perceived effects constitute deterrence. The arms buildup by a potential
target of attack (B) has made an attack less attractive for A. If a counter

arms buildup by A resulted in similar changes in perceptions by the leaders of B, then B would tend to be deterred from an attack on A. Thus, to the extent that arms buildups change the perceptions of rivals in these ways, they would tend to lead to deterrence and to peace.

However, an arms buildup by an adversary (B) may have different effects on the leaders of nation A. An arms buildup by B will tend to *increase* the likelihood that A will attack B if this buildup: (1) leads A to see B as more likely to initiate an attack and/or (2) A sees the value of a resulting fight with B as more negative to itself than a fight that A itself initiates. Obviously, such a perceived situation constitutes a threat to A. If the perceived threat becomes great enough, A's leaders may be tempted to launch a preemptive strike against B in order to end this threat or to improve the outcomes of a likely war.[8] It should be noted that the attractiveness of attack has not increased for A. Rather, the attractiveness of not attacking has decreased so that an attack may have become relatively more attractive.

So far we have considered the possible effects of an arms buildup by an adversary (B) on the perceptions of A's leaders (and thus on A's likelihood of attack). But it is important to consider also the possible impact on A's leaders of an arms buildup by their *own* nation. An arms buildup by nation A will *increase* the likelihood that its leaders will initiate an attack on an adversary, B (or an ally of B), if it causes A's leaders (1) to see B as less likely to fight if B (or an ally) is attacked; and/or (2) to see the value of an attack by itself on B (or B's ally) as higher—i.e., the costs lower or the probability of winning higher.

Changes in perceptions in these directions will increase the incentives for A's leaders to attack B (or B's ally) for whatever gains it believes may stem from such an attack. Of course, as equations 7-1 and 7-2 indicate, the attractiveness of such an attack will depend also on the intrinsic value of an attack (e.g., the political gains seen as stemming from an attack) and on the value of winning a fight—e.g., on the value of gaining territory or gaining military-political dominance as a result of winning.

While an arms buildup may tempt the builders to initiate an attack for gain, it may also have effects that discourage an attack. An arms buildup by nation A will tend to decrease the likelihood that it will attack adversary B to the extent that this buildup leads A's leaders (1) to see B as less likely to initiate an attack and/or (2) to see the value of a war started by B as more favorable to itself (A) than it was previously seen to be—i.e., the costs to A would be lower or A's chances of winning better than before its own arms buildup. Such perceptions would give A's leaders a greater sense of security than they had previously. In other terms, the attractiveness of not attacking would be greater than it was previously.

The overall impact of arms buildups on the likelihood that A will attack B (or B's ally) will depend on the relative size of these various subeffects. This in turn will depend on how an arms buildup by either side affects A's expectations about B's actions (whether B will attack or fight if it or an ally is attacked) and A's perception about the outcomes of a war started by one side or by the other.

The occurrence of a war depends not only on the likelihood that one side will attack the other but on the willingness of the target to fight if it (or an ally) is attacked. Therefore, table 7.1 also indicates how the likelihood that a target (B) will defend itself, or an ally, may be affected by arms buildups. The likelihood that B will fight if attacked by A will be increased by its own arms buildup if it leads B to see the outcome of a fight initiated by A as more favorable to itself. B will be less likely to fight when attacked, and especially if an ally is attacked, if an arms buildup by A leads B to see the results of a fight initiated by A as less favorable to itself. (Of course, additional factors—such as beliefs about the requirements of national honor, political pressures, and concern for setting precedents—may also affect the decision to fight if attacked.)

This analysis of the effects of an arms buildup by one or both sides on the likelihood that A will attack B and that B will fight if attacked may, of course, be reversed. In that case one would consider, in a parallel way, the effects of the arms buildup(s) on B's likelihood of attack and on A's likelihood of fighting in defense.

The overall effect of the arms buildup (by one or both sides) will depend on its effect on the probabilities that each will attack and that each will fight if attacked. If the arms buildup makes A more likely to attack and B more likely to defend, then war is clearly more likely. If A is more likely to attack but B less likely to defend, then the overall effect will depend on the relative size of the increase in A's likelihood of attacking as compared to the decrease in B's likelihood of defending.

Determinants of Perceptions

We have seen that leaders' decisions to attack an adversary depend in part on their expectations about the future actions of their adversaries and about the outcomes of possible armed conflict. Expectations about the actions of the adversary depend, in turn, on perceptions of his capabilities and of his intent (Morgan, 1983). It is, therefore, of great importance to try to understand some of the factors that may shape these vital perceptions. Let us consider first the ways in which the arms situation may affect leaders' perceptions. (For discussions of arms policy, see Frei, 1982; Harvard Nuclear Study Group, 1983; Snow, 1986; Thee, 1986; Harris and Markusen, 1986.)

Arms Situation

The military capability of a nation's weapons depends, in large part, on a combination of their characteristics, their numbers, and their deployment. Weapon systems vary in many characteristics (e.g., their range, speed, accuracy, and explosive force) that affect their capacity to inflict damage on various types of targets. Weapons vary also in ways that affect their own vulnerability to damage from attack, such as in their mobility, their active protection (e.g., defensive missiles on bombers), and their passive protection (e.g., concrete "hardening" of missile sites).[9]

A greater number of weapons of a given type usually will increase a nation's capability to impose damage on targets that such weapons have the capability to hit. In the case of nuclear weapons, if the ratio of the number of warheads on nation A's missiles to the number of nation B's missile launchers is high, then nation A may have the ability to destroy nation B's missiles in a first attack. In addition, particular deployments of weapons will increase their capability to impose damage on certain types of targets. For example, American missiles can hit Soviet missile sites more quickly when deployed in Germany than when deployed in the United States.

The capability of a nation's weapons to impose damage on an adversary's targets depends also on the adversary's vulnerability to attack. Such vulnerability depends, in turn, on the characteristics, numbers, and deployments of the adversary's weapons. For example, the capability of nation A's armed forces to impose damage on the industry of nation B depends in part on the industry's dispersion, on its passive protection (e.g., placement underground), and on the numbers and types of defensive weapons that B deploys.

In addition to considering the factors that determine the present military capability of each side, it is important to consider also trends in the characteristics, numbers, and deployment of weapons. The rates of change in these aspects of arms in previous years—and especially the most recent years—will, when projected into the future, indicate the probable military capabilities of both sides in coming years.

As a result of its own weapons posture (especially the characteristics, numbers, and deployment of its weapons) and the weapons posture of its adversary, a nation may have the following military capabilities:

(1) *Defensive capability.* Its arms are capable of warding off, to some extent at least, the destructive potential of an attack.

(2) *Retaliatory.* In the event of an attack it will have sufficient capability remaining to inflict significant damage on the attacker.

(3) *First strike.* It has the capability to inflict, in a first attack, such great damage on the offensive capability of the adversary that the adversary would lack capability thereafter to do significant damage in retaliation.

Several of these types of capabilities may be related. In particular a defensive capability may be helpful, though it is not essential, in creating either a retaliatory or a first-strike capability. By minimizing damage to its own military force, a defensive capability can help to make retaliation possible. And by minimizing damage to its own cities and industry, defensive capability may make retaliation by an adversary less possible (thus enhancing its first-strike capability).

A number of possible combinations of military capabilities are possible. These include: (1) defensive only; (2) retaliation (perhaps combined with defense); (3) first-strike (perhaps combined with defense); and, (4) retaliation and first strike. What kind of effect will each of these capabilities (and trends with respect to these capabilities) have on the perceptions of each side and therefore on the likelihood of war? This question must be considered from two perspectives: the capability of each single side and the capabilities of both sides taken as a pair. Let us turn first to the effect of the arms posture of a single nation

Defensive only. Although historically nations have not built up military strength that had solely defensive capability, they have at times emphasized defense (e.g., France's military posture of the 1920s and 1930s). Moreover, there has been recent discussion of the possible advantage of a defensive military strategy (e.g., Galtung, 1984; Dankbaar, 1984). A present-day example of defensive weapons is the antiballistic missile.

A buildup by nation A of capability for deflecting attack from nation B would make the outcome of an attack by B less favorable for B. To that extent, it would reduce the incentive for B to attack in hopes of gain. In addition, a capability by A that is defensive only will convince B that it need not expect and fear attack by A. Thus, B will have no incentive to attack preemptively out of fear of A.

However, unless a defensive capability is near-perfect, an attacker will be able to accomplish at least part of his objectives of destruction. Moreover since the attacker does not have to expect retaliation, the cost to him of an attack may be relatively low. Thus, a capability that is defensive only may not serve as a sufficient deterrent to attack.

Retaliatory. Present-day examples of weapons useful primarily for retaliation are long-range bombers, small mobile missiles, and Poseidon submarines. Such weapons (or a substantial portion of them) may survive enemy attack and inflict great damage in return. At the same time they do not have the combination of speed, accuracy, and destructive power necessary to destroy an adversary's military force in a surprise attack. Defensive weapons, as well as passive defensive measures, could contribute to a retaliatory capability by increasing the survivability of retaliatory weapons in the event of enemy attack.

A retaliatory capability should have a deterrent effect on a potential attacker. It would make the outcomes of an attack—in terms of retaliatory damage to be suffered and even the probability of winning a war—appear less favorable to an attacker. At the same time A's retaliatory capability would not appreciably raise B's expectation of a first strike by A since A does not have the capability. Thus, B would have little incentive to attack A preemptively out of fear.

To provide an effective retaliatory capability, such weapons would need to be deployed in numbers sufficient to inflict unacceptable damage on an adversary (allowing for losses suffered in an enemy first strike and in reaching the enemy's targets). However, the number of retaliatory weapons deployed could not be so large that the force begins to acquire, and be seen as having, a first-strike capability. For example, since several small accurate missiles might be able to destroy a hardened missile site, a force of small missiles that could put five missiles on each enemy launcher might constitute a first-strike force. In addition, to maintain its retaliatory-only character, the force would have to be deployed as far from the adversary's borders as possible.

First strike. Examples of weapons whose characteristics are suitable for first strike are the American MX missiles and the Soviet SS18 missiles. The combination of speed, accuracy, and destructive power of such weapons makes them capable of destroying an adversary's offensive weapons in a surprise attack. At the same time, they are—at least when deployed in fixed-site silos—vulnerable to a surprise attack by an enemy. Thus, they are useful primarily as first-strike weapons themselves. Deployed in sufficient numbers (relative to the number of sites for significant enemy weapons), they provide an effective first-strike capability.

Such a first-strike capability raises the probability of a war occurring in two ways. First, it may tempt the side (A) possessing this capability into attack. If it can destroy the adversary's ability to retaliate, then it can expect little damage to itself and a victory over its adversary. At the same time the adversary (B) is given incentive to attack. The fact that A has acquired a first-strike capability is bound to cause B to worry that A may plan to use it. Thus, B may be tempted—especially in a crisis—to attack first itself. At the least B would probably adopt a "launch on warning" policy for its own offensive forces, raising the probability of accidental war. Moreover, since A's leaders will recognize B's incentive to attack preemptively in order to avoid being the victim of a first strike, there may be additional incentive for A to use its first-strike capability while it has the chance.

Even though a given nation does not have a first-strike capability, trends in arms buildups that will result in its acquiring such a capability soon may also lead to war. In particular, the side that sees itself becoming vulnerable in the future may be tempted to attack preemptively before the danger materializes.

It should be noted that defensive measures, which in themselves may reduce the possibility of attack by making the outcomes less favorable for an attacker, will tend to have opposite effects if combined with the buildup (or existence) of a first-strike capability. Under such conditions defensive weapons and defensive preparations may signal to the adversary an intent to create conditions under which one could win a war. Thus, it may signal an intent to attack and may stimulate the adversary to preempt or at least to adopt "launch on warning" procedures. Such a dangerous situation would probably be created, for example, if one of the superpowers deployed—or was close to deploying—an effective "space defense" system while also having a potent offensive force. Similarly, certain civil defense procedures —especially the order to begin evacuation of cities—might, if begun, signal to an adversary that an attack on it is imminent.

Retaliatory plus first-strike capability. Some weapons are suitable either for a first strike or for retaliation against a first attack. One example is the Trident II missile, deployed on U.S. Trident submarines. Submarines can fire these missiles with sufficient speed, accuracy, and destructive power to knock out Soviet missile sites in a surprise attack from a position close to Soviet shores. At the same time, while at sea the submarines are not very vulnerable to being destroyed in a Soviet attack. If deployed in a mobile fashion (as originally planned), the U.S. MX missile would also be suited to both first-strike and retaliatory purposes.

Such weapons will have mixed effects on the likelihood that an attack by an adversary (or by one's own side) will occur. Because of their retaliatory capability, such weapons in sufficient numbers to do unacceptable damage will make the outcomes of an attack less attractive for an adversary, thus having a deterrent effect. To the extent that the adversary is thought to be deterred, the side deploying these weapons will have less fear of a first strike and thus will be less tempted to preempt.

However, because of their first-strike capabilities, if such weapons are deployed in numbers great enough to mount an effective first strike (i.e., enough to hit all the offensive weapon sites of the adversary), then the side deploying them may be suspected of planning to initiate an attack. This perception is especially likely to be present if these weapons have been deployed faster than the other side's, have moved the deployer to a position of superiority in such weapons, or have been deployed close to the adversary's borders (e.g., the U.S. Pershing missiles). Faced with a choice of "use them or lose them" for its own now-vulnerable weapons, the adversary may decide—especially in a crisis—to preempt. At best it may adopt a launch on warning policy that heightens greatly the possibility of firing missiles under a false alarm. Moreover, since the first nation will realize that the other may try to preempt, it will be subject to similar pressures to launch on warning and perhaps to preempt the preemption.

Overall, an arms buildup that provides both a retaliatory and a first-strike capability will result in a greater likelihood of attack—by one side or the other—than an arms buildup that provides only a retaliatory capability.

The capability of both sides. The arms situation should be considered not only in terms of the effects of each nation's arms but also in terms of the combination of the military capabilities of both nations. One, both, or neither side may have a first-strike capability. Where neither side has a first-strike capability, then neither, only one, or both may have a strong retaliatory capability if it is attacked. (If one side has a first-strike capability, then only that same side can have an effective retaliatory capability. If both sides have a first-strike capability then neither can have an effective retaliatory capability.)

How do these situations compare in their susceptibility to war? The situation in which neither side has a strong first-strike capability is least likely to lead to war. If neither side is able to destroy a large part of the military capacity of the other in a first strike, then it would usually have to expect the costs of a fight to be high. These expected costs of a fight would increase as the retaliatory power of the adversary increased. At the same time, if the adversary also does not possess a strong first-strike capability, then the actor is not tempted to attack out of fear of being vanquished by a surprise attack. Moreover, since each side would recognize that the adversary lacks incentives to attack, it would tend not to attribute such an intent to the other. Thus, the most stable situation is one in which neither side has an effective first-strike capability.

If only one side (A) achieves a substantial first-strike capability, the situation becomes more dangerous. The side possessing the first-strike capability may now see that the value of an attack is high since—with retaliation minimal—it would expect to suffer relatively little damage and would expect to win the war easily. This would be even more true if the side with a first-strike capability also had a significant defensive capability against any surviving retaliatory force.

Its adversary (B), realizing that the other may see a net advantage to an attack, may also see the other as intending to attack. The adversary—in this vulnerable position—is likely to be frightened and with good reason. One possible reaction by the vulnerable side is to preempt before the other can launch a successful first strike (or before it attains such a capability fully). However, while possible as an act of desperation, this probably would not be an attractive option since B will not, by our assumption, be able to cripple A's power in a first strike. Only if B is at least equal to A in strength and sees a high probability of a successful first strike by A is preemption in this situation likely to be attractive to B. Otherwise the vulnerable side, B, is likely to try to placate A, granting A what it wants without a fight. Thus, when only one side, A, has a first-strike capability, the result may be political dominance by A but not war.

The most dangerous situation of all is that in which both sides have a substantial first-strike capability. Each side then has a positive incentive to attack the other in order to win its political objectives at relatively little cost. However, since each side knows the other has that temptation and thus may intend to launch a first strike, it has a clear incentive to preempt such an attack with a first strike of its own. Moreover, since each side knows that the other may preempt out of fear, as well as out of ambition, it has all the more incentive itself to preempt. Thus, whether or not either side wants war, each is likely to be poised to attack the other. Any small incident that raises tension and leads to a suspicion that the other may be about to attack can be enough to trigger a holocaust.

Quester (1986) has addressed the question of whether the United States should try to match the Soviet Union if the Soviets should deploy first-strike strategic or conventional weapons. He concludes that such a policy would be foolish, commenting: "Rather than redressing the balance, such a matching procurement on the U.S. side would work to compound and intensify the imbalance, in the sense of making a first strike all the more attractive, in making crisis situations all the more unstable" (Quester, 1986:22).

How about the balance of retaliatory capability between adversary nations? It might happen that one nation has the capability to retaliate against attack by an adversary (e.g., by hitting its cities) while the adversary nation does not have this capability. (This situation might arise if a nation had weapons capable of destroying an adversary's cities and also had defenses effective enough to prevent the adversary from doing great damage to its own cities.) A nation with such a unilateral retaliatory capability would be able to use its forces also to initiate attack on its adversary's cities. It would, therefore, be in a position to bully its adversary into accepting whatever political demands it chooses to make.

If both sides have a good retaliatory capability and potential damage from war is very great, mutual deterrence should tend to be stable. This has been the essential situation existing for the United States and the Soviet Union for the past few decades. A condition of "mutual assured destruction" (in the event of an attack by either on the other) exists. While there is always the danger of miscalculation, technical error, or insanity leading to catastrophe, leaders of both sides are highly likely to try to avoid war.

What if two adversary nations both had only defensive weapons? In such a situation, war would be highly unlikely. The main practical difficulty is in getting to such a situation from a situation in which both sides have many offensive weapons (i.e., the situation for the United States and the Soviet Union today). If during this transition one side acquired the ability to defend itself against attack but retained its offensive capability as well, it would have a unilateral capability to destroy the weapons or cities of its adversary. As noted above, such a situation would be unstable since the nation in the favored position might be tempted to attack its weaker rival, while the rival might be tempted to attack before it was completely vulnerable.

There is another practical difficulty lying in the way of completely eliminating offensive weapons such as nuclear missiles. If any nation succeeded in hiding or producing a few such weapons, all other nations (unless their defenses were 100 percent effective) would be at the mercy of the potential attacker. Therefore it probably is prudent to permit nations already possessing nuclear weapons to retain a small number (i.e., to preserve a retaliatory capability) in order to deter the use, or threat of use of such weapons against themselves.

In summary, the situations most likely to lead to war are those in which one, and especially both, rival nations have a first-strike capability. The situations least likely to lead to war are those in which both nations have an effective retaliatory capability or both have only a defensive capability. However, the transition from a primarily offensive to defensive posture may be dangerous, and a small retaliatory force may continue to be necessary even if this transition is accomplished successfully.

Number of weapons. What is the effect of the number of weapons each side has on the likelihood of war? This question has received attention, especially with regard to the number of nuclear weapons that two rivals possess. Intriligator and Brito (1984) have suggested that the continuing mutual buildup of nuclear weapons by the United States and the Soviet Union may actually have reduced the chances of war. They argue that if each side has a large and approximately equal number of nuclear weapons, each will see an attack as resulting in a large number of casualties to itself (through retaliation) and will therefore be deterred from attacking. To the extent that each side perceives that the high cost of a nuclear attack would similarly deter the other from attack, each side also would have a low incentive to preempt out of fear.[10]

These points about the likely deterrent effect of a large number of weapons on each side seem valid, assuming these weapons have retaliatory capability. However, a buildup of large numbers of weapons by each side is likely to have opposite effects as well that would increase the chance of war. First, such a buildup will tend to give each side greater first-strike capability as well as greater retaliatory capability—e.g., because of its greater ability to knock out the other side's airfields and command and control facilities. Moreover, each of the two sides engaged in an arms race is likely to exaggerate the strength and the rate of buildup of the adversary (Galtung, 1976) and perceive that the other may already have acquired, or be on its way to acquiring, a first-strike capability.

The continuing acquisition of more and better arms by each side is likely to affect also the perceptions each side's leaders have of their rival's intent. They are likely not to see their rival's arms buildup as defensive action, perhaps made in response to their own arms buildup, but rather as indicating an aggressive design (Jervis, 1976). Such perceptions are especially likely to be present if the past behavior and statements of the other side indicate that it is hostile and willing to use force in pursuit of its aims.

Perceiving the arms buildup of the other side as indicating an aggressive intent and a possible first-strike attack, national leaders will be disposed to put their own forces on a heightened state of readiness to respond—perhaps adopting a launch on warning policy. Such a policy is highly dangerous because it may cause a retaliation to be launched on a false alarm. Leaders who fear an attack from an adversary may even decide, especially in a crisis, to attack first themselves.

Intriligator and Brito (1984) also argue that a small and equal number of nuclear missiles on each side would constitute a dangerous situation that could easily lead to war. This conclusion is based on the assumption that under such conditions there would be a "tremendous advantage of striking first" that would make it advantageous for each side to initiate an attack. This might well be true if the few nuclear missiles of each side had a perfect first-strike capability—i.e., were capable of destroying all the missiles of the other side with certainty in a first attack. But it surely seems possible for the two sides to follow weapons policies—either by independent action or by agreement—that would make the weapons of each side relatively invulnerable to those of the other side (e.g., by having them sea-based or mobile). If each side had a small force with a retaliatory capability only, this would create a more stable situation than if each had a large and growing force. Each would be able to inflict only limited destruction on the other (thus removing the temptation of a knockout blow) and each would be deterred by the other's ability to retaliate in kind.[11] Moreover, with each side not building up armaments (and perhaps reducing their numbers), neither side would be so likely to perceive aggressive intent by the other and therefore would be less likely to attack first itself. In addition, of course, if a war should ever occur for any reason, fewer weapons would mean less destruction and less possible effect on the environment.

Overall, then, a situation in which each side has a small and nongrowing number of nuclear weapons (assuming these weapons are not vulerable to first attack) appears to carry less risk of war than a situation in which each side continues to build a larger and larger number of nuclear weapons. It is not, however, the absolute number of nuclear weapons on both sides that is most crucial; rather, it is the extent to which either or both sides have a first-strike capability and the extent to which the arms policy and the other actions of each side have communicated an aggressive intent to the other. The first-strike capability of each side depends not only on the number of nuclear weapons but also on other factors, such as the ratio of each side's nuclear warheads to the other side's missile launchers. Perceptions by each side of its adversary's intent in building up its weapons depend not only on the types of weapons built and the rate at which they are built (discussed above) but also on nonmilitary factors, to which we now turn our attention.

Nonmilitary Determinants of Perception

Arms buildups do not occur in a vacuum. They occur rather in the context of other events and in the context of leaders' beliefs about the adversary and about the outcomes of possible wars. These contextual factors may exert independent effects and perhaps modify the effects of arms buildups on leaders' expectations about the adversary's future actions and about the likely outcome of a war. In particular, the following additional factors are likely to have importance: (1) past experiences with an adversary; (2) statements by the adversary's leaders; (3) perceptions of the adversary's motives; (4) perceptions of the adversary's risk-taking propensity; and, (5) other beliefs. (See chapter 3 for a general discussion of expectations.)

Past experiences. Expectations about the future behavior of an adversary are affected by his past behavior (Deutsch, 1973; Bacharach and Lawler, 1981). When a nation has used its arms offensively before, expectations that it will use them in the same way in the future will rise. For example, the American invasion of Grenada, in the context of previous American intervention in Central America, led Nicaraguan leaders to intensify defenses against a U.S. attack on their nation. The effect of past actions on expectations of future action is likely to be greater as the weapons and situations involved are more similar.

Past experiences also are likely to affect expectations about the likely outcome of a possible war. For example, the swift victories of Israel against Syria in three recent wars would undoubtedly affect perceptions by both sides' leaders about the probable outcome of another war between them.

Statements by the adversary's leaders. Expectations about the behavior of an adversary may be influenced by the adversary's expression of his intentions. For example, statements of a "no first use" policy for nuclear weapons by the Soviet Union may somewhat affect U.S. leaders' expectations while the refusal of the United States to renounce first use of nuclear weapons (at least in defending against conventional attack) may somewhat raise Soviet expectations that such weapons might be used offensively. Perhaps of greater importance than public statements are the statements of military and political officials concerning war doctrine and strategy—e.g., of the possible advantage to the side that strikes first (see, for example, Kaplan, 1983). Such statements may be examined closely by an adversary in order to draw inferences about possible intent.

Statements of policy or strategy will of course be more convincing if they are backed up by action. For example, a statement by American officials that they did not intend early use of nuclear weapons in the event of war in Europe would be more convincing if the United States also moved its tactical nuclear weapons much farther behind the front lines.

Perceptions of the adversary's motives. Regardless of another nation's capabilities or what its leaders say about their intentions, perceptions of their intent will be strongly influenced by perceptions of their motives. As Jervis points out, a nation that is perceived as arming because it fears for its own security is not likely to evoke alarm or much counter-action (Jervis,

1976). Thus, American officials who explained a Soviet bomber buildup in the 1950s in terms of aggressive designs were alarmed while those who saw the Soviet motive as a need for security against the United States were much less concerned. Similarly, the extent to which American or Soviet leaders today feel threatened by a given arms program of the other nation will be affected by their perception of the motives of rival leaders. Such judgments of an adversary's motives, in turn, will be affected by perceptions of his morality, his attitudes toward one's own nation, and his incentives for aggressive versus peaceful behavior (see chapter 3).

Risk-taking by the other. The more the leader of an adversary nation is seen as a risk-taker, the more he will be expected to use his nation's arms under circumstances in which victory is far from certain. For example, American or Soviet leaders would be somewhat more worried about the possibility of a surprise attack by the other if they perceived their adversary's top decisionmaker as willing to take risks or even as reckless.

Other beliefs. National leaders may have other beliefs that affect their expectations about how an adversary will use its arms and about the outcome of a possible test of armed strength. For example, Americans who believe that Communists will never abandon a quest for world conquest, and Russians who believe that capitalist nations are inherently imperialistic will each tend to expect aggressive use of arms by their nation's main adversary. Relevant beliefs also include those concerning whether an exchange of strategic nuclear weapons could be limited or would lead to an all-out exchange and what the world would be like after a war in terms of the physical environment, government, dominance by specific nations, etc.

Overall, then, an arms buildup by an adversary will be interpreted by national leaders according to their relevant beliefs and how they see the past and present relationship between the parties. These factors, combined with the arms situation, will determine their expectations about the future actions of the adversary and about the outcomes of a war. It is important to remember, however, that decisions about whether to attack another nation depend also on the intrinsic values that leaders place on the use of force, on the value to them of the present peace, and on the values they place on winning and losing with respect to issues in dispute (see equations 7-1 and 7-3). These values, which have not been the focus of this chapter, are likely to be influenced primarily by factors other than arms buildups. Figure 7.1 summarizes the previous discussion concerning the effects of arms buildups and other relevant factors on decisions to attack a rival nation.

Figure 7.1   Determinants of National Leaders' Decisions to Attack a Rival Nation

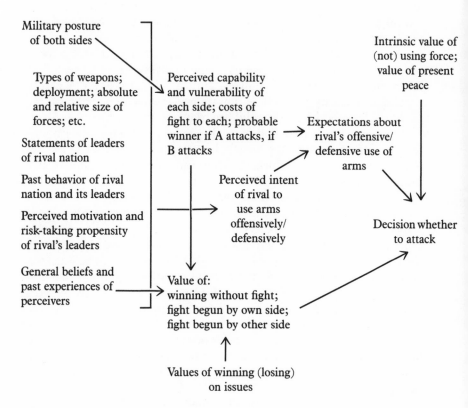

Summary and Policy Implication

When a nation builds up its armaments, a rival nation usually will spend more on arms in order to keep up with its adversary. The greater its relative disadvantage in weapons stockpiles, the greater the rise in the adversary's arms level, and the greater the anticipated future level of the adversary's arms the greater a nation's arms buildup is likely to be. Buildups in each nation's arms also tend to increase as tension with the rival nation increases and as domestic political and bureaucratic pressures for more arms increase. Efforts to lower political tensions between national adversaries will reduce the impetus for arming by each side that stems from perceptions of a hostile and therefore dangerous relationship.

An arms race between two nations is most likely to escalate when the leaders of each nation are highly reactive to arms increases by the other—i.e., when each more than matches the other's increases. National leaders sometimes are tempted to reply to some military increase of the other side by "going them one better." But in order to prevent an arms competition from escalating, national leaders should limit their responses to an adversary's arms buildup to what is truly needed to maintain an adequate defense.

Since each nation will be reluctant to reduce its military spending while a rival nation continues building up its armaments, agreement by both to control or to reduce arms spending can contribute greatly to slowing or reversing an arms competition. Chances for the mutual control of arms increase as political disputes become less intense, as equal power and high costs of war make military means for reaching political goals appear more unattractive, as nonmilitary means for handling disputes become more available, and as verification of mutual restraint becomes more feasible.

When formal agreement on arms limitation is difficult to achieve —perhaps because of mutual hostility and distrust—it may be possible to make some progress by unilateral initiatives. When the desire to limit arms is present on both sides, one nation may be able to get the process under way by taking a first step—e.g., by announcing that it will not test or deploy certain types of weapons if the other does not do so (see Schelling, 1976). One side may also make some reductions in its arsenal of a kind that does not threaten its essential security while inviting reciprocation by the other side (Osgood, 1962; 1984). (See chapters 9 and 10 for a fuller discussion of unilateral initiatives.)

National leaders may build up their armaments with the primary intention of deterring a rival nation from attack. But arms buildups by rival nations tend to be followed by war. To reduce the chances of war, national leaders should follow an arms policy designed to show adversaries (as well as their own side that (1) they will fight if attacked but not attack themselves; (2) the adversary's chances of succeeding in an attack are poor; and, (3) one's own chances of succeeding in an attack are poor. If these perceptions are conveyed, the adversary will be deterred from attack rather than either tempted or frightened into attacking. And one's own side will not attack because it will feel more secure and have little temptation to do so.

What types of arms policy will accomplish these objectives? First, a buildup of defensive weapons (such as antiballistic missiles) or defensive preparations (such as civil-defense measures) may have conflicting effects on the risk of war. By making the outcome of an attack less attractive for an adversary they may help to deter an attack. However, if combined with the buildup (or existence) of a weapons force that has a first-strike capability, vigorous defensive measures may signal to the adversary an intention to attack. A side possessing a good defense against attack and a first-strike capability may in fact be tempted to attack in order to win a political-military victory. But, regardless of its actual intent, its adversary is likely to suspect intent to attack and may therefore adopt a dangerous launch on warning policy or even launch a preemptive attack itself.

Buildup of weapons that provide the capability for either a first strike or retaliation against attack will also have mixed effects on the likelihood of war. Because of their retaliatory capacity, such weapons will help to deter an attack by the adversary. Also, by making their possessors feel more secure against attack, such weapons will reduce their incentive to launch a preemptive attack out of fear. However, because their weapons have a first-strike as well as retaliatory capability, the nation deploying them is likely to be suspected by an adversary of planning a first strike. Such fears may lead this adversary to adopt a launch on warning policy, raising the probability of accidental war and may—especially in a crisis—lead it to launch a preemptive attack.

A buildup of weapons that have a first-strike capability but *not* a retaliatory capability—e.g., the U.S. MX missile or the Soviet SS18 missile in fixed silos—is the most dangerous policy of all. Such weapons are not a real deterrent since they are vulnerable to first-strike attack. At the same time they raise suspicions by the adversary of a first-strike intent. This is likely to lead, as noted above, to a dangerous launch on warning policy or even to a preemptive strike (Steinbruner, 1984).

Assuming that the adversary possesses offensive weapons, the type of weapons buildup that is most likely to reduce rather than to increase the chances of war is that of a force having *only* a retaliatory capability (and not a first-strike capability). Examples of such weapons in the present day are long-range bombers, submarines with older Poseidon missiles, and small, mobile, land-based missiles. Such weapons make the outcome of an attack less attractive to an adversary and thus help to deter such an attack. But because they are not fast enough, and/or accurate enough, and/or destructive enough to destroy an adversary's offensive force before it can be launched, they do not lead the adversary to expect a surprise attack and thus do not frighten him into intentional or unintentional preemption. If both sides have only a retaliatory capability, each is likely to be deterred from attacking the other.

If the adversary does not follow this prescription and instead deploys a force having a first-strike capability, it is *not* in the best interests of one's own side to imitate him. Such actions will make war more likely by providing an incentive for each to strike first. A much safer arms policy is to build up one's own retaliatory capabilities—e.g., by increasing the number of

Poseidon-class submarines, bombers, and small mobile missiles. This would eliminate the first-strike capability of the other and deter it from attack without giving it cause for alarm.

The expectations of each nation's leaders about the future actions of a rival depend on more than just the magnitude and type of the rival's armaments. They are more likely to expect an adversary to use his arms in an aggressive way the more that the adversary has used force aggressively in the past, the more he publicly has left open the option of his using force, the more he is seen as having motivation to use arms aggressively, and the more he is seen as a risk taker.

To be effective, an intelligent arms policy—aimed at removing incentives for the adversary to attack either out of hope of gain or out of fear—needs to be carried out in a context of words and deeds that will lead an adversary's leaders to expect resolute response to attack but not aggressive actions by one's own side. Such a policy would require that national leaders refrain from threats to use arms—especially nuclear weapons —first and from statements of military doctrine that contemplate such first use. (Retaliatory forces would have to be strong enough to serve as a deterrent against first use of arms by the adversary.) National leaders also need to refrain from words or actions that convey an intent to destroy the adversary's system of government or to undermine its vital interests (e.g., for the United States to attempt to undermine the Soviet economy or for the Soviets to attempt to foment social upheaval in Mexico). Instead, national leaders should do things, such as building trade with a rival, that give them (as well as the other) a greater stake in maintaining peaceful relations. Arms acquisitions occurring in a context of actions that indicate a desire for cooperation are more likely to be seen as having a defensive purpose.

Finally, national leaders should be cautious about building a record of actually using force first. Attacks even on small nations (such as on Grenada and Nicaragua by the United States or on Czechoslovakia and Afghanistan by the Soviet Union) will suggest to others a readiness to settle disputes by force. A record of aggressive action therefore will tend to increase expectations by leaders of a major adversary that a nation's arms may be used aggressively against themselves as well.

8 The Use of Coercion

Since there is no central authority in the world, each nation retains the ability and "right" to use coercion against any other nation with which it has a dispute. A wide variety of coercive means may be and have been used.

Sometimes coercion involves the use of physical force. For example, in 1948 the Soviet Union closed the roads leading from West Germany to Berlin; in 1972 the United States bombed heavily the city of Hanoi in North Vietnam; in 1983 Argentina landed troops in the Falkland (Malvinas) Islands, which have been controlled by Great Britain.

In some cases coercive actions involve the imposition of economic costs through the reduction of aid, trade, or credit. For example, in 1965 following a series of anti-American statements and actions by Egyptian President Nasser (including the shooting down of a U.S. civilian plane), the United States reduced its economic aid to that country. When the United States resupplied Israel with weapons during the Yom Kippur War of 1973, Arab oil-producing countries cut back their exports of oil to the United States and other Western nations. When the Soviet Union invaded Afghanistan in 1979, the United States stopped its sale of wheat and other grains to the Soviets.

A variety of other types of punishments may be used against another nation. For example, because of its internal racial policies, South Africa has been ousted from many international organizations; after the imposition of martial law in 1982, the United States restricted air landing rights for Polish planes; and, following the Soviet invasion of Afghanistan in 1979, the United States refused to participate in the 1980 summer Olympic Games held in Moscow.

When is coercion effective in getting another nation to conform with one's wishes? When does coercion lead instead to counter-coercion and perhaps to a spiral of coercion and counter-coercion? This latter question is especially vital when physical violence is used. In this case the question becomes: when is the use of force effective in gaining compliance from an adversary and when does it lead to an exchange of violence, which may escalate to a major, unwanted war?

The Effects of Coercion

Can one side in a dispute get its way by using coercion against—that is, taking actions that punish—the other side? In some cases one side may be able to exert so much force that the other has no choice but to comply. For example, the American defenders of the Phillipines in 1942 had to surrender in the face of Japanese attack when their supplies and ammunition were exhausted. However, we are not concerned here with the use of coercion to overwhelm the other's resistance. That is the subject of military (and perhaps economic) strategy and tactics. Rather we are concerned with the use of coercion as a tactic of influence—what Alexander George and his colleagues (1971) call "coercive diplomacy." We want to know whether and when coercion is an effective way to get the other to concede even though he still has the capability of resisting.

Psychologists have found that punishment often is successful in discouraging unwanted behavior. After reviewing research on punishment, Walters and Grusec state, "If the effectiveness of punishment is assessed in terms of the rapidity and degree of suppression that can be achieved during its application, then there is no doubt that it can be a potent modifier of behavior" (Walters and Grusec, 1977:223). Reviewing evidence about the use of coercion in bargaining situations, Tedeschi and Bonoma (1977) also point out that coercion often is effective in gaining compliance with bargainers' demands, at least in the short run.

However, both these writers and others have also noted extensive evidence that the use of punishment to elicit compliance may lead instead to defiance. Such defiance may be accompanied by counter-aggression and the possibility of an escalating spiral of coercion between the two sides. Tedeschi and Bonoma (1977:235) assert, "An escalation of conflict is usually likely to occur when one party punishes the other. By failing to retaliate against a threat, an individual may leave the impression that he is weak and compliant, thereby inviting further attacks against himself. Even if the target is subjectively willing to accede to a powerful adversary's demands, he may still openly defy the threatener because of this fear that the threatener would be encouraged to make even greater demands in the future."

Even when punishment is effective in eliciting compliance, the effects may not last. When the threat of punishment is removed or surveillance relaxed, behavior the punisher has tried to suppress may reappear in full force (Walters and Grusec, 1977).

In international relations, too, there is evidence both of the possible effectiveness of coercion (at least in the short run) and of the limitations of coercive methods. Barry M. Blechman and Stephen S. Kaplan (1978) have studied the use of American armed forces either to apply or to threaten force in several decades following World War II. They state:

> The weight of evidence is consistent with the hypothesis that discrete uses of armed forces are often an effective way of achieving near-term foreign policy objectives. The aggregate analyses showed clearly that, when the United States engaged in these political-military activities, the outcomes of the situations at which the activity was directed were most often favorable from the perspective of U.S. decision-makers—at least in the short term.
>
> In a very large proportion of the incidents, however, this success rate eroded sharply over time. Thus, it would seem that, to the degree that they did influence events, discrete uses of military forces for political objectives served mainly to delay unwanted developments abroad. (Blechman and Kaplan, 1978:517)

Blechman and Kaplan also found that the use of military forces by the United States generally was more effective in reinforcing ongoing behavior of other nations than in getting them to change their behavior.

Kaplan (1981) has carried out a parallel study of the use of armed forces by the Soviet Union since World War II. Again evidence on the effectiveness of force is mixed. The direct use of force has been successful in getting others to conform to the Soviets' wishes at times, especially in Eastern Europe. However, the use of Soviet armed forces to punish and to threaten other nations has in some instances—notably in the case of China —had little success in securing compliance with Soviet demands.

Blechman (1972) has studied whether Israel's reprisals against Arab nations and political groups for terrorist raids has been successful in discouraging hostile behavior against Israel. He found that the reprisals were effective during some time periods in causing some Arab governments to reduce their support for violence. But the reprisals were not effective in influencing Palestinian terrorists and, even for Arab governments, the positive effects were short-lived. Blechman states: "they have not caused a decrease in violence in the long run" (1972:177).

In addition to research on the use of military coercion, a number of studies of the use of economic coercion also have been made. One wide-spread conclusion is that multilateral economic sanctions rarely achieve their objectives, primarily because they don't achieve universality—i.e., the target has alternative economic partners (Olson, 1979). In addition, a number of writers have pointed out that use of economic sanctions against a nation often leads to increased unity in that nation in defiance of the sanctions (Schreiber, 1973; Olson 1979). After reviewing cases of economic coercion by the United States against small Third World nations, Weintraub (1982) concludes that the success of such coercion in achieving compliance was usually short-lived.

Overall, both the general literature on punishment and coercion as influence techniques and the research on coercion in international relations lead to similar conclusions. Coercion is sometimes successful in gaining compliance with demands, but sometimes it leads instead to defiance or to counter-coercion. Even when coercion is initially successful, this success may be short-lived with the target soon reverting to the prohibited behavior. The key question to be answered then is the following: What are the circumstances in which imposing penalties on the other side in a dispute are most likely to get the other side to concede? On the other hand, under what circumstances is hurting the other likely to be met with noncompliance, with defiance, or with counter-coercion?

The Response to Coercion

When one side in a dispute does something that causes injury to the other, he usually does this in an attempt to get the other to change his behavior —perhaps the position he is taking in the dispute. Alternatively, the side using coercion may intend the injury as punishment for some past undesirable behavior, often with the intent of discouraging its repetition.

The target of the coercion may concede to the wishes of the other, changing his behavior, including perhaps his stand on disputed issues. Alternatively, the target may not change his behavior as the other desires despite the punishment he is enduring or has endured. (If he was punished for a completed behavior, noncompliance would be reflected in a repetition of the "undesirable" behavior.) If he does not comply with the wishes of the other, the target often will employ counter-coercion in an effort to get the other to stop inflicting punishment, as well as for other purposes.

The basic options facing the leaders whose side is the target of coercion are: (1) comply with the other's demands; (2) do not comply but do not use counter-coercion; or, (3) do not comply and use counter-coercion. The choice among these options depends on the decisionmakers' views of the possible advantages (disadvantages) of each alternative action and on their expectancies that various outcomes will result from each action.

Compliance

An important advantage of compliance with the wishes of a coercer is that such concessions usually will bring the punishment to a halt (i.e., end an undesirable status quo). For example, North Vietnamese leaders could expect in 1972 that if they agreed to a peace agreement on American terms the United States would end its bombing of Hanoi. The greater the magnitude of the punishment being inflicted on the target, the greater the potential advantage to him of ending it. Experimental studies have found that as the intensity, the duration, and the frequency of punishment become greater, its effectiveness in securing compliance generally increases (Walters and Grusec, 1977).

Compliance following coercion may be a way not only to end present punishments but also to avoid even larger punishments in the future. National leaders sometimes use low-level coercion against an adversary primarily to signal their determination to inflict much greater punishments if compliance is not forthcoming quickly. American leaders used small-scale bombing of North Vietnam early in that war to signal an intention to devastate that region if the North Vietnamese did not comply with American demands (Thies, 1980). The blockade of Cuba by the United States in 1962 was used primarily to communicate to Soviet leaders the serious American intent to bomb or invade Cuba if the Soviets did not remove their missiles (Abel, 1966). The greater the magnitude of future punishment signaled by present coercion and the more the target expects it to occur if he does not comply, the more likely compliance is to occur.

However, the overall attraction of compliance under coercion will depend also on the magnitude of what would be given up by concessions. George and his colleagues (1971) have pointed out that the motivation of national leaders to comply with coercion is a function of what is demanded. They state also that one of the conditions of effective coercion is that the motivation of the target with respect to the issue be less than that of the coercer. In addition, they argue that to be effective coercion directed toward other nations often must be linked with a "carrot" to make the concessions demanded less onerous.

The importance of the motivation of the target of coercion to persist in his behavior is illustrated by Blechman's (1972) findings concerning the effects of Israeli reprisals for Arab terrorist attacks. Such reprisals had at least short-term effects in curbing support for such attacks by Jordan and

Egypt. But the reprisals had no effect in reducing attacks by Arab Palestinians, the group that cared most about the issue of control of disputed territory.

Writing about the effectiveness of economic boycotts, Weintraub (1982) notes that it was unrealistic to expect an international boycott to cause whites in Rhodesia to give up their privileged position because of the economic costs that such concessions would involve. (Of course, the whites in Rhodesia [now Zimbabwe] did finally give up their control in the face of physical coercive pressure from blacks inside their country.) Similarly, despite the heavy costs in lives and property imposed by American bombing, the intense and long-standing motivation of the North Vietnamese to unify their country led them to endure these costs rather than give up their goal (Thies, 1980).

How much is given up by compliance will depend in part on whether there are alternative ways of reaching important goals other than the behavior that is being penalized. For example, if North Vietnamese leaders had believed that it was possible to arrange national elections to unify Vietnam, they might have had less motivation to persist in their effort to unify the country by force.

In addition to the more pragmatic benefits and costs of compliance under coercion, there are also important consequences of a less tangible kind. These include possible effects on one's status, reputation for resolve, and self-image. We have discussed previously (see chapter 5) the fact that compliance to threats is likely to be seen as lowering one's status and encouraging the threatener (and perhaps others as well) to try to pressure one into further concessions later. Compliance under the pressure of actual coercion is even more likely to be seen as having these effects. Threats can sometimes be made privately, and often the complier can claim that he took (or didn't take) certain actions of his own free will. But actual coercion is almost always public and it is much harder for the target, if it complies with demands, to maintain that it did so voluntarily. Thus, compliance in the face of actual coercion is more likely to be seen as damaging to one's prestige and reputation for standing firm than is compliance under the threat of coercion.

The extent to which the target will be concerned about his reputation for resolve will depend in part on the target's perception of the other—especially the other's hostility, goals, and intentions. If the target believes, as a result of the present coercion and its context, that the other is implacably hostile and has ultimate goals that go beyond his immediate demands, then compliance now will be seen as leading only to further demands accompanied by more coercion. Thus, it may be seen as better to stand firm now than to invite an escalating series of pressures. For example, one of the reasons why American leaders rejected a conciliatory policy at the time of the Berlin blockade is that they believed Soviet actions to be part of a larger design for expansion (Davison, 1958).

Concern with the precedent-setting effects of conceding under coercive pressure is likely to be increased also when the issues at stake are repetitive and are likely to recur. For example, national leaders may be reluctant to submit under coercive pressure to lower their tariffs on certain products because coercive tactics, if successful, may be used again in other tariff disputes.

Compliance with demands under coercive pressure may also involve a cost in personal satisfaction and self-esteem. Coercive acts are likely to cause resentment and anger in the target (Milburn and Watman, 1981). Resentment and anger are likely to increase the more the nature and circumstances of the coercion violate accepted norms of behavior and the less it is seen as justifiable (Tedeschi and Bonoma, 1977). Compliance under such conditions is less likely than when coercion has some legitimate justification (Tedeschi and Bonoma, 1977). For example, the reoccupation of the Rhineland in 1936 by German troops was accepted by Britain and France partly because German military control over all of its own territory was seen as having some legitimacy (Middlemas, 1972). On the other hand, unprovoked oppression of a flagrant kind—e.g., involving wanton killing of civilians—is likely to provoke a feeling of moral outrage in the target that would make it emotionally hard to comply with accompanying demands.

There may be other benefits or costs of compliance under coercion. Leaders who are the targets of coercion may have personal stakes in the policies they are being pressured to change. Thies (1980:13) comments:

> Since a decision to yield in the face of coercive pressures must often be made by the very officials who argued (often long and hard) for going ahead with whatever action brought on the coercive pressures to begin with (and then imposed on subordinates who will very likely have built up a sizeable stake in terms of careers, promotions, and budgets in a continuation of the previous policy), the decision to yield is one that may be fraught with peril for the careers and at times the lives of the officials who must make it, a point that can easily be concealed by dispassionate references to "affecting the enemy's will."

Related to the effects of compliance on leaders' careers is change in political support. Often leaders will have reason to believe that they will be castigated as cowards or traitors if they "surrender" to the demands of a nation using coercion against them. Thus, even after enormous losses to American air and sea power, Japanese political leaders hesitated to end the war because of opposition from diehard nationalists (Ienaga, 1978). On the other hand, in the United States during the later stages of the Vietnam war, political support could increasingly be expected for concessions to the demands of North Vietnam. Of course, as both of these examples illustrate, political support for or opposition to concession will often vary with different groups within the society. Olson (1979) points out that the overall political effects of such coercion in the target state depend on which groups are affected and the importance of each of these groups within the target country.

To summarize, compliance to demands under coercion becomes a more attractive alternative to the target as:

(1) the magnitude of the punishment increases;
(2) the value to him of the concession demanded is less, i.e., his motivation to act otherwise is lower or alternative means to reach his goals are available;
(3) the anticipated future costs due to the effect of concession—in this case on his reputation for resolve—decrease;
(4) the political benefits of compliance increase (costs decrease); and
(5) the personal costs of compliance to his self-esteem decrease.

These perceived benefits and costs are influenced by the nature of the coercion and its context. Compliance will appear most beneficial to the target when the coercion conforms at least minimally to some accepted standards of international behavior, seems to be aimed at limited objectives, and is accompanied by limited demands.

Reacting to Coercion with Counter-Coercion

The attraction of choosing coercion as a *response* to coercion will be determined by the same general set of considerations that lead people to *initiate* the use of coercion—that is, by the value to them of the possible outcomes and their expectancies that each of these outcomes will occur (see chapter 5). However, the fact that the other side has already used coercive means against them is likely to change the value of various possible outcomes and also to change their expectancies about the likelihood of various outcomes occurring.

Direct value of retaliation. We discussed in chapter 5 some of the benefits and costs that are likely to stem directly from the use of coercive means against an adversary, regardless of how the other responds. These benefits and costs may be in the form of resources (financial and other), prestige and reputations, political support, and personal satisfaction.

Sometimes it is more costly to respond effectively with coercion than it is to initiate coercion against an adversary. The initator of coercion is likely to be better prepared to defend against retaliation than is the original target. Thus, greater resources may need to be used by the retaliator to mount a coercive response that stands a chance of being effective. For example, it was necessary for the British to devote more resources to their attempt to retake the Falkland (Malvinas) Islands than it was for the Argentines to initially occupy these lightly defended islands (Hastings and Jenkins, 1983).

However, the political benefits of retaliation are likely to be much greater for responding to coercion in kind than for initiating coercion. Public opinion in any nation is more likely to applaud—and in fact clamor for —retaliation against an attack or injury inflicted by another nation than for initially attacking another. For example, American public opinion swung immediately and almost unanimously in support of war against Japan when Pearl Harbor was attacked, whereas majority opinion had opposed entry into war until then (Cole, 1953).

In addition, leaders are likely to obtain much greater personal satisfaction from inflicting punishment on an adversary who has just injured them than on one that has not done so. The greater the perceived provocation represented by the other side's acts, the greater the anger of the target and the more probable is retaliation (Tedeschi and Bonoma, 1977). The widespread norm of reciprocity that calls for returning bad for bad (as well as good for good) also will lead decisionmakers to feel satisfaction at the prospect of hurting those who have hurt them.

There is another important benefit that can be anticipated from retaliation that is not so relevant when initiating coercion. As we have already noted, a target of coercion who passively accepts such treatment (whether or not it complies with accompanying demands) will lose prestige, and its reputation for resolve to use coercion will be weakened. Adversaries may, therefore, try to bully the target again in the future, expecting that it will refrain again from retaliating. Thus an important benefit of retaliating in kind to coercion is the protection of one's prestige and reputation for firmness, which may help one to get a better outcome in future disputes.

Overall there is likely to be greater direct benefit in countering coercion than in initiating it. Retaliation will be more likely the more that: (a) political support for retaliation increases; (b) the initial coercion has violated accepted norms and aroused anger; and, (c) one's reputation for

resolve is heavily involved, which would be true when similar future interactions are likely to occur.

Possible victory without fight. One possible outcome of using coercion is
that the adversary will concede without a fight. As we have seen, the allure
of this outcome depends on the value of winning in the dispute, weighted
by the expectancy of the other side submitting in the face of coercion (see
chapter 5).

There is no reason to think that the value of winning with respect to the
issues in dispute would be less for the side contemplating retaliation than
for the side considering initial use of coercion. In fact several factors might
raise the value of winning. One is that the target of coercion is more likely
to face a loss (with respect to the status quo) than is the initiator of
coercion, who might be hoping for a gain. We have noted (chapter 4) that
people generally care more strongly about losses then they do about gains
of an equivalent size. Moreover, the arousal of strong feelings of anger at
being injured by the adversary may raise the value of "beating" the other
(i.e., focus attention on relative versus absolute payoffs).

While the value of winning may be somewhat greater when one has been
the target of coercion than otherwise, the expectancy that the adversary
will concede in the face of one's own coercion is apt to be lower for a party
considering retaliation than for one considering first use of coericion. The
side that has been injured by the other has just seen evidence of the other's
willingness to use coercion. This action is likely to be seen as evidence of
the other's motivation to use further coercion in this dispute. Moreover, in
the process of using coercion, the initiator is likely to have considerably
raised the stakes to itself (in prestige, material commitment, etc.) of giving
in.

In judging the likelihood that the initiator of coercion would continue or
even escalate coercion, the potential retaliator is likely to take into account
the extent to which the initiator has committed itself to further action. If it
has not, the target may see the initial coercion as just a probe and believe
that a firm response will cause the initiator to back down (Snyder and
Diesing, 1977). For example, when the Soviet Union blocked Western
access to Berlin in 1948 (and in later years), it did so in a way (e.g.,
claiming road and railway repairs) that stopped short of committing the
Soviets to a permanent bar to Western access. Some U.S. officials recommended sending an armed convoy through Soviet barriers in the expectation that the Soviets would then back down (Davison, 1958). (However,
top American officials were never confident enough of this outcome to give
such an order.)

In general, the side considering retaliation is not likely to have much confidence that by such action it can get the initiator of coercion to concede. It is more likely to expect that if it retaliates a fight will ensue. The more the initiator of coercion has committed itself to persist in any fight, the less likely is the target to retaliate.[1]

The value of a fight to a retaliator. Alexander George and his colleagues (1971) state that the more the target of coercion fears escalation, the more effective is coercion as a tool of national diplomacy. In other words, the less the value of a fight to the target of coercion, the less likely it is to retaliate.

As previously noted, being the target of initial coercion will likely raise the value to a potential retaliator of winning a fight because he may be faced otherwise with a loss and because, in his anger, he wishes to triumph over his injurer. On the other hand, the fact that the other has struck the first blow may lower one's expectations of winning a fight. This would be the case where the initial coercive move has changed the power situation in the attacker's favor—e.g., when the preemptive strike by Israel in 1967 destroyed a large part of Egypt's air force on the ground. The initial blow may also provide information about the capability of the initiator, the vulnerability of one's own side, and perhaps about the reaction of third parties, which might have bearing on the probable outcome of a fight. In general, we may expect that the more the initial coercive action has given the initiator an advantage in a fight the less likely the target is to retaliate.

In summary, the attraction of using coercion is determined by the same general factors for the potential retaliator as for the potential initiator. However, the direct value of using coercion is likely to be higher for the retaliator to the extent that norms, public opinion, and personal standards dictate striking back against an aggressor. The value of winning also will tend to be higher for the potential retaliator compared to the potential initiator of coercion, especially if it is faced with a potential loss and if its anger at the attacker leads it to focus on getting a better outcome than its adversary.

While the value of using coercion and of winning may be high for the target of initial attack, its expectancy that retaliatory coercion will cause the adversary to concede is likely to be low, especially if the initiator has committed itself to its course of action. The potential retaliator's expectancy of winning a fight will also be reduced to the extent that the initiator of coercion has gained advantage in the fight as a result of its action.

It is important to note also that the alternatives to the use of coercion differ for leaders who themselves have been targets of coercion and are considering retaliation as compared to those considering the initial use of coercion. For the decisionmaker considering retaliation, his principal alternative is conformity to the demands of the attacker, with resultant tangible losses and humiliation. The alternatives available for decisionmakers considering first use of coercion (e.g., continuing the status quo, seeking compromise) usually are more numerous and more attractive.

Escalation and Conflict Spirals

It happens frequently that when one side to a dispute uses coercion, and the other responds in kind, there ensues a sequence of coercive actions and counter-actions by which the parties inflict progressively greater injury to each other. A process by which the use of punishment by one side leads to the use of punishment by the other, and so on, occurs for conflicts in a variety of settings (Bacharach and Lawler, 1981; Pruitt and Rubin, 1986).

This process of action and reaction, usually involving an escalation of the magnitude of coercion as it continues, has been described for internation disputes by many writers (e.g., North, Brody, and Holsti, 1964; Azar, 1972; Smoke, 1977; Phillips, 1973; Milstein, 1974; Ward, 1982). For example, Milstein (1974) describes the dynamics of interaction between the United States and North Vietnam in the late 1960s, during which each responded to coercive moves by the other with coercive responses, often of a greater magnitude, of its own. Azar (1972) reports that during the escalation of conflict between nations, hostile interaction tends to be symmetrical and close in time.

The concept of escalation of hostile actions often has been used to describe the growth in the frequency, and especially in the magnitude, of coercive actions. Thomas Schelling (1966) has pointed to an important aspect of such possible increases in coercive action: that there usually are not only quantitative increases but *qualitative* increases in coercive action that may occur. For example, while an increase in American bombing in Vietnam represented a quantitative increase in violence, the initial bombing of North (in addition to South) Vietnam represented a qualitative increase. Similarly, if the United States had later begun to use nuclear weapons rather than only conventional weapons in Vietnam, this would have represented another qualitative change in coercive action. Schelling refers to those clear demarcations between different types or kinds of coercion as "salient points." He and others following his usage have used the term escalation to refer to an action that crosses a salient point (Schelling, 1960, 1966; Smoke, 1977).

Sometimes what starts out as a trading of threats and of low-level coercive actions will continue and grow in magnitude (passing one or more salient points as it increases) until it culminates in an all-out war. In other cases, there is an initial trading of coercive action and counter-action, and perhaps some growth in the frequency or magnitude of such actions, but this process is halted and perhaps reversed before it explodes into all-out conflict.

What are the key factors that lead to the escalation of coercion in a dispute? When will this process continue until it spreads out of control and ends in war? How can it be controlled or reversed? In the following sections, I consider these important issues.

Purposes of Escalation

To understand why escalation of coercion occurs in a conflict we need to understand the consequences it has for the side that escalates and the purposes it is intended to serve. By raising the level of coercion it uses in a fight, a nation not only increases the punishment it inflicts on the other but also raises its own costs as well. These costs include those of administering the punishment and also, more importantly, of other losses it inevitably will suffer as a result of this action. For example, in escalating the war in Vietnam from operations solely in the South to a bombing campaign against the North, the United States could anticipate suffering not only the financial costs of the raids but, more important, loss of American planes and pilots, increased political opposition at home, and loss of support by some of its allies. In addition, by escalating the conflict, the United States increased the risks of direct confrontation with the military forces of China and the Soviet Union.

There may be a number of reasons why an actor in a dispute is willing to suffer the costs and risks of escalation to himself. Sometimes there is some direct, immediate benefit that is anticipated. For example, American officials believed that by carrying the war to North Vietnam, they would raise the morale of the South Vietnamese forces (Milstein, 1974). Also, there may be personal satisfactions in striking a harder blow at one's adversary than he has just struck at you.

However, the basic reason why either side in a fight escalates the level of coercion is that, by this means, it hopes to win in the issue at dispute (Nicholson, 1967). The increase in the level of coercion is intended to get the opponent to concede by (a) increasing the costs and risks of the fight to the adversary as well as to oneself, while at the same time, (b) demonstrating one's own determination to persevere in the fight and bear the added costs necessary for victory. Escalating the level of coercion that one is applying to an adversary will seem to have a greater chance of success in getting him to concede, and therefore is more likely to tried, if the adversary is "force-vulnerable"—i.e., the application of greater coercion will make it in his interest to concede (see chapter 2).

Thus, the basic purpose of the decision to begin the bombing of North Vietnam was to make the war much more costly for the North Vietnamese while demonstrating United States resolve to continue the war. American policymakers believed that heavy bombing of their cities would make it in the interest of North Vietnam's leaders to concede—i.e., to stop their support of rebellion in South Vietnam. Similarly, the North Vietnamese leaders believed that increasing attacks on and casualties among Americans would force the United States to withdraw (Milstein, 1974).

Each side in a dispute may begin with a relatively small level of force —seeking to minimize its own costs—and then gradually increase its level of coercion, continuing to expect that the other side will eventually give in under pressure. Thus a process of escalation may stem from the initial commitment of both sides to winning and the initial expectations of both sides that the other can be forced to concede.

However, to understand why escalation of coercion often occurs in a dispute, we need to look also at the *changes* that occur during a conflict that often make escalation of coercion seem more attractive than other alternatives. These include changes in (a) the costs of the fight to each rival; (b) each side's motivation and the value it places on possible outcomes of the dispute; and, (c) each side's expectations about the actions of the other and about winning. In addition, previous inhibitions on the use of coercion may be changed.

Changes in the Costs of Fight

As an exchange of punishments continues during the course of a fight, the burden of such costs may become more difficult for one or both sides to bear. This is particularly apt to be true if the frequency and magnitude of the punishments have increased and if the fight has gone on for a long time. In such a case leaders of one or both of the participant nations may feel that they must do something to keep the fight from dragging on and their losses from continuing indefinitely. If, for various reasons (to be considered below), they do not wish to make concessions in an effort to end the conflict, they may decide to escalate the fighting in order to get the other side to concede.

An example is found in the actions of Iraq during the war with Iran that began in 1980. In 1984, after four years of war, the Iraqis were still suffering large costs in money and lives, their oil exports had been cut off, and no end of the war was in sight. Since Iraq's President Sadam Hussein did not wish to make the concessions Iran demanded as conditions for ending the war (including replacing his own government with one acceptable to Iran), he escalated to a new type of military action—bombing ships attempting to load oil at Iran's oil terminal (Kharg Island). These actions were intended explicitly to pressure Iran into negotiating a peace agreement acceptable to the Iraqi regime. (The Iranian reaction was to escalate in turn to a new level of military action—bombing the ships of nations trading with Iraq's allies.)

Changes in Motivation

As a fight develops and continues, important changes in the motivation of the participants may occur. These motivational changes may make the desired outcomes of escalating coercion seem more attractive. Such changes may include: (a) having a new goal of countering the effects of the previous coercive action of the adversary; (b) placing a greater value on winning with respect to the initial issues of the dispute; (c) placing greater value on triumphing over the adversary—i.e., having an outcome better than that of the other; (d) raising one's objectives concerning terms for settling the initial dispute; (e) expanding one's goals in terms of the issues with respect to which one seeks to improve one's position; and, (f) greater motivation to hurt the other side.

Countering the other's action. When the coercive action of one nation creates a difficult situation (status quo) for its adversary, the second nation is often motivated to respond with an even higher level of coercion in order to neutralize or end the losses it is suffering. Milstein (1972) has analyzed the reciprocal and often escalating pattern of violence between Israel and Arab states from this perspective. He points out that violent attacks by an adversary increase the stress on national leaders and leads them to try to force the enemy to reduce his attacks by violent attacks of their own.

A good example of this process is provided by the war of attrition between Israel and Egypt in 1969 (Shlaim and Tanter, 1978). Egyptian shelling of Israeli positions along the Suez Canal was causing a mounting number of casualties among Israeli soldiers. To try to force the Egyptians to stop the shelling, the Israelis launched a series of deep-penetration raids against industrial and military targets inside Egypt. (These raids were unsuccessful in achieving their purpose; the Egyptians themselves escalated further by calling in direct assistance from the Soviet Union.)

Another example of an escalating action motivated by a desire to counter the actions of the adversary is Iran's bombing of "neutral" shipping in the

Persian Gulf in 1984 in the course of its war with Iraq. This action was taken to counter Iraq's attack on ships carrying Iran's oil in an attempt to get the neutral nations (some of whom had been helping Iraq) to put pressure on Iraq to stop its air attacks on Iranian shipping (Goldstein, 1984).

Increased value of winning. As fighting in a dispute continues and grows in magnitude, winning often becomes more important to the participants than it was initially. As this happens, each side may become less willing to concede or to compromise. Conversely, it may become more willing to suffer the costs and take the risks of escalating the fight in hopes of achieving the victory so important to it.

As a fight continues and grows in magnitude, each side may see itself as having a greater stake in winning. After having expended much treasure and perhaps much blood, its leaders feel that they must have some gain to show for this loss. Having committed themselves to the struggle, they feel that the prestige of their nation and themselves as leaders is at stake. Also, they are emotionally involved in the fight.

The process by which people become entraped in escalating conflicts as they commit more and more of their resources and therefore feel they have a greater and greater stake in winning has been described for experimental settings by Brockner and Rubin (1985). Reviewing the escalation of inter-nation conflicts, Smoke (1977) has emphasized the importance of rising stakes as one of the fundamental causes of escalation. A good example is the Vietnam war, where American leaders spent many billions of dollars, suffered many thousands of casualties, and made victory a central test of American resolve and their own statesmanship. Thus even when the costs of the war became enormous and winning became even more elusive, they preferred for a long time to escalate the fighting rather than to withdraw.

Rising goals. In addition to feeling an increased stake in achieving their initial aims in the dispute, winning may become very valued because a nation's leaders have raised their goals and aspirations in the course of the dispute. Smoke (1977) mentions the elevation of objectives that often occurs during a dispute. Singer (1979) has noted that, following the mobi-lization of public support for one's own national cause, the rising level of public hostility toward the rival nation raises general expectations of a satisfactory settlement and makes it difficult for leaders to accept less. As a fight continues and escalates, there also is often an expansion of the issues involved (Kriesberg, 1982). For example, while the initial aim of the North in the U.S. Civil War was to preserve the Union, the elimination of slavery was added as an objective as the war continued and made victory seem even more important for many. When such an expansion of goals occurs, victory seems to promise more positive outcomes on a number of issues.

"Beating" the other. Finally, winning may become more valued as a fight progresses because it comes to seem even more important to "beat" the other (Deutsch, 1973). The fight magnifies the element of competition in strength and resolve. Winning may become an end in itself, regardless of whether one's own absolute position is improved or whether the benefits of winning are greater than the costs of the fight.

A spiral of hostile actions during the course of a dispute is accompanied and paralleled by a spiral of hostile feelings. This pattern has been described for national leaders in World War I (North, Brody, and Holsti, 1964; Holsti, Brody, and North, 1969). For example, both for nations of the Dual Alliance (Germany and Austria) and those of the Triple Entente (Russia, France, and Britain) there was a high correlation between a nation's own frequency of hostility and its leaders' perceptions of their nation as a target of hostility (North, Brody, and Holsti, 1964). While there usually are strategic reasons for retaliating coercion, several analysts of conflict have emphasized the important role that anger and resentment also play in this process (Milburn and Watman, 1981; Tedeschi and Bonoma, 1977; Pruitt and Rubin, 1986). Feelings of anger at injury to oneself—especially when such coercion is seen as illegitimate—usually lead to heightened desires to see the other hurt in turn and to triumph over the adversary.

Changes in Expectations

As a conflict continues there often are changes in the expectations of each side about the likely actions of the other side and about the likely outcomes of the dispute. Such changes in expectations may lead to an escalation in the use of coercion.

Changes in the perceived probability of winning. When a fight has gone on for some time, one of the participants may begin to realize that it is losing. It may come to believe that if things go on as at present, the end result will be that it will be defeated and will have to concede in the issue at dispute. If the side that sees itself losing does not wish to accept this prospect, it may try to raise its chances of winning by escalating the level of coercion. It may believe (or hope) that in a fight of greater magnitude it will have advantages that it does not have at the lower level of coercion—e.g., that it will be able to inflict more damage on the other than vice versa. It may believe (or hope) also that the other side will be less willing than itself to continue to sustain losses at the new higher level of coercion and will therefore give up first.

American actions in Vietnam illustrate this process. In 1965 the limited American military actions in Vietnam were not succeeding in stemming the growth of Communist power in the South. American officials saw the military situation as deteriorating. In an attempt to halt and perhaps reverse this deterioration, the United States escalated its military action to a new level by bombing Hanoi and other areas in North Vietnam. This action, it was believed, would raise the costs of the war to the North Vietnamese much more than it would for the United States and might therefore get them to give up their aims in the South (Milstein, 1974). (The result, instead, was a counter-escalation by the North Vietnamese, who began for the first time to move their main-line army units into the South.)

Expectations about coercion by the other side. As a conflict continues and grows in intensity, each side may come to expect a higher level of coercive action by the other. In part this may occur because increasingly strident rhetoric and increasingly assertive actions by each may lead the other to believe that its opponent's goals in the dispute have been raised (Kriesberg, 1982). It may be also that the previous actions of one or both sides have gone beyond the explicitly or implicitly agreed boundaries of coercive conduct, thus leaving each uncertain about what the limits, if any, of the other's future coercive action may be. If one side expects the other to raise its level of coercion, then it will feel less inhibition about increasing its own coercive actions. In fact, it may believe that there is advantage in escalating first. For example, when U.S. forces crossed the 38th parallel in Korea and advanced toward the Chinese border, the Chinese perceived this action as reflecting an important increase in American aims (perhaps including a crippling of Chinese installations that bordered Korea) and an action that shattered previous bounds within which U.S. action was taken (i.e., remaining within South Korea). In this fluid situation of suspicion of American aims and unclear expectations about the limits of American actions, the Chinese attacked the advancing American forces (Heller, 1977).

Expectations of peaceful resolution. As a dispute continues and grows in intensity, each side may also see less and less chance for peaceful resolution of the dispute, either by compromise or by finding some solution acceptable to both sides. It becomes more difficult to think of the adversary as anything other than a hostile enemy or to see plausible ways in which the situation could develop other than toward acute conflict. Richard Smoke has studied the escalation process in five wars and emphasizes the importance of such changes in expectations, saying:

As the escalation sequence subsequently proceeded, the range of expectations steadily narrowed. The number and variety of plausible futures decreased and the expected value of policy instruments short of direct military action declined. Plausible images of the near future became fewer, until extremely acute crisis and very possibly war seemed to be the only realistic expectations. Negotiations, signals, and outright military demonstrations all came to seem less and less promising ways to secure objectives; only military action seemed feasible. (Smoke, 1977:282)

If decisionmakers come to see no realistic prospect of a negotiated settlement and see a struggle based on strength and resolve to be the only possible outcome, then they are apt to take whatever measures they think necessary for achieving victory. Such measures may well include actions that escalate the conflict to new and higher levels of coercion.

Effect of Escalation on Expectations

While changes in expectations may lead to escalation in the use of force, the reverse also may occur. The use of higher levels and new types of coercion is likely to affect expectations about future actions and outcomes. Smoke (1977) points out that escalation of violence by one (or both) sides in a war may alter policymakers' expectations about the course and outcome of the war. Moreover, as noted already, use of more or new types of coercion by one side may make its adversary expect further increases.

A party that escalates its use of coercion usually is trying to change the expectations of the other. It wants to convince the other that it is resolute and to make the other believe that the course and outcome of the dispute must inevitably favor its side. However, as several writers have pointed out (Smoke, 1977, Schelling, 1966), the coercive actions of one side may not have the intended effects on the expectations of the other. Smoke (1977:278) comments: "In action-reaction sequences, then, each escalation is undertaken on the basis of expectations likely to be not entirely known by those on whom the escalation is inflicted, and has its most important impact on expectations likely to be not entirely known by those who undertook it. Each side's field of expectation shifts with the leverage of every escalation, and each side's is partially hidden from the sight of the other."

Several unanticipated and sometimes dangerous effects on the other side's expectations may occur. First, while the side using more coercion may wish to convince its opponent of its own resolve and of the futility of resistance, it may instead convince the opponent of its own hostile intentions and of the likelihood that it will take further dangerous and aggressive actions in the future (Schelling, 1966). Given such perceptions and expectations, the opponent may believe more than ever that it is important to take swift decisive action to defeat its threatening adversary and thus escalate in turn.

By definition, an act that escalates the kind of coercion used is one that goes beyond the previous boundaries (explicit or implicit) of "allowable" coercion. The effect of such an act on the expectations of the adversary will depend in part on whether the act itself, and any accompanying explanations, establish new boundaries of allowable action. Schelling (1966) has urged that a nation that escalates its level of force should stop at another clear boundary.

By indicating a new boundary for its actions, a nation signals its intention to keep the level of coercion controlled and indicates also the new limits it is placing on its own actions. It thereby implicitly (or explicitly) proposes the same limits for the other's action. If a new boundary is not made clear, the adversary may conclude that all rules have been discarded and feel forced to respond with an even higher level of coercion. Holsti and his colleagues (1969) also have emphasized the importance of a nation making clear the limits of its aims and intent to use coercion.

Inhibitions About the Use of Coercion

In most disputes between nations each side initially is very reluctant to use coercion—especially violence—to get its way. Such action is probably contrary to most norms of international behavior; it risks disrupting positive ties of commerce, etc., with the adversary; and, most importantly, it risks wider, more costly conflict. Young has described the reluctance of the United States, the Soviet Union, and China to initiate the use of force in four disputes following World War II. In the Berlin crisis of 1948–1949, for example, Young asserts that, "Both sides went to considerable lengths throughout the crisis to avoid being the first to use violence or to take steps which would make the outbreak of violence inevitable. . . . Throughout the crisis both sides were circumspect about undertaking unusual mobilizations or movements of troops and military equipment" (Young, 1968:313–315).

If the overt use of coercion does occur, each side still may desire to limit the magnitude and scope of the struggle in order to minimize losses. However, once coercion is used the inhibitions on escalating its use seem to weaken greatly. Experimental studies on aggression have often found that once people begin to administer punishments (usually electric shocks) to others, they tend to escalate the levels of punishment as time goes on (Goldstein, Davids, and Herman, 1975). Goldstein and his associates suggest that, once the individual decides to act aggressively, proaggressive norms become psychologically more potent while antiaggressive norms become less important. In addition, there is evidence that the aggressor tends to devalue his victim in order to justify his actions.

These same psychological mechanisms seem to be relevant in international disputes. Once force or other coercion begins, each side tends to regard the usual norms for settling disputes as no longer applicable and as having been broken by the other side in any case. Norms concerned with defending national honor and national security become more salient. Moreover, the other side begins to be seen in a stereotyped way as an evil, perhaps subhuman, people who deserve whatever harm is being inflicted on them (Smoke, 1977) and who understand only force (Kriesberg, 1982).

Inhibitions against punitive action may also be lowered by a reduction or elimination of positive ties with the adversary. Before the outbreak of hostile actions, each side may have had some economic, political, scientific, cultural, and other ties. As a conflict intensifies, such ties are likely to end. Initiating a fight is likely to entail the costs of disrupting such exchanges. But once such ties are ended, further escalation of coercion does not bring further costs of this type.

To summarize the discussion of escalation, national leaders are likely to escalate their use of coercion in disputes when the following set of conditions is present:

(1) The present costs of the dispute to them are high.
(2) Winning is (increasingly) important to them. As a dispute continues, winning tends to become more important to leaders as their commitment of resources and prestige increases, as their goals relevant to the original issue rise, as the issues expand, and as winning the contest assumes more importance in itself.
(3) They expect that the adversary will concede when coercion reaches a higher level. Such expectations will become greater as the adversary is seen as more vulnerable and less determined than their own side.
(4) The costs to their own side of raising the level of coercion are seen as tolerable.

In addition to this basic set of conditions, escalation of coercion will become more probable as:

(1) Leaders expect more that the adversary will unilaterally increase its own level of coercion, and that this will give the adversary an advantage.

(2) Leaders have lower expectations that a peaceful resolution of the dispute is possible.
(3) Inhibitions about the use of coercion decline—as positive ties with the adversary decrease, negative stereotypes become stronger and norms opposing coercion become less salient.

De-escalation of Coercion

Just as participants in a dispute may increase the level of coercion, so too they may decrease it. When will this occur? There appear to be several key conditions that tend to promote de-escalation. Two of these conditions are the same ones that may contribute to escalation of coercion: heavy costs of the ongoing fight and lack of success of present methods (especially the current level of coercion) in getting the adversary to concede (Azar, 1972; Kriesberg, 1982).

As we have seen, these conditions may lead a disputant to escalate the use of coercion in an attempt to put so much pressure on the opponent that victory will be achieved. However, there are a number of additional factors that may make further escalation seem less attractive or de-escalation more attractive. As the costs of a fight mount and the prospects of winning appear to fade, one side may lose the will to persist. Not only are the costs—in money and perhaps in blood—disheartening but also the goals for which the fight was initiated may be devalued (Kriesberg, 1982). For example, as the costs of the war to keep control of Algeria increased for France, government leaders as well as large parts of the population began to question the importance and even the legitimacy of the goal. The goal of winning a dispute with one nation also may seem less important as another conflict with a different nation assumes primacy (Kriesberg, 1984).

Secondly, the possible costs (financial, political, and human) of pushing the fight to a higher level of violence may appear to be very great. For example, in the spring of 1968 American leaders confronted a war in Vietnam that was costly but not succeeding. The U.S. commander, General William Westmoreland, requested a large increase in American military forces, and other escalation options—such as using nuclear weapons—were also available. However, President Johnson and his advisers judged the costs of a further escalation to be very great. It would cost billions more dollars and thousands more American lives. It would further inflame large segments of the public, which already was in vigorous opposition to the war. It would further alienate other nations, including allies, who were already critical of the war, and increase the dangers of a major war with

China or the Soviet Union. Such costs seemed too large to justify for the stakes involved (Milstein, 1974).

A decision to de-escalate rather than escalate a fight that is going badly will also be facilitated by a perception that satisfactory terms can be obtained through negotiation. Signals from the adversary that it is willing to try to settle the dispute on "reasonable" terms may help to foster this perception. Offers by third parties who have ties to both sides to mediate a settlement also may help to encourage the expectation that a satisfactory solution can be found by means other than increased coercion of the adversary.

Changes that lead to de-escalation of coercion (like those that lead to escalation) are not necessarily only changes in the values and expectations of the same leaders. When a costly fight continues a long time without a clear prospect of success, there are likely to be changes in political alignments and perhaps in leadership. The numbers of those calling for a change in policy are likely to grow and competition for the leadership is likely to increase (Kriesberg, 1982). Thus, as the costly war in Vietnam dragged on inconclusively, the number of American groups opposing continuation of the war grew, and challengers (Eugene McCarthy and Robert Kennedy) to the renomination of Lyndon Johnson arose within the Democratic party. In France, the long, bitter Algerian war led eventually to the collapse of the Third Republic and the return to power of General Charles de Gaulle, who brought the war to an end.

Even when leadership does not change, the leaders may be forced to decrease their coercive actions if they are subject to strong political pressures to do this. However, as Kriesberg (1982) points out, when there are serious divisions within a group about what actions to take (e.g., whether to escalate or de-escalate an unsuccessful fight), it may be difficult for leaders to move very far in any direction. A more politically secure leader is better able than an insecure leader to make clear changes in policy. For example, the prestige and authority of General de Gaulle, a national hero, permitted him to withdraw France from the Algerian war—a step the leaders before him lacked the political support to take.

When one side in a dispute reduces its level of coercion, it is possible that the other will follow suit. An action-reaction process may result, leading to lower and lower levels of threat and coercion, a reverse of the process that often leads to spiraling escalation. However, it is also possible that when one side reduces its use of coercion the adversary—taking this as a sign of weakness and seeing an increased chance for complete victory —will continue or even increase its own level of coercion.

The reaction of the adversary—whether or not it reciprocates a reduction in coercion—may depend on its perception of the intention of the side de-escalating and on the relative power of the two sides. If the side that has reduced its level of coercion is seen as doing so in an attempt to reach agreement through noncoercive methods, but is seen also as having both the power and the will to continue the struggle if necessary, then reciprocation of its de-escalation is more likely than otherwise (Osgood, 1984).

In summary, de-escalation of coercion may occur when the present fight is costly and the prospect of winning it soon with present methods are low. In addition, one or more of the following conditions must also be present:

(1) winning the dispute has been devalued;
(2) the costs of a more intense fight are seen as very high;
(3) expectations of winning a more intensive fight (or of the other conceding immediately in the face of more coercion) are low; and,
(4) a substantial expectation of being able to get minimally satisfactory terms by negotiation exists.

The subject of efforts to induce reciprocal de-escalation of threat and coercion will be discussed further in chapter 10.

Escalation from Conventional to Nuclear War

An extremely important case of possible escalation is that from conventional war to nuclear war. If Arab states and Israel were to go to war again, under what circumstances might such a war escalate to the use of nuclear weapons (assuming both sides had acquired these)? If the United States and the Soviet Union were to get embroiled in a shooting war in Central Europe (say, over Berlin) or in the Middle East (say, over Iran or Pakistan, or in support of their respective Israeli and Arab allies), what might lead such hostilities to escalate to nuclear war?

One basic set of conditions that leads participants to escalate the use of force in a conflict (as described above) is the following: they value highly their goal of winning but find the current state of the conflict unacceptable because it is very costly and there is no clear prospect of winning soon. Such circumstances could easily arise if a conventional war were to occur for example between the NATO allies and the Soviet Union (Warsaw Pact) armies in Europe. The usual scenario (e.g., Hampson, 1985) is that the NATO forces might be pushed back by numerically superior Soviet forces and face the prospect of defeat and Soviet occupation of Western Europe if the current situation continued. The motivation of American leaders to avoid such an outcome—initially high because of the economic and political stakes involved—might well be heightened following the outbreak of actual fighting. After American troops had been committed to battle and some number killed, American resolve had been publicly stated by the president, and the passions of leaders and the public had been aroused, winning would come to seem even more important than before.

Faced with a deteriorating battlefield situation but unwilling to concede defeat, Western (especially American) leaders would consider the use of tactical nuclear weapons—e.g., short-range nuclear missiles. (In fact, current plans call for their use if necessary.) The purpose of using small nuclear weapons would be not only to try to reverse defeats on the battlefield but to make the fight very costly to the other side and to show one's resolve to use whatever weapons are necessary to win. The hope would be that the adversary, the Soviets, would see that continuing the fight was becoming so costly and so risky (in terms of further nuclear escalation) that it would withdraw or agree to favorable terms for ending the fighting.

Such a strategy could conceivably work, particularly if a fight involving the use of tactical nuclear weapons was much more costly to the Soviets than to the West and if the Soviets were much more fearful of the risks of further escalation to more powerful nuclear weapons than was the West. American attempts to establish "escalation dominance"—i.e., an ability to wreak greater destruction on the Soviet Union at each level of warfare (see, e.g., Jervis, 1984)—is intended to discourage the Soviet Union from either initiating or escalating war at any level.

However, our previous analysis of escalation dynamics suggests some reasons why escalation to tactical nuclear weapons by one side may result in further escalation by the other side. Let us follow the example of American first-use of nuclear weapons in Europe. First, to the extent that such weapons were successful in turning the tide of battle in favor of NATO, Soviet leaders would be faced with the same dilemma described earlier for Western leaders—i.e., whether or not to permit a present situation that was very costly and seemed likely to lead to defeat to continue. Assuming that Soviet leaders had initiated the fighting, their motivation to attain certain political and economic goals must have been high at the start. Once the fighting had begun, their motivation to win would have increased. Their prestige, reputation, and probably their political survival would depend on a successful conclusion of the military adventure. If they believed that their own tactical nuclear weapons could cause as much or more damage to Western forces as vice versa, and that the strength of their strategic nuclear forces would make American leaders equally or more fearful to escalate further, they might well choose to match the Americans' use of tactical nuclear weapons with the use of similar weapons of their own. They might even use somewhat larger weapons over a somewhat larger area. Their hope would be to make the costs for the West so high and, by exhibiting their own resolve, show the risks of continuation to be so great that Western leaders would have to accept defeat. Further escalation to use of more numerous and powerful nuclear weapons over a wider area by each side might follow this same dynamic: each side trying to raise the costs and risks for the other (at the same time that it raises its own) in an effort to get the other to give up.

But there is another possible contributor to escalation (as previously discussed) that could be even more dangerous. This is the effect of unfolding events on the expectations of each side's leaders. If the United States were to use tactical nuclear weapons on the battlefield in Europe—or fire a demonstration nuclear weapon as General Alexander Haig suggested—this would represent a crossing of the boundary between conventional and nuclear weapons. Where would the next boundary line, if any, be drawn? Would nuclear weapons be used to hit staging areas behind the lines? Military bases and airfields? Industrial targets? Targets in Soviet territory? How large would the nuclear weapons be? Might the United States at some point launch an all-out nuclear attack on Soviet missile sites and cities? The point is that once the boundary between conventional and nuclear weapons had been crossed by one side, the other side's leaders would have no clear expectation of the limits, if any, to the other's use of force. Even a stated intention by the other side to use nuclear weapons first if necessary—as the United States has proclaimed—will create uncertainties for the leaders of the other side about the limits, if any, on use of nuclear weapons. Such uncertainties may serve to help deter a potential aggressor from an attack. But if for any reason fighting should occur, then such uncertainties about an adversary's use of nuclear weapons may lead to preemptive action. Thus a limited use of nuclear weapons by the United States (or even a stated intention to do so) might trigger a large-scale nuclear response by Soviet leaders. Similarly, a retaliatory use of nuclear weapons by the Soviets might trigger a large-scale premptive strike by the United States. Such escalation would be especially likely if another condition mentioned in our previous analysis was present: namely, that the leaders of one or both sides had lost hope of a peaceful resolution of the dispute and believe that it will be decided inevitably by force. Such expectations could easily arise in a conventional war and—if combined with the use of some nuclear weapons—could easily cause the leaders of one or both sides to believe that they must launch an all-out nuclear strike before the other does so to them.

Thus, despite the fact that the leaders of nations today know the awful risks of all-out nuclear war, it seems quite possible for any conventional war to escalate to full-scale nuclear war for the same reasons that conventional wars may escalate to higher levels. The chances of this occurring would be less if each side refrains from using even small nuclear weapons and also states its intention to refrain from doing so.[2] Mechanisms for facilitating possible peaceful resolutions to a conflict, such as mediation efforts by other nations, may also help to reduce the likelihood of escalation (nuclear or otherwise) by permitting national leaders to see the chance for resolution of a conflict other than by the stronger prevailing.

Summary and Policy Implications

Evidence from experimental studies of conflict and historical evidence from inter-nation conflicts is consistent in showing that the use of coercion usually is met by retaliation rather than by compliance. However, this is not always the case. When will the other side concede in the face of coercion and when is it likely to retaliate instead with coercive action of its own?

When the choice for the decisionmaker is between compliance with demands accompanying coercion and retaliation, he must compare the attractiveness of these alternative actions. The attractiveness of compliance will increase as the magnitude of the present punishment being suffered and of any future punishment it may signal grows and as the probability that compliance will end this punishment increases. Thus, the side using coercion must make it clear that it will end the punishment it is inflicting as soon as compliance occurs.

The attraction of compliance will increase also as the value of what is being given up becomes smaller. To encourage compliance, the users of coercion should keep their demands to a minimum and even include "carrots" to reduce the net value of what they are asking the other side to give up.

The attraction of compliance will also increase as such action is seen as less unpopular, less humiliating, and less likely to encourage the adversary to repeat and even increase the use of coercion in the future. The nature of the coercion and its context are important in affecting such perceptions. The target of coercion is likely never to approve its use. But if the adversary uses coercion in a way that conforms generally to accepted standards, in a context of limited objectives and limited demands, then such action may not arouse the extreme outrage, and alarm about the adversary's intentions, that would make compliance to its current demands almost impossible.

What about the attraction of retaliating against coercion? The attraction of using coercion in retaliation is affected by the same general factors that affect the initial use of coercion—i.e., the intrinsic value of such action, the values of winning and losing, the expectancy that the adversary will retaliate, and the value of a fight. But these values and expectancies will tend to be different in some ways for the use of coercion in retaliation rather than in first use.

The more an adversary using coercion has violated norms of behavior and thus aroused the target's anger, the greater the political support (or demand) for retaliation, and the more that a continuing interaction between the parties puts the target's reputation for resolve at stake, the greater the intrinsic value of retaliation will be for the target. For leaders of a nation that has been the target of coercion, anger, political support, and concern for its reputation for resolve all are likely to be high and thus make retaliation more intrinsically attractive than a first use of coercion would be. To maximize the chances of compliance with its demands, the side that initiates coercion should try to make the intrinsic benefits of retaliation less powerful by choosing and explaining its actions in a way that minimizes the outrage of the target's leaders and public and minimizes the salience of the present events for future interactions.

While the target of initial coercion often will find retaliation to have a high intrinsic attraction, he usually cannot expect that the adversary will accept his retaliation passively or comply in the face of his retaliation. Thus, his expectancy that use of coercion will lead to winning without a fight is likely to be lower when considering retaliation than when considering the initial use of coercion. However, sometimes the target of coercion may believe that the adversary is using coercion merely to frighten him or to see his reaction and that the initiator will back down when faced with a firm counter-response. The more the initiator of coercion commits himself to continue his coercive behavior if resisted, the less likely the target is to retaliate. To discourage retaliation, the initiator of force must make clear that he is not bluffing and that retaliation will lead to a fight.

When deciding whether to retaliate, the target of coercion must also consider the value of a fight. The more abhorrent he finds the prospect of a fight (based on its costs, the values of winning and losing, and his expectancy of winning), the less likely he is to retaliate. The value of winning a fight will not be less when retaliating than when initiating the use of coercion. Winning may even seem somewhat more important because of the anger the coercion of the adversary has aroused. However, the fact that the other side has struck first may lower the target's expectation of winning a fight. Thus, the more that the first blow by the other side has given it an important advantage for winning a fight the less likely is the target to retaliate.

The first user of coercion may discourage retaliation by displaying an overwhelming strength or by making its first blow a decisive one for the outcome of a fight. However, even where victory seems remote, the target of an attack may retaliate because organizational arrangements are such that response is automatic or because the intrinsic benefits of resistance (preserving honor, discouraging future aggression, etc.) are believed to be great.

As conflict in a dispute continues, either or both sides may increase the amount or type of coercion it uses. The basic purpose of such an escalation of coercion usually is to make the conflict so costly for the other side that it will concede on the issues in dispute. However, an escalation by one side often is matched or exceeded by the other side and a spiral of ever-increasing coercion, possibly ending in all-out war, may follow.

National leaders will become more likely to escalate their use of coercion the more the following combination of conditions is present.

(1) The present costs of the dispute are onerous.
(2) The other side is not expected to concede soon (if at all) if the present situation continues.
(3) The value of winning the dispute remains high or has increased. Winning becomes more important during a dispute as the commitment of resources and prestige increases, as issues expand, and as the contest itself becomes more important.
(4) The possible costs of an expanded fight to one's own side are seen as acceptable.
(5) The adversary is expected to concede when subjected to a higher level of coercion.

Additional factors that make escalation of coercion more likely are: greater expectation that the adversary will not be restrained in its own use of coercion, lower expectation that a negotiated settlement is possible, and lowered inhibitions against use of coercion.

Just as a party to a dispute may increase the scope and intensity of its coercive actions, so too it may decrease them. Like escalation of coercion, de-escalation is likely to occur when a policy of limited coercion loses its attraction, due to high or prolonged costs and an apparently poor prospect of the adversary conceding soon. Such a disagreeable situation is likely to lead to a reduction rather than an increase in coercion the more the following additional conditions are met: (1) the goal of winning the dispute has been devalued; (2) the costs of carrying on a larger fight are seen as very high; and, (3) expectations of winning a larger fight (or of the adversary conceding in the face of more coercion) are seen as low. These three conditions contribute to making continuation or expansion of the fight less desirable. In addition, de-escalation becomes more probable as the alternatives to coercion become more attractive. In particular, given the other conditions stated, the more decisionmakers expect to be able to get satisfactory terms by negotiation the more likely they are to de-escalate the use of coercion.

What can be done to counter the tendency for the use of coercion to escalate? How can movement in the opposite direction be encouraged instead? First, in order to discourage escalation it is important for the adversaries to avoid dangerous misinterpretation of each other's actions and intentions. When using coercion, each side must be careful to make clear the limits of its objectives and the boundaries it is setting on its own use of coercion. Otherwise, the adversary may believe that its objectives are much greater than they are in fact and that there is no limit to the amount and type of force that it may soon use to pursue its aims. In the face of what it sees (perhaps mistakenly) as an imminent threat, the adversary may find unattractive the option of continuing (or reducing) its own level of coercion. One way for a user of coercion to make clear the boundaries it accepts on its own methods is to use coercion only up to perceptually prominent "salient points." For example, one side in a war may use (and state its intention to use) only nonnuclear weapons. Once the nuclear boundary has been crossed it is much harder for the other side to know what the limits of force are.

It is important also to prevent the value of winning from increasing during the course of a dispute and if possible to reduce it. Each side needs to avoid expanding the issues of the dispute, raising its aspirations and demands, or turning a pragmatic dispute into a contest in resolve and prestige. On the contrary, efforts to reduce the actual and perceived stakes of both sides—by narrowing the issues and by persuading leaders and public that their goals are not as vital as initially believed—may help to de-escalate the level of violence.

Escalation of a fight can also be discouraged by changing the perceived value of (increased) fighting. For example, providing full information about the possible catastrophic health, social, ecological, climatic, and other consequences of a nuclear war can help to discourage the temptation to escalate the use of nuclear weapons. In addition, full and vivid information about the material, human, and other costs of an ongoing fight—such as reached the American public during the Vietnam war—can help to provide incentives for de-escalation from a present level of fighting.

Escalation of a dispute also can be discouraged (and de-escalation encouraged) by actions that reduce each side's expectations that using more coercion will force the other to concede. By demonstrating its ability and will to resist further coercion, an adversary can discourage increased use of coercion against itself. By threatening that it will step in to aid a "victim" if coercion against the victim is increased (as the Soviets and Chinese tacitly did in Korea and Vietnam), third parties can reduce the expectancy of winning the dispute through greater coercion. In addition, the possibility of victory can be made to appear Pyrrhic if leaders can be convinced that there will be no winner in a large-scale fight.

Finally, the escalation of coercion may be discouraged and de-escalation encouraged by making conciliatory options seem more attractive and more realizable. Possible compromise solutions can be suggested to leaders by those within their own nation, by third parties, and by their adversaries. This is another reason why it is desirable that some communication between the adversaries continue even during a fight: so that each may be aware when and if the other is amenable to a compromise settlement. Third parties can also play an important role in facilitating communication between the parties, either directly or by serving as an intermediary to convey intentions, "feelers," and actual proposals.

9   The Use of Positive Incentives

Influence between nations need not stem solely from each side's use or threat of punishment against the other. As an alternative to the use of punishment, one nation may give or promise rewards to encourage the actions it desires.

For example, in 1954 Austria promised the Soviet Union that it would maintain neutrality in the East-West conflict if the Soviet Union (along with the Western nations) withdrew their occupation troops. In 1963 President Kennedy announced suspension of U.S. nuclear tests in the atmosphere and asked the Soviet Union (and other nations) to follow suit. In 1965 President Johnson offered large-scale economic aid to North Vietnam if that nation would accept American terms for ending the war in Vietnam. In 1977 President Sadat of Egypt offered a peace agreement to Israel if that country would withdraw from all occupied Egyptian territory. When Egypt moved away from the Soviet Union and made peace with Israel, the United States followed with substantial economic and military aid, with the apparent purpose of keeping Egypt on its new pro-Western, nonbelligerent course.

In some cases, including most of those just mentioned, the use of rewards or promises has been effective in helping to elicit the behavior desired from another nation. In other cases—such as Johnson's effort to tempt the North Vietnamese with economic aid—the influence attempts have been unsuccessful.

As several writers (Rosecrance, 1981; Kriesberg, 1981) have pointed out, while the use of punishment has received a great deal of attention in the literature of international politics, the role of positive incentives has been relatively neglected. These writers have pointed to the need to try to clarify the conditions under which promises and rewards are most appropriate and most effective. In this chapter, I will discuss this issue, drawing on relevant work both on influence in general and on influence in internation relations in particular. My aim will be to see what conclusions seem warranted concerning this question: under what conditions are positive incentives most likely and least likely to be effective?

The Effectiveness of Conciliatory Actions

When one nation uses conciliatory methods in an attempt to influence the behavior of another nation, how successful is such action likely to be? There is considerable evidence that the usual tendency is for each side in a dispute to reciprocate the behavior of the other side—i.e., to match concessions with concessions as well as firmness with firmness. This general tendency has been found in many experimental studies (Druckman, 1983; Pruitt, 1981). Reciprocation has also been found to be common in internation negotiations (Jensen, 1963, 1968, 1984; Hopmann, 1974; Hopmann and King, 1976). Much recent evidence comes from arms-control negotiations. While Jensen found some evidence that firmness sometimes led the other side to concede more in arms talks, he also found that concessions by either side in American-Soviet arms talks tended to be reciprocated by the other during most of the periods he studied. For example, Jensen (1984) found a positive correlation of .49 between American and Soviet concessions during the twenty-three rounds of Strategic Arms Limitation talks from 1969 to 1979.

Using diplomatic events data for European nations during the nineteenth century, Alexandroff (1979) found that cooperative initiatives led to cooperative responses about 70 percent of the time. In their study of interaction between the Western Allies and the Soviet Union from 1946 to 1963, Gamson and Modigliani (1971) found that each of the sides was likely to respond in kind to conciliatory actions by the other. Specifically, in seven out of eight instances in which the Western nations took conciliatory actions toward the Soviets, the latter reciprocated with conciliation; in twelve of seventeen instances in which the Soviets were conciliatory, the Western nations responded in kind. This pattern was in contrast to a tendency toward "refractory" actions (those increasing disagreement) by each side when confronted by refractory action by the other.

Leng (1980) studied the use of threats and of promises in dyadic disputes between nations ranging over three historical time periods. He found that the target of threat was likely to respond either with outright compliance or outright defiance. Promises were slightly less likely than threats to lead to compliance but were less likely to result in defiance and more likely to produce placating responses. Leng's data suggest that, on balance, promises were more effective than threats in producing desired changes in another nation's behavior.

While conciliatory actions often are reciprocated, sometimes they are met with a lack of cooperation. Larger previous concessions by the other side might lead a negotiator to expect that the other will continue to concede if he himself remains firm in his position (Cross, 1969). Some experimental studies have found such a pattern of behavior—i.e., that larger concessions by one side were met with lack of reciprocity by the other (Bartos, 1974; Druckman, 1983; Pruitt, 1981). There is some evidence suggesting that such a pattern has sometimes occurred also in U.S.–Soviet arms negotiations (Jensen, 1984). Hopmann and Smith (1977) found that when U.S. decisionmakers perceived the Soviets in more positive terms (and presumably expected Soviet flexibility), they tended to toughen their negotiation terms in arms-control talks; when they tended to see the Soviets in negative terms, (and presumably expected Soviet intransigence), they softened their negotiating posture.

Experimental studies of cooperation and conflict also show that when one side acts in a cooperative and rewarding way, his partner sometimes attempts to exploit this behavior in order to enjoy an advantage (Shure, Meeker, and Hansford, 1965; Oskamp, 1971). Historical cases in which conciliation by one side was met with increased belligerence by another side also are not hard to find. The actions by Adolf Hitler, who responded to Neville Chamberlain's conciliatory moves with increased belligerence and new demands, is a dramatic instance.

The key question then is not whether conciliation (i.e., rewards, usually in the form of concessions, or promises of rewards) always works or never works. Rather we need to know under what conditions conciliatory actions are effective in eliciting cooperation. To answer this question my strategy again is to consider the rewards and costs that may be expected to result from reciprocating conciliatory actions as compared to the net benefits expected from alternative actions.

Using the same theoretical framework as that employed previously (see chapter 5), we may see the decision to reciprocate a conciliatory move by an adversary to depend on:

(a) the intrinsic rewards and costs of responding positively to rewards or offers of rewards;

(b) the value of the possible outcomes of such reciprocation—especially the value of agreement with or harmonious relationships with the other side;

(c) the expectancy that responding positively will lead to a rewarding relationship with the other side; and,

(d) the attraction of alternative responses, such as making threats and new demands on the other side.

To understand the effect of conciliatory actions on the target, we need to know how such actions affect these perceptions. What is there about a conciliatory action, and about the context in which it is taken, that will make reciprocation appear likely to be more rewarding than alternative actions?

Intrinsic Rewards and Costs

Responding to rewards (or promises of rewards) by the other side with rewarding actions of one's own may involve some immediate benefits and/or costs. These include the direct costs of rewards or concessions given to the other, moral satisfactions, effects on personal and national status, effects on the other side's attitudes, and political benefits or costs.

Direct costs. Making concessions in response to positive incentives offered by another party may involve costs in money, territory, trading advantages, political control over some area or institution, military strength, or in some other desirable good or position. For example, in order to get the large-scale economic aid promised by the United States in 1965, North Vietnam would have had to abandon its effort to reunify Vietnam under its control. Israel had to give up its control over the Sinai area and to make certain other political concessions in exchange for a peace treaty with Egypt. The cost of such concessions to a nation will depend on the importance of the "objects" involved to its own central aims and in some cases on the resources (such as money) it has that affect the scarcity of such objects. In the case of North Vietnam the concessions asked were too great because reunification of Vietnam was highly important to them. For Israel, on the other hand, control over the Sinai was not of central importance, and so it was willing to make this concession in order to obtain peace with Egypt.

Moral satisfactions. When leaders of one nation receive a reward or concession from another or a promise of such reward, they may believe that it is right and appropriate to reciprocate. Such beliefs may rest on general values about proper ways to act toward other people or toward leaders of other nations in particular. Or a belief in reciprocity may derive from a norm—i.e., widely held expectations of proper behavior—that has arisen to cover particular relationships. In international relations such norms are likely to apply to the relations among nations of approximately equal status, especially when they are generally friendly and interdependent. In a dispute between Britain and France, for example, the leaders of each nation are likely to feel some moral obligation to reciprocate concessions.

In some situations, however, national leaders will feel no moral pressure to reciprocate a rewarding action or promise by another nation. They may distrust the sincerity and motives of the other, they may believe that the other's action was prompted by necessity or weakness, or they may regard the relationship as one of such rancorous conflict that norms of reciprocity do not apply. For example, Syrian leaders would not be likely to feel a moral obligation to reciprocate a concession by Israel on issues in dispute between these nations.

Personal and national status. One's response to a promise of reward from another party that is contingent on one's own rewarding action may be affected by the symbolic meaning of that offer. In general, promises are seen as more legitimate than threats and are thus viewed more favorably. However, offers of reward in return for concessions may sometimes be seen as coercive or demeaning. This may occur if the offerer is much more powerful than the other side and when the target of the offer perceives pressure that restricts its free choice about whether or not to respond positively to the offer (Deutsch, 1973; Knorr, 1975). In such cases making concessions to the other side may involve some loss of personal and/or national status. Reluctance to accept such a humiliation was probably one factor that influenced North Vietnam to refuse to give up its military efforts in return for money from the United States, since the American offer was combined with threats and coercion. To do so would have been seen by the Vietnamese as a serious blow to their self-esteem and their esteem in the eyes of others.

Effect on adversary. Reciprocating a reward from another party or responding positively to an offer of reward may be expected to please the other and make him view you more favorably. Responding to rewards or offers in a harsh or negative way may be expected to displease or anger the other side and make him view you less favorably. How much national leaders value the goodwill of another nation's leaders will be affected by their dependence on the other side. Thus, in deciding whether or not to reciprocate specific trade concessions or offers by Japan, American leaders would be influenced not only by the advantages of the particular exchange but also by the advantage of maintaining the goodwill of a nation with which they have considerable economic interdependence.

Political advantages (costs). As with any possible action, the political advantages of one's response to a reward or offer of reward have to be considered by national leaders. Domestic opinion may express weariness of a serious dispute or desire to avoid one and may exert pressure on decision-makers to reciprocate concessions. Thus, if the Soviet Union were to make a generous offer to cut their armaments in return for similar U.S. concessions, an American president could anticipate general public approval for accepting the offer. On the other hand, if the public is in a militant mood toward another nation, reciprocal concessions toward the other would probably bring general public censure. For example, after the S.S. *Maine* was sunk in Havana Harbor in 1898, the clamor for war was so strong in the United States that it is doubtful that any offer of compromise by Spain would have induced the American government to accept.

Response to reward by the other side may also bring approval or disapproval from other nations. Thus, when conciliatory proposals are floated by Arab leaders in Egypt or Jordan, Israel stands to benefit from U.S. approval if it indicates a willingness to reciprocate concessions and to suffer U.S. disapproval if it does not. The more dependent a nation is on support from other nations, the more important obtaining the approval of such other nations will be.

To summarize the discussion in this section: the recipient of a reward or promise of reward is likely to see greater intrinsic benefits from responding in a rewarding manner (and therefore is more likely to do so) as the following conditions are met.

(1) His values and resources make the cost of the rewards he reciprocates low.
(2) He believes—because of ideology, the existence of norms, etc.—that it is right to reciprocate conciliatory actions.
(3) There is not coercive pressure from the other to cooperate that would cause a loss of status as a result of cooperation.[1]
(4) The actor is generally dependent on the goodwill of the other side.
(5) Cooperation is supported by domestic factions and/or other nations on which the actor is dependent.

Value of Cooperation with Other Side

Reciprocating a rewarding action or concession or promises of reward by the other side may result in a situation of agreement and cooperation that involves a (continued) receipt of rewards from the other side. The value of such an outcome to decisionmakers will depend on the relevance of the possible rewards of cooperation to their needs, the magnitude of possible rewards, the specificity of rewards promised, the timing of rewards, and the dependence of the decisionmakers on these rewards.

Relevance of rewards to needs. The value to national leaders of compromise, cooperation, and mutual exchange of rewards with another nation will depend in part on the goals of those leaders. If they aim for an outcome of harmony on a basis of equality and mutual benefit, such an outcome may be very attractive. On the other hand, if their goals include dominance over and perhaps exploitation of the other side, then the outcome of an agreement based on mutuality of concession and reward would not be highly valued.

The value of rewards from the other will depend also on the nature of such rewards. For example, some national leaders may feel great need for material rewards (e.g., grants or loans of money to their nation) while for others the need for symbols of high status (e.g., visits by prominent world figures, inclusion in international conferences) may be more important. Deutsch (1973) has pointed out that promises may be ineffective in securing concessions if the rewards being promised are seen by the target as inappropriate or even insulting.

Magnitude of rewards. The value of possible rewards for cooperation will in general be greater as the magnitude of the reward increases (Favell, 1977). However, promises of rewards that are seen as excessive for the given circumstances may be ineffective, in part because they may lack high credibility.

Specificity of rewards. The more clear and specific a promised reward is the more it is apt to influence the actions of the target of influence. Leng (1980) found that national leaders were more likely to respond with compliance to requests that were coupled with promises from another nation when the nature of the promised actions was clearly specified rather than unspecified. Snyder and Diesing (1977) found that clear, explicit offers of concession were more likely than vague offers to facilitate settlements of serious disputes between nations. They state that explicit concessions are likely to break through the "noise" of various communications, are likely to be taken seriously by the other side, and present the other with a clear option. Deutsch (1973) has suggested also that vagueness about the rewards promised may lead the target to conclude that the promisor has little power to deliver.

Timing of rewards. When a given behavior is followed quickly by rewards it is more likely to be repeated than if the reward is appreciably delayed (Favell, 1977). As Deutsch (1973) states, the timing of promised rewards is likely to have similar effects: promises that are to be fulfilled far in the future will have less potent effects on compliance than promises of quick rewards. Thus, we would expect that a nation that promises some trade concession to another nation in return for some act of cooperation will be more successful in its influence attempt if the promised trade concession is made immediately after compliance by the other rather than following a new round of talks scheduled in two years.

Dependence on the rewarder. An anticipated reward will be valued more as one becomes more dependent on the other party to provide such rewards. In his analysis of the successful use of rewards in relations between nations, Rosecrance (1981) asserts that rewards are successful when the receiver cannot do without these rewards, cannot obtain them elsewhere, and cannot seize them by force. Under such conditions the recipient will value highly the rewards currently being obtained or promised.

To summarize, the value of the rewards of cooperation with the other side (and therefore the likelihood of reciprocating cooperation) will increase as:

(1) the rewards of cooperation are relevant to the actor's goals—most important, that his aim is not domination of the other;
(2) the rewards are large;
(3) the rewards are clear and specific;
(4) the rewards will follow closely in time; and,
(5) the actor is dependent on the other side to provide the rewards—i.e., he cannot easily do without them, cannot easily obtain them elsewhere, and can't easily seize them by force.

Expectancy That Reward Will Follow Cooperation

The expected benefits of reciprocating rewards or offers of rewards will depend not only on the possible value of cooperation but also on one's expectancy that (further) cooperation by the other will follow one's own cooperation. National leaders will expect that rewards will follow their own cooperative actions (more than they would follow other actions) if: (a) the other side has made its continued rewards contingent on their cooperation, and (b) the other side's promises are credible.

Concessions by one side have been found effective in getting the other to reciprocate only if those concessions are made contingent on concessions by the other (Komorita and Esser, 1975). Unconditional cooperation by one side is not effective in getting the other side to cooperate (Oskamp, 1971). In such circumstances the recipient of rewards learns that he will receive them (or continue to receive them) regardless of his own behavior.

When reward is made conditional on cooperation by the other, then this promise must be credible to be effective. Morton Deutsch (1973) has discussed the conditions under which promises are most credible. Promises, like threats, Deutsch asserts, will be more credible as the other side is seen as more determined to influence; as the other is seen as having more capability to implement the promise at acceptable cost to himself; as the other's perceived commitment to implement the promise increases; and as the appropriateness of the promised reward to what is desired from the target increases. Deutsch suggests that a promise that is inappropriate in kind (or in magnitude) is less believable than an appropriate one because social restraints are more likely to inhibit implementation.

The credibility of the promise will increase also as the target has greater ability to reward and to punish the promisor (Pruitt, 1981). Such capability by the target makes it in the promisor's interest to honor his promise.

In addition to these aspects of the present situation, the credibility of promises will be affected by past behavior of the promisor—i.e., how well he has kept past promises (Gahagan and Tedeschi, 1968; Pruitt, 1981). In this connection, Tedeschi, Schlenker, and Lindskold (1972) report that a promisor who previously was exploitive was ineffective in gaining compliance. Apparently his previous exploitive behavior made the target suspicious of his intentions. Even if the immediate promises of a previously exploitive party are believed, the target may be reluctant to cooperate because he suspects the long-range intentions of the other.

To summarize: a decisionmaker's expectation that rewards from the other side will follow one's own cooperation (and thus his likelihood of responding positively to promises or rewards) will increase as:

(1) the other side has stated, and shown by his past behavior, that his cooperation will follow one's own cooperation but is contingent on such cooperation;
(2) the other has the capability to implement his promises (continue rewards) at an acceptable cost to himself;
(3) the other's attitudes, commitments, and incentives (including one's own ability to reward or punish) give him the motivation to fulfill promises or provide rewards; and,
(4) the reward promised is appropriate to the cooperative behavior requested of one's own side.

Attraction of Alternatives to Cooperation

Whether or not national leaders will reciprocate rewards or respond to offers of rewards will depend also on the attractiveness of possible alternative responses. In particular they may consider the benefits and costs of using coercion, or threat of coercion, to attain their goals. As noted in chapter 5, the attraction of using coercion will depend on its intrinsic benefits and costs, the value of winning in a dispute and the value of a fight (as well as the value of other outcomes), and expectancies about how an adversary will respond to coercion and who the winner of a fight would be.

There is no need to repeat here the lengthy discussion of factors influencing use of coercion that was presented in chapter 5. However, we may consider now the way in which the use of reward or promise of reward may affect the appeal of using coercion.

First, when one's own side is rewarded or promised reward for cooperation by the other side, the intrinsic value of using coercion tends to be reduced. It has been noted (chapter 5) that coercion may seem an appropriate and satisfying action if the decisionmaker believes that the adversary has violated relevant norms of behavior or has otherwise acted illegitimately or provocatively. Such perceptions are unlikely when the other side has provided some reward and invited reciprocation or has promised reward in return for some desired action. Such actions are likely to be viewed positively and to result in more positive attitudes toward the source of reward (Knorr, 1975; Deutsch, 1973). Thus, there usually will be little moral satisfaction in responding to reward or promise with coercion. On the contrary, insofar as norms of reciprocity are relevant, such a coercive response might entail a cost of moral unease. The more that rewards or promises are seen as appropriate and as not demeaning to the target the greater will be the moral discomfort of responding to reward with coercion (or even with inaction).

Secondly, use of reward or promise by the other side will tend to reduce the value of winning a dispute. It has been noted (chapter 8) that heightened competition and rancor in a dispute may make a relative advantage over the adversary appear more important, even at the cost of absolute advantage to oneself; that is, "beating" the other seems as or more important than doing well oneself. But when the other side rewards one's own side or promises rewards for cooperation, the question of who will "win" may become less salient and the prospect of mutual advantage may become more salient. Therefore, coercive methods used to obtain a victory may become less attractive.

Finally, the use of rewards or promises by the other side may affect one's own expectancy that use of coercion will be successful in winning over the other. Sometimes the use of rewards or promises may be seen as indicating softness or a weak resolve to compete successfully.

Whether concessions by one side will be reciprocated or will be met instead with greater toughness will depend on the context of the concessions and the interpretation the opponent puts on them (Druckman, 1983;

Pruitt, 1981; Bartos, 1974). If the side making large concessions is seen by its opponent as doing so out of weakness and desperation, then his concession will tend to be seen as signaling an imminent total collapse of his resolve. Therefore the other may choose to wait for further concessions. On the other hand, if the conceder is seen as strong, then his concessions are likely to be viewed as showing only a willingness to cooperate. The other side may not expect further concessions if he himself does not reciprocate; rather, he may expect the other to become angered and perhaps to harden its position again. In such circumstances the original beneficiary of concessions is likely to reciprocate them. Consistent with this reasoning, Michener and his co-workers (1975) found that a bargainer's concession is more often matched when he has greater threat capacity than his partner. Also, matching of concessions has been found to be more likely when the conceder is seen as having a hard-line constituency (Wall, 1977).

In order to avoid the appearance of weakness, national leaders who take accommodative actions toward an adversary are likely to accompany them with words or actions that indicate a resolve to resist pressures (Snyder and Diesing, 1977). (The ways in which conciliatory actions may be combined with coercive actions and the effects of such strategies will be discussed in the next chapter).

To summarize: the attractiveness of coercive responses to conciliatory behavior by the other will depend on a wide range of factors discussed in chapter 5. Conciliatory actions by another are likely to make the use of coercion less attractive in some ways because: (a) a coercive response to conciliation violates common norms of behavior, and (b) the other's conciliatory actions may make competition less salient. On the other hand, when conciliatory actions are made out of apparent weakness they will tend to be seen as indicating a lack of resolve and therefore make coercive actions seem more likely to succeed. For this reason, national leaders who offer rewards or promises often combine these with words or actions intended to show strength and firmness.

Summary and Policy Implications

If one nation takes conciliatory actions toward another nation with which it has disputes, will such actions be effective in gaining the cooperation of the other? Evidence derived from studies of interaction between contending nations indicates that there is a strong tendency for conciliatory actions to be reciprocated. Also, promises by one nation appear generally to be more effective than threats in influencing an adversary in desired directions. However, conciliatory actions are not always reciprocated; sometimes such actions are met with continued or increased belligerence and an apparent effort to exploit any "softness."

To the target of conciliatory actions, the intrinsic value of responding in a rewarding way (and thus the chances of his doing so) will increase as the costs to him of such actions are lower, as he sees norms of reciprocity to be more relevant, as political support for reciprocation—both domestic and foreign—is greater, as he is more dependent on the goodwill of the other side, and the less the promises of the other side are made in a context of coercion that makes a positive response seem demeaning.

For nation A to make its conciliatory overtures effective in eliciting cooperation from nation B, it should avoid asking for reciprocal actions that are excessively costly for B. It is desirable for A to place its actions within the framework of whatever international norms of cooperation and reciprocity may be relevant. And while it should not hide the fact that noncooperation will not bring the same benefits as cooperation to nation B, it should avoid explicit threats and pressures that would make it humiliating for the other side to respond positively to promises.

The likelihood that nation B will respond with cooperation to rewards or promises of rewards from nation A will depend also on the value to nation B's leaders of the rewards associated with mutual cooperation. The value of the rewards of cooperation will increase as these rewards are more relevant to their important goals, as the magnitude of the promised rewards increases, as the promised rewards of cooperation are more explicit and specific, as the rewards of cooperation are expected more speedily, and as nation B is more dependent on nation A for the relevant rewards.

To make its own conciliatory actions effective in securing cooperation from the other side, national leaders need first to offer the prospect that cooperation will bring benefits that are relevant to the basic goals of the other side. For example, if the other nation is concerned primarily with acceptance as a political equal, then offers of political acceptance may be more effective than an offer of economic aid. National leaders also need to make promises of rewards or concessions that are substantial enough to arouse the interest of the other side without being so great as to arouse suspicion. Promises also need to be specific; vagueness may be seen as indicating either a lack of seriousness or an inability to deliver on the promise. The promised rewards need to be forthcoming quickly as rewards to be enjoyed far in the future tend to be discounted. Finally, it may be possible to make cooperation with one's own nation more valuable by increasing the extent to which the other nation is dependent on the rewards one can provide. Increasing ties of trade, investment, technological exchange, political cooperation, etc., can create greater dependence by both sides.

Whether a conciliatory action by nation A is successful in eliciting concessions from nation B will depend also on the expectations of nation B's leaders about whether mutual cooperation with nation A, however desirable, is realistically possible. B's leaders may wonder: if nation A has made some concessions, will it continue to be cooperative or is its action merely a trick to lull us into a false sense of security (and perhaps into disarming so they can then strike at us)? If nation A has promised rewards in exchange for concessions from us now, will it fulfill these promises?

Decisionmakers will be more likely to expect that (continued) cooperation from a rival will follow their own conciliatory actions the more that: the other has expressed an intention to do so and has done so in the past, the other has the resources to fulfill his promises at an acceptable cost to himself, the other has incentives (including those stemming from vulnerability to their own punishments) to fulfill his promises or continue cooperation, and the rewards promised are appropriate to the cooperative behavior requested of their own side.

To make a policy of conciliation effective, the leaders of nation A must convince their counterparts in nation B that their promises of (continued) rewards are credible. Any promises made should be clearly within their capability to fulfill; for example, offers of economic aid should not be beyond their budget capacity. Rewards promised should be appropriate and roughly proportional to the concessions asked in return. Commitments—such as public statements by top leaders—may aid the credibility of promises. And, national leaders should try to establish a record of behavior—of not attempting to exploit others and of honoring past promises—that makes any current promises of cooperation more credible.

It also is important for leaders using a policy of conciliation to make clear by word and deed that their own (continued) cooperation is contingent on reciprocity from the other side. If the other side believes that it can continue to enjoy rewards regardless of its own behavior, it may prefer to try to exploit the conciliatory side rather than to cooperate with it.

Finally, whether or not nation B will reciprocate conciliatory actions by nation A depends on the relative attractiveness of alternative responses, including especially coercive actions. Factors that determine the attraction of using coercion are discussed in chapter 5. But it has been noted here that conciliatory actions by nation A will tend to make coercive action less appealing to nation B for several reasons. First, to respond to rewards with punishments may be viewed as morally wrong and likely to bring condemnation from others. Secondly, the value of winning over the other nation may be lowered by the other's conciliatory behavior; the value of mutual cooperation may increase in salience while that of triumphing over a hated enemy may decrease in salience. However, conciliatory behavior by nation A will tend to make coercion appear more attractive to nation B's leaders if A's concessions or promises occur in a context of apparent weakness and thus are interpreted as showing a lack of resolve to resist coercion.

To increase the chances that their conciliatory behavior will be reciprocated, national leaders need to do the things (discussed in chapter 5) necessary to make coercion appear costly and unsuccessful to the other side. When offering rewards to induce the other side to cooperate, they need to make clear also their ability and intention to resist any effort by the other side to exploit their own willingness to cooperate. Sometimes this requires a combination of both conciliatory and coercive actions, as will be discussed in the next chapter.

10 Strategies That Mix Conciliation and Coercion

In previous chapters I have discussed separately the effectiveness of conciliatory and of coercive actions in eliciting cooperative responses from an adversary. While it is important to understand the effect of particular kinds of actions, the parties to a dispute often do not use either conciliatory or coercive tactics to the total exclusion of the other. Each may direct some combination of threats, promises, rewards, and penalties toward its adversary.

What kind of strategies that combine reward and punishment in some way are likely to be most effective? There is relevant evidence on this issue from a fairly substantial experimental literature on use of different strategies in conflict situations as well as a smaller but growing literature on the use of alternative strategies in inter-nation disputes. In the following sections, I will review this literature so that we may see what conclusions may be drawn.

Noncontingent Strategies

A decisionmaker will sometimes use a predetermined strategy toward the other side: cooperating consistently, competing consistently, or mixing these actions in some proportion.

Consistent Cooperation

Experimental studies have found that in Prisoner's Dilemma situations (in which the actors prefer a fight to surrender),[1] a player generally can elicit more cooperation from the other by displaying a high level of cooperation himself (Oskamp, 1971). However, often a person who cooperates unconditionally will be exploited by the other (Shure, Meeker, and Hansford, 1965; Deutsch et al., 1967; Reychler, 1979). A strategy of unchanging cooperation appears to be least successful in eliciting cooperation from another in a Chicken situation, in which the payoff for a fight is lower than that for being exploited.[2] In such situations, unconditional cooperation usually results in being exploited by the other (Sermat, 1964, 1967).

Similar outcomes seem to occur frequently on the international scene. Leng and Wheeler (1979) found that in six cases in which a nation used a policy of consistent appeasement against an adversary the result was a diplomatic defeat for the appeaser in five cases and war in the sixth.

Consistent Competitiveness

A completely opposite policy of consistent competition is used sometimes. This strategy may sometimes work when the other side prefers surrender to a fight. In experimental Chicken situations a strategy of consistent competition was more successful than a policy of consistent cooperation in eliciting cooperation from the other side (Sermat, 1964, 1967). In their study of crises between nations, Snyder and Diesing (1977) also found that coercive tactics often are effective in Chicken or "Called Bluff" situations; i.e., where one or both sides prefer giving in on a disputed issue to going to war. In such situations, firmness and belligerence by a clearly stronger side may convince the weaker party to yield.

However, an unconditionally competitive strategy runs a serious risk of resulting in a struggle with an adversary that may bring low payoffs to both. This is especially true when the two sides are about equal in strength and resolve. In Prisoner's Dilemma situations studied in the laboratory, a long string of competitive responses by one side usually is matched in kind by the other—resulting in a "lock-in" on a mutually destructive struggle (Rapoport and Chammah, 1965). Even in Chicken situations, in which one's opponent will receive a better outcome by giving in than if both sides compete, a strategy of consistent competitiveness is successful in causing an opponent to cooperate in only about half the trials; the other half of the time both sides compete and both get poor outcomes (Sermat, 1964, 1967). After trials in which mutual competition and low outcomes occur, both players choose a competitive strategy again on the next trial in at least half, and usually more, of the trials; i.e., both sides refuse to back down despite the fact that to do so would certainly improve their outcomes (Rapoport and Chammah, 1969). They may continue to compete out of the belief that their persistence and willingness to sustain a temporary loss will lead the other side to give in first (Brams, 1985). But if the other side proceeds on the same assumptions, the mutually costly struggle may continue and intensify.

The limitations of a policy of consistent competitiveness are apparent too in studies of inter-nation relations. Leng and Wheeler (1979) found that in thirteen cases in which one nation's leaders consistently bullied an adversary (i.e., used threats and force against it), the result was a diplomatic victory for the bully in two cases, compromise in another two cases, but war in nine cases.

Overall, then, neither unconditional cooperation nor unconditional competitiveness appears to be a very effective way of getting another to cooperate and obtaining good outcomes for one's own side.

Competition, Then Cooperation

It is also possible to change the relative frequency of conciliatory and coercive actions over time so that one becomes more conciliatory or less conciliatory as the interaction progresses. In experimental studies, a strategy that moves from an initial zero level of cooperation to an eventual 100 percent cooperation has been more effective in eliciting cooperation from another than has a strategy of complete cooperation from beginning to end. Also, a change from a low to a high level of cooperation over time is more effective in eliciting cooperation than is the reverse (Oskamp, 1971).

There is some parallel to these experimental results from studies of disputes between nations. In their study of inter-nation crises, Snyder and Diesing (1977) distinguish among P-bargaining, which emphasizes firmness and coercion; T-bargaining, which clarifies one's own minimum demands; and R-bargaining, which involves concessions and the search for compromise. Writing of Prisoner's Dilemma (PD) crises, they state: "The evidence from our cases shows that one cannot begin the solution to a PD crisis with R-bargaining, as a soft-line actor might wish, but must precede R by T and P bargaining" (Snyder and Diesing, 1977:100). They further assert that because P-bargaining establishes one's resolve and makes clear to the other side the danger of war if the other side does not compromise, it makes possible the success of later cooperative efforts. In other types of crisis situations, such as Chicken (in which both nations prefer giving in rather than going to war), Snyder and Diesing (1977:chapter 3) also found that an initial period of coercive bargaining was necessary to clarify the relative bargaining power of the two sides; after this initial period one or both sides would then make concessions.

Using quantitative events data, Leng and Walker (1982) studied ten inter-nation crises, including eight of the same crises studied with qualitative methods by Snyder and Diesing. Leng and Walker also found that successful outcomes for a nation involved in a crisis were associated with use of a relatively high level of coercion during the initial confrontation period. However, their findings also suggest that a willingness to reciprocate cooperation, even during the early confrontational period, is useful in order to prevent a mutual escalation of coercion.

Overall, the evidence indicates that an initial willingness to use threat or coercion often is necessary to gain eventual cooperation from an adversary. Having realized that it cannot exploit its opponent and after having experienced low outcomes during the initial period, the adversary may come to welcome an opportunity for the mutual cooperation it earlier scorned.

However, as Leng and Walker (1982) indicate, the strategy of using threat and coercion to demonstrate one's resolve has dangers. It may begin the two sides on a spiral of escalating coercion that could lead to war. Morever, an initially competitive strategy may make it difficult later to elicit cooperation from an adversary, especially one who began with a cooperative orientation and has become disillusioned (Komorita, 1973). Often an early experience of mutual cooperation can set a pattern of continued cooperation (Oskamp, 1971) and avoid the danger of mutually destructive competition.

Contingent Strategies

Rather than following a preset series of moves, an actor may use a contingent strategy—i.e., one in which he adjusts his actions in some consistent way to the actions of the other side. Both experimental studies (Oskamp, 1971) and studies of strategies followed by national leaders (Leng and Wheeler, 1979) indicate that contingent strategies are more effective than noncontingent strategies in securing the cooperation of an adversary. Contingent strategies also are likely to be of greatest relevance to real-world conflicts since national leaders are likely to adjust their actions to the cooperativeness or belligerence of an adversary.

Two main types of contingent strategies may be distinguished. The first chooses between conciliatory and coercive moves according to how successful each type of move has been in eliciting compliance from the other side. The second chooses his action according to the latest action of the other side, usually reciprocating the other's action.

Trial and Error

The first type of contingent strategy decides whether to be conciliatory or coercive depending on how the other side has responded to one's conciliation or coercion in the past. This type of strategy has not received extensive investigation but several relevant studies have been done.

Robert Axelrod (1980, 1984) has conducted "tournaments" in which experts in conflict submitted strategies for playing the Prisoner's Dilemma game, which were then played out against other strategies by computer. One strategy, submitted by Leslie Downing, estimates after each move the probability that the other side will cooperate after one's own side cooperates as well as the probability that the other will cooperate after one defects (i.e., makes a move that will benefit oneself at the other's expense). These estimates are based on the other side's past responses to one's own cooperation or defection. If the opponent seems to respond similarly whatever one does, then it pays to defect. But if the other tends to cooperate after one's own cooperative move but not after one's defection, then it is best to cooperate. The success of this general strategy was affected greatly by whether one assumed initially that the other would be cooperative or noncooperative (i.e., by whether one began with cooperation or defection). When one began by assuming goodwill on the part of the other and thus cooperated (a revision Axelrod made in the original Downing strategy), this strategy was quite successful in securing favorable outcomes for its user.

The effectiveness of a strategy based on the previous responses of the other side to one's own conciliation or coercion also has been studied in inter-nation disputes. Leng and Wheeler (1979) studied the effectiveness of several strategies followed by national leaders in twenty serious disputes occurring in the twentieth century. One strategy they studied is the "trial and error" strategy. They describe this strategy as follows: "The actor simply adjusts his choice of inducements (i.e., positive or negative) based on the target's response to the previous influence attempt. Inducements that produce positive responses are repeated; inducements that produce negative responses are not" (Leng and Wheeler, 1979:662).

A predominately trial-and-error strategy was followed by five nations in the disputes studied. In four of these cases the nation using this strategy achieved a compromise while in the fifth case it suffered a diplomatic defeat; no wars resulted. The trial-and-error strategy was more effective then a bullying (consistently coercive) strategy, which resulted in war in nine of thirteen cases. It also was better than an appeasing (consistently rewarding) strategy, which resulted in diplomatic defeat in five of six cases and in war in the sixth.

Overall, the limited evidence available suggests that trial-and-error strategies—i.e., choosing those actions that have been successful in the past—sometimes can be effective in promoting mutual cooperation. However a trial-and-error strategy is not likely to be successful against a bullying opponent—i.e., one who is consistently coercive so long as its opponent does not comply fully with its demands. In none of the cases studied by Leng and Wheeler was a trial-and-error strategy used against a bullying opponent. They hypothesize that, when used against such a bully, the trial-and-error strategy will result in either a victory for the bully or in war.

When faced with a bully, Leng and Wheeler comment, the trial-and-error strategist will jump continually from positive to negative inducements and back again (since neither will succeed in gaining the bully's cooperation). The user of the trial-and-error strategy will therefore appear indecisive or unstable, and a clear resolve to resist threats is lacking. Moreover, they note, "it would be the trial-and-error strategist that would be conditioned to change by adopting an appeasing strategy, rather than the other way around" (Leng and Wheeler, 1979:666).

Reciprocation (Tit for Tat)

Most contingent strategies choose one's own next move according to the previous move of the other side. The most straightforward and most common contingent strategy is that of reciprocity, or "tit for tat" (TFT). If in the last move the other has acted in a rewarding or cooperative way, then one responds with cooperation; if the other has acted most recently in a competitive or coercive way then one responds in kind.[3]

A simple TFT matching strategy appears generally to be quite effective in eliciting cooperation from an adversary and securing good outcomes for the user. In experimental studies, a TFT matching strategy has been found to elicit greater cooperation from an adversary than a noncontingent strategy having the same level of cooperation (Oskamp, 1971; Wilson, 1971). A simple TFT strategy also has been more effective than a variety of more complex strategies in producing favorable outcomes in the computer tournaments conducted by Axelrod (1980, 1984).

While these studies have used Prisoner's Dilemma situations, there is no reason to believe that a TFT strategy would be any less effective in a Chicken situation. In fact one might expect it to be even more effective since an adversary suffers his worst outcome when his competitive move is reciprocated in Chicken, as compared to suffering his next-to-worst outcome when this occurs in Prisoner's Dilemma. While to my knowledge no studies have compared the effectiveness of TFT strategies in Chicken versus Prisoner's Dilemma situations, several experiments conducted by Sermat (1967) showed that a TFT strategy (preceded by some cooperative moves) elicited from 58 to 70 percent cooperative responses from an adversary in Chicken situations.

A TFT strategy appears usually to counter the temptation for the other side (B) to preempt (raise his level of competition first) in a Chicken situation (Brams, 1985). If B expects reciprocation of a competitive move, there will be little incentive for him to preempt since the result would be his lowest payoff.[4] And since B will not expect A (who is following a TFT strategy) to preempt, B will not try to beat A to the punch by preempting first.

Leng and Wheeler (1979) have studied the use of a reciprocating (TFT) strategy in serious disputes between nations. They hypothesized that if a nation used the reciprocating strategy against an opponent who employed a bullying strategy (i.e., continuing negative inducements until the other complied), the outcome of a dispute would be war. However, they actually found that a generally reciprocating strategy was fairly successful in dealing with opponents who used bullying strategies. Of eight such cases, two resulted in wars, three ended in compromise, and three resulted in victories for the reciprocator. Thus, the reciprocating strategy did better than hypothesized against bullies.

When a nation used a reciprocating strategy against an opponent who followed a trial-and-error strategy, the outcome was compromise in two cases (as hypothesized by Leng and Wheeler) and a victory for the reciprocator in one additional case. In one case in which two reciprocators interacted in a dispute, the result was compromise (as predicted). And in three cases in which a nation followed a reciprocating strategy against an appeaser, the result was victory for the reciprocator in all three cases.

The overall evidence presented by Leng and Wheeler indicates that a reciprocating strategy was generally effective when used by national leaders in disputes with nations that followed a variety of strategies. The outcomes obtained were better than the outcomes following use of a bullying (consistently coercive) strategy or an appeasing (consistently rewarding) strategy. It was the only strategy generally effective against a bullying opponent. Leng and Wheeler concluded that, "The findings support the central hypothesis that a reciprocating strategy is the most effective means of avoiding a diplomatic defeat without going to war, especially when it is employed against a bullying opponent" (Leng and Wheeler, 1979:655). However, it should be noted that the successful strategies used by the nations studied by Leng and Wheeler were not strictly ones of reciprocity but included unilateral conciliatory initiatives as well. (We will return to this important point in the section on conciliatory initiatives.)

There are several ways in which the basic reciprocity (tit-for-tat) strategy may be varied. One variation is in the speed with which the other side's actions are reciprocated. Bixenstine and Gaebelein (1971) varied separately the quickness of reciprocity to cooperation and to competition by the other side in a Prisoner's Dilemma game. They found that an imbalance in quickness of responding to cooperation and to competitiveness was least effective in eliciting cooperation from the other side. A strategy quick to reciprocate cooperation but slow to reciprocate competition encouraged the other side to take advantage of oneself. On the other hand, quickness to reciprocate competitiveness but slowness to reciprocate cooperation encouraged a "lock-in" on mutual competition.

Bixenstine and Gaebelein (1971) also found that a slow response to both cooperative and competitive behavior by the other was somewhat more successful than a quick response to each kind of behavior. However, Axelrod (1984:184–185) argues that quick reciprocal actions are desirable. Discussing competitive acts by the other, he writes: "The results . . . demonstrate that it is actually better to respond quickly to a provocation. . . . The longer defections are allowed to go unchallenged, the more likely it is that the other player will draw the conclusion that defection can pay. And the more strongly this pattern is established, the harder it will be to break it."

As Axelrod notes elsewhere, the optimal quickness of retaliation against a competitive move may vary with the aims and strategy of one's opponent. When the opponent is not trying systematically to exploit one, a quick reciprocation of a competing move may be counterproductive, leading to a spiral of mutual competition desired by neither side; a tit only after two tats may be a better strategy with a generally cooperative opponent.[5] However, if the opponent is seeking to exploit one's weakness, then being too forgiving of an occasional defection may stimulate further exploitive moves and be destructive of long-run cooperation.

Another way in which reciprocating strategies may vary is in the strength and consistency of their reciprocation. A person might believe that by generally reciprocating cooperation but "sneaking in" an occasional competitive move, one can keep the other side cooperating while gaining some advantage. One of the strategies that competed in the computer tournament conducted by Axelrod was of this kind. This strategy started with tit for tat and gradually lowered its probability of cooperation following the other's cooperation to .5 by the two-hundredth move. It always defected after a defection (competitive move) by the other. Another strategy in the Axelrod tournament that gave less than full cooperation followed a rule of cooperating 90 percent of the time after a cooperation by the other. It too always defected after a defection by the other.

Neither of these strategies was effective in gaining good outcomes for the user. Both did considerably worse than a simple tit for tat that always reciprocated cooperation. Apparently neither strategy was able to lull or fool the other by cooperating most of the time but sneaking in an occasional competitive move. A competitive move often set off a chain reaction of mutually competitive moves that resulted in poor outcomes for both sides.

Of course, the effect of trying to obtain a unilateral advantage occasionally will depend on the reactions of the opponent. An occasional competitive move may not be damaging to long-run cooperation against an opponent who is slow to retaliate or quick to forgive after retaliating; but it may effectively end future cooperation against an opponent who does not forgive (i.e., is consistently competitive) after experiencing an unprovoked competitive move by one's own side. In general, the attempt to gain an occasional advantage by not consistently reciprocating cooperation does not appear to pay off in the long run.

Tit-for-tat strategies may also differ in the strength or severity of the reciprocation made when the other acts competitively or coercively. A person may believe that by hurting the other more than he has been hurt, one will teach the other a lesson and so dissuade him from repeating competitive or coercive acts. However the available evidence does not support such a belief. Gruder and Duslak (1973) compared three types of response to efforts at exploitation by the other: (a) strong retaliation (reducing one's own payoff to zero and the other's to a loss); (b) milder retaliation (reducing both sides' payoffs to zero); and, (c) no retaliation. They found that cooperation from the other was elicited more by mild retaliation than by either a strongly retaliatory or nonretaliatory strategy. Wilson (1971) found that a strategy that responded to a competitive action by the other with two competitive choices was less effective than a simple tit-for-tat (one-for-one) strategy in gaining cooperation from the other.

Two of the strategies entered in Axelrod's tournament of strategies also used strong retaliations. One strategy increased the number of one's own defections every time the other side defected (i.e., the second time the other makes a single defection, one defects two times, etc.). This strategy was less effective than a simple (one-for-one) tit-for-tat strategy in securing cooperation from the other and good outcomes for its users.

Commenting on the general principles of retaliating against competitive moves by the other side, Axelrod (1984) states that often the stability of cooperation is improved if retaliation is slightly less than the provocation. The reasoning behind this statement is that there is a danger of retaliation and counter-retaliation that may cause the two sides to get locked into a continuing and possibly escalating series of mutually competitive actions. By making one's retaliation slightly less than the other's competitive act, one may show him that competition doesn't pay and yet start a process of de-escalation in mutually coercive actions. Gruder and Duslak (1973) suggest that strong retaliation may evoke anger or fear and thus lead to counter-retaliation, either as a defensive move or in an effort to gain victory in the competition.

Strengths and limitations of tit for tat. The simple tit-for-tat strategy appears generally to have great effectiveness in encouraging cooperation from an adversary and leading eventually to good outcomes for both sides. Axelrod (1984) has pointed to four properties that tend to make this decision rule successful: it avoids unnecessary conflict, by cooperating as long as the other side does; it avoids being exploited, by retaliating to competitive actions by the other side; it does not unnecessarily prolong conflict, by its readiness to resume cooperation after it has retaliated; and it is a clear strategy to which the other side can adjust easily.

The success of the simple tit-for-tat strategy also requires few assumptions or special conditions (Axelrod, 1984). Neither side has to be rational; it merely has to repeat behavior that has been rewarded and change behavior that has been punished (or perhaps follow a norm of reciprocity). Altruism is not needed and neither is trust since defection is unproductive. The players do not have to exchange messages or commitments; deeds speak for themselves. And no central authority is needed; cooperation based on reciprocity can be self-policing.

However, there are some special conditions that are necessary for tit for tat to be effective. First, the situation must be one in which the payoffs to each side are greater when they both cooperate than when they both compete. For example, if one side perceives greater advantage in mutual competition than in mutual cooperation, a tit-for-tat policy by the other side will not be effective in eliciting cooperation.

Another important aspect of the situation is the importance of future interactions between the parties (Axelrod, 1984). If each side is concerned only with a present interaction, it may try to get the better of the other by trying to trick or defeat him. However, an attempt to win unilateral advantage today will lead to mutual competition and mutually low outcomes (in most cases) in the future. Cooperation at any point in time requires therefore that both sides place sufficient importance on cooperation in the future to induce them to refrain from competing in the present. A tit-for-tat strategy is most likely to be effective when the relationship between the parties is frequent and durable and where the issue of today does not seem so vital to either side that it is willing to sacrifice future cooperation in order to win current advantage.

There are also some important problems that may arise in the interaction process necessary in order for a TFT strategy to be successful. First, it may be hard to get reciprocal cooperation started. The usual rule in experimental studies is that a party using the tit-for-tat strategy will make its first move a cooperative one; but that assumes that the interaction is just beginning. In real-world cases in which a new strategy is being considered, the interaction is ongoing, and if the other side has just taken a competitive action the tit-for-tat rule would be to reciprocate with a competitive action.

Whether or not a mutual reciprocation of cooperation can ever get started, there is another serious problem inherent in a strict TFT strategy. This is that if ever, and whenever, a single competitive move is made by one side, the two sides may get "locked in" on mutual competition. The first competitive move by side A may be reciprocated with a competitive move by side B, which is in turn reciprocated by a competitive move by side A, and so on. Axelrod has acknowledged this strategic weakness, commenting that, "The result would be an unending echo of alternating defections. In this sense, tit-for-tat is not forgiving enough" (Axelrod, 1984:176). Wilson (1971) points out that in order for the TFT strategy to do well, the other player must be willing to break out of a lock-in on mutual competition and follow a "more generous" strategy.

The problem of a lock-in on mutual competition appears to be more serious in Prisoner's Dilemma situations than in Chicken situations. However, even in Chicken, where mutual competition results in the lowest outcome for each side, in a majority of cases neither side switches to cooperation following a mutually competitive, mutually punishing, trial (Rapoport and Chammah, 1969).

Reciprocity Plus Conciliatory Initiatives

A strategy that is intended to overcome the major problem of tit for tat—i.e., the difficulty of breaking out of a "lock-in" on mutual competition—combines elements of reciprocity with conciliatory initiatives taken independently of the other's actions. An influential statement of such a strategy has been made by Charles Osgood (1962, 1980, 1984), who labels his program Graduated Reciprocation in Tension Reduction

(GRIT). Osgood proposes that American leaders initiate a series of conciliatory moves toward our major adversary, the Soviet Union. Each of these moves might be one of a variety of types—e.g., reductions in, or less threatening, deployment of some military force (bombers, missiles, submarines, troops, etc.); an economic concession; provision of scientific information; a political concession. None of these moves, singly or in combination, would be of a nature and magnitude that would endanger basic U.S. security. The basic program of initiatives would be announced in advance and explained as an effort to reduce tensions and to enhance cooperation between the two sides. Each cooperative move also would be announced in advance. Reciprocation by the other side would be invited. The size and nature of future conciliatory initiatives by the United States would be adjusted according to the degree of reciprocation that the adversary displayed. However, the program of initiatives would be continued for a considerable time, regardless of how much reciprocation was initially forthcoming.

The GRIT strategy would not abandon the possible use of coercion. If the Soviet Union used coercive tactics, perhaps in an attempt to exploit what they might see as signs of U.S. weakness, such coercive moves would be resisted in kind.

The basic aim of the GRIT strategy is to encourage an eventual pattern of mutual cooperation. It is intended also to lower the level of mutual mistrust and hostility to a point where negotiated agreements for arms reductions and further cooperation could be made.

The possible effectiveness of the GRIT strategy has been investigated in several experimental studies. Some evidence from inter-nation relations also is available.

Pilisuk and Skolnick (1968), Lindskold and Collins (1978) and Lindskold, Walters, and Koutsourais (1983) all studied the effectiveness of a GRIT-type conciliatory strategy[6] as compared to the effectiveness of other strategies in Prisoner's Dilemma games. All three studies found that the conciliatory strategy was more effective than a tit-for-tat strategy in eliciting more and/or earlier cooperation from the other side. (The conciliatory strategy also was more effective than 100 percent cooperation, than 50 percent cooperation, and than natural sequences of play.) The GRIT strategy was as effective for groups as for individuals. It also was as effective among subjects who were generally competitive as among those who were generally cooperative, as shown by their previous play. Lindskold (1978) also has reviewed a wide experimental literature relevant to the GRIT proposal and finds the evidence generally consistent with the GRIT strategy.

Evidence concerning the possible effectiveness of the conciliatory GRIT strategy comes not only from laboratory studies but also from interactions between nations. One of the most dramatic examples of the use of unilateral initiatives occurred in American-Soviet relations during the early 1960s in what Etzioni (1967) calls the "Kennedy experiment." On 10 June 1963 President Kennedy delivered a speech in which he took a conciliatory tone toward the Soviet Union and outlined a "strategy for peace." The President also announced that the United States was unilaterally stopping all nuclear tests in the atmosphere and would not resume them unless another nation did. (The Soviets reciprocated by not testing their own nuclear weapons in the atmosphere.) On June 15 Soviet Premier Khrushchev welcomed Kennedy's speech and announced that he had ordered that the production of strategic bombers be halted.

In the following months, from June through October, a series of further unilateral conciliatory moves were made by each side. For the United States, these actions included removing its objections to full status for the Hungarian delegation to the United Nations, proposing that the United States and the Soviet Union explore the stars together, and approving the sale of U.S. wheat to the Soviets. Unilateral conciliatory actions by the Soviets included removing their objection to Western-backed proposals to send observers to war-torn Yemen, agreeing to a direct communications link between the United States and the Soviet Union, and calling for a nonaggression pact between Warsaw Pact members and nations of the North Atlantic bloc. In addition, several agreements between the two countries were reached: a U.S.-Soviet treaty banning the testing of nuclear weapons in the atmosphere was signed in Moscow and the two nations agreed to ban weapons of mass destruction from space. Also there was an exchange of released spies.

The momentum of mutual cooperation slowed during the American election year of 1964, in part because of domestic political reasons in the United States and also because of the opposition to détente from the hard-line chancellor of America's ally Germany. Despite President Kennedy's assassination, the United States resumed some conciliatory initiatives in early 1965, but by that time the Vietnam war was escalating, putting the United States and the Soviet Union on opposite sides of a major conflict and the "Kennedy experiment," which had started so promisingly, petered out.

In reviewing the events of 1963–1964, which clearly produced a reduction of tension between the United States and the Soviet Union, Etzioni concludes that this "effect can be most directly tied to the unilateral initiatives; it started with them, grew as they grew, and slowed down only as they decreased" (Etzioni, 1967:375). He comments also that an important purpose of the Kennedy policy was to change American public opinion to be more accepting of cooperative moves toward the Soviet Union. Overall, he asserts, "The policy of unilateral initiatives can be said to have worked, and the experiment to have been successful" (Etzioni, 1967:380).

A national policy that combines firmness in resisting coercion with conciliatory initiatives also has been found effective in a recent study by Leng (1984). He studied the relation between American actions and Soviet responses in three crises: the Berlin blockade of 1948–49, the Berlin crisis of 1961, and the Cuban missile crisis of 1962. Leng found that when the United States combined threats with positive inducements, or used positive inducements alone, it was much more successful in getting Soviet cooperation than when it used threats alone. He comments: "The most effective U.S. influence attempts were carrot-and-stick inducements combining a demonstration of resolve with cooperative initiatives" (Leng, 1984:353). These results are consistent with the Leng and Wheeler (1979) study of twenty inter-nation crises.

In describing the reciprocating strategies that were successful against a bully, (Leng and Wheeler, 1979:677) say: "In each case, a firm-but-fair attitude on the part of the reciprocating opponent is combined with a face-saving way out for the bully in the form of a modest unilateral positive inducement." Later, in discussing the role of third parties in ". . . encouraging the positive inducements that led to the deescalation of the dispute, . . ." they assert: "In the cases at hand, we may be observing a two step process in which the third party convinces one of the disputants to abandon a simple tit-for-tat strategy which are then seized by the disputant that has found itself in the weaker bargaining position" (Leng and Wheeler, 1979:679). Clearly, then, the strategy found successful by Leng and Wheeler is not one of strict reciprocity but one that combines a general disposition to reciprocity with unilateral conciliatory actions that break any cycles of mutual competition and coercion. In this respect the strategies they found successful in inter-nation disputes are consistent with the GRIT program. Further evidence of the effectiveness of concessions offered in combination with a firm approach has been presented in comparative case studies of coercive bargaining in recent American foreign policy by George, Hall, and Simons (1971) and in a variety of international crises by Snyder and Diesing (1977).

Some possible limitations or problems of the conciliatory GRIT strategy should be noted. Under certain conditions, the adversary whom one is attempting to influence may try to exploit one's willingness to take conciliatory initiatives. The adversary may continually lag behind in reciprocation and in this way attempt to do better than its partner (Pilisuk and

Skolnick, 1968). More seriously, it may attempt to get the conciliatory side to surrender completely to its demands.

Such attempts by a target of the GRIT program to exploit and dominate its partner, rather than to cooperate with him, may stem from the target's basic aims. In presenting his GRIT program for promoting U.S.-Soviet cooperation, Osgood (1962) makes clear that the program assumes that the prime Soviet objective is for security, not domination. In words still relevant a generation later, he writes:

> It assumes that the Soviet people *and* their leaders are more like us than the bogey men our psychology creates, and that therefore we can do business with them. It assumes that their prime motive, like ours, is security, not world domination, and that they are as eager as we are to avoid full-scale nuclear conflict. . . . And, finally, therefore, it assumes that the Russians would accept an unambiguous opportunity to help reduce world tensions—for reasons of good sense even if not for reasons of good will. (Osgood 1962:136–137)

Kaplowitz (1984) also asserts that the success of a "firm but cooperative" strategy depends on the aims of the other side. He defines this strategy as one that employs positive inducements to influence its opponent, although it also uses negative sanctions to resist exploitation if necessary; it aims at mutual satisfaction of both parties. This strategy seems very similar to and certainly consistent with that of GRIT.

Used against an opponent who is following a "totalist" strategy (i.e., emphasizing negative sanctions and seeking complete victory over its adversary), Kaplowitz says that the firm-but-cooperative strategy will be interpreted as weakness and the end result will be a high level of conflict. However, he argues, when used against an opponent who is willing to accept an accommodation with its adversary (even if it initially emphasizes use of negative sanctions), the firm-but-cooperative strategy will move the interaction toward constructive, cooperative outcomes.

The possibility that an adversary will try to exploit cooperative initiatives usually is greatest in a Chicken situation. Because the adversary knows (or believes) that one's payoffs will be even lower in a fight than they will be by giving in, he may interpret a conciliatory initiative as a sign of lack of resolve. He may expect that by making threats, exerting other pressures, or simply waiting, other concessions will follow until the conciliator has accepted all of his terms.

Thus, while a conciliatory move often is useful to signal one's own willingness to cooperate, it is important—especially when the opponent may be tempted to try to exploit such action—to make clear also one's resolve to reciprocate competitive moves. To make such intentions credible requires among other things that one's side has sufficient strength to be able to withstand a period of mutual competition for as long as or longer than the other side can do so (Brams, 1985).

Consistent with these remarks, experimental evidence indicates that conciliation is most likely to be effective in eliciting cooperation when the conceder is perceived by his adversary as strong and as having made the concessions willingly rather than as having been compelled to do so (Komorita, 1973). Also an opponent is more likely to cooperate in response to a strategy of conciliation when the initiator of conciliation is equal in power to or stronger than the other side (Linkskold and Aronoff, 1980; Chertkoff and Esser, 1976).[7] I know of no systematic evidence concerning how relative power affects the success of a conciliatory strategy used by nations. However, it may be noted that in the most widely cited use of GRIT by national leaders, the Kennedy administration initiated its successful policy of concessions toward the Soviet Union soon after a strong United States had "faced down" the Soviets in the Cuban missile crisis.

Though the limits of its application need to be recognized, a conciliatory strategy like GRIT appears to be a very promising way to use the basic strengths of a reciprocating strategy without getting locked-in on mutual competition. It appears to offer a feasible way to reverse a spiral of mutual competition and turn it into a pattern of mutual cooperation.

One possible way in which the GRIT strategy can be combined with a straight reciprocating (tit-for-tat) strategy has been advanced by Pilisuk and Skolnick (1968). They suggest that a conciliatory (GRIT) strategy may be most useful for inducing movement toward cooperation but that once the advantages of mutual cooperation have grown apparent, a tit-for-tat strategy may be best to push it all the way to full mutual cooperation.

This suggestion is consistent with the pattern of behavior found by Leng and Wheeler to be most successful against a bullying adversary in internation disputes. They state: "we find a remarkable regularity to the reciprocating pattern observed in five of the six cases. Each of these began with a series of unyielding and threatening responses to the consistently negative inducements of the bullying adversary. These were followed by one or two unilateral positive inducements. Then the reciprocator returned to tit-for-tat responses to the bully's mix of cooperative and conflictive actions for the remainder of the dispute" (Leng and Wheeler, 1979:680).[8] Apparently the conciliatory initiatives were successful in breaking the cycle of mutual punishments and moving the adversaries toward a more satisfying pattern of reciprocal cooperation.[9]

Summary and Conclusions

A policy of unconditional cooperation tends to bring exploitation by an adversary while a policy of consistent coerciveness tends to lead to war. However, a strategy that begins with firmness—including the threat or use of coercion—in the early stages of a dispute and then switches to conciliation appears generally to be effective in securing cooperation from an opponent. Apparently the demonstration of one's willingness to use coercion and the poor outcomes of an initially competitive relationship usually cause an adversary to welcome, and respond positively to, a later chance for cooperation.

This does not mean that, when a dispute arises with another nation, leaders should routinely begin by issuing threats and acting coercively against the other in order to demonstrate their resolve. Such actions can be dangerous; they can escalate quickly into mutual threats and coercion —perhaps erupting into an open clash—and it may be difficult to reverse this momentum. Moreover, in many cases an initially conciliatory overture may be successful in eliciting cooperation and in setting a pattern for continuing cooperation.

However, the evidence does suggest that, especially when confronting a competitive adversary, it may be necessary to exhibit firmness before a more conciliatory approach can be successful. If threat and even mild coercion is used in an early stage of a dispute, it should be done in a way that makes clear that one's aim is to resist domination and not to dominate or exploit the other. Such a firm-but-fair posture can prepare the way for later conciliatory moves aimed at breaking out of a pattern of mutual threat and coercion.

While certain patterns of behavior—such as initial firmness followed by cooperation—tend to be successful, the most effective strategies are those that adjust one's own behavior to the actions of the other side. One such strategy is that of trial and error—i.e., discarding those actions that are unsuccessful and repeating those that are successful in gaining positive responses from the other side. There is some evidence that this strategy is often successful in obtaining the cooperation of an adversary. However, if used against a bullying opponent who will not respond positively to anything less than complete surrender to his demands, the trial-and-error strategy is likely to lead either to surrender or to war.

More widely used is the strategy of reciprocity (tit for tat), which returns reward for reward and punishment for punishment. This strategy avoids unnecessary conflict, by cooperating as long as the other side does; avoids being exploited, by retaliating to competitive actions by the other side;

does not unnecessarily prolong conflict, by its readiness to resume cooperation after it has retaliated; and is a clear strategy to which the other side can adjust easily. A strategy of basic reciprocity has been found generally to be effective in gaining the cooperation of an adversary in experimental settings and also in inter-nation disputes.

Available evidence indicates that cooperation and competitiveness by the other side should be reciprocated with equal vigor. To respond more slowly to competition than to cooperation invites exploitation by the adversary. But to respond more slowly to cooperation than to competition invites a lock-in on mutually unrewarding competition.

Inconsistency in reciprocating cooperation tends to destroy the chances for sustained mutual cooperation. Even an occasional attempt to take advantage of the other's cooperation tends to result in a pattern of repeated mutual competition. In addition, responding to an adversary's competitive move with an even stronger competitive move of one's own appears to perpetuate mutual competition. Rather than teaching the other side a lesson, "topping" the adversary in coercion tends to generate hostility and a feeling by the other that he needs to get even. A strategy that reciprocates a competitive move in equal measure, or preferably in slightly smaller magnitude, will indicate firmness in resisting exploitation by the adversary while signaling a desire for de-escalation and cooperation.

It appears desirable then for national leaders to follow a policy of basic reciprocity, responding in kind equally (and reasonably promptly) to conciliatory and to coercive moves by an adversary. They should not attempt to take advantage of the other side's cooperation even occasionally, since such actions will seriously damage the chances for sustained cooperation. Also, while resisting competitive actions by the other, they should not respond with punishments that are stronger than those used by the other side; in fact, somewhat milder punishments should suffice to show resolve while encouraging de-escalation of mutual coercion.

While a strategy of reciprocity has some important strengths, in its pure form this strategy also has some important, sometimes fatal, weaknesses. The basic problem is that once a pattern of mutual competition has started, it may be very difficult to break. In fact, if both sides follow strictly a strategy of reciprocity, a single competitive move will be enough to start an unending series of reciprocal competitive moves.

To break such lock-ins on mutual competition, usually accompanied by mutual hostility and distrust, a strategy that combines unilateral conciliatory initiatives with a general policy of reciprocity is desirable. Such a policy, termed Gradual Reciprocation in Tension Reduction (GRIT), has been proposed by Charles Osgood.

Evidence from experimental studies of conflict provides support for the GRIT program. Moreover, a similar strategy combining basic reciprocity with conciliatory initiatives has been found to be effective in studies of inter-nation disputes. National leaders achieved successful outcomes in serious disputes with other nations (including bullying adversaries) if they followed a policy of general reciprocity (including firmness against attempted coercion early in a dispute) but also initiated conciliatory moves (e.g., making some concessions) to break a dangerous competitive stalemate.

A policy of general reciprocity, plus conciliatory initiatives when needed, would not be expected to work against all adversaries. It assumes that the adversary is primarily concerned with its own security and not in achieving domination. Thus, an adversary who is more powerful than one's own side and has exploitive aims might not respond positively to the reciprocity-plus-conciliatory initiatives strategy.

However, in most cases—including the present Soviet-American situation—neither side has a power so preponderant that it can afford realistically the costs of attempting to dominate the other (whatever its wishes might be). Thus, the task of national leaders is to manage the relations between their nations in such a way that destructive competition and coercion is kept to a minimum and a maximum of mutually beneficial cooperation occurs. For these ends, a basic strategy of reciprocating both rewarding behavior and punishing behavior by the other, combined with using conciliatory initiatives to break out of competitive spirals, seems to be effective.

11 Settling Disputes

Every dispute eventually comes to an end. Occasionally it ends with one side physically imposing its will on the other, or even destroying the other, as when Rome destroyed Carthage. In the vast majority of cases, however, a dispute is ended by agreement between the parties. The agreement is reached by a process of explicit or implicit negotiation or bargaining.

When do the parties to a dispute reach agreement on the issue or issues separating them and when do they not reach agreement? Our consideration of this subject will primarily involve the subject of negotiation as it involves the exchange of demands, offers, and concessions. However, we will view the process of negotiation in the context of bargaining as a broader process that involves not only bids and counterbids but also actions such as threat and coercion by which each side may attempt to influence the other to make concessions. Thus, the discussion of negotiation in this chapter will be linked to the discussion in previous chapters of the use of threat, of coercion, and of positive incentives.

Much of the work on negotiation has been done in economics, growing out of interest in such relations as those between labor and management and between buyers and sellers (see, for example, Bacharach and Lawler, 1981). Social psychologists also have devoted considerable attention to negotiation processes and have carried out many experimental studies on this topic (see, for example, Rubin and Brown, 1975; Pruitt, 1981). Most of the work in both fields has been done at a high level of generality so that it may be applied to negotiation between parties in a wide variety of settings. I will draw on this body of work concerning negotiation as a general process and will try to apply it to negotiation of disputes between nations. In addition, I will draw on work dealing directly with negotiations between nations. I will consider in a general way the nature of an agreement reached in terms of how much it favors each side. But there will not be an attempt to predict the precise nature of an agreement in any case. Rather, the emphasis will be on the process by which two sides may move toward some agreement and the circumstances that result either in success or failure of such efforts.

Differences in Perceptions

If the parties to a dispute knew how it would be settled eventually, they could reach agreement quickly, without suffering the costs of prolonged bargaining (which sometimes include a long, painful test of coercive strength). As Snyder and Diesing remark with respect to crises between nations: "If two states could agree on each other's relative capabilities, willingness to take risks, interests, and intentions, there would be little to bargain about. If each side agreed on who was weaker (though both might be mistaken), the weaker side would not challenge and, if challenged by the stronger, would yield quickly . . ." (Snyder and Diesing, 1977:290).

The basic reason disputants often do not reach quick agreement is that each side may have a different view of how the dispute will eventually be settled and the costs to each during the bargaining period. Snyder and Diesing note concerning nations in disputes: "At the beginning of a crisis, each party is expecting the other to give way on some disputed point and is not expecting to give way itself, and as long as these differences persist there can be no settlement" (1977:290). In another place, they say: "A crisis occurs only when the net balance of interests and material power is even enough that both sides can plausibly see some chance of winning, or at least, for the challenger, some chance of improving his position, or for the resister, some chance of salvaging something better from resisting than he would lose by immediate capitulation" (1977:193).[1] Consistent with this line of reasoning, there is evidence that war becomes more likely as the identity of the victor in a struggle becomes less clear (Blainey, 1973).

A good example of how divergent perceptions by the two sides about their relative strengths may lead to continuation of a conflict is the territorial dispute between India and China that led to war between these nations in 1962. Lebow (1985:209) comments that this military confrontation

. . . was the result of different estimates of the relative political and military strengths of the two sides. As Chinese leaders considered themselves very definitely the stronger party in any military confrontation, they believed that restraint on their part might encourage compromise by India, but because the Indians saw themselves as militarily superior, they interpreted Chinese restraint as lack of resolve and became more intransigent in their position.

Differences in perceptions of the two sides about their relative resolve leads to different expectations about the final outcome of the dispute. The wider the initial gap in expectations between the two sides, the more difficult and the more time-consuming it will be for them to reach agreement. Experimental evidence in support of this plausible proposition is provided by Siegel and Fouraker (1960), who found that optimistic expectations by bargainers will delay a settlement.

Expectations of decisionmakers, including leaders of nations, usually are slow to change (Jervis, 1976; Lebow, 1981). Usually sudden, dramatic unanticipated events or a long succession of disconfirming events are necessary before changes in the expectations of national leaders occur (Snyder and Diesing, 1977). The wider the initial divergence in expectations, the longer and more difficult its reduction will be.

When expectations about the final outcome of the dispute differ greatly, nations may be reluctant even to enter negotiations to resolve the dispute. Pillar (1983) found that when leaders of a nation involved in a war had very different expectations from their opponent about what the outcome would be, they preferred to delay peace negotiations until the other side came around to their view. For example, Pillar points out that during the first year of the Korean war, the Communist side (North Korea and later China) and the United States had differing expectations about the outcome. During the ebb and flow of the battle, first one side and then the other expected to push its opponent off the Korean peninsula while the adversary had other plans. However, the failure of the Chinese offensive in May 1951 "marked the end of contradictory expectations. Each side now knew—and knew the other knew—that the Communists could not push the UNC (United Nations Command) out of Korea. It was also fairly clear that the UNC was capable of advancing farther north, but only at the cost of heavy casualties" (Pillar, 1983:61). Negotiations opened soon afterward, though further fighting occurred before a truce was finally concluded.

The differing expectations by the parties about the outcome of the dispute reflects the fact that each expects the other to make all or most of the concessions. This difference in expectations stems in turn from different perceptions of the strength of values and interests held by each side and of the costs and probable outcome of a (continued or expanded) test of strength between the two sides.

Because each side is acutely aware of its own interests in the issue and may have little close contact with the other, it may believe that the strength of its own motivation (and thus the value it places on favorable outcomes) is greater than that of its adversary. It may believe too that, in the event of a coercive struggle, the other side will suffer more and that its own side will ultimately win. Therefore it will believe that the other side puts a more negative value on a fight and is more anxious to avoid such a fight. Given such perceptions, it will see itself in a more powerful bargaining position and will expect the other side to back down. For example, in their dispute with North Vietnam, American leaders believed that their greater capacity to impose damage gave them a clear superiority in bargaining power that would lead North Vietnam to give in. However, the North Vietnamese believed that they would be prepared to endure sacrifices for a much longer time than the Americans and that eventually they would prevail.

Walton and McKersie (1965) assert that widely incompatible differences in the position of management and workers occur because of differences in perceptions about the strength of preferences and about strike cost realities. Writing about serious disputes between nations, Snyder and Diesing (1977) emphasize the same basic point: that an initial wide gulf between two nations' positions stems from differences in their perceptions of the power balance, i.e., of the relative strength of the values each side puts on various outcomes, including winning, losing, compromise and war.

In order for the perceptions and expectations of two sides to converge, it is necessary that they have similar information about the interests, strengths, and preferences of each side. This requires that free and full information be available to each (Cross, 1978). In the case of nations relevant information includes that concerning each nation's military and economic capabilities and its alternatives for making up for resources that might be denied to it by an adversary in the event of a war. Also relevant is evidence bearing on the value that each side places on various outcomes of the dispute, such as winning or compromise on the issue. Such evidence can be provided by the clear presence of incentives—such as the need for raw materials or for satisfying domestic political factions. For example, there was clear evidence by 1968—from newspaper editorials, congressional statements, polls, and public demonstrations—that the American public had turned against the war in Vietnam and that there were political advantages for the administration to settle on terms far short of victory. In general, the more complete the flow of information during the bargaining period, the more easily and rapidly the expectations and positions of the two sides will converge.

While some relevant objective information often is available to both sides, there usually is considerable ambiguity and uncertainty about the true balance of capability and of motivation. Each side in a dispute may try to mislead the other about its own interests, strength, preferences, and intentions in order to win some advantage. Even when objective information is available concerning specific elements of an adversary's strength (e.g., tanks, artillery, men under arms), it is difficult for national leaders to make overall estimates of the other side's capabilities and especially of its motivations. Among the many uncertainties that are likely to be present are those of how completely the adversary is willing to mobilize its resources for a fight, how much outside help each adversary would get in a fight, and what the effect of coercion would be on the morale of the adversary (Iklé, 1971:chapter 2).

When information is available to national leaders, they interpret it in the context of their prior beliefs and expectations (see chapter 3). Leaders may approach a present situation convinced that an adversary is weak, irresolute, and anxious to avoid a fight. For example, Israeli leaders after their 1967 victory had such an image of their Egyptian adversary and distorted information that the Egyptian president preferred to fight rather than to accept the status quo. National leaders often hold general hard-line or soft-line beliefs about the preferences of adversaries—that they prefer backing down to engaging in a fight or vice versa. (See chapter 3 for a discussion of such beliefs.) While perceptions about an adversary based on general beliefs, on stereotypes, or on past experiences may be correct, they are more likely to be wrong than those based on good current information. Thus, the more fixed and inflexible the beliefs about the adversary that leaders of two sides bring to a dispute, the more likely are their perceptions of their relative bargaining power and resolve to diverge.

Bargaining Tactics

Given a situation in which two sides initially make widely different demands, each side is likely to want to learn more about how serious the other really is about sticking to its demands. It may also at the start not be completely clear about how serious it itself is. Each side would like of course to influence the other to accept all (or at least most) of its own demands. Bargaining, as Walton and McKersie (1965) assert, serves to estimate the utility of outcomes and to alter them.

Clarifying the Situation

Each side in a dispute may not be sure about how highly its opponent values the stakes in the dispute nor how willing it is to fight to gain its ends. Is it truly committed or is it mainly bluffing? Writing about the disputes between nations that reached crisis proportions, Snyder and Diesing (1977:393) comment:

> From the opponent one needs to know his intentions and objectives as well as the amount of risk he is willing to take for his objective. One also would like to know the minimum concession that would induce him to settle peacefully. In short, one would like information about his constraints and his levels of aspiration and acceptability. However, this is precisely the information the opponent wishes to keep secret, either because he is not clear about it himself and wishes to keep his options open or, if he is clear, because it can be used to manipulate him.

Information about the opponent's values and intentions may be obtained from a variety of sources, including intelligence sources. But the most important device to gather information is the probe, an action of one's own intended to test the other's responses. Probes can be either coercive or accommodative. When a nation uses a coercive probe, it applies military, economic, or diplomatic pressure of some kind in order to see how firmly the other will react. For example, during the lengthy second Berlin crisis, the Soviets and their East German clients carried out a number of probes in 1960–1961 aimed at testing Western resolve to stay in Berlin. These included imposing travel restrictions to Berlin and East Berlin border regulations (both accepted) and air-traffic regulation for West Berlin, which was rejected (Schick, 1971). Such probes provided information to the Soviet Union and to East Germany about what rights and Western allies considered most vital in Berlin and how far they were prepared to give in to demands of the Eastern bloc.

Accommodative probes are hints (not firm statements) of one's own willingness to make certain kinds of agreements in order to learn what concessions the other might be prepared to make. For example, during the Berlin crisis, the U.S. ambassador to Moscow suggested some hypothetical Western concessions to Soviet Premier Khruschev to learn if these would induce Khruschev to agree to German reunification with free elections. (These ideas were dropped because they did not have the support of West German Chancellor Adenauer.)

In addition to trying to learn more about the values of its opponent—i.e., how committed it is to its objectives and how ready it is to risk a fight in order to get its way—each side may need to ask the same questions of itself. The initial period of probes and counter-probes may force each to face these questions. Snyder and Diesing (1977:395) comment:

When a bargainer is probed coercively, he must ask himself "Is this specific point worth a war to us?" This is not a speculative question but a practical one requiring immediate reply. When he receives an accommodative probe, he must ask "Are we willing to concede that?" These questions require the examination of constraints at specific points, at the margin, rather than in general and in the abstract. The prober must also evaluate his aspiration and acceptability levels when he is planning a probe, and also when his probes are repulsed. Probes are expensive and risky and must be limited to securing really important information; and when a probe is repulsed the question again arises "Is this specific point worth a war, or can we be satisfied with some other point instead?"

The bargaining period—especially in its early phase—also may help to clarify the costs of a possible (expanded) fight and the probable winner. Each side may learn more about the resources and unity of the other side and about its own as well. Furthermore, each side may attempt to learn more about the likely actions of relevant third parties, including possible allies in any fight. Such information helps national decisionmakers to assess the probable consequences of a fight and therefore affects the strength of their relative preferences for various outcomes, such as compromise or losing versus war.

Exerting Influence

Of course, the process of bargaining involves much more than attempts by each side to clarify the preferences of the opponent. Central to the bargaining process is the attempt by each side to change the preferences of its opponent so that the relative strength of the value the opponent gives to winning or to a fight decreases while the value it gives to losing (or at least compromising) increases.

The bargaining tactics used by each side are intended to change the perceived (and sometimes the objective) bargaining power of the two sides (Bacharach and Lawler, 1981; Snyder and Diesing, 1977). Each side attempts to do this by taking actions that affect the values the other places on various outcomes of the dispute (including a fight) and the other's perception of one's own values and intentions. The choice among possible actions intended to influence the other side, and the effectiveness of most actions, have been discussed at length in previous chapters. Here we may consider influence methods only briefly.

Persuasion. The first and least expensive means for influencing the other side is verbal persuasion. Side A may give real or fictitious information to Side B that is intended to show one or more of the following: (a) winning the dispute is not as important for side B as it has believed; (b) winning is more important for side A than B has realized; (c) a fight will be more costly to B than B has recognized; (d) A has the strength to prevail in a (continuing) fight; and, (e) A will not concede (much) and is willing to fight "if necessary." For example, during the Berlin crisis of 1958–1962, the Soviet Union attempted to convince the Western allies that changing the status of Berlin and signing a peace treaty with East Germany merely represented the normalization of an abnormal situation carried over from World War II and thus should not be of great concern for the West. At the same time they argued that a change in the status quo was a matter of great importance to their side in order to stabilize the German Democratic Republic (East Germany). They stressed the great costs of a war begun in Central Europe but made clear their belief that their superior conventional forces would result in a Soviet victory. On the other hand, the United States and other Western powers tried to convince the Soviets of the great importance they placed on maintaining control of Berlin and attempted also to convince the Soviets that a war in Central Europe would escalate to the use of nuclear weapons in which the Soviets would be the loser (Schick, 1971).

While persuasion may have some effect, usually each party will be distrustful of arguments advanced by its opponent. Therefore, influence methods that actually affect the opponent, or express one's intention to do so, are often used.

Threat. Through threats one side affects the expectatons of its opponent that, unless concessions are made, it will face an expanded fight and additional costs. One example is the threat made by the Kennedy administration to the Soviet Union that it would bomb and invade Soviet bases in Cuba if Soviet missiles there were not removed.

Even when a war is already in progress, threat of escalation may be used to change the opponent's expectations about one's future action. For example, after Eisenhower was inaugurated president in 1953 he hinted that the United States would use atomic weapons and strike directly at China if the Chinese did not agree to an end to the war in Korea. Eisenhower's words were accompanied by a number of actions, including the movement of nuclear missiles to Okinawa and a partial alert of the Strategic Air Command, which served to give credibility to the veiled threats (Pillar, 1983:183–84). Eisenhower's words and actions caused the Chinese to revise their expectations about future American actions, which probably contributed to the armistice agreement that followed shortly.

Coercion. Rather than threatening future actions, a disputant may actually take actions that impose costs on its opponent. For example, the United States launched heavy bombing raids against North Vietnam in 1965 and in later years in an effort to influence North Vietnam to accept a settlement of the Vietnam dispute on American terms. Similarly, in trade disputes, one nation may raise tariffs on another nation's goods in order to pressure it to agree to terms acceptable to the first (Nicholson, 1967). The main purpose of using coercive action is to make the status quo so costly for the opponent that it will prefer a quick agreement to continuation of the struggle. In addition, the use of coercion may be intended to signal to the opponent one's own determination to stand firm in the dispute and the likelihood that one will take further coercive actions if the dispute remains unresolved. For example, the American blockade of Cuba during the missile crisis of 1962 not only created some immediate difficulties for the Soviets but, more importantly, communicated American resolve and made much more credible to the Soviets the American threats to take further coercive action (i.e., bombing or invasion).

In order for coercion to be effective in influencing an opponent to make concessions, it usually is necessary that the costs imposed on the opponent are much greater than those suffered by the user of the coercion (Pillar, 1983:chapter 4). Thus, in both the Korean war and the Vietnam war, the aim of American policymakers became that of imposing high costs on the opponent while keeping their own costs (especially in casualties) relatively low—thus showing the opponent that it had more to gain by a settlement than the United States did. General Mark Clark, who commanded United Nations' forces in the last year of the war put the matter in the following way: "Since it was not our government's policy to seek a military decision, the next best thing was to make the stalemate more expensive for the Communists than for us, to hit them where it hurt, to worry them, to convince them by force that the price tag on an armistice was going up, not down" (Clark, 1954:69).

Occasionally coercion may be used to demonstrate to the opponent one's own determination to prevail, even if the costs to oneself are very high. For example, Pillar (1983:187) makes this comment about the Tet offensive of the Vietnamese Communists in 1968:

> The Tet offensive vividly demonstrated the fanaticism with which the Communists intended to pursue their objectives despite immense losses to their own side. It drove home a point which McNamara's 1966

memorandum had made: that the leaders in Hanoi were too highly motivated to back down, even in the face of the terrible human costs to their countrymen who trod southward along the infiltration routes.

Promises and concessions. Rather than using threat or coercion, either side may use more positive incentives to influence concessions by the other side. One method is to promise rewards if the other side agrees to one's terms. This may be considered a kind of "side payment" on issues other than the one in dispute. For example, in 1965 President Johnson promised large-scale American aid to North Vietnam if its leaders would agree to settle the war in South Vietnam on terms acceptable to the United States.

A disputant also may offer concessions on the issues in contention in an effort to induce concessions by the other. In 1968 the United States softened its own terms for settling the war in Vietnam (e.g., abandoning its insistence that the Communists withdraw their forces from South Vietnam) in the hope that the other side would drop some of its own extreme demands (e.g., that the United States depose the government of President Thieu in South Vietnam). In the 1986 arms-control negotiations between the United States and the Soviet Union, the Soviets offered to reduce their offensive missiles force if the United States abandoned plans to pursue its Strategic Defense Initiative ("Star Wars") plans.

Concessions by one side may induce concessions by the other side for several reasons. Often a norm of reciprocity exists that creates pressure to respond in kind. Second, a concession by side A is apt to raise B's expectation that a reciprocating concession from B may lead to still another concession from A (since A has demonstrated his goodwill and desire to reach agreement). Third, the initial concession by A has narrowed the gap between what B has demanded and what A is now offering. As a result, it is less worthwhile for B to suffer the continuing (and possibly escalating) costs of disagreement in order to get its way. To put it another way, B's critical risk—the risk of war it is willing to take to get its own way—will decrease as A's concession reduces the gap between what the two sides are asking (Zeuthen, 1930; Crawford, 1980; Wagner, 1982). For example, when the United States agreed to allow the Communist forces to remain in South Vietnam and to participate in administrative structures in that country, it became less worthwhile for the North Vietnamese to remain firm in their own demands and thereby suffer the continuing costs of bombing and possible further escalation.

Interaction During Bargaining

The actions of each side in a dispute cannot be considered in isolation from those of its opponent. The action of one affects the actions of the other, which in turn affect the actions of the first, and so on. We may consider two types of interaction: that involving coercive actions and that involving concessions.

Coercive Interaction

As noted previously, a party that uses coercive actions (or threatens them) intends to make the status quo of disagreement more costly for the other side and/or to cause the other to expect future actions that are costly to him. In these ways the user of coercion hopes to pressure his opponent to make concessions in order to escape a high level of present and future costs.

Use of such coercive tactics may be successful, as when Hitler's threats led Britain and France to concede part of Czechoslovakia to Germany and when heavy American bombing of North Vietnam in late 1972 and early 1973 apparently succeeded in getting North Vietnamese leaders to make additional concessions during peace negotiations. However, the more common reaction of the target of threat or coercion is to counter in kind (see, for example, Smoke, 1977; Ward, 1982).

While the initial coercion may have been successful in raising the present and anticipated costs of the struggle to the target, the target may value its goals in the dispute so highly that it is willing to suffer high costs in the belief (or hope) that it will be able to win eventually. Furthermore, the opponent's use (or threat) of coercion may have raised the target's motivation to carry on the struggle. Because it has probably been angered by the other's coercive tactics, and because giving in under duress is probably seen as humiliating, it may value winning the dispute more and value losing it more negatively than before. Moreover, the opponent's use of coercive tactics may have led the target's leaders to conclude that a peaceful resolution of the dispute is not possible.

Therefore, rather than submit in the face of coercion, the target may use the same tactics that its opponent has already used. By coercion and threat it may try to raise the present costs to the other side so high that the other, not itself, is forced to concede. In other words, a contest to see who can impose and threaten greater costs on the other, and which side is willing to bear such costs longer, may have started. This is basically what happened during the war in Vietnam. By a bombing campaign in 1965 the United

States attempted to raise the costs to North Vietnam of continuing the war; the North Vietnamese countered by moving mainline units into South Vietnam and increasing their level of attacks on U.S. troops and installations; the United States responded with further actions (search-and-destroy strategy, wider bombing) that were intended to raise the costs to the enemy and convince him that he could not win. But each U.S. action was countered by further escalation by the Communist side, which attempted to accomplish the same ends (Milstein, 1974). Many of the events of the war between Iran and Iraq represent a similar pattern of mutual escalation, with each trying to force the other to give in by making the war more costly and the other responding in kind.

A pattern of mutual escalation of coercion may spiral up and up, resulting eventually in an all-out war without any restraint. This is what happened during the period that led to World War I. Threats and coercive actions by the Central Powers were met by threats and preparations for war by the Allied Powers (especially Russia), which in turn led to more threats and more war preparations by their opponents, until the national leaders involved felt powerless to stop the slide into general and total war.

In many other cases the process of coercion and counter-coercion de-escalates before it gets completely out of control. This is what finally happened, for example, in the Cuban missile crisis and in Vietnam.

Coercive interaction is likely to de-escalate when one or both sides comes to believe one or more of the following: (a) the costs of a more intense fight will be very high; (b) the value of winning is not as great as previously thought; (c) the probability of winning a more intensive fight is low; and (d) a substantial probability of being able to get satisfactory terms by negotiation now exists.

A convergence in certain perceptions will facilitate de-escalation of coercion. Mutual escalation is likely to occur when the perceptions of the two sides differ regarding which side can cause the other more damage and the relative determination of each to endure the pain. In such circumstances both sides will expect their own costs to be lower than those of their adversary and will be confident of eventual victory. A convergence of perceptions—i.e., both realize that one side is stronger or more determined or that both are equally strong and determined—will lead to agreement on how much each side must concede. (See chapter 8 for further discussion of escalation and de-escalation.)

Interaction of Concessions

A dispute may be settled by mutual, reciprocated concessions by the two sides; one side may make all, or almost all, the concessions; or, after one side makes some concessions, the other side may fail to reciprocate and the dispute may continue unresolved.

A pattern of reciprocated concessions is frequently found in negotiations between nations. For example, Jensen (1984) found that the United States and the Soviet Union generally reciprocated the other side's concessions in a number of arms-control negotiations.

The process of mutual concessions is not necessarily one in which each side makes a continuing series of small concessions along a single continuum (e.g., of territory or tariff rates) until their demands converge. Rather, as Zartman (1978) has pointed out, a crucial part of the process often is the proposal by one or both sides of formulas that indicate the shape of a holistic final agreement. For example, in their negotiations with great Britain to end the War of 1812, American representatives made a package proposal in which the United States would concede on the maritime issues in dispute and the British would give up their territorial demands (Pillar, 1983:226).

The importance of general formulas is not inconsistent with the possibility of trading concessions, leading to a convergence of positions. A general formula proposed by one side may represent in itself a concession from some previous set of principles espoused by that side. And, once the two sides agree on a general formula for settlement, they still may trade concessions in implementing the principles. For example, even after the French and Algerians had agreed on the main principles of Algerian independence, they needed to reach compromises (and traded concessions) on such important arrangements as the schedule for withdrawal of French troops and the length of leases on French bases (Pillar, 1983:131).

There are a number of reasons why a pattern of reciprocating concessions may occur. Often there are norms that have grown up in the relations between the parties that dictate reciprocity. Thus, over a series of arms-control negotiations between the United States and the Soviet Union, each has come to expect that genuine concessions of its own will be matched by the other. Moreover, given such norms, each may believe that agreement can come only through a process of mutual concessions. Furthermore, as either side makes concessions, the gap between what each is asking and what the other is offering has decreased. Thus, there is less incentive for either side to continue to stand firm in its demands, at the cost of continued disagreement and the risks of conflict between the two sides. Finally, regardless of the incentives for each side to reciprocate concessions in the current negotiation, both sides may be accommodating in order to maintain good working relations on broader issues and future interactions.

While a pattern of reciprocating concessions frequently occurs in bargaining, concessions may be much more one-sided. John Cross (1978) has argued that the larger the concessions made by one side in a dispute, the smaller the concessions made by the other side. According to this perspective, larger concessions by side A lead side B to expect greater future concessions from side A, so that side B is willing to stand firm and await further concessions by A. (Cross also suggests that there will be an equilibrium point for the two concession rates where the interdependent concession functions of the two sides intersect.)

There are many empirical instances in which the type of nonreciprocal pattern predicted by Cross has been found. For example, the concessions made by Chamberlain to Hitler were not reciprocated; rather, they led Hitler to stiffen his demands and await further British concessions. The Soviet Union has sometimes tended to increase its rate of concessions in arms-control talks following a period of little movement in the American position (Jensen, 1984).

In their study of sixteen international crises, Snyder and Diesing found a pattern of alternating concessions in only one case, the Agadir (Morocco) crisis between France and Germany in 1911. Usually, they found "one party simply concedes everything, although it may receive a 'carrot' or 'face-saver' along the way" (Snyder and Diesing, 1977:206). One good example is the Berlin blockade of 1948–1949 in which the Soviets eventually gave in and lifted the blockade in exchange for the scheduling of a rather meaningless foreign ministers conference. Other examples include the Munich crisis of 1938, the Iranian crisis of 1945–1946 (in which the Soviets, under heavy American pressure, withdrew their troops from northern Iran) and, to some extent, the Cuban missile crisis.

When will a pattern of reciprocation in bargainers' concessions be found, and when will primarily one-sided concessions occur? First, the likelihood of reciprocation will be enhanced by the presence of strong norms that support reciprocity and by the existence of strong long-term mutual interests between the parties that make it in the interest of both to maintain cordial relations (Gouldner, 1960).

Second, focusing more directly on the issue in dispute, reciprocation is likely when each believes that concessions by the other side indicate a willingness to cooperate but not great weakness that will result in a continuation of concessions regardless of whether reciprocation occurs (Pruitt, 1981; Druckman, 1978). Such mutual perceptions are most likely to occur when the bargaining power of the two sides—based on their motivation to prevail on the issue and their ability to impose and withstand costs in a fight—is about equal. In such circumstances the parties come to realize that they are about equally resolved. Then, as Snyder and Diesing (1977:197) note, "both give ground grudgingly until a mutually acceptable settlement is found." This was basically the situation during the negotiations to end the Korean war and those to end the Vietnam war (Pillar, 1983).

The pattern of one-sided concessions is likely to occur when one side is perceived by both itself and the other as making concessions because it has been forced to do so by the relatively great pressures on it; e.g., the high costs of the struggle, political pressures, the demands of third parties. Such pressures on the initial conceder reflect its weaker bargaining position. The realization of both sides of this asymmetry in the two sides' bargaining positions, and thus in their relative resolve to stand firm, leads both to expect that the initial concessions of the weaker side will be followed by still others, even if not reciprocated. Snyder and Diesing (1977: 206) comment: "Once superior resolve is established, it is not affected or is even enhanced by the other party's concessions; there is no reason for the superior party to stop pushing until is has gotten everything."

Of course, the process of concessions—either reciprocal or one-sided —may stop before agreement is reached. It may be that Side A makes a concession, Side B does not reciprocate, and there the matter rests, at least temporarily. This pattern of events is most likely to occur when the two sides differ in their perceptions of the power balance and of the meaning of the concessions being made. The initiator of concessions may intend its own actions to signal a willingness to compromise but not see its own bargaining position as appreciably weaker than that of the other nor intend to concede further without some reciprocation. However, its opponent may believe that the balance of bargaining power is in its favor and interpret the other's concession as showing that the other's resolve has begun to crack. Thus it may believe that it need only await further concessions. Eventually, as a result of the absence of such further concessions, as well as by other events in the bargaining process (e.g., persuasion, threats, or coercion by either) the perceptions and the behaviors of either or both sides may change and one or both may make new concessions. In the negotiations to end the Vietnam war initial concessions by the United States were met only by repetition of the original hard-line North Vietnamese position. The Vietnamese believed that the United States was anxious to withdraw from the war and would make further concessions. Only after a lengthy period in which the United States showed surprising perseverence and imposed new costs on North Vietnam (by further bombing) did the North Vietnamese alter their perception of the relative bargaining power of the two sides and make concessions of their own (Zagare, 1978).

Phases in Bargaining Tactics

During bargaining it is necessary for the parties to air and contest over their differences but it is also necessary to coordinate their actions (e.g., in setting an agenda for discussion) and their terms for settlement (Gulliver, 1979). While there may be some mixture of these antagonistic and cooperative activities throughout the course of bargaining, it is common for a primarily antagonistic and coercive phase to come first, followed by a phase characterized by greater emphasis on coordination and accommodation (Gulliver, 1979; Pruitt, 1981; Snyder and Diesing, 1977). For example, in the Cuban missile crisis, it was only after a period of mutual threats of military action, statements of determination to stand firm, and some use of force (the blockade of Cuba by the United States) that serious efforts to settle the crisis (especially through the exchange of letters between Khrushchev and Kennedy) were made.

An initial period of threat and coercion may serve to clarify the relative power of the two sides; i.e., by showing more clearly the relative strength of interest each side has in the outcomes, their relative capacity to damage each other, and the strength of the resolve of each side to remain firm even at the risk of a (wider) fight. On the basis of these changed perceptions, each side is likely to become clearer about what the other side—and itself as well—would be willing to settle for rather than to fight (or to continue or expand an ongoing fight).

The relative power and resolve of the two sides—as they both come to see it—is reflected in the terms of the eventual agreement (Bacharach and Lawler, 1981). For example, in the Cuban missile crisis, Soviet Premier Khrushchev initially believed that the United States would accept a fait accompli of Soviet missiles in Cuba rather than risk a war. The words and actions of the Kennedy administration soon caused him to change these expectations and to conclude that the balance of interests and military power, and therefore of resolve, favored the United States. The terms that settled the crisis, including acceptance of the key American demand for removal of the Soviet missiles, reflected the now-mutual perceptions of the two sides that the balance of resolve in this case favored the United States.

The Attraction of Making Concessions

We have seen that settlement of a dispute between two nations becomes more likely as the leaders of two sides come to agree more in their perceptions of their relative bargaining power and resolve. But this alone is not enough to guarantee that leaders of either or both nations then will make concessions leading to agreement. It is possible for both sides to be convinced of the resolve of the other side to stand firm, and to realize that a trial of force is likely to result, but for each to prefer a continued stalemate or even war to any agreement it sees as possible. This appears to have been the case in the dispute between Japan and the United States in 1940–1941 over Japanese control over Southeast Asia. War did not come because either side mistakenly believed that the other side would soon give in. Rather, by late 1941 each recognized that the other was determined to stand firm in its demands and that war was approaching; but neither was willing to make significant concessions to avoid war. Clearly, if both sides prefer continued disagreement or even war to compromise (or loss) then no settlement is possible.

The attraction to decisionmakers of making concessions (compared to the attraction of other actions) has been discussed in chapter 5. The attraction of making concessions was seen to be greater to leaders as: (1) the value to them of having an agreement increases (e.g., because they wish to use their resources for other purposes); (2) the value they put on a specific agreement increases (e.g., because their aspirations are low or because what is conceded does not affect their vital interests); (3) the status quo of nonagreement becomes more costly; (4) the value of a fight decreases for them (because it is seen as more costly or the chances or winning a fight are seen as low; (5) they see making concessions as having intrinsic advantages (e.g., it is expected to be politically popular); and, (6) they expect concessions to lead to an acceptable agreement (e.g., because the other has reciprocated concessions in the past).

Here we may take note of several additional aspects of the bargaining situation that may affect the values of agreement and nonagreement and therefore affect the attractiveness of making concessions. These aspects are the presence of deadlines, the nature of the available solutions, and the relative power of the two sides.

Deadlines

Agreement between the two sides may be affected by the existence of a deadline for agreement. In labor-management relations, such a deadline may arise from the automatic expiration of a previous contract or represent a date chosen by a union for a strike. In international relations a deadline might exist because of the expiration of a treaty (such as the SALT II arms-control treaty) or be created by an election that could turn one of the negotiating parties out of office (such as the U.S. presidential election in 1980 that set a deadline for the Carter administration's negotiations with Iran in the hostage crisis); or be set arbitrarily by one side, as when in 1958 Soviet Premier Khrushchev set a six-month deadline for settlement of the status of Germany, including Berlin, after which he would unilaterally end Western occupation rights in Berlin.

Several studies of bargaining behavior have found that there sometimes is an "end spurt" as the deadline for agreement approaches (Bartos, 1974; Pruitt, 1981). Since expiration of the deadline without an agreement usually brings increased costs to both sides, there is an incentive for both sides to make additional concessions at this time to avoid such costs. Moreover, each side may have been holding back some of its concessions for the last minute so as not to make "premature" concessions or be pressured into additional concessions at the deadline.

However, the willingness of a party to make concessions to meet a deadline may depend on its interpretation of the significance and legitimacy of the deadline. If the other side has arbitrarily stated a deadline, and the party believes that conceding in the face of such a deadline would be humiliating and weaken its long-term reputation for resolve, it may purposely ignore the deadline. Thus, the United States under President Eisenhower, while agreeing to negotiate in the Berlin dispute, did not make extra concessions to meet Khrushchev's deadline. Overall, we may conclude that the presence of a deadline will tend to make bargainers reduce their demands (and thus make agreement more likely) to the extent that agreement before the deadline will avoid new costs while not being itself costly to their reputation for resolve.

The Nature of Possible Solutions

The likelihood of agreement in a dispute may be affected also by the types of solutions that are available to the parties. Of particular relevance are (a) the possibility of compromise; (b) prominent solutions; and (c) integrative solutions.

Possibility of compromise. Some issues concern matters that are divisible — for example, money, tariff rates, or territory. In such disputes compromise is possible; the goods in question can be divided. Thus, the United States and Canada can settle a boundary dispute by dividing a disputed piece of territory. Other disputes, however, concern outcomes that are not divisible easily, if at all. Control over the government of a nation or the principle of the unity of a nation are important examples. Thus, once the central issue in the Vietnam war was defined by the adversaries as whether Vietnam would be unified under a Communist government or whether South Vietnam would remain separate under a non-Communist government, the struggle could not easily be compromised. The more the issues of a dispute are defined by the parties in a way that is amenable to compromise, rather than in a way that allows only for total victory by one side, the more likely is agreement to occur.

Prominent solutions. Agreement tends to be facilitated by the existence or discovery of a prominent solution—i.e., one that stands out as salient in the perceptions of both sides (Schelling, 1960; Pruitt, 1981). Examples include the principle of equality (e.g., equal tariff reductions for both sides), a precedent—like the terms of a previous treaty—or an outstanding geographical feature such as a river, which might be used to divide disputed territory. A prominent solution may serve to coordinate the expectations of the two sides. That is, each may see the prominent solution as a likely solution.

However, expectations based on the power balance between the parties may not coincide with expectations based on the existence of some prominent solution. Thus, if both parties see A as much more resolved than B, this would lead both to expect a solution favoring A rather than a solution that gave each equal rewards.

Expectations are more likely to be coordinated on the basis of shared perceptions of the power balance than on the basis of a prominent solution since the party with stronger bargaining power and greater resolve can force an agreement to its advantage. A prominent solution that is not consistent with the (perceived) power balance is not likely to be agreed to by the stronger side. However, when the relative power of the two sides is fairly equal, or the power balance is unclear, the existence of prominent solutions will tend to facilitate agreement.

Integrative solutions. Our discussion sometimes has assumed that outcomes that benefit one side more must thereby benefit the other side less. However, disputes differ with respect to the degree of conflict of interest between the two sides. Not only may both sides share a common interest in avoiding a costly fight but there may also be possible outcomes that are fairly desirable—though not the most preferred—for both sides. In some cases it is possible even for the parties to discover or devise "integrative" solutions that bring substantial benefits to both sides (Walton and McKersie, 1965; Pruitt, 1981). For example, in negotiations to reduce armaments it seems possible to find solutions that would reduce the expenditures and increase the security of both sides. When such integrative solutions can be found to cover at least some of the issues in a dispute, it becomes more possible (though not necessarily easy) to achieve agreement.

Relative Power

As previously noted, the terms of an agreement are likely to reflect the parties' perceptions of the relative power of the two sides. However, Bacharach and Lawler (1981:chapter 7) suggest that agreement is easier to reach when the power of the two sides is equal rather than unequal. They argue that when power is equal, a "splitting the difference" rule is not only consistent with the equality of power but also may appear to each to be a normatively justifiable (i.e., fair) way to resolve the conflict. However, when power is unequal, the question arises for both bargainers of how the power relationship should be reflected in the agreement. The result is that they may get bogged down in normative issues (e.g., does might make right?). Bacharach and Lawler report experimental results that support their argument that the likelihood of agreement is highest when the power of the bargainers (as measured by the alternatives open to each side) is equal. They found also that when total power for the bargainers was high (as indicated by each being highly dependent on the other), the probability of agreement was high. These results are consistent with evidence that when two sides are equal in power and have the capacity to do great damage to each other, they tend to develop norms to avoid the use of coercion (see chapter 2). However, if approximate equality of power leads to ambiguity and divergent perceptions of relative power, then it could be an impediment to agreement. A reasonable conclusion would be that equality of power will tend to facilitate agreement so long as the two sides agree in this assessment of their relative power.[2]

A schematic overview of the major factors affecting agreement is presented in figure 11.1.

Summary and Policy Implications

An essential reason why most disputes are not settled at their outsets is that each side has a different view of how the dispute will actually be settled. Each may believe that the other will back down in its position sooner and further than it is in fact prepared to go. This disparity in the expectations of the two sides stems from a difference in their perceptions of the balance in bargaining power—based on the relative strength of each

Figure 11.1   Factors Determining Whether Agreement Is Reached*

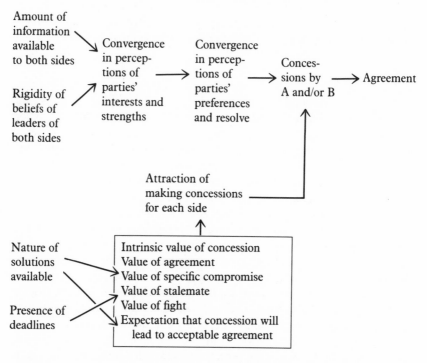

side's interests in the issues at stake and on their relative capability.

The more the two sides to a dispute diverge in their perceptions of the bargaining power of the two sides, and thus in their judgments of their relative resolve, the wider the gap in their demands is likely to be. The less information is available to leaders of the two sides, and the more rigid their prior beliefs, the more likely are their perceptions of relative bargaining power and resolve to differ.

Bargaining serves two main functions in moving disputing sides toward agreement: clarification of the situation and changing the preferences and expectations of the parties. First, each side tries to learn more about its opponent: how highly it values the issues at stake, its willingness to stand firm and even to fight to gain its ends, and the minimum outcome acceptable to it. One important way of obtaining such information is by probes designed to test the other side's willingness to stand firm and to make

---

*See chapter 5 for discussion of other determinants of values and expectations that affect the attraction of making concessions.

concessions. While learning more about the opponent's values and intentions, each bargainer also may clarify its own goals and intentions. In addition, the bargaining period may help to clarify for both sides the probable costs of a (expanded) fight and the likely winner of such a fight.

Besides trying to learn more about each other, bargainers try to influence each other. Each side may try to change its opponent's preferences among outcomes so that it places lower values on winning and on a fight and higher values on agreements that give it less than it had originally asked. Each side also may try to change the other's expectations about its own actions—to convince its opponent that it will stand firm in its demands and/or that it will impose penalties on the other unless the other concedes and/or that it is willing to cooperate in reaching a mutually acceptable agreement. To influence the opponent's perceptions and expectations in these ways, each side may use some combination of persuasion, promises, threats, and concessions of its own. In addition, each side may try to influence the other to concede by using coercive tactics to make the status quo of disagreement more costly to the other.

As each bargainer attempts to influence the other, there is an interaction between them. The use of coercion by one side may lead the other to concede. More likely, the other will respond in kind. A contest of escalating coercion may then ensue to see which side can impose greater costs on the other and which can bear the costs longer.

Mutual escalation becomes more likely as the two sides differ more in their perceptions concerning their relative strength and resolve. De-escalation of coercion tends to occur when one or both sides sees the balance of costs to potential benefits as becoming unacceptable and when the two sides come to agree in their perceptions of the relative ability of the two sides to impose and to bear higher costs.

Interaction involving concessions also may follow different patterns. Concessions may tend to be mutual, or one side may continue to make concessions without reciprocation, or concessions may begin but stop after not being reciprocated. The target of a concession is likely to reciprocate when it perceives its opponent as acting out of a desire to cooperate but not out of weakness. Both sides are most likely to interpret their opponent's concessions in this way when bargaining power (based on their motivations and fighting capabilities) is about equal.

If and when perceptions of the two sides concerning their relative bargaining power and resolve become similar, agreement becomes possible. If it is clear to both sides that side A is more resolved, then side B will move most of the way toward A's position. If both sides see that their bargaining power and resolve are roughly equal, then both will make concessions.

Thus, the terms of agreement—as well as its occurrence at all—will reflect the shared perceptions of the two sides concerning their relative bargaining power and resolve.

The convergence of expectations depends on each side getting a more realistic view of the other side's interests and capabilities and of the terms it is willing to accept rather than to stand firm or fight. It is desirable, therefore, to give both parties more full and accurate information without their going through a long, costly, and dangerous period of bluffs, threats, and coercion. This goal is difficult to achieve because each side is motivated to try to convince its opponent of its strong interests, strong capability, and firm resolve in order to get better terms. Each side may be especially reluctant to provide accurate information because it fears its opponent will be dishonest and thereby gain advantages.

While there is no simple solution to this problem, some steps may be possible to encourage a clarification of the power balance that is less long and costly. One possibility is to make arrangements to provide more complete objective information to each nation about the military and economic strength of its opponent. This might be done through direct exchange of verifiable information or by enlisting a third nation or international organization to compile and transmit such information.

Reliable information about the strength of each side's preferences among various outcomes would be harder to obtain and exchange but the good offices of third parties as mediators or intermediaries might be useful for this purpose. Such third parties—hopefully trusted by both sides—might be able to transmit to each side a fuller picture of the essential concerns and goals of the other side. If both sides quickly formed a generally accurate view of the interests and capabilities of both sides, the period of mutual probes and pressures might be made shorter, less costly, and less dangerous.

Even when national leaders have similar perceptions of their relative bargaining power and resolve, agreement cannot be reached unless one or both sides sees concessions as more attractive than continued stalemate or war. Factors that affect the attractiveness of making concessions were discussed in chapter 5. That discussion suggested that national leaders may be influenced toward agreement by information or actions that cause them to downgrade the value of winning, of stalemate, and of a fight, and/or lead them to raise the value they give to compromise (or even losing) on an issue. Such changes may stem, for example, from information that suggests that the long-run cooperative advantages stemming from agreement are greater than previously believed, from domestic political pressures from factions that support compromise as opposed to stalemate or war, and from pressures from third-party nations that threaten withdrawal of support or penalties in the event of a refusal to accept compromise terms.

Several additional factors that may affect the attractiveness of making concessions were discussed in the present chapter. The presence of a deadline will tend to make bargainers reduce their demands (and thus make agreement more likely). The costs of nonagreement usually will increase after a deadline has passed and so a compromise settlement before the deadline becomes relatively more attractive. However, if a deadline is imposed arbitrarily by an adversary, then making concessions may be costly to one's reputation for resolve and the positive incentives of conceding prior to the deadline will tend to be canceled out. To facilitate agreement, it seems desirable for both sides mutually to agree on a deadline or for a deadline to be proposed by a third party.

The attraction of making concessions may be affected also by the kinds of possible solutions available. First, the more the issues of a dispute are defined by national leaders in a way that permits compromise, rather than only total victory, the more likely is agreement to occur. It sometimes will facilitate agreement between disputing nations if their leaders avoid thinking in either-or terms about possible solutions. For example, if the United States wants to establish a pro-Western government in a small Third World country while the Soviet Union wants a pro-Soviet government, agreement may be facilitated by proposals to establish a government that is somewhere between those poles. Thus, the United States and the Soviet Union were able to agree on a neutral government for Laos in 1962.

Finding proposals or formulas that embody perceptually prominent or salient solutions will tend to bring the expectations and demands of the two sides together. Solutions may be perceptually prominent because they reflect widely shared norms, well-established precedents, or outstanding features of the situation (e.g., a river boundary as the solution to a territorial dispute). For example, in arms-control talks between the United States and the Soviet Union, solutions based on equal (or equivalent) numbers of weapons are perceptually salient because (among other reasons) they reflect a widely shared norm of equality. However, perceptually prominent solutions are not likely to be acceptable if they are inconsistent with the parties' perceptions of the balance of bargaining power between the two sides. To facilitate agreement, both the parties themselves and outsiders should search for solutions that are perceptually prominent while at the same time being consistent with the balance of bargaining power.

Finally, agreement can be facilitated by finding possible solutions that, at least in some respects, increase the welfare of both sides. While there are genuine conflicts of interest in most disputes, there often are potential areas where jointly beneficial outcomes are possible. For example, rather than viewing possible solutions to trade disputes as ones in which a fixed amount of wealth is to be divided, it may be possible to find solutions that raise the total amount of production, trade, and profit to be shared by the two sides. Similarly, while there are genuine conflicts of interest in arms-control negotiations, it is possible to find solutions that will reduce the costs and increase the security of both sides.

12 Summary and Conclusions

This book has focused on these questions: (1) How do national leaders come to choose coercive or conciliatory actions in disputes with other nations? (2) How effective are various kinds of actions (threats, coercion, promises, concessions, etc.) and strategies combining various kinds of actions for defending national interests while avoiding war? and (3) When will disputes between nations be settled?

I have approached this subject from the perspective of conflict resolution as a general process that occurs in a variety of specific settings. The relationship between the two sides in a dispute has been viewed from the perspective of strategic interaction. The actions of the leaders of each side are affected by their expectations about the response of the other, and the outcomes to each side depend on their joint actions.

Within this general framework I have examined and tried to integrate findings of research on a number of separate but interrelated topics, including perceptions, decisionmaking, the use and effectiveness of various influence techniques, and bargaining and negotiation. For each of these topics I have summarized the major general findings, especially those drawn from social-psychological research. In addition, I have examined findings in each area dealing specifically with conflict between nations. The major aim has been to see what conclusions may be drawn, even if only tentatively, about how disputes between nations may be settled most effectively and with least cost.

A substantial number of generalizations have been stated in previous chapters and I will not attempt to repeat all of them here. I will, however, summarize some of the major conclusions and suggest some of their implications for national leaders and for citizens concerned about problems of peace and war.

The Choice Among Actions

At any time during a dispute national leaders may choose among a variety of possible types of actions, including threatening or using coercion, promising or giving rewards, and making concessions on the issues in dispute. When will they use coercive and when more conciliatory means?

Sometimes national leaders choose an action not by deliberating among alternatives but simply by following pre-established rules. For example, in shooting down the Korean airliner that flew over their territory in September 1983, Soviet officials appear to have followed standard operating procedures for such eventualities. To reduce the chances of war, it is important to reduce the number and scope of formal or informal rules that dictate the automatic use of force. It is particularly important not to delegate to military commanders (or to computers) the right to follow standardized rules about when to attack an adversary.

In most cases national leaders choose their actions not by following rules but by evaluating the merits of alternative actions. The first step in this process is to screen out those options that would not achieve their minimum goals. The use of coercive action is less likely when decisionmakers make the avoidance of war a clear and high-priority constraint than when war avoidance is not made a top policy requirement.

In a dispute the focus of the decisionmakers' attention tends to be on changing the situation or of preventing the other side from doing so. Other objectives or constraints, such as avoiding war, tend to be given secondary consideration. Moreover, national decisionmakers may not be clear on how great a risk of war they are prepared to run until a crisis situation has deteriorated and the danger of war has increased. It is desirable for government leaders to try to build into their decision processes an early consideration of what priority they wish to give to avoiding war (relative to other goals) and how much risk of war they are prepared to take in order to win other objectives. Clarity about these vital questions would help to avoid the possibility that national leaders will, without clear reflection and intent, take excessive risks of war that are not justifiable even in terms of their own priorities.

When several alternative actions (including doing nothing) are considered as viable options, decisionmakers may be expected to choose on the basis of how much they value different possible outcomes of the dispute (e.g., winning, compromise, war) and their expectations about what actions will result in what outcomes.

Coercion, or the threat of coercion, is most likely to be used by national leaders under the following set of conditions:

(1) they place great value on winning the dispute, i.e., getting agreement on their own terms;

(2) the ongoing dispute is costly to them, and thus they want to bring it to an end quickly;

(3a) a (wider) fight is seen as tolerable (because costs would be low and/or one's own side would win); and/or

(3b) a (wider) fight is seen as unlikely to result from one's threat or use of coercion, e.g., because the other is seen as likely to concede when coercion is used or threatened; and

(4) the use or threat of coercion is seen as being legitimate and popular with the public of one's own nation and with one's allies.

Under such circumstances national leaders are likely to see coercive tactics as useful to end an ongoing costly dispute and win the goals they value so highly. They are not deterred by the possibility that their use of coercion may lead to a fight, either because they expect the other side to give in under pressure or because they are not frightened by the prospect of a fight. Nor are they deterred by moral considerations or by public opinion. They are likely to use threat first and then, if it is not successful, to actually impose punishment on the adversary.

National leaders are likely to place great value on getting their own way in a dispute and thus are likely to use coercion when they see the issues in dispute as vital, when they are convinced of the legitimacy of their position, and when they see other outcomes as putting (or leaving) their side in a highly undesirable position that falls below their minimum goals. In such circumstances decisionmakers often are willing to take some risk of large losses (such as they might suffer if a war occurs) in order to avoid the certainty of remaining in, or falling into, what they consider an intolerable position. It is important for national leaders to try to avoid pushing an adversary into a corner, where the adversary may be willing to take desperate gambles to escape an "unacceptable" situation. Instead, it usually is in the enlightened self-interest of a nation to try to satisfy to a reasonable degree the legitimate interests of its adversaries.

The importance of winning a dispute also becomes greater to national leaders (and the use of coercion more likely) as their personal prestige becomes involved, as the outcome becomes more relevant as a precedent, as political pressures for winning increase, and as great hostility between the two sides makes "beating" the other an end in itself. To help reduce the likelihood that leaders will use coercive means, it is useful for adversaries to avoid personalizing the dispute, to try to separate the present dispute from other disputes, to avoid whipping up the public's emotions about the issues, and to try to keep the dialogue between the adversaries at a businesslike, nonrancorous level.

National leaders become more likely to use coercion when they expect such tactics to be successful in getting an adversary to concede without a fight. Such expectations are greater when leaders hold general beliefs about the effectiveness of hard-line tactics, when the statements and especially the past behavior of the adversary have shown a willingness to concede under pressure, and when the adversary is currently seen as having weak motivation to resist coercion—because of low stakes or commitments in the dispute, fear of war based on its vulnerability, low political support for use of coercion, etc. The leaders of a nation that is the potential target of coercion by an adversary may help to discourage such actions by making clear its determination to resist coercion. It may do this by actions (public statements, deployment of troops, treaties, etc.) that establish commitments to resist, by building up its defensive capabilities, and by establishing a record of responding to coercion in kind. While attempting to make clear their determination to resist bullying, national leaders should be careful not to project an image of aggressiveness nor to commit themselves to defending positions that are not really vital to them.

Since the use of coercion may lead to war, it is important also to consider the conditions under which national leaders are prepared to accept the possibility of a fight. The prospect of a fight will have a more positive (or less negative) value to decisionmakers as the perceived costs of a fight decrease, as their expectancy of winning the fight increases, and as the value to them of winning (discussed above) increases.

The costs of a fight will be seen as greater and the chances of winning as lower the greater the relative power and the resolve of the adversary and the less its vulnerability to a first strike. The costs of a fight will also be seen as greater as more scarce resources are needed to engage in a fight, as there are more beneficial ties with the adversary that would be disrupted by a fight, and as more political opposition to engaging in a fight exists. The more that the leaders of an adversary nation, as well as those opposed to confrontation within their own nation, provide information and take actions that show decisionmakers that a fight will have high costs and that chances of winning a fight are low, the less attractive tactics of coercion will appear.

Whether or not national leaders will threaten or use force or other forms of coercion in a dispute will depend also on the relative attraction of alternative types of actions. One other option for national leaders is to do nothing and wait for the other side to concede. The attraction of this option for decisionmakers will tend to be high when the situation of nonagreement is not very costly or they expect that the adversary will concede soon.

However, national leaders also have to consider the possibility that the adversary will attack them first if they do nothing. Such expectations of a first strike by the other will tend to be high when they perceive the adversary to be seeking domination, possible gains from attack for the adversary are seen as high, the adversary has used force first in the past, the adversary has built up a capability for first attack, and there is a substantial (military) advantage for the side that attacks first. Where suspicions of an attack by the adversary are high, and where a fight initiated by the other side is judged to be much more disastrous than one begun by one's own side, then doing nothing may appear very unattractive.

In addition to the use of coercion or doing nothing, national leaders may of course pursue other options. They may try to get an adversary to make concessions by using persuasion to change the adversary's view of the situation, by promising rewards for concessions, or by rewarding positive actions in order to encourage (further) concessions. Promising or giving rewards are more attractive options when decisionmakers have available resources (e.g., money) that are needed by the other and that would not be excessively costly to give. Also, promising or giving rewards becomes a more attractive option for decisionmakers when they expect that the other side will respond cooperatively to such incentives. Such expectations of a positive response are likely to be greater when the overall relations and the present dispute between the parties are not intensely hostile, when the other has responded to positive incentives in the past, and when the other is seen as having additional incentives (e.g., political pressures) to cooperate.

Another option for national leaders embroiled in a dispute is to make concessions themselves in order to reach agreement. Such action will end their chance of achieving the full demands they have been making. However, they may gain the benefits of having an agreement, end the costs of the ongoing dispute, and avoid a fight. Making concessions will be most attractive to decisionmakers under the following conditions.

(1) The status quo of nonagreement is costly—e.g., in money and in manpower devoted to conducting that dispute.

(2) Having an agreement has positive advantages—e.g., in freeing resources for domestic goals, for use in other disputes, or in leading to or restoring mutually beneficial relations with the adversary.

(3) The terms of agreement proposed meet their minimum aspirations, are consistent with accepted norms, and do not threaten their other important interests (e.g., maintaining domestic political support).

(4) They expect that the adversary will respond to concessions with

cooperation rather than with attempts to dominate and exploit their side. Such expectations are based on the adversary's past behavior and on perceptions of his present motives and goals.

(5) Making concessions is not seen as humiliating or greatly damaging to the reputation for resolve of the leaders themselves or of the nation they represent.

Thus, to encourage the leaders of a nation to make concessions, the adversary's leaders (as well as advocates of conciliation within their own nation) should try to show the advantages of reaching agreement—e.g., by suggesting mutually beneficial relationships such as trade and political cooperation that could follow such an agreement. They should also communicate that they are asking only for an agreement that meets the basic goals of the other nation. They need to indicate that concessions will be met with reciprocation and not with demands for complete surrender. Finally, they need to try to reduce any humiliation and damage to a leader's reputation that could be attached to making concessions—by such means as providing for face-saving formulas, refraining from "crowing" about gaining advantage, and trying to distinguish the present agreement from any future agreements for which it might be a precedent.

Effectiveness of Influence Methods

During the course of a dispute, the leaders of one nation attempt to influence the actions of the adversary; in particular, they try to induce the other side to make concessions and to dissuade the other from taking coercive actions against their own side. To be successful each side must make the consequences of conciliatory actions appear more attractive and those of coercion less attractive to the adversary. To do this, the leaders of one nation must change the values and expectancies of the adversary concerning one or more of the following outcomes: (a) continuation of a situation of nonagreement or stalemate; (b) war (or, if a limited war already has begun, an expanded war); and, (c) possible agreements. We may consider attempts by one side to influence the other—by persuasion, threats, promises, coercion, and concessions—in terms of how such influence methods affect the values and expectancies of the adversary concerning these outcomes.

Threatening Penalties or Promising Rewards

The leaders of one nation may try to get an adversary to agree to its demands by threatening penalties if the other side does not accept these terms. At the same time (or instead) national leaders may promise rewards to an adversary if the leaders of that nation will agree to their demands.

Threats. Threats are sometimes effective. As would be expected from decision theory, the greater the magnitude of a threat and the greater its credibility, the more likely the target is to comply with the demands of the threatener. Thus, national leaders sometimes are able to force concessions from an adversary, especially a weaker one, by threatening substantial penalties—e.g., a trade embargo, a cutoff of loans, a bombing attack—and making such threats in a credible way. To make their threats credible, they need first to establish their capability of carrying out the threat—e.g., of having sufficient military power to launch an effective attack. In addition, they can make threats more credible by showing that the issue at stake is important to them, that the costs to them of carrying out the threat (e.g., from retaliation by the target) will not be unacceptably high, and that the costs of not carrying out the threat (e.g., because of commitments made) are high. Also, national leaders can enhance the credibility of their threats by making them explicit, by having them issued by the highest-level officials, and by making preparations to carry out the threats. However, while such steps build credibility, they may commit the threatener so far that, in the event of noncompliance by the target, he will feel forced to carry out threats that might provoke a dangerous confrontation.

Even when threats of serious penalties are credible, they are frequently met with defiance by the target, who often responds with counter-threat and even by striking out at the threatener. This is especially apt to occur when the two sides have about equal power.

Threat is less likely to be effective in changing behavior if the target sees this behavior as the only way it can reach goals it deems to be vital. National leaders should be careful not to issue threats that try to force an adversary to give up a means for reaching goals it values highly without allowing or providing alternative means to reach such goals. For example, a threat to punish a nation for using forceful means to recover lands it believes to be an integral part of its own country are not likely to be successful permanently unless some alternative means (e.g., negotiations) for reaching this central goal are provided.

The target of a threat may defy the threatener not only because the tangible costs of compliance are too high but also because he views compliance as humiliating or as damaging his long-term relationships with adversaries by creating an impression of weakness under pressure. Users of threat should try to reduce as far as possible the costs in prestige and reputation that compliance will bring to the target. Possible methods for doing this include making threats privately rather than publicly, emphasizing common norms that justify one's demands (thus making acceptance of them less humiliating), pointing to the uniqueness of the present situation (to make the other's reputation for resolve less salient), and providing for face-saving formulas that permit the other to retreat gracefully.

The likelihood that threat will be effective in securing compliance also depends on the target's perceptions of the threatener's general intentions. If the target interprets the demands and threats of his adversary as reflecting general hostility and indicating a continuing policy of aggression, then it may believe that concession now will lead only to further demands and threats. It may believe that the only way to stop coercion by the other side is to stand firm and show that it can't be intimidated. To be effective, threats—if used at all—need to be made in a way that indicates that they do not reflect hostile intent or unlimited demands.

Arms buildups. To threaten other nations, to coerce them, and to defend against threat and coercion, nations build armaments. While arms buildups are affected by internal forces within each nation (such as bureaucratic momentum and economic pressures), a nation in rivalry with another nation tends to increase its arms as the arms of the rival increase and as tension with the rival increases. How far and how fast an arms race progresses depends on whether each side reacts to increases by the other by matching these increases, undermatching them, or overmatching them. To keep an arms race from spiraling rapidly upward, it is important that the leaders of each side not overreact to arms increases by the other.

Arms races tend to lead to war, especially when the nations involved are of equal power and the arms buildup is accelerating. However, an arms buildup may lead to a situation in which both sides are deterred from attack. Whether an arms buildup contributes to war or to deterrence depends on the effect of such buildups on leaders' expectations about (a) the adversary's intent to use its arms offensively and/or defensively; and (b) the outcomes of a war begun by a particular side.

To reduce the chances of war, national leaders should follow an arms policy designed to show adversaries (as well as their own side) that (1) they will fight if attacked but not attack themselves; (2) the adversary's chances of succeeding in an atttack are poor; and (3) one's own chances of succeeding in an attack are poor. If these perceptions are conveyed, the adversary will be deterred from attack rather than being either tempted or frightened into attacking. And one's own side will not attack because it will feel more secure and have little temptation to do so.

To create these necessary conditions for reducing rather than increasing the chances of war, a nation should build a military force that has a retaliatory but *not* a first-strike capability. Such an arms policy—aimed at removing incentives for either side to attack out of hope of gain or out of fear—can be most effective if it is supported by leaders' declared intentions and, more importantly by their other actions. National leaders need to make clear that, while they will defend their interests against attack, they have no aggressive designs against other nations.

Promises. Rather than using threats, leaders of one side in a dispute may try to influence the other by promising some reward—e.g., economic or military aid, improved trade terms, loans, or political cooperation. Promises by one nation appear generally to be more effective than threats in influencing the actions of an adversary.

However, promises are not likely to be effective if they require the adversary to give up vital goals in order to receive the promised reward. For example, President Johnson's promise to give economic aid to North Vietnam did not succeed in getting the Vietnamese to accept American terms because this would have meant giving up their central goal of reunifying Vietnam.

To increase the chances that their promises will be successful in influencing the other side to cooperate or make concessions, leaders need first to offer rewards that are relevant to important goals of the other side. For example, if the other nation is concerned primarily with acceptance as a political equal, then offers of political acceptance may be more effective than an offer of economic aid. National leaders also need to make promises of rewards or concessions that are substantial enough to arouse the interest of the other side without being so great as to arouse suspicion. Promises also need to be specific; vagueness may be seen as indicating either a lack of seriousness or an inability to deliver on the promise. The promised rewards need to be forthcoming quickly as rewards to be enjoyed far in the future tend to be discounted. Finally, it may be possible to make cooperation with one's own nation more valuable by increasing the extent to which the other nation is dependent on the rewards one can provide. Increasing ties of trade, investment, technological exchange, or political cooperation can create greater dependence by both sides.

Promises of reward are less likely to be successful in eliciting concessions if the requests made of the target are seen as illegitimate and humiliating. For example, Soviet leaders in the 1970s would not change some of their internal policies (especially on allowing more emigration) in order to obtain trade advantages with the United States at least partially because they viewed such demands as illegitimate intrusions into their domestic affairs.

For promises to be effective in affecting behavior, the target must not only value the promised rewards but also have a high expectancy that his cooperation will in fact bring these rewards. The credibility of a promise will be increased if the promiser has kept his word in the past. The promiser also needs to make clear both his capability to deliver on the promise at an acceptable cost to himself and his motivation to do so (based on his attitudes, commitments, and other incentives). For example, when promising substantial aid to Egypt if that country agreed to a peace treaty with Israel, U.S. President Carter had to make it clear to Egyptian President Sadat that he had the necessary support in the Congress to get the necessary money appropriated and that because of high U.S. concern about maintaining peace and stability in the Middle East, his administration had the motivation to fulfill the promises made.

Making a Fight Seem Less Attractive or More Likely

The more unappealing or frightening the leaders of a nation find the prospect of a fight to be, and the more they believe that some action will lead to a fight, the less likely they are to choose that action. Thus, the leaders of an adversary nation (or third parties, or people within their own nation) may be able to influence leaders' choices by changing the value they give to a fight or their expectations of it occurring as a result of certain types of actions.

Value of fight. The value of a fight to a decisionmaker depends on (a) the direct costs and benefits of the fight itself, (b) the values he places on winning (and losing) the fight, and (c) his expectancy of winning.

The prospect of a fight may be made more repugnant to decisionmakers by convincing them that such a struggle will be costly in terms of money, property, damage, lives, and even political support. The value of a fight also can be reduced by making winning seem less important. A nation's adversary may help to make winning a fight less attractive by making its own demands and objectives reasonable ones. For example, Soviet leaders would be likely to value victory over the United States less if they believed that the United States was not aiming to destroy their social system (and vice versa). The importance of winning over the other side may also be reduced if each side's leaders avoid conducting the dispute in a rancorous way or in a way that engages their own personal prestige or that of the other side's leaders. Otherwise, "beating" the other side may become an end in itself, irrespective of the practical advantages it may bring.

In the long run, the importance of winning particular disputes with another nation may be reduced by establishing ties of common interests. For example, establishing stronger ties of economic interdependency (of trade, finance, or technology) can help to make the stakes of winning a dispute seem less vital in the wider context of shared interests.

The overall value of a fight to decisionmakers may be reduced also by decreasing their expectations of winning such a fight. The adversary can help to create such reduced expectations of victory by increasing its ability to defend itself successfully, by forming alliances, and by providing evidence of its will and ability to persist in a struggle. It is important, however, that in attempting to demonstrate their own nation's strength and resolve, national leaders should be careful not to create the impression that their own side has aggressive plans. If such an impression is created, it may frighten the other side into making a preemptive attack.

Expectancy of winning a war can also be reduced if leaders realize that the very process of fighting a war—especially a nuclear war—today will make the concept of winning meaningless. If they see the outcome of a next war as mutual annihilation and a long nuclear winter, then winning will cease to have meaning.

Expectancy that actions will lead to a fight. If decisionmakers see a fight as very costly, they are apt to avoid coercive action if they believe that such action will result in a fight. This expectation depends in turn on their anticipation about how their adversary will respond to coercion. The adversary—i.e., the potential target of coercion—can influence these expectations by its record of past behavior and by statements of intent—e.g., that it will retaliate against any coercive act.

The potential target also can influence the other's expectations by demonstrating that it has strong incentives for resistance to coercion. It may show (and even create) such incentives by such means as strengthening formal commitments to resist coercion (e.g., by treaty), by increasing its stakes in resistance (e.g., by increasing its economic or military presence in some disputed area), by building greater political support for resistance, and by building a military capability sufficient to reduce the costs of resistance and raise the chances of the resistance being successful.

In addition to the question of whether their use of threat or coercion will lead to a fight, decisionmakers may also consider the likelihood that doing nothing (or even making concessions) will lead to a fight. They may believe —perhaps because of a military buildup that the other side sees as defensive —that the other side is determined to attack them whatever they may do. When such expectations are formed, national leaders may decide to attack first, especially when they see an advantage to the side that strikes first. This was, for example, the basis of the preemptive Israeli attack on Egypt in June 1967. To reduce the chance that an adversary will use coercion, it is important not to give him reason to think that he will be struck first unless he acts.

Raising the Costs of Disagreement: The Use of Coercion

The greater the net costs of a dispute and the longer such costs are expected to continue, the more likely decisionmakers are to try to bring the dispute to an end. Knowing this, the leaders of one nation may try to pressure its adversary to concede by increasing the costs of the conflict to it—for example, by imposing greater physical damage on the adversary or by raising the conflict to a level that strains the adversary's resources. National leaders who use such coercive methods may intend them also to signal their own resolve to stand firm, thus convincing the adversary that the costs it is experiencing will continue indefinitely if it does not concede on the issues in dispute.

Sometimes the use of coercion is successful. The chances of success increase as the magnitude of the penalties imposed becomes greater, as the target expects the penalties to continue longer unless he submits, as the concessions demanded of the target are less onerous, as the target sees the long-term objectives of the coercer as more limited, as the prospect of an expanded fight becomes more repugnant for the target, and as there is more political support for concessions in the target nation.

However, even when coercion succeeds in getting the leaders of a nation to submit to the demands of the adversary, this success is often only temporary. As soon as the opportunity arises, the original target of coercion usually attempts to and often succeeds in undoing the settlement imposed on it.

Moreover, the general tendency is for coercion to be met initially not with compliance but with counter-coercion. The leaders and the public of the target nation are almost certain to be angered by the use of coercion against them, which they usually see as unjustified and provocative. Typically they want to "get even" with the adversary and may see retaliation as necessary to preserve the chance for an eventual favorable agreement. Retaliation may be seen as showing the adversary that one's own nation cannot be bullied into concessions and as making the dispute costly enough for the adversary that it will be forced to make concessions.

If each side believes that it can continue to increase the costs of the other while suffering lower (or at least more tolerable) costs itself, a cycle of escalating coercion and counter-coercion may ensue. Such a pattern of escalating violence occurred in disputes between the United States and North Vietnam, between Israel and Egypt, between Iran and Iraq, and in many other instances.

Escalation of coercion does not occur solely as the result of rationally calculated attempts by each side to get the other to concede. Rather, as a dispute continues and intensifies, the motivations and expectations of each side tend to change. First, the intrinsic value for decisionmakers of using coercion tends to increase. As a fight continues and grows more intense, hostile feelings against the opponent increase; hurting him becomes more of a goal in itself, more satisfying, and more acclaimed by the public.

Secondly, the value of winning the dispute tends to increase. Having expended much treasure and perhaps blood, the leaders of each side become emotionally involved in the fight; they feel they must win to justify the costs and the sacrifices already made. Furthermore, winning may become more valued because the leaders have raised their goals and aspirations in a dispute.

Finally, as a fight progresses, it seems increasingly important to beat the other side, apart from the immediate advantages this may bring. Leaders of both sides have committed their prestige to the struggle and have become emotionally involved in it. Moreover, as winning is seen as affecting the outcome of future disputes, winning becomes important in itself.

Escalation of coercion in a dispute may be caused also by changes in expectations held by the leaders of each side. As a conflict continues and grows in intensity, each side may come to expect a higher level of coercive action by the other; moreover, it may be uncertain about what limits on coercion, if any, the other side has accepted. In such a situation, each side will feel less inhibition about increasing its own coercive actions beyond previous bounds. It may believe that there is advantage in escalating first.

In addition, as a dispute continues and grows in intensity, each side may see less and less chance for a peaceful resolution. If leaders see force as the only plausible way for the dispute to be settled, then they are likely to take whatever measures they think necessary for victory.

Just as changed expectations may help to produce escalation of coercion, escalation in turn may affect each side's expectations. By escalating its level of coercion, leaders of one side aim to convince the other of the costliness of resistance and of their own resolve to win. However, they may instead convince the adversary of their hostile intentions and of the likelihood that they will take dangerous aggressive actions in the future. Rather than being motivated to concede, the target of coercion may believe that it must take swift decisive actions to defeat its dangerous enemy and thus escalate its own use of coercion.

What can be done to counter the tendency for the use of coercion to escalate? How can movement in the opposite direction—toward a lower level of coercion—be encouraged instead? First, in order to discourage escalation, it is important for the adversaries to avoid dangerous misinterpretation of each other's actions and intentions. When using coercion, each side must be careful to make clear the limits of its objectives and the boundaries it is setting on its own use of coercion. Otherwise the adversary may believe that its objectives are much greater than they are in fact and that there is no limit to the amount and type of force that it may soon use to pursue its aims. In the face of what it sees (perhaps mistakenly) as an imminent threat, the adversary may find unattractive the option of continuing (or reducing) its own level of coercion. One way for a user of coercion to make clear the boundaries it accepts on its own methods is to use coercion only up to perceptually prominent "salient points." For example, one side in a war may use (and state its intention to use) only nonnuclear weapons. Once the nuclear boundary is crossed, it is much harder for the other side to know what the limits of force are.

It is important also to prevent the value of winning from increasing during the course of a dispute and, if possible, to reduce it. Each side needs to avoid expanding the issues of the dispute, raising its aspirations and demands, or turning a pragmatic dispute into a contest in resolve and prestige. To the contrary, efforts to reduce the actual and perceived stakes of both sides, by narrowing the issues and by persuading leaders and the public that their goals are not as vital as were initially believed, may help to de-escalate the level of violence.

Escalation of a fight can also be discouraged by raising the perceived costs of (increased) fighting. For example, providing full information about the possible catastrophic health, social, ecological, climatic, and other consequences of a nuclear war can help to discourage the temptation to escalate a war to the use of nuclear weapons. In addition, full and vivid information about the material, human, and other costs of an ongoing fight—such as that which reached the American public during the Vietnam war—can help to provide incentive for de-escalation from a present level of fighting.

Escalation of a dispute also can be discouraged (and de-escalation encouraged) by actions that reduce each side's expectations that using more coercion will force the other to concede. By demonstrating its ability and will to resist further coercion, an adversary can discourage increased use of coercion against itself. By threatening that it will step in to aid a "victim" if coercion against the target is increased (as the Soviets and Chinese tacitly did in Korea and Vietnam), third parties can reduce the expectancy of winning the dispute through greater coercion.

Finally, the escalation of coercion may be discouraged, and de-escalation encouraged, by making conciliatory options seem more attractive and more realizable. Possible compromise solutions can be suggested to leaders by those within their own nation, by third parties, and by their adversaries. This is another reason why it is desirable that some communication between the adversaries continue even during a fight—so that each may be aware when and if the other is amenable to a compromise settlement. Third parties can also play an important role in facilitating communication between the parties, either directly or by serving as an intermediary to convey intentions, "feelers," and actual proposals.

Making Agreement More Attractive

One way to encourage one or both adversaries in a dispute to make concessions is to make agreement more valued for them. If agreement is highly valued, then leaders of each side are more likely to make concessions if they believe that such actions are likely to lead to an acceptable agreement.

The value of agreement per se. The leaders of an adversary nation as well as third parties (such as neutral nations or international organizations) can take actions that make agreement per se more attractive to national leaders. They can do this by creating or making more salient and concrete possible benefits that could flow from good relations with the present adversary. These might include proposals for increased trade, joint space explorations, joint water projects, cooperative efforts to reduce environmental pollution, and scientific cooperation. The possible benefits of an improved relationship also include enormous savings of resources currently being spent on armaments. In addition, the benefits may include cooperative action against one or more other nations that pose a danger of some sort. For example, the desire of both the United States and China to settle outstanding disputes in the 1970s was based in part on the benefits both saw in cooperating to restrain Soviet influence in Asia. American and Soviet leaders at various times in the 1960s and 1970s saw improved relationships (détente) as helping to keep small wars in Africa and Asia from getting out of control and as helping to control nuclear proliferation throughout the world.

The value of agreement per se is increased also as competing demands are made for the scarce resources that are being devoted to the dispute. Sometimes national leaders are anxious to settle a dispute with one adversary so that they can turn their attention and allocate their resources more fully to another dispute that has assumed greater priority. Competing demands for resources may come also from constituencies within a nation involved in an external dispute. The more that domestic groups insistently urge the implementation of plans for reaching such goals as improved medical care, better schools, improved transportation, greater economic development, and reduction of environmental pollution, the more national leaders will feel the need to use money and manpower resources for such programs. Therefore, settling a dispute that diverts money and manpower from such purposes will be more attractive.

There are signs that the Soviet government under the leadership of Mikhail Gorbachev would like a relaxation of tensions and arms-control agreements with the United States so that it can devote more resources to building its domestic economy. In the United States the huge budget deficits and the loss of a competitive advantage by many U.S. industries may provide an incentive for American leaders to improve relations with the Soviets so that less money is spent on the military and more on economic development.

However, making settlement of a dispute appear attractive to decision-makers will not necessarily lead them to make concessions. They must also believe that conciliatory actions are likely to lead to an acceptable agreement (and that coercive actions will not). To promote such expectations by an adversary, national leaders need to indicate clearly that their own aims are limited and that they will respond to conciliatory moves with reciprocal cooperation rather than by trying to exploit the other's concessions. Since actions usually speak louder than words, positive responses to concessions by the other side in one or more previous disputes will raise an adversary's expectations that conciliatory actions will lead to a settlement.

The value of a specific agreement. The overall value of an agreement to national leaders depends not only on their general desire to settle the dispute but also on the specific terms of the settlement. To encourage an adversary to accept one's own offer or to make concessions it often may be necessary to make the terms of a possible agreement more attractive to them.

The attractiveness of any outcome to decisionmakers depends in part on their frame of reference, specifically on their goals and on the point below which they would prefer no agreement to a settlement. Sometimes it may be possible to modify national leaders' goals and/or what they define as an essential minimum. By skillful persuasion, leaders of other nations or domestic constituencies may be able to convince them that a given goal (e.g., maintaining the status quo or restoring a previous situation) is less desirable than they have believed. For example, Peace Now activists in Israel may be able to convince some Likud party leaders that a goal of maintaining Israeli control over the West Bank area is undesirable because of the disadvantages of an eventual Arab majority in Israel.

The goals of national leaders may be modified also by getting them to see certain goals as unrealistically high. Information that makes clear the bargaining strength of the other side—i.e., its capability and resolve—may cause leaders to lower their aspirations concerning the type of settlement they can attain.

The lower limit for bargainers depends on their alternatives to agreement. To keep national leaders from setting their minimum conditions for agreement too high, it is desirable to make clear to them the unattractiveness of a situation of no agreement. In particular, the costs of no agreement need to be made clear and vivid. For example, American and Soviet leaders may tend to lower their minimum terms for an arms agreement as each becomes more concerned about the costs of no agreement in terms of the burden to their economy and the increased risk of nuclear war.

It is not always possible to modify the goals or the minimum acceptable terms that decisionmakers hold. National leaders may have a deep feeling of dissatisfaction with present political arrangements—e.g., with territorial boundaries, access to raw materials, trade terms, or political control in areas of vital concern—and believe that the goal of changing the status quo is highly important. They may be tempted to use force to try to change the present situation. For example, Japanese leaders were willing to go to war with the United States in 1941 in order to gain access to vital raw materials. In other cases national leaders may be deeply committed to preserving present arrangements and to maintaining what they see as their vital interests. For example, American leaders have been committed for many decades to keeping Central and South America free of control by outside Communist nations.

Especially when an adversary is committed to its goals, it is dangerous to put it in a position where it must choose between surrendering or using force. To encourage conciliatory moves by the adversary, it must be offered terms that are at least minimally acceptable—terms it can "live with," even though reluctantly.

*Expectations.*Conciliatory behavior will depend not only on leaders' perceptions that an acceptable agreement is available but also on their expectations that making concessions is the way to achieve it. Often national leaders will not even offer concessions if they do not expect them to be reciprocated. For example, President Sadat of Egypt would not have offered recognition and peace to Israel if he did not expect the Israeli government to make concessions on territorial boundaries. Sometimes national leaders—in order to project an image of resolve and perhaps to rally domestic support—create an impression of total inflexibility that may discourage an adversary from making concessions. To encourage concessions from the other side, national leaders need to convey, by their statements and by the record of actions they build, a general willingness to meet the other side halfway.

Making Concessions

What if one side does make some concessions to an adversary, perhaps in the hope of reaching terms that are acceptable to the other side as well as to itself: will the adversary reciprocate? There is a strong tendency for conciliatory actions by one nation toward another to be reciprocated. However, this does not always occur; sometimes concessions are met with continued intransigence and even belligerence. The adversary may believe that an initial concession is a forerunner of more to come and that he need only wait for the other side's position to collapse completely.

The target of a concession is most likely to reciprocate when it perceives its opponent as acting out of a desire to cooperate or compromise but not out of weakness. Both sides are most likely to interpret their opponents' concessions in this way when their bargaining powers (based on their motivations and fighting capabilities) are about equal.

To encourage reciprocation for their concessions, then, national leaders need to make clear to their adversary that continued cooperation and concession on their side is dependent on reciprocation. This can be done best not only by words (which may not be believed) but by maintaining the necessary strength and political support to persist in their position if necessary.

Overall Strategies

Strategies that rely on coercion and those that rely on cooperation both have serious limitations. A consistently coercive strategy usually leads to conflict with the adversary and, in international relations, to war. A strategy of consistent (and unconditional) cooperation usually leads to exploitation by an adversary and, in international disputes, to diplomatic defeat.

Strategies that combine coercive and conciliatory actions appear to be more successful in eliciting cooperation from an adversary. Using "tough" tactics early in a series of interactions with an adversary and then switching to more cooperative actions generally elicits greater cooperation from the other than does a consistently cooperative or consistently competitive strategy. The "first firm, then conciliatory" strategy may show the adversary initially that it cannot exploit its opponent and that competition is costly and therefore make it more receptive to cooperative actions than it would have been at the start. If threat and even mild coercion are used early in a dispute, it should be done in a way that makes it clear that one's aim is to resist exploitation and not to dominate or exploit the other. Otherwise a pattern of mutual escalating coercion may be started.

The most effective strategies that combine coercive and cooperative actions are those in which actions of one's own side are contingent on the actions of the other side. A strategy of reciprocating the other's actions (tit for tat) has been found to be successful generally in leading to mutual cooperation. The tit-for-tat strategy seems to work best when the user matches consistently and with equal vigor both cooperative and competitive actions by the other side. When responding to a competitive move by the other, the reciprocator should not "over-match" the other's move—i.e., respond with a higher level of coercion. Rather he should slightly "under-match" the other's competitive action to de-escalate the conflict while showing that he cannot be exploited.

While a strategy of reciprocity has some important strengths, it also has some serious weaknesses. Once a pattern of mutual competition has begun, the two sides may get "locked-in" on it. Moreover, if both sides follow a strict policy of reciprocity, a single competitive move by either side will start an unending series of reciprocal competitive moves.

To break a "lock-in" on mutually competitive and mutually costly actions, a program of unilateral conciliatory initiatives has been proposed for the United States. This program would retain the nation's basic defenses and would continue to react firmly to any attempt by an adversary to exploit the United States. But by a series of conciliatory actions, to which reciprocation by the other side would be invited, the program aims to begin a pattern of mutual cooperation to replace that of mutual coercion.

Such a strategy of unilateral initiatives has been found to be effective in promoting cooperation both in experimental settings and in international relations. Probably the best example is that of American-Soviet relations in 1963–1964. A strategy of combining firmness against coercion with offering concessions to break competitive stalemates has been found to be effective in many other international disputes as well. The strategy that appears to be most successful is not one of strict reciprocity but one that combines a general posture of reciprocity with the use of unilateral conciliatory actions to break out of a cycle of mutual coercion.

A strategy that makes use of conciliatory initiatives is not likely to be successful if the adversary has superior power and aims to dominate. Conciliation is most likely to be effective in eliciting cooperation when the conceder is perceived by his adversary as strong and as making concessions willingly rather than under compulsion.

In the case of the most important international relationship today—that between the Soviet Union and the United States—neither side is so strong that it can hope realistically to dominate the other. While each would like to outdo the other in ideological and political competition, the leaders of each country are acutely aware that their first concern must be to avoid a terrible nuclear war. Thus the conditions exist for successful use of the firm-but-cooperative strategy by our national leaders. A general strategy of reciprocity, combined with the use of a program of unilateral initiatives to break out of competitive deadlocks, appears to offer a feasible way to halt costly and dangerous conflict and move toward a pattern of mutual cooperation.

Reaching Agreement

Almost every dispute is settled eventually. Why, then, is not every dispute settled quickly, without the cost and possible agony of a long struggle? The basic reason is that, in many cases, the leaders of each side have incompatible expectations about the terms of settlement. Each side's leaders expect the adversary to yield to all or some major part of their own demands within a reasonable time. In some cases they may expect that a test of strength—i.e., a fight—will be necessary before the other concedes, but they expect to win the fight and believe that the costs of the fight will be justified by the gains they finally make. So long as both sides have similar expectations of eventual victory, at acceptable cost (or prefer a stalemate to any available settlement), the dispute will remain unresolved.

The actions of each side in a dispute—including persuasion, threats, promises, coercive actions, and concessions—are all part of a process of bargaining in which each side tries to shape the terms of final settlement to its liking. The process of bargaining serves two basic functions for the parties in a dispute. First, each tries to learn more about how far the other side is willing to concede and the circumstances under which it would be willing to use force to defend its interests. Second, each side tries to influence the preferences and the expectations of the other in order to get it to make further concessions and to discourage it from using coercion.

As a result of the interaction that occurs between the parties during the period of bargaining, the relative bargaining power of the two sides (based on their capabilities and the strength of their motives) is clarified. Most important, what each side is willing to settle for, rather than endure a stalemate or a fight, becomes clearer to both. If both sides realize that side A is more resolved, then side B will move most of the way toward side A's demands—assuming side B prefers that outcome to continued stalemate or a (wider) fight. If leaders of the two sides see that they are both equally resolved, each of the two sides will move its position closer to that of the other, again assuming that each would prefer a compromise agreement to no agreement.

It may be noted that a strategy that combines firmness against exploitation with willingness to make concessions (as discussed before) can help facilitate agreement. The element of firmness in the face of threat of coercion makes it clear to the adversary that he cannot force a one-sided outcome in his favor. The willingness to compromise (and even to initiate unilateral concessions) provides the adversary with the possibility of a settlement that is attractive enough that he prefers it to a continued stalemate or an expanded fight.

To reach an agreement in a dispute between two nations, then, it is necessary to get the leaders of both sides to see the situation in the same way, especially regarding the eventual willingness of each side to accept given terms. How can such a convergence of expectations be promoted?

First it is desirable to try to keep the gap in expectations (and thus in demands) from becoming too wide at the start of the dispute. Each side should make its own intentions clear enough at the outset that it does not encourage unrealistically high expectations by the other.

The convergence of expectations and demands also may be facilitated by the availability of more information to both sides. Each needs to obtain a more realistic view of the other side's interests and capabilities (as well as its own) and of what terms each is willing to accept rather than to stand firm and/or fight. If both parties receive accurate information quickly, they will not need to go through a long, costly, and dangerous period of bluffs, threat, and coercion.

However, it is difficult for each side to obtain (or to believe) accurate information about the other because each is motivated to mislead the other in order to win an advantage and fears the same behavior from the other. While it is difficult to completely overcome this problem, several types of approaches may be helpful. Nations might exchange additional information bearing on their military and economic strengths, either directly or through third nations or international organizations. Third parties may also be able to transmit to each side a fuller picture of the vital concerns and goals of the other side. If leaders of both sides were able early in the dispute to get a good understanding of the aims and capabilities of both sides, the period of probes and pressures might be made shorter, less costly, and less dangerous.

A convergence of expectations and demands of two nations in a dispute may also be facilitated by the introduction of certain kinds of possible agreements. A perceptually prominent solution based on shared norms, precedents, or salient features of the situation may provide a focus on which the two sides' expectations may converge. For example, in arms-control negotiations between the United States and the Soviet Union, a proposal based on equal numbers of weapons is more likely than other proposals to win agreement because (among other reasons) it represents a perceptually salient point on which expectations can converge. However, for a perceptually prominent solution to be acceptable to both parties, it should also be consistent with the parties' perceptions of their relative bargaining power.

Agreement also may be facilitated by discovering or devising solutions that, in some respects at least, benefit both sides. While some conflicts of interest cannot be denied, more attention needs to be paid to areas in which jointly beneficial outcomes are possible. For example, in trade disputes it often may be possible to devise agreements that increase the total production, trade, and profit of both sides. Similarly, while each party in an arms-control negotiation may hope to win some military advantage, both sides have mutual interests in reducing costs and reducing the danger of war, which provide the basis for mutually acceptable agreements.

Coordinating Actions

If leaders of two rival nations each try to maximize their own self-interest in competition with the other nation, the result may be bad for both sides. Both may find themselves locked into a costly arms race that neither side can win. Moreover, the two sides may find themselves embroiled in disputes — e.g., for influence and dominance over smaller nations — that bring a real danger of a war neither side wants.

Both sides may be better off if they coordinate their actions in order to limit their competition. Leaders of both sides may realize this. Yet they may continue along the path of relatively unrestrained competition because each side distrusts the other and does not want to be taken advantage of.

How can the two sides escape this dilemma? First, as the previous discussion indicates, leaders of each nation can take actions independently to encourage mutual cooperation. Most notably, a strategy of reciprocity plus conciliatory initiatives to break out of competitive deadlocks appears to be successful. In addition, there are some ways to facilitate cooperation that require the combined actions of both sides (and sometimes of outsiders as well). One important condition is to maintain effective channels for and flow of communication. Certain kinds of communication are necessary for effective cooperation; both sides must communicate clearly and accurately their own intentions and expectations. But each side should not need to have complete trust in the honesty of the other. In cases where actions are not obvious—e.g., in building some kinds of weapons—effective methods of verification need to be devised and mutually accepted in order to give each side assurance that the other side is living up to its stated intentions.

Both by the independent, reciprocal actions of each nation, and through explicit agreements, norms or rules of cooperation need to be developed in order to settle disagreements without mutually costly and dangerous confrontations. Disputing parties are most likely to develop norms to control the use of force in their relationship when they have equal power and have the capacity to inflict a great amount of damage on each other. This is precisely the situation that exists today for the United States and the Soviet Union. Some small steps have been taken to regulate competition in arms buildups and in the use of force. But these few faltering steps have not been sufficient to reduce greatly the dangers. The basic conditions for agreeing on rules exist. More rapid progress is urgently needed.

A Final Word

Some or all of the conclusions presented in this book are subject to challenge. Though they are backed by evidence, some of the evidence is incomplete; some is open to different interpretation; some relevant factors may have been overlooked or not given enough weight. As with all attempts at scientific explanation, new theories and especially new evidence may force a modification or even a rejection of some of the conclusions presented.

Yet, though the ideas and evidence presented here are subject to revision and improvement, I believe that they represent a useful summary and interpretation of much that we know that is relevant to resolving conflicts between nations. Most important, I believe that they represent an advance over "commonsense" thinking, which is often simplistic and contradictory.

Many people, including many government officials, approach disputes with another nation, such as that with the Soviet Union, with the belief that the way to peace is through strength and firmness. They are convinced that history and experience shows this to be true. But the evidence we have reviewed shows that this approach, while having some elements of validity, is—in itself—often ineffective and dangerous.

A very different approach is championed by many people in the "peace movement." They argue that the way to peace is through making concessions and reducing arms. Again, while this approach has some merit, the evidence suggests that a policy based only on cooperation and concession often will lead to either surrender or war.

The basic message that underlies many of the specific conclusions presented in this book is that a successful policy—one that maintains the essential interests of one's own side while avoiding war—is one that combines both a measure of firmness and a measure of flexibility, both a willingness to vigorously resist coercion by an adversary and a willingness to reciprocate and sometimes to initiate concessions. By words, and especially by deeds, it is important to show the adversary that one will not be exploited but also that one is ready to cooperate. The adversary should be convinced that he has little to gain by coercion and much to gain by cooperation.

Such a basic policy should be supported by a compatible arms policy. In order to maintain peace rather than provoke war, the number, types, and deployment of arms should convince an adversary that he could not profit from attack but also that one's own side does not intend and could not profit from an attack.

Choices of action for officials and for the public in specific disputes will never be easy. Knowledge of the specifics of each particular situation and of the personalities involved are important. But actions in specific situations need to be guided by more general principles derived from the widest available evidence. I hope that the general framework and conclusions presented here can help to provide some broad guidelines for choosing actions in specific circumstances that will lead to peace rather than to war.

Notes

Chapter 1

1. I use the term theoretical framework rather than theory because, while I identify the key types of variables affecting the choice of actions and indicate generally the relationship among them, I do not attempt at this point to identify more specific variables nor to state the relationship among the variables with precision or detail. Some attempts to specify variables and relationships further are made in later chapters of the book.
2. Figure 1.1 does not assume any specific order of moves by the two sides. If one assumes that the two sides act in a strict sequence (i.e., each acts only after the other's last move), the situation may be depicted in a somewhat different way (see, for example, Brams, 1985).
3. It is, of course, desirable to estimate preferences as well as expectancies of each side from information other than its actions; otherwise the reasoning becomes circular.
4. Further distinctions in preference could perhaps be made—e.g., whether U.S. leaders would have preferred a small-scale fight in the Caribbean to one elsewhere—but the gross distinctions made here are sufficient for my purpose.
5. See chapter 4 for a discussion of the concept of "maximizing expected utility."
6. In a study of the decision by Israel's cabinet to launch a preemptive attack on Egypt in 1967, Wagner (1974) averaged the preferences and perceived probabilities of members of the Israeli cabinet as expressed in interviews after this crisis. He then applied what is basically an individual model of utility maximization to account for the Israeli cabinet's choice.
7. It also is possible to study the actions of government as an organizational process (e.g., Halperin, 1974).

Chapter 2

1. The two basic categories of concession and firmness, omitting the category of no action, are used in this chapter in order to simplify the analysis and make it consistent with previous work on this topic. The firmness category is used here to include both taking no concessive actions and taking actions penalizing to the adversary.

2. The PLO is not a nation, of course, although it represents a people who have aspirations for nationhood.

3. Having a measure of each side's strength of preferences among outcomes is especially useful when the sum of the rank order preferences for a win and a fight is equal to the sum of preferences for a compromise and a loss.

4. Rapoport and Guyer (1966) have used the concepts of threat-vulnerability or force-vulnerability with regard to equilibrium situations. Here the concept is used for a wider range of situations. Also, I have added the condition that the user of threat or force suffer less than his opponent if he were to act.

5. Rummel (1979:254) also discusses reasons why a weaker nation may resist a stronger.

6. Bueno de Mesquita (1981) has argued that there is no theoretical reason to expect a particular distribution of power in the international system to be related consistently to war. However, he focuses on power distributions among a set of nations and not on the relative power of two potential adversaries.

7. Equal and great power induce caution if there are incentives for each to attack first.

8. An equilibrium outcome is "such that neither player can unilaterally 'depart' from it (i.e., shift his strategy while the other retains his) without diminishing his own payoff" (Rapoport and Guyer, 1966:3). Brams (1985) has discussed "non-myopic equilibria" in which each player may make a temporary gain by changing his move but would not benefit in the long run.

9. The term Prisoner's Dilemma derives from an anecdote concerning two criminals who are being questioned separately about a joint crime (see Rapoport and Chammah, 1965). The term Chicken derives from a game in which two persons drive their cars straight toward each other to see who will veer off first. For a discussion of how inter-nation crises fit these and other types of situations, see Snyder and Diesing (1977).

10. Reasons why some laboratory Prisoner's Dilemma games may have only limited applicability to inter-nation relations have been suggested by Wagner (1983).

11. In both historical and simulation studies, Schwartz (1972) did not find a reduction in nations' "receptivity to communication" as perceptions of unfriendliness and threat increased. However, he did not measure actual volume of communication.

Chapter 3

1. Stein (1982) has argued that misperceptions by national leaders of an adversary's intent do not necessarily facilitate war. He discusses the conditions under which misperceptions may contribute to war.

2. Different assumptions about reactions of the Soviet Union to actions of the United States are discussed by Gamson and Modigliani (1971).

3. In addition, national leaders sometimes project their own intentions onto adversaries. For example, Lockwood (1983) describes the tendency of both Soviet and American military officials to perceive their adversary as having military intentions similar to their own, even when this is untrue.

4. Deutsch also found that three other elements of communication increased expectations of cooperation: the other's expectation that one would also cooperate, that the other would respond to noncooperation with sanctions, and "absolution" for past noncooperation.

5. See chapter 2 for a discussion of Prisoner's Dilemma and Chicken situations.

6. Ignoring information about possible dangers has been termed perceptual defense by psychologists (Dember and Warm, 1979:366). Jervis (1976:372–378) suggests that

this mechanism of perceptual defense is most likely to operate when individuals can do little to ward off the danger.

7. While there is evidence to support the influence of expectations on attention, several other competing theories have been advanced (see Dember and Warm, 1979:chapters 9 and 10).

Chapter 4

1. March (1982) states that current rules store information generated by previous experience and analyses. These in turn may be affected by the nature of the situations that the decisionmaker has faced in the past (e.g., conflict of interest, relative power). March also points out that decision rules may be based on moral principles and on the individual's self-image (i.e., what kind of action is necessary to be the kind of person one wishes to be).

2. It could be argued conversely that use of standard rules would permit more unexamined use of rewarding, friendly actions. However, rules which specify the occasions for such positive action appear to be much rarer than those specifying when to use coercive action.

3. This is an issue in which one of the requirements of effective deterrence—i.e., the credibility of a response to attack—may conflict somewhat with the desirability of keeping firm control over the use of military force. However, a small reduction in the effectiveness of a deterrent threat seems an acceptable price to pay for minimizing the chance of a war caused by error.

4. Another way in which decisionmakers may screen out unacceptable alternatives is "elimination by aspects" (Tversky, 1972). The decisionmaker first eliminates any options that do not meet his most important criterion, then he eliminates any that do not meet his second most important criterion, and so on.

5. Decision theorists have also explored other possible bases for choice—e.g., maximizing the minimum return.

6. Fischhoff, Goitein, and Shapira (1982) maintain that the ability of the expected utility model frequently to predict behavior may simply reflect the fact that it includes relevant variables but does not necessarily show that it reflects the process by which decisions are made.

7. In many cases people tend to choose the option that has the lower expected value.

8. Preference for the riskier option may occur even when the probability of the larger loss is high (see Kahneman and Tversky, 1979:268). Kahneman and Tversky explain it primarily in terms of the certainty principle, but the differential value for positive and negative outcomes is also relevant.

9. Where two choices both offer the possibility but not high probability of gains, people generally choose the prospect that offers the larger gain (Kahneman and Tversky, 1979).

10. This would be true only within limits since beyond a certain point large losses may be seen as unacceptable.

11. The equation for the subjective value of a "prospect" (option) is similar to that for the "expected utility" of an action used by other theorists. The value of each outcome is multiplied by a weight associated with a subjective probability rather than by the probability itself. When outcomes are all positive or all negative, the equation for a prospect is modified.

Chapter 5

1. Another possibility is for one side to purposely weaken itself militarily, perhaps in order to reassure the other side of its peaceful intent.
2. The outcome of a dispute may include advantages or disadvantages on matters not part of the dispute. For example, one side may promise trade concessions or political cooperation if it gets a favorable outcome in a territorial dispute.
3. Kelley and Thibaut (1978) have discussed the ways in which the valuation of one's objective outcomes may be transformed by considering the other's (relative) outcomes.
4. A fight usually involves a mutual exchange of penalties. However, sometimes a fight may be very one-sided, involving primarily or entirely the imposition of penalties by one side on the other.

Chapter 6

1. Modified forms of defiance are to promise to comply with the threatener's demand at a later time or to comply partially with the demand.
2. The value of having the penalty imposed is equivalent to the value of a one-sided fight. Thus, the value of this outcome is a subcategory of the term "value of a fight" in the choice model presented in chapter 5.
3. The question of whether or not the threat is limited to the present situation is related to Schelling's (1966) discussion about whether there is a clear delimitation of the demand.
4. See Pruitt (1981:82) for a listing of some additional noncompliant ways of dealing with threats.

Chapter 7

1. Anderton (1985) has presented a categorization and analysis of efforts at modeling arms races.
2. This was true for some measures of spending used by Cusack and Ward. When other spending measures were used, neither tension nor arms spending by the other had any substantial effect on arms spending.
3. Note however that war mobilization may be related to tension with rivals. Cusack and Ward also studied variation in defense spending by China but were not very successful in explaining this.
4. Note that Hollist's conclusions regarding an arms race between Iran and Iraq, and between the United States and the USSR, differ from those of Majeski and Jones.
5. I assume that there is a central decisionmaker who makes the final decision to use force. See Hoagland and Walker (1979:130) and Bueno de Mesquita (1981a:28) for defenses of this assumption.
6. The value of winning a fight and the value of losing it are not necessarily equal in absolute value. The value of a draw or indecisive outcome is not included here in order to simplify the analysis and presentation.
7. The Soviet Union has used proxy forces to fight against American-backed regimes—e.g., North Korean forces against South Korea, North Vietnamese against South Vietnam, and Cubans against American-supported factions in Angola.
8. As J. Snyder (1985) points out, a nation's leaders also have an incentive to attack a rival when an ongoing arms buildup by the rival makes them anticipate an adverse change in the relative power of the two sides.

9. Additional factors, including the efficiency of command and control systems, intelligence accuracy, and skills of military personnel also affect overall military capability. The focus here is on weapons.

10. Mayer (1986) has shown that the conclusions of Intriligator and Brito depend on their special assumptions about the conditions under which nuclear attack might be initiated or deterred and about the nature of nuclear war itself.

11. It can be argued that a small number of nuclear weapons is less of a deterrent threat against an adversary beginning a conventional war than is a large nuclear arsenal. However, if the adversary also has a large nuclear force, then the threat of retaliating with nuclear weapons against his conventional attack is not likely to be very credible since it would be suicidal (see chapter 6). A strong conventional force would be a better deterrent, though the same cautions about avoiding first-strike capability and the communication of aggressive intent made with respect to nuclear weapons would apply to conventional forces as well.

Chapter 8

1. Blechman and Kaplan (1978) have found that the use of force by the United States was more effective when the United States was more committed.

2. It should be recognized that stating an intention not to use nuclear weapons in the event of a war, and taking actions consistent with this intent (e.g., removing tactical nuclear weapons from one's forces), may reduce deterrence of attack by a potential aggressor. However, such deterrence can be maintained by other ways, such as strengthening one's conventional defenses against attack.

Chapter 9

1. Coercive pressure may make compliance with an adversary's wishes more attractive in order to escape (or end) punishment at the same time that it decreases the attractiveness of compliance because of the status loss of complying under pressure.

Chapter 10

1. In a Prisoner's Dilemma situation, the relative payoffs are: Winning (T) > Mutual Cooperation (R) > Mutual Competition (P) > Losing (S); and $2R > T + S$.

2. In a Chicken situation, payoffs are: Winning (T) > Mutual Cooperation (R) > Losing (S) > Mutual Competition (P); and $2R > T + S$.

3. More complex strategies of a generally reciprocating nature, "linked tit for tat" and "quid pro quo," have been discussed by McGinnis (1986). These strategies are relevant when there are two or more separate "games." There is little or no systematic evidence on their effectiveness. Often, though there are several issues in a dispute, they may be considered part of a single overall "game."

4. In a Chicken situation, it is especially difficult to make credible one's intention to reciprocate competitive moves. See Brams (1985) for a discussion of ways to make credible threats in a Chicken situation.

5. A policy of slowness to reciprocate competitive moves (tit only after two tats) did well in one computer tournament of strategies but not in another such tournament (Axelrod, 1984).

6. The exact operational meaning of the GRIT strategy differed in these studies.

7. There is some evidence also that retaliation to another's competitive moves either before or during the use of a GRIT strategy is most effective in eliciting cooperation from the other when the power of the two sides is equal (Lindskold, Bennett, and Wayner, 1976; Lindskold and Aronoff, 1980).

8. This pattern is similar to that found most successful in a Prisoner's Dilemma game by Harford and Solomon (1967): initial noncooperation, then unconditional cooperation, followed by conditional cooperation.

9. Komorita (1973) has suggested that Osgood's GRIT strategy is most valid in the later stages of a negotiation, when deadlock has continued for an extended period. This suggestion seems generally consistent with the Leng and Wheeler results.

Chapter 11

1. Similarly, Walton and McKersie (1965) assert that the chance of a strike occurring is high when the expectations of labor and of management about the outcomes of the dispute are divergent.

2. In this section the term power is used in the sense of capability to impose costs on the other side. Bargaining power includes capabiity plus strength of motivation to prevail on the issues. Thus, two sides may agree in their perception of their relative power in the sense of capabilities but not in their perceptions of relative bargaining power.

References

Abel, E. *The Missile Crisis.* Philadelphia: J. B. Lippincott, 1966.

Abelson, R. P., and Levi, A. "Decision-Making and Decision Theory." In *Handbook of Social Psychology*, 3rd ed., edited by G. Lindsey and E. Aronson. New York: Random House, 1985.

Acheson, D. "Testimony before the Senate Committee on Appropriations." *Supplemental Appropriations for 1951*, p. 272.

Alexandroff, A. *Symmetry in International Relations.* Ithaca, N.Y.: Cornell University Press, 1979.

———, and Rosecrance, R. "Deterrence in 1939." *World Politics* 39 (1977): 404–424.

Allison, G. *Essence of Decision: Explaining the Cuban Missile Crisis.* Boston: Little, Brown, 1971.

Allison, G. T., and Morris, F. A. "Armament and Arms Control: Exploring the Determinants of Military Weapons." In *Arms, Defense Policy and Arms Control*, edited by F. A. Long and G. W. Rathjens. New York: W. W. Norton, 1976.

Allison, G. T.; Carnesdale, A.; and Nye, J. S., Jr. *Hawks, Doves and Owls: An Agenda for Avoiding Nuclear War.* New York: W. W. Norton, 1985.

Altfeld, M. F. "Arms Races?—and Escalation? A Comment on Wallace." *International Studies Quarterly* 27 (1983): 225–231.

Anderton, C. H. "Arms Race Modeling: Categorization and Systematic Analysis." Paper presented at International Studies Association meetings, Washington, D.C., March 1985.

Asch, S. E. "Effects of Group Pressure upon the Modification and Distortion of Judgment." In *Groups, Leadership and Men*, edited by H. Guetzkow. Pittsburgh: Carnegie Press, 1951.

Atkinson, J. W. *An Introduction to Motivation.* Princeton, N.J.: Van Nostrand, 1964.

Axelrod, R. "Conflicts of Interest: An Axiomatic Approach." *Journal of Conflict Resolution* 11 (1967): 87–99.

———. *Structure of Decision: The Cognitive Maps of Political Elites.* Princeton, N.J.: Princeton University Press, 1976.

———. "Effective Choice in the Prisoner's Dilemma." *Journal of Conflict Resolution* 24 (1980): 3–25.

———. *The Evolution of Cooperation.* New York: Basic Books, 1984.

Azar, E. E. "Conflict Escalation and Conflict Reduction in an International Crisis: Suez 1956." *Journal of Conflict Resolution* 16 (1972): 183–201.

Bacharach, S. B., and Lawler, E. J. *Bargaining*. San Francisco: Jossey-Bass, 1981.

Baldwin, D. A. "The Power of Positive Sanctions." *World Politics* 24 (1971a): 19–38.

——. "Thinking about Threats." *Journal of Conflict Resolution* 15 (1971b): 71–78.

——. "Power and Exchange." *American Political Science Review* 72 (1978): 1229–42.

Barnet, R. J. *Real Security: Restoring American Power in a Dangerous Decade*. Beaverton, Oreg.: Touchstone Books, 1981.

Bartos, O. J. *Process and Outcome of Negotiations*. New York: Columbia University Press, 1974.

——. "A Simple Model of Negotiation." In *The Negotiation Process*, edited by I. W. Zartman. Beverly Hills: Sage, 1978.

Beach, L. R., and Mitchell, T. R. "A Contingency Model for the Selection of Decision Strategies." *Academy of Management Review* 3 (1978): 439–449.

Ben-Zvi, A. "American Preconceptions and Policies toward Japan, 1940–41: A Case Study in Misperception." *International Studies Quarterly* 15 (1975): 228–248.

Beres, L. R. *Apocalypse: Nuclear Catastrophe in World Politics*. Chicago: University of Chicago Press, 1980.

Bixenstine, V. E., and Gaebelein, J. "Strategies of 'real' Opponents in Eliciting Cooperative Choice in a Prisoner's Dilemma Game." *Journal of Conflict Resolution* 15 (1971): 157–166.

Blainey, G. *The Causes of War*. New York: Free Press, 1973.

Blechman, B. M. "Impact of Israel's Reprisals on Arab Behavior." *Journal of Conflict Resolution* 16 (1972): 155–181.

——, ed. *Preventing Nuclear War: A Realistic Approach*. Bloomington: Indiana University Press, 1985.

Blechman, B. M., and Kaplan, S. J. *Force Without War: U. S. Armed Forces as a Political Instrument*. Washington, D.C.: Brookings Institution, 1978.

Boyle, R., and Bonacich, P. "The Development of Trust and Mistrust in Mixed-Motive Games." *Sociometry* 33 (1970): 123–139.

Brams, S. J. *Superpower Games: Applying Game Theory to Superpower Conflict*. New Haven, Conn.: Yale University Press, 1985.

Brams, S. J.; Davis, M. D.; and Straffin, P. D., Jr. "The Geometry of the Arms Race." *International Studies Quarterly* 23 (1979): 567–588.

Brecher, M. *Decisions in Crisis: Israel, 1967 and 1973*. Berkeley: University of California Press, 1980.

Brockner, J., and Rubin, J. Z. *Entrapment in Escalating Conflicts: A Social-Psychological Analysis*. New York: Springer-Verlag, 1985.

Brody, R. "Some Systematic Effects of the Spread of Nuclear Weapons Technology." *Journal of Conflict Resolution* 7 (1963): 665–753.

Brown, R. B. "The Effects of Need to Maintain Face on the Outcomes of Interpersonal Bargaining." *Journal of Experimental Social Psychology* 4 (1968): 107–121.

Brzezinski, Z. *Power and Principle*. New York: Farrar, Straus, Giroux, 1983.

Bueno de Mesquita, B. *The War Trap*. New Haven, Conn.: Yale University Press, 1981a.

——. "Risk, Power Distributions, and the Likelihood of War." *International Studies Quarterly* 25 (1981b): 541–568.

Byrne, D. *The Attraction Paradigm*. New York: Academic Press, 1971.

Carnesdale, A.; Doty, P.; Hoffman, S.; Huntington, S. P.; Nye, J. S., Jr.; and Sagan, S. D. *Living With Nuclear Weapons*. Cambridge, Mass.: Harvard University Press, 1983.

Chertkoff, J. M., and Esser, J. K. "A Review of Experiments in Explicit Bargaining." *Journal of Experimental Social Psychology* 12 (1976): 464–487.

Clark, M. *From the Danube to the Yalu.* New York: Harper, 1954.

Claude, I. L., Jr. *Power and International Relations.* New York: Random House, 1962.

Cohen, R. *Threat Perception in International Crisis.* Madison: University of Wisconsin Press, 1979.

Cole, W. S. *American First: The Battle Against Intervention, 1940–1941.* Madison: University of Wisconsin Press, 1953.

Crawford, V. P. "A Note on the Zuethen-Harsanyi Theory of Bargaining." *Journal of Conflict Resolution* 24 (1980): 525–536.

Cross, J. G. *The Economics of Bargaining.* New York: Basic Books, 1969.

———. "Negotiation as a Learning Process." In *The Negotiation Process,* edited by I. W. Zartman. Beverly Hills: Sage, 1978.

Cusack, T. R., and Ward, M. D. "Military Spending in the United States, Soviet Union and the People's Republic of China." *Journal of Conflict Resolution* 25 (1981): 429–469.

Cyert, R. M., and March, J. C. *A Behavioral Theory of the Firm.* Englewood Cliffs, N.J.: Prentice-Hall, 1963.

Dankbaar, B. "Alternative Defense Policies and the Peace Movement." *Journal of Peace Research* 21 (1984): 141–156.

Davison, W. P. *The Berlin Blockade.* Princeton, N.J.: Princeton University Press, 1958.

Dember, W., and Warm, J. S. *The Psychology of Perception,* 2nd ed. New York: Holt, Rinehart and Winston, 1979.

de Rivera, J. *The Psychological Dimensions of Foreign Policy.* Columbus, Ohio: Charles E. Merrill, 1968.

Detzer, D. *The Brink: Cuban Missile Crisis, 1962.* New York: Thomas Y. Crowell, 1979.

Deutsch, M. *Conditions Affecting Cooperation.* Final Technical Report for the Office of Naval Research, February 1957.

———. "Conflicts: Productive and Destructive." *Journal of Social Issues* 25 (1969): 7–41.

———. *The Resolution of Conflict.* New Haven, Conn.: Yale University Press, 1973.

Deutsch, M.; Epstein, Y.; Canavan, D.; and Gumpert, P. "Strategies of Inducing Cooperation: An Experimental Study." *Journal of Conflict Resolution* 11 (1967): 345–360.

Deutsch, M., and Krauss, R. M. "The Effect of Threat Upon Interpersonal Bargaining." *Journal of Abnormal and Social Psychology* 61 (1960): 181–189.

Diehl, P. F. "Arms Races to War: Testing Some Empirical Linkages." Paper prepared for delivery at annual meeting of The American Political Science Association, September 1983a.

———. "Arms Races and Escalation: A Closer Look." *Journal of Peace Research* 20 (1983b): 205–212.

Druckman, D. "Boundary Role Conflict: Negotiations as Dual Responsiveness." In *The Negotiation Process,* edited by I. W. Zartman. Beverly Hills: Sage, 1978.

———. "Social Psychology and International Negotiations: Processes and Influences." In *Advances in Applied Social Psychology, Vol. 20* edited by R. F. Kidd, and M. J. Saks. Hillsdale, N.J.: Lawrence Erlbaum, 1983.

Engel, E. "Binocular Methods in Psychological Research." In *Explorations in Transactional Psychology,* edited by F. P. Kilpatrick. New York: New York University Press, 1961.

Etzioni, A. "The Kennedy Experiment." *Western Political Science Quarterly* 20 (1967): 316–380.

Favell, J. E. *The Power of Positive Reinforcement.* Springfield, Ill.: Charles C Thomas, 1977.

Feis, H. *The Road to Pearl Harbor.* Princeton, N.J.: Princeton University Press, 1950.

Ferris, W. H. *The Power Capabilities of Nation-States.* Lexington, Mass.: Lexington Books, 1973.

Fischer, D. *Preventing War in the Nuclear Age.* Totowa, N.J.: Rowman and Allanheld, 1984.

Fischhoff, B.; Goitein, B.; and Shapira, Z. "The Experienced Utility of Expected Utility Approaches." In *Expectations and Actions: Expectancy-Value Models in Psychology,* edited by N. T. Feather. Hillsdale, N.J.: Lawrence Erlbaum, 1982.

Freedman, L. *U.S. Intelligence and the Soviet Strategic Threat.* Boulder, Colo.: Westview, 1977.

Frei, D. *Risks of Unintentional Nuclear War.* Geneva, United Nations Institute for Disarmament Research, 1982.

——. *Assumptions and Perceptions in Disarmament.* New York: United Nations, 1984.

French, J. R. P., Jr.; Morrison, H. W.; and Levinger, G. "Coercive Power and Forces Affecting Conformity." *Journal of Abnormal and Social Psychology* 61 (1960): 93–101.

Gahagan, J. P., and Tedeschi, J. T. "Strategy and the Credibility of Promises in the Prisoner's Dilemma Game." *Journal of Conflict Resolution* 12 (1968): 224–234.

Galtung, J. "Balance of Power and the Problem of Perception." In *Peace, War, and Defense: Essays in Peace Research,* vol. 2. Copenhagen: Ejlers, 1976.

——. "Transarmament: From Offensive to Defensive Defense." *Journal of Peace Research* 21 (1984): 127–140.

Gamson, W., and Modigliani, A. *Untangling the Cold War.* Boston: Little, Brown, 1971.

George, A. "The Causal Nexus between Cognitive Beliefs and Decision-Making Behavior: The 'Operational Code.'" In *Psychological Models in International Politics,* edited by L. W. Falkowski. Boulder, Colo.: Westview, 1979.

George, A.; Hall, D. K.; and Simons, W. E. *The Limits of Coercive Diplomacy.* Boston: Little, Brown, 1971.

George, A., and Smoke, R. *Deterrence in American Foreign Policy.* New York: Columbia University Press, 1974.

Gibson, J. S. "Group Decisions and Foreign Policy." In *Group Decision-Making,* edited by W. C. Swap. Beverly Hills: Sage, 1984.

Goldblat, J. *Arms Control Agreements: A Handbook.* New York: Praeger, 1983.

Goldstein, J. H.; Davids, R. W.; and Herman, D. "Escalating of Aggression: Experimental Studies." *Journal of Personality and Social Psychology* 31 (1975): 162–170.

Goldstein, W. "The War Between Iraq and Iran: A War That Can't Be Won or Ended." *Middle East Review* 11 (1984): 41–50.

Gooch, G. P. *Before the War.* London: Longmans, 1938.

Gouldner, A. W. "The Norm of Reciprocity: A Preliminary Statement." *American Sociological Review* 25 (1960): 161–179.

Gray, C. S. *The Soviet-American Arms Race.* Lexington, Mass.: Lexington Books, 1976.

Gruder, C. L., and Duslak, R. J. "Elicitation of Cooperation by Retaliatory and Nonretaliatory Strategies in a Mixed-Motive Game." *Journal of Conflict Resolution* 17 (1973): 162–174.

Gulliver, P. H. *Disputes and Negotiations: A Cross-Cultural Perspective.* New York: Academic Press, 1979.

Halberstam, D. *The Best and the Brightest.* New York: Random House, 1972.

Halperin, M. H. "The Decision of Deploy the ABM: Bureaucratic and Domestic Politics in the Johnson Administration." *World Politics* 25 (1972) 62–95.

——. *Bureaucratic Politics and Foreign Policy.* Washington, D.C.: Brookings Institution, 1974.

Hampson, F. O. "Escalation in Europe." In *Hawks, Doves, and Owls,* edited by G. T. Allison, A. Carnesdale, and J. S. Nye, Jr. New York: W. W. Norton, 1985.

Handel, M. "The Yom Kippur War and the Inevitability of Surprise." *International Studies Quarterly* 21 (1977) 461–502.

Harford, T., and Solomon, L. "'Reformed Sinner' and 'Lapsed Saint' Strategies in the Prisoner's Dilemma Game." *Journal of Conflict Resolution* 11 (1967): 104–109.

Harkabi, Y. *Nuclear War and Nuclear Peace*. Jerusalem: Israel Program for Scientific Translations, 1966.

Harris, J. B., and Markusen, E. eds. *Nuclear Weapons and the Threat of Nuclear War*. San Diego: Harcourt Brace Jovanovich, 1986.

Hart, J. A. "Cognitive Maps of Three Latin American Policy Makers." *World Politics* 30 (1977): 115–140.

Harvard Nuclear Study Group. *Living with Nuclear Weapons*. Cambridge, Mass.: Harvard University Press, 1983.

Hastings, M., and Jenkins, S. *Battle for the Falklands*. New York: Norton, 1983.

Heller, F. *The Korean War: A 25-Year Perspective*. Lawrence: Regents Press of Kansas, 1977.

Hersh, S. M. *The Price of Power: Henry Kissinger in the Nixon White House*. New York: Summit Books, 1983.

Higgins, T. *Korea and the Fall of MacArthur*. New York: Oxford University Press, 1960.

Hoagland, S. W., and Walker, S. G. "Operational Codes and Crisis Outcomes." In *Psychological Models in International Politics*, edited by L. S. Falkowski. Boulder, Colo.: Westview, 1979.

Hogarth, R. M. *Judgement and Choice: The Psychology of Decision*. New York: John Wiley, 1980.

Hollist, W. L. "Alternative Explanations of Competitive Arms Processes: Tests on Four Pair of Nations." *American Journal of Political Science* 21 (1977): 313–341.

Holsti, O. R. "Cognitive Dynamics and Images of the Enemy: Dulles and Russia." In *Enemies in Politics*, edited by D. J. Finlay, O. Holsti, and R. Fagen. Chicago: Rand McNally, 1967.

————. *Crisis, Escalation, War*. Montreal: McGill-Queen's University Press, 1972.

Holsti, O.; Brody, R.; and North, R. C. "The Management of International Crisis: Affect and Action in American-Soviet Relations." In *Theory and Research on the Causes of War*, edited by D. G. Pruitt, and R. C. Snyder. Englewood Cliffs, N.J.: Prentice-Hall, 1969.

Hopmann, P. T. "Bargaining in Arms Control Negotiations: The Seabeds Nuclearization Treaty." *International Organizations* 28 (1974): 313–343.

Hopmann, P. T., and King, T. "Interactions and Perceptions in the Test Ban Negotiations." *International Studies Quarterly* 20 (1976): 105–142.

Hopmann, P. T., and Smith, T. C. "An Application of a Richardson Process Model: Soviet-American Interactions in the Test Ban Negotiations, 1962–3." *Journal of Conflict Resolution* 21 (1977): 701–726.

Horai, J., and Tedeschi, J. T. "The Effects of Credibility, Magnitude of Punishment, and Compliance to Threats." *Journal of Personality and Social Psychology* 12 (1969): 164–169.

Horelick, A. L., Johnson, A. R., and Steinbruner, J. D. *The Study of Soviet Foreign Policy: Decision-Theory-Related Approaches*. Beverly Hills: Sage, 1975.

Hornstein, H. A. "The Effects of Different Magnitudes of Threat Upon Interpersonal Bargaining." *Journal of Experimental Social Psychology* 1 (1965): 282–293.

Hosoya, C. "Characteristics of the Foreign Policy Decision-Making System in Japan." *World Politics* 26 (1974): 353–369.

Hough, J. E. "The Evolution of the Soviet World View." *World Politics* 32 (1980): 509–530.

Houweling, H., and Siccama, J. "The Arms Race-War Relationship: Why Serious Disputes Matter." ECPR Joint Session of Workshops. Lancaster, England, 1981.

Huntington, S. P. "Arms Races: Prerequisites and Results." *Public Policy* 8 (1958): 41–86.
Huth, P., and Russett, B. "What Makes Deterrence Work? Cases from 1900 to 1980." *World Politics* 36 (1984) 496–526.
Ienaga, S. *The Pacific War: World War II and the Japanese, 1931–45*. New York: Pantheon Books, 1978.
Iklé, F. C. *Every War Must End*. New York: Columbia University Press, 1971.
Intriligator, M., and Brito, D. "Can Arms Races Lead to the Outbreak of War?" *Journal of Conflict Resolution* 28 (1984): 63–84.
Janis, I. *Groupthink*. 2nd ed. Boston: Houghton Mifflin, 1982.
Janis, I., and Mann, L. *Decision-Making: A Psychological Analysis of Conflict, Choice and Commitment*. Glencoe, Ill.: Free Press, 1977.
Jensen, L. "Soviet-American Bargaining Behavior in the Post-War Disarmament Negotiations." *Journal of Conflict Resolution* 9 (1963): 522–541.
———. "Military Capabilities and Bargaining Behavior." *Journal of Conflict Resolution* 9 (1965): 155–163.
———. "Approach-Avoidance Bargaining in the Test Ban Negotiations." *International Studies Quarterly* 12 (1968): 152–160.
———. "Negotiating Strategic Arms Control, 1969–1979." *Journal of Conflict Resolution* 28 (1984): 535–559.
Jervis, R. "Bargaining and Bargaining Tactics." In *Nomos 14: Coercion*, edited by J. R. Pennock, and J. Chapman. Chicago: Aldine Atherton, 1972.
———. *Perception and Misperception in International Politics*. Princeton, N.J.: Princeton University Press, 1976.
———. "Deterrence Theory Revisited." *World Politics* 31 (1979): 289–324.
———. *The Illogic of American Nuclear Strategy*. Ithaca, N.Y.: Cornell University Press, 1984.
Jervis, R.; Lebow, R. N.; and Stein, J. G. *Psychology and Deterrence*. Baltimore: Johns Hopkins University Press, 1985.
Jones, E., and Nisbett, R. "The Actor and the Observer: Divergent Perceptions of the Causes of Behavior." In *Attribution: Perceiving the Causes of Behavior*, edited by E. Jones. Morristown, N.J.: General Learning Press, 1972.
Kahneman, D., and Tversky, A. "Prospect Theory: An Analysis of Decision Under Risk." *Econometrics* 47 (1979): 263–291.
———. "Variants of Uncertainty." In *Judgement Under Uncertainty: Heuristics and Biases*, edited by D. Kahnaman, P. Slovic, and A. Tversky. Cambridge: Cambridge University Press, 1982.
———. "Choices, Values and Frames." *American Psychologist* 39 (1984): 341–350.
Kaplan, F. *The Wizards of Armageddon*. New York: Simon and Schuster, 1983.
Kaplan, S. J. *Diplomacy of Power: Soviet Armed Forces as a Political Instrument*. Washington, D.C.: Brookings Institution, 1981.
Kaplowitz, N. "Psychopolitical Dimensions of International Relations: The Reciprocal Effects of Conflict Strategies." *International Studies Quarterly* 28 (1984): 373–406.
Kelley, H. H. "Experimental Studies of Threats in Interpersonal Negotiation." *Journal of Conflict Resolution* 9 (1965): 79–105.
Kelley, H., and Thibaut, J. *Interpersonal Relations*. New York: John Wiley, 1978.
Kennedy, L. *Pursuit: The Chase and Sinking of the Bismarck*. London: Collins, 1974.
Kennedy, R. F. *Thirteen Days: A Memoir of the Cuban Missile Crisis*. New York: W. W. Norton, 1969.
Kissinger, H. *The White House Years*. Boston: Little, Brown, 1979.

————. *Years of Upheaval*. Boston: Little, Brown, 1982.

Knorr, K. *The Power of Nations*. New York: Basic Books, 1975.

Komorita, S. S. "Concession Making and Conflict Resolution." *Journal of Conflict Resolution* 17 (1973): 745–762.

Komorita, S. S., and Esser, J. T. "Frequency of Reciprocated Concessions in Bargaining." *Journal of Personality and Social Psychology* 32 (1975): 699–705.

Kriesberg, L. "Non-Coercive Inducements in International Conflicts." *Peace and Change* 7 (1981a): 37–46.

————. *Social Conflicts*, 2nd ed. Englewood Cliffs, N.J.: Prentice-Hall, 1982.

————. "Social Theory and the Deescalation of International Conflict." *Sociological Review* 32 (1984): 471–491.

Lambelet, J. "Do Arms Races Lead to War?" *Journal of Peace Research* 12 (1975): 123–128.

Lebow, R. N. *Between Peace and War: The Nature of International Crisis*. Baltimore: Johns Hopkins University Press, 1981.

————. "Miscalculations in the South Pacific: The Origins of the Falklands War." In *Psychology and Deterrence*, edited by R. Jervis, R. N. Lebow, and J. G. Stein. Baltimore: Johns Hopkins University Press, 1985a.

————. "The Deterrence Deadlock: Is There a Way Out?" In *Psychology and Deterrence*, edited by R. Jervis, R. N. Lebow, and J. G. Stein. Baltimore: Johns Hopkins University Press, 1985b.

————. "Conclusions." In *Psychology and Deterrence*, edited by R. Jervis, R. N. Lebow, and J. G. Stein. Baltimore: Johns Hopkins University Press, 1985c.

Lenczowski, J. *Soviet Perceptions of U.S. Foreign Policy*. Ithaca, N.Y.: Cornell University Press, 1982.

Leng, R. J. "Influence Strategies and Interstate Conflict." In *The Correlates of War: Vol. 2, Testing Some Realpolitik Models*, edited by J. D. Singer. New York: Free Press, 1980.

————. "Reagan and the Russians: Crisis Bargaining Beliefs and the Historical Record." *American Political Science Review* 78 (1984):338–355.

Leng, R. J., and Walker, S. G. "Comparing Two Studies of Crisis Bargaining: Confrontation, Coercion and Reciprocity." *Journal of Conflict Resolution* 26 (1982): 571–591.

Leng, R. J., and Wheeler, H. G. "Influence Strategies, Success, and War." *Journal of Conflict Resolution* 23 (1979): 655–684.

Lindskold, S. "Trust development, the GRIT proposal, and effects of conciliatory acts on conflict and cooperation." *Psychological Bulletin* 85 (1978): 772–779.

Lindskold, S.; Bennett, R.; and Wayner, M. "Retaliation Level as a Foundation for Subsequent Conciliation." *Behavioral Science* 21 (1976): 13–18.

Lindskold, S., and Aronoff, J. R. "Conciliatory Strategies and Relative Power." *Journal of Experimental Social Psychology* 16 (1980): 187–198.

Lindskold, S., and Collins, M. G. "Inducing Cooperation by Groups and Individuals." *Journal of Conflict Resolution* 22 (1978): 679–690.

Lindskold, S.; Walters, P. S.; and Koutsourais, H. "Cooperators, Competitors, and Response to GRIT." *Journal of Conflict Resolution* 27 (1983): 521–532.

Lockhart, C. "Problems in the Management and Resolution of International Conflicts." *World Politics* 29 (1977): 370–403.

Lockwood, J. S. *The Soviet View of U. S. Strategic Doctrine*. New Brunswick, N.J.: Transaction Books, 1983.

Loomis, J. L. "Communication, the Development of Trust and Cooperative Behavior." *Human Relations* 12 (1959): 305–315.

MacCrimmon, K. R.; Stanbury, W. T.; and Wehrung, D. A. "Real Money Lotteries: A

Study of Ideal Risk, Context Effects, and Simple Processes." In *Cognitive Processes in Choice and Decision Behavior,* edited by T. S. Wallstein. Hillsdale, N.J.: Lawrence Erlbaum, 1980.

McClelland, D. C., and Liberman, A. M. "The Effect of Need for Achievement on Recognition of Need-Related Words." *Journal of Personality* 18 (1949): 236–251.

McGinnis, M. D. "Issue Linkage and the Evolution of International Cooperation." *Journal of Conflict Resolution* 30 (1986): 141–170.

Maghoori, R., and Gorman, S. *The Yom Kippur War: A Case Study in Crisis Decision-Making in American Foreign Policy.* Washington, D.C.: University Press of America, 1981.

Majeski, S. J., and Jones, D. L. "Arms Race Modeling: Causality Analysis and Model Specification." *Journal of Conflict Resolution* 25 (1981): 259–288.

Mandel, R. "The Effectiveness of Gunboat Diplomacy." *International Studies Quarterly* 30 (1986): 59–76.

Maoz, Z. *Paths to Conflict: International Dispute Initiation, 1816–1976.* Boulder, Colo.: Westview, 1982.

March, J. G. "Theories of Choice and Making Decisions." *Transaction: Social Science and Modern Society* 20 (1982): 29–39.

March, J. G., and Simon, H. A. *Organizations.* New York: John Wiley, 1958.

May, E. R. "Conclusions: Capabilities and Proclivities." In *Knowing One's Enemies: Intelligence Assessment Before the Two World Wars,* edited by E. R. May. Princeton, N.J.: Princeton University Press, 1984.

Mayer, T. F. "Arms Races and War Initiation: Some Alternatives to the Intriligator—Brito Model." *Journal of Conflict Resolution* 30 (1986): 3–28.

Michener, H. A.; Vaske, J. J.; Schleifer, S. L.; Plazewski, J. G.; and Chapman, L. J. "Factors Affecting Concession Rate and Threat Usage in Bilateral Conflict." *Sociometry* 38 (1975): 62–80.

Middlebrook, P. N. *Social Psychology and Modern Life,* 2nd ed. New York: Knopf, 1980.

Middlemas, K. *Diplomacy of Illusion.* London: Weidenfeld and Nicolson, 1972.

Milburn, T. W., and Watman, K. H. *On the Nature of Threat: A Social-Psychological Analysis.* London: Praeger, 1981.

Milstein, J. S. "American and Soviet Influence, Balance of Power, and Arab-Israeli Violence." In *Peace, War and Numbers,* edited by B. Russett. Beverly Hills: Sage, 1972.

———. *Dynamics of the Vietnam War.* Columbus: Ohio State University Press, 1974.

Mitchell, C. R. *The Structure of International Conflict.* New York: St. Martin's Press, 1981.

Mogy, R. B., and Pruitt, D. G. "The Effects of a Threatener's Enforcement Costs on Threat Credibility and Compliance." *Journal of Personality and Social Psychology* 29 (1974): 173–180.

Moll, K. D., and Luebbert, G. M. "Arms Race and Military Expenditure Models: A Review." *Journal of Conflict Resolution* 24 (1980): 153–185.

Morgan, P. M. *Deterrence: A Conceptual Analysis,* 2nd ed. Beverly Hills: Sage, 1983.

Morgenthau, H. *Politics Among Nations: The Struggle for Power and Peace.* New York: Knopf, 1963.

Naroll, R. "Deterrence in History." *Theory and Research on the Causes of War,* edited by D. G. Pruitt, and R. Snyder. Englewood Cliffs, N.J.: Prentice-Hall, 1969.

Nicholson, M. "Tariff Wars and a Model of Conflict." *Journal of Peace Research* 6 (1967): 26–38.

Nixon, R. M. *RN: The Memoirs of Richard Nixon.* New York: Grosset and Dunlap, 1978.

North, R. C.; Brody, R. A.; and Holsti, O. R. "Some Empirical Data on the Conflict Spiral." *Peace Research Society Papers* I (1964).

Olson, R. S. "Economic Coercion in World Politics with a Focus on North-South Relations." *World Politics* 31 (1979): 471–494.

Organski, A. F. K. *World Politics*. New York: Knopf, 1958.

Organski, A. F. K., and Kugler, J. *The War Ledger*. Chicago: University of Chicago Press, 1980.

Osgood, C. E. *An Alternative to War or Surrender*. Urbana: University of Illinois Press, 1962.

――――. "The GRIT Strategy." *Bulletin of Atomic Scientists* May (1980): 58–60.

――――. "Disarmament Demands GRIT." In *Toward Nuclear Alternatives*, edited by G. H. Weston. Boulder, Colo.: Westview, 1984.

Oskamp, S. "Effects of Programmed Strategies on Cooperation in the Prisoner's Dilemma and Other Mixed-Motive Games." *Journal of Conflict Resolution* 15 (1971): 225–259.

Ostrum, C. W., Jr. "A Reaction Linkage Model of the U.S. Defense Expenditure Policymaking Process." *American Political Science Review* 72 (1978): 941–956.

Paige, G. D. *The Korean Decision*. New York: Free Press, 1968.

Payne, J. W. "Task Complexity and Contingent Processing in Decision-Making." *Organizational Behavior and Human Performance* 16 (1976): 366–387.

Phillips, W. R. "The Conflict Environment of Nations." In *Conflict Behavior and Linkage Politics*, edited by J. Wilkenfeld. New York: McKay, 1973.

Pickles, D. *Algeria and France*. New York: Praeger, 1963.

Pilisuk, M., and Skolnick, P. "Inducing Trust: A Test of the Osgood Proposal." *Journal of Personality and Social Psychology* 8 (1968): 122–133.

Pillar, P. R. *Negotiating Peace: War Termination as a Bargaining Process*. Princeton, N.J.: Princeton University Press, 1983.

Postman, L.; Bruner, J. S.; and McGinnies, E. "Personal Values as Selective Factors in Perception." *Journal of Abnormal and Social Psychology* 43 (1948): 142–154.

Pruitt, D. G. "Definition of the Situation as a Determinant of International Action." In *International Behavior: A Social-Psychological Analysis*, edited by H. C. Kelman. New York: Holt, Rinehart and Winston, 1965.

――――. *Negotiation Behavior*. New York: Academic Press, 1981.

Pruitt, D. G., and Rubin, J. Z. *Social Conflict: Escalation, Stalemate, and Settlement*. New York: Random House, 1986.

Quester, G. *The Future of Nuclear Deterrence*. Lexington, Mass.: Lexington Books, 1986.

Ramazani, R. *The United States and Iran: The Patterns of Influence*. New York: Praeger, 1982.

Rapoport, A. "Lewis F. Richardson's Mathematical Theory of War." *Journal of Conflict Resolution* 1 (1957): 249–299.

――――. "A Note on the 'Index of Cooperation' for Prisoner's Dilemma." *Journal of Conflict Resolution* 11 (1967): 100–103.

Rapoport, A., and Chammah, A. M. *Prisoner's Dilemma*. Ann Arbor: University of Michigan Press, 1965.

――――. "The Game of Chicken." In *Game Theory in the Behavioral Sciences*, edited by I. R. Buchler, and H. G. Nutini. Pittsburgh: University of Pittsburgh Press, 1969.

Rapoport, A., and Guyer, M. "A Taxonomy of 2×2 Games." *General Systems* 11 (1966): 203–214.

Raser, J. R., and Crowe, W. J. "A Simulation Study of Deterrence Theories." In *Social Processes in International Relations*, edited by L. Kriesberg. New York: John Wiley, 1968.

Rattinger, H. "Armaments, Detente, and Bureaucracy: The Case of the Arms Race in Europe." *Journal of Conflict Resolution* 19 (1975): 571–595.

――――. "From War to War to War: Arms Races in the Middle East." *International Studies Quarterly* 20 (1976): 501–531.

Raymond, G. A., and Kegley, C. W., Jr. "Third Party Mediation and International Norms: A Test of Two Models." *Conflict Management and Peace Science* 9 (1985): 33–52.

Reychler, L. "The Effectiveness of a Pacifist Strategy in Conflict Resolution: An Experimental Study." *Journal of Conflict Resolution* 23 (1979): 228–260.

Richardson, L. F. *Arms and Insecurity.* Pittsburgh: Boxwood, 1960.

Rokeach, M., ed. *The Open and Closed Mind.* New York: Basic Books, 1960.

Rosecrance, R. "Reward, Punishment and Interdependence." *Journal of Conflict Resolution* 25 (1981): 31–46.

Rubin, J. Z., and Brown, B. R. *The Social Psychology of Bargaining and Negotiation.* New York: Academic Press, 1975.

Rubin, J. Z., and Lewicki, R. J. "A Three-Factor Experimental Analysis of Promises and Threats." *Journal of Applied Social Psychology* 3 (1973): 240–257.

Rummel, R. J. *War, Power, and Peace*, Vol. 4 of *Understanding Conflict and War.* Beverly Hills: Sage, 1979.

Russett, B. M. "The Calculus of Deterrence." *Journal of Conflict Resolution* 7 (1963): 97–109.

Russett, B. M., and Starr, H. *World Politics: The Menu for Choice.* San Francisco: W. H. Freeman, 1981.

Schelling, T. C. *The Strategy of Conflict.* Cambridge, Mass.: Harvard University Press, 1960.

———. *Arms and Influence.* New Haven, Conn.: Yale University Press, 1966.

———. "A Framework for the Evaluation of Arms-Control Proposals." In *Arms, Defense Policy, and Arms Control*, edited by F. A. Long, and G. Rathjens. New York: W. W. Norton, 1976.

Schelling, T. C., and Halperin, M. "Preemptive, Premeditated, and Accidental War." In *Theory and Research in the Causes of War*, edited by D. Pruitt. Englewood Cliffs, N.J.: Prentice-Hall, 1969.

Schick, J. *The Berlin Crisis, 1958–62.* Philadelphia: University of Pennsylvania Press, 1971.

Schlesinger, A. M. *A Thousand Days: John F. Kennedy in the White House.* Boston: Houghton Mifflin, 1965.

Schreiber, A. P. "Economic Coercion as an Instrument of Foreign Policy." *World Politics* 25 (1973): 387–413.

Schwartz, D. "Decision-Making in Historical and Simulated Crises." In *International Crises: Insights from Behavioral Research*, edited by C. F. Hermann. New York: Free Press, 1972.

Sermat, V. "Cooperative Behavior in a Mixed-Motive Game." *Journal of Social Psychology* 62 (1964): 217–239.

———. "The Effect of an Initial Cooperative or Competitive Treatment Upon a Subject's Response to Conditional Cooperation." *Behavioral Science* 12 (1967): 301–313.

Sherif, M. *The Psychology of Social Norms.* New York: Harper and Row, 1936.

Shlaim, A., and Tanter, R. "Decision Process, Choice and Consequences: Israel's Deep-Penetration Bombing in Egypt, 1970." *World Politics* 30 (1978): 483–516.

Shure, G. H.; Meeker, R. J.; and Hansford, E. H. "The Effectiveness of Pacifist Strategies in Bargaining Games." *Journal of Conflict Resolution* 9 (1965): 106–117.

Siegel, S., and Fouraker, L. E. *Bargaining and Group Decision-Making.* New York: McGraw-Hill, 1960.

Simon, H. "Rational Decision Making." *American Economic Review* 69 (1979): 493–513.

Singer, J. D. "Threat-Perception and the Armament-Tension Dilemma." *Journal of Conflict Resolution* 2 (1958): 93–94.

———. "Escalation and Control in International Conflict: A Simple Feedback Model." In *The Correlates of War, Vol. 1*, edited by J. D. Singer. New York: Free Press, 1979.

————. "Accounting for International War: The State of the Discipline." *Journal of Peace Research* 18 (1981): 1–18.

Singer, J. D.; Bremer, S. A.; and Stuckey, J. "Capability Distribution, Uncertainty, and Major Power War, 1820–1965." In *The Correlates of War, Vol. I*, edited by J. D. Singer. New York: Free Press, 1979.

Singer, J. D., and Small, M. "Foreign Policy Indicators: Predictors of War in History and in the State of the World Message." In *The Correlates of War: Vol. I*, edited by J. D. Singer. New York: Free Press, 1979.

Sisson, R. L., and Ackoff, R. L. "Toward a Theory of the Dynamics of Conflict." *Peace Research Society: Papers, V.* Philadelphia: Peace Research Society, 1966.

Slovic, P.; Fischhoff, B.; and Lichtenstein, S. "Behavioral Decision Theory." in *Annual Review of Psychology, 1977*, edited by M. R. Rosensweig, and L. W. Porter. Palo Alto, Calif.: Annual Reviews, 1977.

Smoke, R. *War: Controlling Escalation.* Cambridge, Mass.: Harvard University Press, 1977.

Smith, T. C. "Arms Race Instability and War." *Journal of Conflict Resolution* 24 (1980): 253–284.

————. *Trojan Peace: Some Deterrence Propositions Tested.* Denver, Colo.: Graduate School of International Studies, University of Denver, 1982.

Snow, D. M. "Current Nuclear Deterrence Thinking: An Overview and Review." *International Studies Quarterly* 23 (1979): 445–486.

————. *National Security: Enduring Problems of U.S. Defense Policy.* New York: St. Martin's Press, 1986.

Snyder, G. "Deterrence and Power." *Journal of Conflict Resolution* 4 (1960): 163–178.

Snyder, G., and Diesing. P. *Conflict Among Nations.* Princeton, N.J.: Princeton University Press, 1977.

Snyder, J. L. "Rationality at the Brink: The Role of Cognitive Processes in Failures of Deterrence." *World Politics* 30 (1978): 345–365.

————. "Perceptions of the Security Dilemma in 1914. In *Psychology and Deterrence*, edited by R. Jervis, R. N. Lebow, and J. G. Stein. Baltimore: Johns Hopkins University Press, 1985.

Snyder, R. C., and Paige, G. D. "The United States' Decision to Resist Aggression in Korea." *Administrative Science Quarterly* 3 (1958): 341–378.

Sonnenfeldt, H. "Soviet Negotiating Concept and Style." In *A Game for High Stakes*, edited by L. Sloss and M. S. Davis. Cambridge, Mass.: Ballinger, 1986.

Steele, M. W., and Tedeschi, J. T. "Matrix Indices and Strategy Choices in Mixed-Motive Games." *Journal of Conflict Resolution* 11 (1967): 198–205.

Stein, A. A. "When Misperception Matters." *World Politics* (1982): 505–526.

Steinbruner, J. "Launch Under Attack." *Scientific American* 250 (1984): 37–47.

Stoessinger, J. G. *Why Nations Go To War*, 3rd ed. New York: St. Martin's Press, 1982.

Svenson, O. "Process Descriptions of Decision-Making." *Organizational Behavior and Human Performance* 23 (1979): 86–112.

Swingle, P. G., and Santi, A. "Communication in Non-Zero Sum Games." *Journal of Personality and Social Psychology* 23 (1972): 54–63.

Taylor, T. "Arms Control: The Bankruptcy of the Strategists' Approach." In *The Arms Race in the 1980s*, edited by D. Carleton, and C. Schaerf. New York: St. Martin's Press, 1982.

Tedeschi, J. T.; Bonoma, T. V.; and Schlenker, B. R. "Influence, Decision, and Compliance." In *The Social Influence Processes*, edited by J. T. Tedeschi. Chicago: Aldine, 1972.

Tedeschi, J. T., and Bonoma, T. V. "Measures of Last Resort: Coercion and Aggression in Bargaining." In *Negotiations: Social-Psychological Perspectives*, edited by D. Druckman.

Beverly Hills: Sage, 1977.

Tedeschi, J. T.; Schlenker, B. R.; and Lindskold, S. "The Exercise of Power and Influence." In *The Social Influence Processes*, edited by J. T. Tedeschi. Chicago: Aldine-Atherton, 1972.

Thee, M. *Military Technology, Military Strategy, and the Arms Race*. London: Croom Helm, 1986.

Thibaut, J. W. "The Development of Constructed Norms in Bargaining: Replication and Variation." *Journal of Conflict Resolution* 12 (1968): 102–112.

Thibaut, J. W., and Faucheux, C. "The Development of Constructed Norms in a Bargaining Situation under Two Types of Stress." *Journal of Experimental Psychology* 1 (1965): 89–102.

Thibaut, J. W., and Gruder, C. L. "Formation of Contractual Agreements Between Parties of Unequal Power." *Journal of Personality and Social Psychology* 11 (1969): 59–65.

Thibaut, J. W., and Kelley, J. H. *The Social Psychology of Groups*. New York: John Wiley, 1959.

Thies, W. J. *When Governments Collide: Coercion and Diplomacy in the Vietnam Conflict, 1967–1968*. Berkeley: University of California Press, 1980.

Trachtenberg, M., "The Influence of Nuclear Weapons in the Cuban Missile Crisis." *International Security* 10 (1985): 137–163.

Tversky, A. "Elimination by Aspects: A theory of Choice." *Psychological Review* 79 (1972): 281–299.

VanEvera, S. "Why Cooperation Failed in 1914." *World Politics* 38 (1985): 80–117.

Verba, S. "Assumption of Rationality and Non-rationality in Models of the International System." In *The International System*, edited K. Knoor, and S. Verba. Princeton, N.J.: Princeton University Press, 1961.

Wagner, A. R. *Crisis Decisionmaking: Israel's Experience in 1967 and 1973*. New York: Praeger, 1974.

Wagner, R. H. "Deterrence and Bargaining." *Journal of Conflict Resolution* 26 (1982): 329–358.

———. "The Theory of Games and the Problem of Internation Cooperation." *American Political Science Review* 77 (1983): 330–346.

Wall, J. A., Jr. "Intergroup Bargaining: Effects of Opposing Constituents' Stance, Opposing Representatives' Bargaining, and Representatives' Focus of Control." *Journal of Conflict Resolution* 21 (1977): 459–474.

Wallace, M. D. "Arms Race and Escalation: Some New Evidence." *Journal of Conflict Resolution* 23 (1979): 3–16.

———. "Armaments and Escalation: Two Competing Hypotheses." *International Studies Quarterly* 16 (1982): 37–56.

Walters, G. C., and Grusec, J. E. *Punishment*. San Francisco: W. H. Freeman, 1977.

Walton, R. E., and McKersie, R. B. *A Behavioral Theory of Labor Negotiations*. New York: McGraw-Hill, 1965.

Ward, M. D. "Cooperation and Conflict in Foreign Policy Behavior." *International Studies Quarterly* 26 (1982): 87–126.

———. "The Political Economy of Arms Races and International Tension." *Conflict Management and Peace Science* 7 (1984): 1–24.

Weede, E. "Conflict Behavior of Nation-States." *Journal of Peace Research* 3 (1970): 229–235.

———. "Arms Races and Escalation: Some Persisting Doubts: Response to Wallace's Article, JCR, March 1979." *Journal of Conflict Resolution* 24 (1980): 285–287.

———. "Preventing War by Nuclear Deterrence or by Detente." Paper presented to annual meeting of Peace Research Society, University of Maryland, November 1982.

––––––. "Extended Deterrence by Superpower Alliance." *Journal of Conflict Resolution* 27 (1983): 231–254.

Weintraub, S., ed. *Economic Coercion and U.S. Foreign Policy*. Boulder, Colo.: Westview, 1982.

White, R. K. "Images in the Context of International Conflict: Soviet Perceptions of the U.S. and the U.S.S.R." In *International Behavior: A Social-Psychological Analysis*, edited by H. C. Kelman. New York: Holt, Rinehart and Winston, 1965.

––––––. *Nobody Wanted War: Misperception in Vietnam and Other Wars*. Garden City, N.Y.: Doubleday, 1968.

––––––. *Fearful Warriors*. New York: Free Press, 1984.

Wicklund, R. A., and Brehm, J. W. *Perspectives on Cognitive Dissonance*. Hillsdale, N.J.: Lawrence Erlbaum, 1976.

Wilmot, C. *The Struggle for Europe*. London: Collins, 1952.

Wilson, W. "Reciprocation and Other Techniques for Inducing Cooperation in the Prisoner's Dilemma Game." *Journal of Conflict Resolution* 15 (1971): 196–198.

Wright, G. *Behavioral Decision Theory*. Beverly Hills: Sage, 1984.

Wright, P., and Barbour, F. "Phased Decision Strategies: Sequels to an Initial Screening." In *Studies in the Management Sciences*, edited by M. K. Starr, and M. Zeleny. Amsterdam: North Holland, 1977.

Wright, Q. "The Escalation of International Conflict." *Journal of Conflict Resolution* 9 (1965): 434–449.

Wyer, R. "Prediction of Behavior in Two-Person Games." *Journal of Personality and Social Psychology* 13 (1969): 222–238.

––––––. "Effects of Outcome Matrix and Partner's Behavior in Two-Person Games." *Journal of Experimental Social Psychology* 7 (1971): 190–210.

Young, O. R. *The Politics of Force: Bargaining During International Crises*. Princeton, N.J.: Princeton University Press, 1968.

Zagare, F. C. "A Game-Theoretic Analysis of the Vietnam Negotiations." In *The Negotiation Process*, edited by I. W. Zartman. Beverly Hills: Sage, 1978.

Zartman, I. W. "Negotiation as a Decision-Making Process." In *The Negotiation Process*, edited by I. W. Zartman. Beverly Hills: Sage, 1978.

Zeuthen, F. *Problems of Monopoly and Economic Warfare*. London: Routledge and Kegan Paul, 1930.

Zinnes, D. A. "A Comparison of Hostile Behavior of Decision-Makers in Simulate and Historical Data." *World Politics* 18 (1966): 474–502.

––––––. *Contemporary Research in International Relations: A Perspective and Critical Appraisal*. New York: Free Press, 1976.

Zinnes, D. A.; Zinnes, J. L.; and McClure, R. D. "Hostility in Diplomatic Communication: A Study of the 1914 Crisis." In *International Crises: Insights from Behavioral Research*, edited by C. F. Hermann. New York: Free Press, 1972.

Zuk, G., and Woodbury, N. R. "U.S. Defense Spending, Electoral Cycles and Soviet-American Relations." *Journal of Conflict Resolution* 30 (1986): 445–468.

Index

About the Author

Martin Patchen is Professor of Sociology at Purdue University. He has been at Purdue since 1968. Previously, he taught at the University of Michigan and was Senior Study Director at the Institute for Social Research there. Dr. Patchen's interests are in social cooperation and conflict and the resolution of conflict. His research has centered on conflict and cooperation between groups in a variety of settings, including labor-management relations, race relations, and international relations.